Break Your Chains

I0260775

Table of Contents

Introduction

This book is arranged so that the first half covers the “problem”, or rather, the challenges that we face as a human race, and the second half covers the solutions. To present one without the other would mean drawing a picture which is less than integral or whole.

Before we discuss the two halves, I will take a moment here to introduce a key phrase when it comes to the worldwide conspiracy: the New World Order (NWO). The NWO refers to a group as well as the agenda being carried out by this group.

So what is the NWO exactly? It is a rich and powerful group of mostly genetically-related individuals, including many of the world’s top politicians, international bankers, military and intelligence chiefs, corporate bosses and so-called “royal” bloodlines, whose agenda is to create a totalitarian, militaristic One World Government (which would be both fascist and Communist, since there is no meaningful difference between the two in terms of respect for self-determination, individual rights and human freedom). Their plan is to back this planetary-wide centralized dictatorship with a one world currency and army, and wipe out the middle class to leave a hierarchical society with just rulers and servants (or slaves). In order to achieve complete domination and secure their power indefinitely, they want to have the servant class digitally chipped or tagged, as well as mind controlled – so they can control every aspect of life and stop a potential rebellion before it happens. The New World Order is really an ancient agenda, an Old World Order, which has always been the greatest conspiracy the Earth has ever faced. Now, with the rapid advent of ever more invasive and powerful technology, the NWO is the biggest threat to a free and peaceful humanity.

Other terms which are basically synonymous with the NWO are becoming widely used, especially "Shadow Government" and "Deep State." A 2018 poll by Politico[1] found that 74% of Americans either believed (either definitely or probably) that a Deep State existed, meaning an unelected government operating above the rule of law, free from all checks and balances and immune to public scrutiny.

The plan for a NWO is a very old plan, whose roots can be found in Sumer, which was a very advanced civilization ruled by a religious class. Many authors and researchers such as David Icke, Bill Cooper and others have gone in depth to illustrate the trail from that time and place to this time and place, which is beyond the scope of this book. However, to give those new to this topic a brief overview, a series of mystery schools purporting to teach humanity "esoteric secrets" and "enlightenment" arose in Sumer, influenced subsequent philosophies, schools and religions in Egypt, Greece, Rome and other nations. Although enlightenment is a noble goal, their version of enlightenment was sinister. It wasn't purely about

---

[1] https://www.politico.com/story/2018/03/19/poll-deep-state-470282

improving one's self, but rather gaining power over others. Eventually the mystery schools went underground and ended up influencing the formation of Secret Societies that exist to this day, the most famous of which is Freemasonry, which exerts a massive and inordinate amount of influence on world affairs and the governments of many nations. Almost all of the Founding Fathers of the USA were Freemasons, as have been numerous US presidents.

In addition to Secret Societies, another key aspect of the NWO is the collusion of very rich and powerful families, most of whom control international banking. The two key families are the Rothschilds and Rockefellers.

After they had commandeered medicine, forcing homeopathy underground and virtually pioneering an entirely new brand of drugs-vaccines-surgery medicine known as allopathy, they set their sights on controlling education. After all, they reasoned, the greatest way to change the world would be to change the minds of the next generation, who would then go on to create a new world. They would just need to be patient while they gradually seized control of the curriculum. To do this, they used their aforementioned tax-exempt foundations to give generous funds and grants to universities – with strings attached. The money was given on the condition that the universities accept foundation members on their boards. So Rockefeller agents began to populate university boards all over the USA, then step by step influencing and eventually controlling the curriculum.

What exactly were the Rockefellers trying to produce by altering the curriculum? More aware, knowledgeable, intelligent or astute citizens? Of course not! Just the opposite. In fact, they admitted their plans in plain English:

I don't want a nation of thinkers. I want a nation of workers.

– John D. Rockefeller

Over a century later, the mal-effects of the Rockefeller driven drive to alter the curriculum can be seen on the state of US education and the US citizenry in general. The late and great American comedian George Carlin summed it up very well:

There's a reason education sucks, it's the same reason that it will never, ever, ever be fixed. It's never going to get any better, don't look for it, be happy with what you got. Because the owners of this country don't want that. I'm talking about the real owners, now. The real owners, the big wealthy business interests that control things and make all the important decisions. Forget the politicians, they're an irrelevancy. The politicians are put there to give you the idea that you have freedom of choice. You don't. You have no choice. You have owners. They own you. They own everything. They own all the important land. They own and control the corporations. They've long since bought and paid for the Senate, the Congress, the statehouses, the city halls. They've got the judges in their back pockets. And they own all the big media companies, so that they control just about all of the news and information you hear. They've got you by the balls. They spend billions of dollars every year lobbying – lobbying to get what they want. Well, we know what they want; they want more for themselves and less for everybody else.

But I'll tell you what they don't want. They don't want a population of citizens capable of critical thinking. They don't want well-informed, well-educated people capable of critical thinking. They're not interested in that. That doesn't help them. That's against their interests. They don't want people who are smart enough to sit around the kitchen table and figure out how badly they're getting fucked by a system that threw them overboard 30 fucking years ago.

You know what they want? Obedient workers – people who are just smart enough to run the machines and do the paperwork but just dumb enough to passively accept all these increasingly shittier jobs with the lower pay, the longer hours, reduced benefits, the end of overtime and the vanishing pension that disappears the minute you go to collect it.

The NWO megalomaniacs didn't stop at the control of education. Their next objective was to gain even more power by controlling the food supply. At first, this was done by buying out large corporations that owned crop plantations. History is full of examples of Western corporations stealing or buying up land in 3rd world nations on the cheap, growing food there, exploiting discount labor, then making a massive profit by selling the food back in the corporations' home country. Often, the US military was brought into poorer, weaker countries, purely to protect the commercial interests of the US ruling class. One instance was the US-led coup in Guatemala in 1954, where the US army illegally intervened in a sovereign nation to help the United Fruit Company, a US corporation with connections to the Dulles brothers, John and Allen (Allen Dulles was director of the CIA, and evidence shows was the mastermind of the JFK assassination).

It didn't stop with exploiting 3rd world nation land and labor. The very same network of interlocking families and bloodlines was also connected to I.G. Farben, the massive German industrial and chemical corporation that was at one point in history the largest in the world. After the Nazis lost the war, I.G. Farben was broken up into several smaller companies including BASF and Bayer, however these companies continued on in a similar vein. Pretty soon they producing the chemical fertilizers which fueled the growth of agricultural pesticide use in the 1950s – and began the slow poisoning of the food supply. Then, with the advent of biotechnology, the NWO controllers had the means at their disposal to completely dominate the food supply in a way never before imagined.

Monsanto, voted the most hated corporation in the world many times, was acquired by Bayer in 2018. Monsanto's history is filled with dark episodes including the production of dioxin-laced Agent Orange (used to deform and kill millions in Vietnam), DDT, rBGH, aspartame and glyphosate, the main ingredient in RoundUp. Monsanto began producing GM (genetically modified) crops based on them owning the GM seed. By altering the genes of the organism (in a random and unhealthy way), Monsanto and other biotech companies claimed they had invented something new (because, by law, no one is allowed to own Nature) and thus were granted patents for their "proprietary inventions." Thus, they had found a way to patent and own Nature, and food itself! It was Monsanto that first pursued the diabolical idea of developing pesticide resistant GM crops that could be sprayed with their toxic glyphosate but not die. Monsanto also developed "terminator seeds" that reversed millions of years of evolution. Their seeds would not reproduce; they would produce crops that would be sterile and would produce no further seeds, so the farmers would be forced to pay Monsanto every year to buy new seeds. In this way, Big Biotech created a whole new dependent market and began to seize control of the food supply. Their ultimate aim, of course, is to genetically modify everything, thus own everything, and thus require everyone to come to them to buy seeds to grow food to eat. It is nothing sort of complete dominance of the global food supply, but then again, these guys don't think small – their ability to think big is only just outdone by their capacity for greed and lust for power.

So far I have outlined the NWO evolution in a nutshell – banking (control of the money supply), oil (control of the energy supply), chemicals/medicine (control of health), education (control of the mind/ perception) and chemicals/GMOs (control of the food supply). The last part that ties all this together is the eugenics (control of human breeding/population). Some say eugenics is a science that aims to improve the human race by controlling breeding so as to increase the occurrence of desirable heritable characteristics. However it many ways it is unscientific; many of those writing in favor of eugenics believed they could somehow erase entirely subjective qualities like "feeblemindedness" from humankind, or to forever rid the world of those deemed "unfit." Even before Hitler and the Nazis, eugenics had a dark past. It was used in the US in the early 1900s as an excuse to sterilize single young women who were deemed to be too unfit to bear children. Many respected and famous personalities were eugenicists, including people such as author H. G. Wells, playwright George Bernard Shaw, former UK Prime Minister Winston Churchill, former US President Theodore Roosevelt, explorer Jacques Cousteau, scientist Francis Crick (who discovered DNA in 1953), inventor Alexander Graham Bell, biologist Julian Huxley (brother of Aldous Huxley, author of the famous dystopian novel Brave New World) and philosopher Bertrand Russell, who had this to say about it:

Gradually, by selective breeding, the congenital differences between rulers and ruled will increase until they become almost different species. A revolt of the plebs would become as unthinkable as an organized insurrection of sheep against the practice of eating mutton.

In short, eugenics offered the NWO criminals a pseudoscientific excuse to cloak their genocidal desires. It offered an apparently plausible yet ultimately spurious intellectual foundation for the NWO psychopaths to justify their grand goal: depopulation. After the Nazis implemented eugenicist ideas in their quest to preserve the master Aryan race and eliminate the undesirables, the term eugenics become associated with the Nazis, and so the men in the shadows – who had funded both sides of the war during WWI and WWII, and who had helped fund Hitler's rise to power – realized that their movement needed a PR facelift.

The eugenically-led drive for the NWO powerbrokers, and others of their ilk, to dominate the world and have the ultimate power of who lives and dies, eventually materialized as official governmental policy. On December 10th 1974, notorious war criminal and then US National Security Advisor under Nixon, Henry Kissinger, oversaw the final drafting of National Security Study Memorandum 200 (NSSM 200), entitled "Implications of Worldwide Population Growth for U.S. Security and Overseas Interests." On November 26th 1975, Kissinger was Secretary of State. His successor as National Security Advisor, General Brent Scowcroft, issued National Security Decision Memorandum 314, which adopted NSSM 200 as US policy. Depopulation had become the legal and official course of action for a world superpower intent on cornering the majority of the world resources for itself.

As we shall see, the idea has always been to control Life itself – via the stepping stones of oil, banking, education, medicine, mass media, food and biotech.

So this book is divided into two halves. The first half is the conspiracy, the danger, the threat. It is imperative that we fully understand the depth of this conspiracy and the nature of this danger, for without such a realization, it is unlikely we will collectively find the motivation to respond to it appropriately, to change and to tackle the issue head-on. The point of sharing the information in the first half of the book is not to scare, alarm, disempower or anger you – although you may well feel afraid, shocked, depressed, angry and a whole range of emotions as you go through the information. Such reactions are understandable and natural. However, the aim is to empower you with awareness, so that you may move beyond your initial reactions to a place of knowing and power. From this place, you are able to look with eyes wide open at the whole issue, know what needs to be done, and have the presence, power and courage to play your part in doing it. Ignorance is never really bliss, because ignorance and denial are temporary states which can only resist the truth of reality for a certain period – until it all comes crashing down.

In today's world where a practically infinite amount of information is at your fingertips, ignorance is a choice. You can stick you head in the sand and pretend nothing's wrong when a cyclone or hurricane is coming, but you're still going to get whacked, and you'll get hit far worse than the guy who saw it coming, accepted the fact it was coming, and made preparations to deal with it before it was too late. Denying a problem allows it time in the darkness to fester and grow far worse than if we'd just dealt with it at the beginning.

So, once you understand what we're up against, it's time to place your focus where it needs to be: on solutions. The second half lists many solutions, arranged into various "planes" (aspects, levels or areas). The conspiracy cuts deep, affecting us on many levels; therefore, the solutions have to be multi-faceted also. The more levels we can tackle this on, the better, and as always, it's best to address the root cause. As Henry Thoreau famously said, "There are a thousand hacking at the branches of evil to one who is striking at the root."

Most of all, you need to remember this: the whole deal is a challenge to push us to greater heights, to awaken us out of our slumber, to help us integrate our individual and collective shadows sides. In the end, truth is more powerful than lies, and love is more powerful than fear. However, there is still much work to be done right here, right now, to make that a reality for all to share.

Chapter 1 – The State of the World

THE PARADOX OF OUR TIMES

Is that we have taller buildings, but shorter tempers
Wider freeways, but narrower viewpoints
We spend more, but we have less.

We have bigger houses, but smaller families
More conveniences, but less time.
We have more degrees, but less sense
More knowledge, but less judgement
More experts, but more problems
More medicines, but less wellness.

We have multiplied our possessions, but reduced our values.
We talk too much, love too seldom, and hate too often
We have learnt how to make a living, but not a life.
We have added years to life, but not life to years.
We've been all the way to the moon and back
But have trouble crossing the street to meet the new neighbour.
We have conquered outer space, but not inner space.
We've cleaned up the air, but polluted our soul.
We've split the atom, but not our prejudice.
We've higher incomes, but lower morals.
We've become long on quantity but short on quality.

These are the times of tall men, and short character;

Steep profits, and shallow relationships.
These are the times of world peace, but domestic warfare,
More leisure, but less fun; more kinds of food, but less nutrition.

These are the days of two incomes, but more divorces;
Of fancier houses, but broken homes.
It is a time when there is much in the show window, and nothing in the stockroom.

– Dalai Lama

It is no measure of health to be well adjusted to a profoundly sick society.

– Jiddu Krishnamurti

To live in this process is absolutely not to be able to notice it... Each step was so small, so inconsequential, so well explained or, on occasion, 'regretted,' that, unless one were detached from the whole process from the beginning... one no more saw it developing from day to day than a farmer in his field sees the corn growing. One day it is over his head.

– Milton Mayer, *They Thought They Were Free*

Just look at us. Everything is backwards, everything is upside down. Doctors destroy health, lawyers destroy justice, psychiatrists destroy minds, scientists destroy truth, major media destroys information, religions destroy spirituality and governments destroy freedom.

– Michael Ellner

*****

We live on a slave planet.

Those people who run the world – whom I refuse to call the "elite" since there's nothing noble, refined, superior, respectable, or dignified about their brand of psychopathy – have helped, in one way or another, to shape society into a structure where a few sit atop the pyramid, harvesting the energy and life force of everyone below them. This group has the goal of implementing a worldwide totalitarian dictatorship, which over the decades and centuries they have been calling a New World Order (NWO). Many of the seemingly separate issues and affairs which will be mentioned in this book are actually connected agendas in the pursuit of this goal. Since the NWO refers to both this nefarious agenda itself and to the dangerous group of people promoting it, for clarity, I will be referring to this dangerous group as "NWO controllers," "NWO conspirators," and "NWO manipulators" throughout this book.

"NWO" has been their pet phrase for a long time, at least as far back as Woodrow Wilson, US president during and after WWI, who used it to promote his League of Nations, a group that ultimately failed but was replaced by the United Nations. Adolf Hitler used the phrase; George H. W. Bush used it repeatedly; Bill Clinton, Gordon Brown,

Tony Blair, George Soros, Henry Kissinger, Zbigniew Brzezinski, David Rockefeller, Barack Obama, and Joe Biden also used it. It is the code word for a One World Government or "Global Governance" as they like to call it, which implies a global institutional framework for codifying international rules where everyone and everything is regulated, including features such as a One World Bank and a One World Army. The agenda is that everyone must submit to being governed by this One World Government. Autonomy and independence would become things of the past.

If you take a look around you, the world is in a precarious state. On an individual level, a huge percentage of humanity is stuck in survival mode, living hand-to-mouth and week to week, dependent on handouts, welfare, food banks, and other forms of charity to survive. On the next economic rung up, those in the "lower class" may have jobs, but they are just barely scraping by to make ends meet, with many of them stuck in unsatisfying, low-paying jobs with little chance of ever owning a house. Next up are those in the "middle class." They have a secure job, enough food to eat and are often paying off a mortgage, but they are usually overworked and stressed, feeling that it's impossible to slow down: for if they ever get off the hamster wheel, everything could come crashing down. Above them is the "upper class", who own assets (like real estate, houses, investments) and are economically secure.

However, all of these classes are being eroded by a super class – the 1% of the 1%--who are sucking more and more wealth upward every year, if this

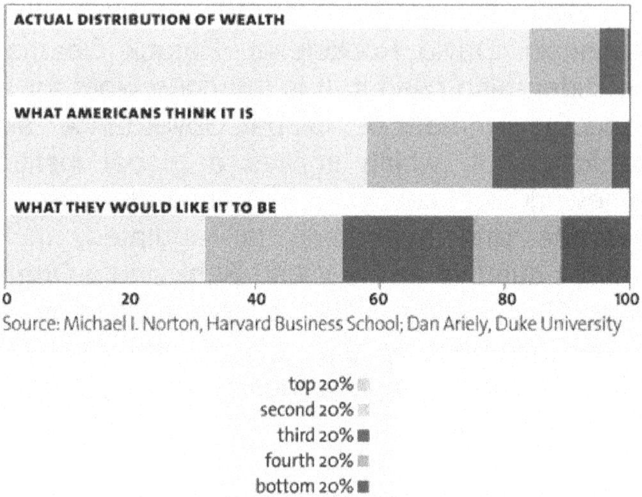

The perceived and actual wealth distribution in the USA.

2010 Harvard study[2] by Michael Norton is accurate. The lower class is expanding, and both the traditional middle classes and upper classes are shrinking. We are moving into a world where there will be just two classes: the rich and powerful who control things and everyone else who will be servants and slaves to this class. It's becoming a world of sharp contrasts – of "haves" and "have nots." This is all by design, as we shall see.

Governments have gone crazy. They were set up to be a helpful and humble servant to the people but have fast become a horrific master. Governments are so out of control they have been the number-one

---

[2] https://www.hbs.edu/faculty/Publication Files/ Norton_Michael_Building a better America One wealth quintile at a time_4c575dff-fe1d-4002-b61a-1227d08b71be.pdf

leading cause of death of all people worldwide, killing an estimated 262 million in the twentieth century, according to political scientist R. J. Rummel, who revivified and redefined the word "democide" (death by government). He arrived at this figure by studying more than eight thousand reports of government-caused deaths. Even when not at war and killing foreign peoples, governments have admitted to experimenting on their own citizens, including drugging them and sterilizing them without their knowledge or consent. In the US, the amount of property stolen by police from average citizens through "civil forfeiture" exceeded the dollar amount of property stolen via burglary in 2014.[3]

Individually, there are many problems people have to struggle with, including lack of sanitation, rising prices of basic goods, stagnant wages, lack of affordable housing, massive unemployment rates, inflation, excessive regulations, excessive taxation, police brutality, racial profiling, predatory lending, unpayable debt and more.

On a collective level, there are just as many problems. Environmental pollution, disappearing habitats and species, radiation leaks, poisoned waterways, nations going into default by not paying back their "debts" (thus forfeiting their critical infrastructure and resources), and a readiness to choose militaristic rather than diplomatic solutions to conflict. Numerous nations either openly possess nuclear weapons, possess them but officially pretend

---

[3] https://www.washingtonpost.com/news/wonk/wp/2015/11/23/cops-took-more-stuff-from-people-than-burglars-did-last-year/?utm_term=.b3cd4c2ec1cd

they don't (Israel), or have obtained them and won't let them go (North Korea). The nations that possess nuclear weapons are often in conflict: for instance, India and Pakistan, or the US and Russia.

Some would look at the world today and believe humanity is doing okay, since the standard of living has risen for most people compared to a hundred years ago. This may be true, but it is a limited perspective. To stop your analysis at that would be to miss a huge piece of the puzzle. The point is that it doesn't have to be like this. We are allowing a tiny minority to control a massive amount of the world's power, wealth, and resources and dictate to us how things will be. Besides, there's absolutely no guarantee the standard of living for the vast majority will just "keep improving." In fact, trends suggest just the opposite. Technology may have helped the standard of living improve for most people in the last fifty to a hundred years, but ironically, that same technology is about to strip jobs away and threaten the entire economy. Robots and other forms of AI (Artificial Intelligence) are becoming increasingly prevalent in the workforce, and not only can they do the simple jobs (waitress, bartender, retail assistant, bank teller) but even more technical and creative jobs (driving, writing, creating art, doctor).

Given just all these things, the world is already in a precarious condition; but on top of that, humanity is under attack from various manmade threats.

Humanity Under Assault from Manmade Environmental Threats

Not only is humanity contending with the rather massive problems listed above, both individually and collectively, but we are also actively under assault. That's right: the NWO controllers have also created a whole array of toxic and lethal hazards which affect our daily lives. I am referring to the barrage of chemicals, toxins, poisons and dangers which have been released into society – all of which have the result of weakening, dumbing down, and killing people, often in a "soft-kill" or "slow-kill" way that escapes immediate detection.

After all, the NWO obsession with eugenics has manifested itself in politics as depopulation. Arch-globalist and NWO insider Henry Kissinger, who was US Secretary of State under Nixon and Ford, oversaw the completion of the 1974 document NSSM 200 (*National Security Study Memorandum 200: Implications of Worldwide Population Growth for U.S. Security and Overseas Interests*) as mentioned in the Introduction which states:

Whatever may be done to guard against interruptions of supply and to develop domestic alternatives, the U.S. economy will require large and increasing amounts of minerals from abroad, especially from less developed countries. That fact gives the U.S. enhanced interest in the political, economic, and social stability of the supplying countries. Wherever a lessening of population pressures through reduced birth rates can increase the prospects for such stability, population policy becomes relevant to resource supplies and to the economic interests of the United States.

NSSM 2000 was adopted as official US policy by President Ford in November 1975. Although the report was ostensibly discussing the US attitude toward foreign populations, the principles were eagerly embraced by the US leaders (or rather US misleaders) at the time. It is clear that to the ruling class it is far easier to control a small population than a large one. It is also far preferable to govern a sick, dying, and weakened population rather than a healthy, vibrant, and active one that is much more likely to revolt. Big Pharma, the cartel of multinational pharmaceutical companies, has mastered the art of "managing" disease without healing it, as we shall see.

Processed, poisoned, and modified food is one of the biggest threats we face today. Food is obviously essential for life. Since our bodies use the material from food to literally make new cells, if we take in food that is compromised in some way, this will adversely affect our bodies sooner or later. You cannot maintain a state of health and power if your primary "fuel" fails to give you what you need. Most supermarket food today is highly processed and refined, with the important and health-giving nutrients stripped away. On top of that, ever since the 1950s in most developed nations, crops which are conventionally grown are sprayed with chemical fertilizers and an array of synthetic pesticides (herbicides, fungicides, insecticides, etc.). These chemicals are absorbed by the plants as they grow and thus cannot be simply washed off when you buy them from the shop or market. The poison goes into the plant and stays there; then it goes into your body after you ingest the plant. Monoculture agrofarming now relies heavily on these chemical sprays (which also incidentally have been fundamental in stripping away nutrients from the topsoil). Thus, even if you were able to rid the food of pesticide once you buy it (which is impossible in most cases), you can't change the fact that the soil is depleted of minerals that used to be present. If the soil doesn't contain those minerals, the plant cannot absorb them, meaning that our food is lacking these key essential nutrients.

So far I have outlined the problems with food that has been overly processed, refined, and sprayed with synthetic chemicals. That's bad enough; however, there is an even greater problem: GMOs or Genetically Modified Organisms. A GMO is created when the DNA of a plant is spliced with the DNA of another organism, resulting in an entirely new organism (never seen before in Nature) which is able to be owned and patented by the corporations doing it – the multinational biotechnology companies such as Monsanto (now acquired by Bayer), Dow, DuPont, Pioneer, Syngenta, and BASF. Collectively, many are calling them Big Biotech, and they are closely related to Big Pharma as can be seen by the Bayer-Monsanto acquisition. Although Big Biotech puts out the propaganda that GMOs are "substantially equivalent" to non-GMO food, scientific studies have shown GMOs wreak havoc on the body and can lead to serious diseases such as infertility, autism, organ failure, and cancer. If you eat GM (genetically modified) food, you are literally taking foreign proteins and DNA into your body, which then starts to replace your own DNA. Thus, as horrible as it sounds, by eating GMO food, you are literally participating in genetically modifying yourself.

Fluoride is another unnecessary manmade health threat which many people are subjected to because of the mass fluoridation of municipal water supplies. It's mass drugging. Fluoride damages organs, leads to dental fluorosis, carries aluminum across the blood-brain barrier[4], and can lead to cancer. It also accumulates in the pineal gland, the body's physical link to spiritual realms, and shuts it down. Putting fluoride in water is essentially just a hazardous waste management tool. It has nothing to do with dental health whatsoever. (Fortunately, there are ways to naturally remove fluorides from your body, as will be discussed in the solutions section.) Fluoride is a lot harder to remove from drinking water than chlorine, another substance which is not good for health (at least not in the form in which it's used in tap water). Yes, chlorine in water kills algae and "bad" bacteria, but it's also the main element in bleach. Why would you want to drink a chemical disinfectant every time you're thirsty? There are other ways to disinfect water and keep it clean without needing to resort to chemicals, such as using ozone (O_3) as is widely done in France.

Speaking of Big Pharma, there are many manmade threats which emanate from the pharmaceutical cartel, which is itself an offshoot of the oil industry created by the late robber baron John D. Rockefeller. Western medicine is Rockefeller medicine in many ways. When Rockefeller was

---

[4] https://pubmed.ncbi.nlm.nih.gov/16892590/

making his fortune from oil, he investigated other ways in which his "black gold" could be sold and found that there was a market for petrochemical derivatives which could be turned into "medicine." Thus, synthetic drugs were born, which have proven to be useful for eliminating symptoms of a disease but highly inadequate for addressing the root cause of disease. However, masking symptoms and not addressing causes has been the basis of a very lucrative business model for Big Pharma. Meanwhile, doctors are routinely bribed to push as many pills as possible, and much of the US (and the world) is now suffering from an out-of-control opioid crisis.

Antibiotic proliferation and overuse are other manmade threats to be aware of. Even if you don't use antibiotics, this issue will still affect you. The over-prescription and overuse of antibiotic drugs has resulted in many bacterial and microbial lifeforms mutating to develop resistance to the drugs, which are no longer effective. This in essence creates superbugs: bacterial, viral, and fungal strains which become so virulent they can no longer be stopped with drugs. Antibiotic residue is often found in municipal water supplies, meaning that you may well be ingesting someone else's drugs unless you're thoroughly cleaning and filtering your water before drinking it.

Vaccines are another huge topic about which entire books could be written. Big Pharma and its cohort Western Medicine prance around repeating the mantra that vaccines are "safe and effective" while the evidence shows that they are neither. Unvaccinated children are consistently shown to be healthier than vaccinated ones in studies (such as this comprehensive survey of 7600 children[5] from numerous nations). Meanwhile, vaccines typically contain a shocking amount of toxic ingredients and adjuvants, such as mercury, aluminum, formaldehyde (all of which are carcinogenic), MSG, antibiotics, GMOs, polysorbate, squalene, nagalese (an immunity-destroying enzyme that can impede one's ability to fight cancer) and common allergens such as peanut oil. Vaccines themselves usually are made from cloned cells of an aborted fetus, often usually a chicken egg as the substrate. They therefore contain human and animal cells. Vaccines have been known to be contaminated, as happened in the 1960s with the polio vaccines in the US, which were laced with SV-40 (simian virus 40), a monkey virus which was shown to cause cancer.

On top of all that, research has shown that vaccines lead to blood sludge, hypoxia, and ischemia (i.e., localized "strokes" in your body). Other possible side effects include autism (or diseases along the autism spectrum), paralysis, and death. Italian courts ruled in both 2012 and 2014[6] that it was conclusively established that the MMR vaccine had caused autism in a child and awarded damages to the family; US courts have also made similar rulings. The herd immunity myth has been busted; it turns out that those taking the vaccine are actually more likely to contract and/or pass on a disease than those

---

[5] www.thehealthyhomeeconomist.com/survey-results-are-unvaccinated-children-healthier/

[6] https://www.globalresearch.ca/u-s-media-blackout-italian-courts-rule-vaccines-cause-autism/5430940

unvaccinated due to viral shedding, whereby live viruses shed for varying amounts of time in the body fluids of a vaccinated individual – and can be transmitted to others. You can absolutely catch the virus (or bacterium) from someone who has just been vaccinated against that disease. Lastly, it has been exposed that vaccines have been used as tools to conduct sterilization programs against people (especially in poorer nations such as the Philippines and Kenya). In 2015, a Catholic priest whistleblower[7] discovered that a tetanus vaccination program (sponsored by the WHO and UNICEF) contained vaccines laced with HCG or Human Chorionic Gonadotropin. This is a hormone that the human embryo produces after conception to enable it to be implanted in the womb. However, when the body takes in HCG via a tetanus vaccine, it treats the HCG as an antigen (a foreign substance) and makes antibodies to the HCG. Those antibodies cause the woman's body to reject future embryos, effectively sterilizing her.

So far, all these threats are in the realm of the seen, but there are invisible threats which are just as hazardous. Many of today's electronic devices rely upon wireless technology: cordless phones, mobile or cell phones, tablets, wi-fi, Bluetooth, and so on. This technology operates in frequencies massively higher than the Earth's natural frequency (mobile handsets require gigahertz, and the new 5G network will be using the 28, 37 and 39 GHz bands, also known as millimeter wave (mmW) spectrum).

---

[7] https://vaccinefactcheck.org/2015/03/20/vatican-unicef-and-who-are-sterilizing-girls-through-vaccines/

Wireless radiation in the MHz, GHz, and THz is, respectively, literally millions, billions, and trillions of times the Earth's Schumann Resonance of 7.83 Hz.

Everything has a cost or a price, and this EMF (Electromagnetic Frequency) and RF (Radio Frequency) radiation is no exception. By bathing our cities, our animals, our plants, and ourselves in this radiation, we are creating an electromagnetic soup and exposing everyone and everything inside of it to unnatural and unhealthy frequencies. At our core, we are energetic beings, and this type of wireless radiation is contorting our energy fields. Multiple studies[8] have indicated the harmful effects of wi-fi on plants, bees, and children. The 5G grid is designed to work in conjunction with what former CIA head David Petraeus called the Internet of Things or IoT. Many people are encouraging the advancement of 5G by their desire for convenience and speed (give me my multiple gigabit downloads now!). People are foolishly valuing this over privacy, safety, and health. 5G is not merely an upgrade of wireless infrastructure; it is a giant leap toward the erection and installation of a total technological control grid. The rollout of 5G and the smart grid electromagnetic blanket is happening so quickly (including wi-fi being beamed down from satellites owned by corporations like Facebook), that unless drastic changes happen, it will end up covering every square inch of Earth, and thus its effects will adversely affect every living thing on this planet.

---

[8] https://www.aph.gov.au/DocumentStore.ashx?id=d038a736-ceb1-4287-b6bb-d13dcadc1fb4&subId=672825

Speaking of covering the entire planet, we come to the next troublesome global issues: geoengineering, chemtrails, climate remediation, solar radiation management, and weather manipulation. These all are terms describing the ongoing worldwide operation to saturate the skies with chemicals under the name of fighting "global warming." The terms are very revealing: geoengineering is the attempt to "engineer" the "geo" (world); chemtrails are "chemical" "trails" of heavy metals and synthetic nanoparticles laid out in the stratosphere and other levels of the upper atmosphere; climate remediation is an example of Orwellian newspeak (remediation is defined as "the correction of something bad or defective", so the implication is that the climate is somehow bad or wrong and has to be fixed by human [governmental] intervention); solar radiation management (SRM) is another corporate-sounding euphemism which glosses over the very real crimes against humanity which are being perpetrated by the indiscriminate spraying of these toxic aerosols, including various light and heavy metals, fungi, viruses, other pathogens, and synthetic lifeforms.

The 2010 documentary *What in the World Are They Spraying?* did a great job of exposing the horrific consequences of geoengineering. It showed firsthand evidence of extremely elevated levels of aluminum, barium, and strontium in the soil, which is killing plants and trees and inevitably making its way into the food supply. There has been a mass awakening about the existence of chemtrails, as more and more people are noticing that instead of being blue, the sky is crisscrossed with long white lines hanging in the air for lengthy periods and eventually breaking down into a gray haze. The chemtrail program, also known as Project Cloverleaf, is extremely compartmentalized; even the pilots themselves have no real idea of why they are actually spraying. For years the government has denied the existence of chemtrails, falsely claiming that they were merely contrails, the water vapor that comes out of jet engines and disappears after ten to twenty seconds. However, the truth is that chemtrails don't emanate from the engines but rather from the nozzles above the engines, which are fed by tubes from inside the plane. Chemtrails linger in the air for hours, often covering the sky, blocking the sun, and resulting in very unnatural cloud formations. In addition to blanket denial, the US Government has been using the excuse and phony science of global warming to justify the spraying.

What are the aims of chemtrails? There are several. Firstly, similar to other depopulation plans such as the use of vaccines, fluoride, and aspartame, the objective is to gradually poison the masses but do it so slowly that no one can discern the true cause. People find it harder to heal their diseases and stop the perpetrators if they don't know the origin of their illnesses. Aerosol spraying is particularly effective since everyone has to breathe, and once it's sprayed overhead in an area, people can't easily escape and are essentially forced to ingest the toxic particles. The idea is to make people sick, infertile, and trapped in survival mode, where they are so focused on just getting by that they have little or no energy to investigate what is happening and mount an effective resistance.

Secondly, large biotech corporations profit from the spraying. When the chemtrails fall to Earth, they land in the soil and raise its pH, making it too alkaline and unable to support crops. Monsanto is developing aluminum-resistant crops so they can monopolize the market, force organic crops out, and get everyone to buy their GM (Genetically Modified) seeds. These "terminator" seeds produce no further seeds when planted, so farmers have to keep buying seeds from Monsanto every year.

Thirdly, HAARP and chemtrails are working together in a program of "iron fertilization" in which the planes specifically dump millions of tons of iron and barium into the seas, which changes their composition. HAARP then magnetizes these metals in the water to create high- and low-pressure systems, allowing it to control the weather and create storms and floods at will. Likewise, other particles found in chemtrail cocktails may be enabling HAARP to manipulate our thoughts by energizing the otherwise nonconductive air we breathe, so HAARP is a mind control weapon, too.

Fourthly, we need to broaden our horizons on this issue. Historically, we have always gone through periodic solar cycles. Sometimes the sun has been very active (e.g., by putting out large solar flares). For all we know, the light from the sun (which is, after all, information) could be a type of catalyst that has the potential to activate our DNA and propel us forward in our evolution. The NWO controllers fear a global awakening and are desperate to keep their grip on the planet. It is entirely possible they are dumping these toxic metal particles in the stratosphere to act as a shield, block the sun's rays, and possibly obstruct the activation of humanity's DNA.

We urgently need to upgrade our idea of what is possible. We need to put this weapon on our radar and become aware of its existence and operations.

Fakery Everywhere

In addition to all the manmade environmental threats listed above, humanity is also involved in another type of battle: an information war. To take false information into the mind is just as bad for you as to eat junk food or drink toxic water. The truth is that we are indeed surrounded by an immense amount of fakery. To deconstruct and expose all that fakery would take many voluminous tomes, so for now, we'll keep it brief and just highlight a few examples.

Let's start with words. Almost everyone uses language to communicate, whether in writing or speech. Yet so much of our language perpetuates the fakery. There is so much doublespeak around, by which I mean euphemisms (mild expressions designed to hide harsher or more direct ones), deliberately ambiguous terms (expressions designed to hide the truth), or actual inversions (outright lies that state the opposite of the truth). Although he never used the term in his book *1984*, George Orwell is often associated with the idea of "doublespeak." After all, it was Orwell who famously wrote that the motto of the totalitarian ruling party in *1984* was *"War is Peace, Freedom is Slavery, Ignorance is Strength"* – an example of an inversion. Orwell did, however, use the term "newspeak" to refer to a new kind of language that drastically reduced the scope of available words and terms so as to concurrently reduce the scope of possible free thought among the ruled population. Seeing how people communicate via texting today evokes shades of Orwell. Can you imagine him bending over his smartphone and texting in emoticons?

Many doublespeak terms are oxymorons: terms themselves that are inherently contradictory. Many hide the truth because it is too raw, unpalatable, uncomfortable, or outright horrifying. Some modern doublespeak terms include *terrorist* (a foreign militia member or soldier designated as the "enemy") and *extremist* (just about anyone who questions the "official" version of reality. The US DHS [Department of Homeland Security] listed each of the following as a potential extremist: patriot, veteran, alternative media journalist, border control advocate, animal rights advocate, gun control advocate), are *freedom fighters* or *moderate rebels* (mercenaries, soldiers and other guns for hire who are branded "allies" who are in essence paid to do the dirty work), *ethnic cleansing* (genocide), *enhanced interrogation* (torture), *extrajudicial killing* (assassination), *humanitarian intervention* and the *responsibility to protect* (invasion or preemptive attack under the false pretext of saving a foreign nation's people from its leader), *collateral damage* (the killing of civilians and other nonmilitary people), *eliminate*, *neutralize*, *depopulate* (kill), *quantitative easing* (excess printing of fiat currency backed by no new economic growth, which has the effect of stealing from you by robbing the value of your money) and *conspiracy theory* and *theorist* (a term amplified by the CIA after the JFK assassination to shut down genuine investigation into governmental lies). These days, anyone who questions the official COVID narrative or COVID restrictions is considered an extremist by the government.

It is vitally important we watch our language because it greatly affects how we shape our world and create our reality. In many ways, by unconsciously using these terms instead of more accurate or truthful ones, we are quietly lying to ourselves (or at a minimum acquiescing to the process of being lied to and programmed). Political correctness (see chapter 7) is a great example of how language control, thought control, and doublespeak can be introduced to an entire population without people realizing they are being deceived and manipulated.

Fake News

The MSM (Mainstream Media) refers to the giant multinational corporate cartel, which is mostly composed of these six giants[9]:

- News Corp (Fox, Wall Street Journal, New York Post, National Geographic)
- Time Warner (CNN, HBO, Time, Warner Bros)
- Disney (ABC, ESPN, Miramax, Marvel Studios)
- Comcast (NBC, CNBC, Universal Pictures)

---

9 https://www.webpagefx.com/data/the-6-companies-that-own-almost-all-media/

- National Amusements (CBS, Viacom, MTV, Paramount Pictures)
- Sony (Tri Star)

These players have many different brands, outlets, media (e.g., TV, internet, radio, newspaper, magazine, etc.) and channels; however, they all broadcast from a centralized source, so just because there are thousands of access points doesn't mean you're getting a variety of perspectives.

The MSM plays a dominant role in today's society because it controls much of the news and information flow (although this is changing with the rise of the internet and alternative media). Information control = perception control = mind control. It was more than ironic when the MSM began to complain during the end of 2016 (during the last phases of the US presidential election) that there was too much "fake news" around. You have to hand it to the MSM: they win the chutzpah award every time. The MSM has always been the biggest purveyor of fake news on the planet. After this, the term "fake news" itself went mainstream and became a talking point for many politicians, journalists, and members of the public, including President Trump who has accused CNN multiple times of being a "fake news" outlet. CNN is likely no worse than the rest of the MSM; however, it is a fact that they have been busted on several occasions for blatantly inventing the "news." In one famous example, they pretended they were broadcasting on air from Saudi Arabia while being bombed and attacked. It turned out to be a total lie, as they were broadcasting from their US studio[10]. Another day, another lie; it's all part of the business. Back when CNN pulled this mendacious stunt, very few people would have believed that they were lying. The MSM propaganda was so effective that it would have been virtually unthinkable. Now, however, times have changed; it has become more obvious that the MSM routinely broadcasts lies—so that at least is a good sign that humanity is waking up from its slumber.

The MSM has been controlled by the CIA (Central Intelligence Agency) ever since the 1950s via their project codenamed Operation Mockingbird. More on this is exposed in chapter 7.

The Falsification of History

News, which is current affairs, has long been compromised and infiltrated by purveyors or fakery. Sadly, our history books, the records of past affairs, have been just as compromised. Orwell famously wrote in *1984* that "Who controls the present, controls the past; who controls the past, controls the future." What he meant by this was that if you are in control now (the present), you can control what happened (the past) by altering all the records of the past (e.g. books and documents) which by necessity must exist in the present. Once such alterations are done, you can influence people's idea of who they are, who you are, what is possible, where they are going, and what they can expect (the future).

---

10 https://www.bitchute.com/video/tFarFGdXUHED/

It is no exaggeration to say that the history of practically every major event in the world, especially the history of Europe and the USA, has been falsified to hide the true perpetrators and prevent people from seeing the grander pattern and agenda.

There are countless examples of this, but in the interest of brevity, I will list just a few. The Spanish-American War of 1898 was started not because Spain attacked the USA, but because the US blew up its own ship (USS Maine) to make it look like they were being attacked by the Spaniards. This would garner more sympathy and public support for war than if the US had just openly attacked Spain, since it would then have been seen as the naked aggressor. This trick is called a "false flag" attack and an effective method of hoodwinking people (more on this in the section). Similarly, America's entry into WWI, WWII, and the Vietnam War were also the result of false flag attacks where certain US officials either planned or knew about the attacks in advance (i.e. had foreknowledge). The sinking of the *Lusitania* in 1917 was allowed to happen; Pearl Harbor in 1941 was allowed to happen; and the Gulf of Tonkin incident of 1964 is a complete fabrication where US ships shot at nothing in the ocean. I encourage all readers to do their own research on these events since a more detailed explanation is beyond the scope of this book.

The burning of the German Reichstag (Parliament) building in 1933 was reported to be a false flag attack engineered by the Nazis in order to justify persecuting the Jews. On the other hand, there has also been a massive amount of exaggeration and embellishment about the Holocaust (done to further the Zionist cause) including the mysterious "6 million" figure that was being bandied around even before WW1, let alone WW2. The attack on the USS Liberty in 1967 was carried out by Israeli jets against their supposed ally (the US) in an attempt to make it look like Egypt was attacking the USA. The assassinations JFK, MLK, and RFK in the 1960s were all the result of coordinated, grand conspiracies orchestrated by people at the highest levels of government; the official cover story of "lone wolf" shooters is absurd.

The official version of historical events is a whitewash and a lie. We know that history is written by the victors. In the majority (but not all) cases, you will be closer to the truth if you invert the official story and believe the exact opposite of what it says.

False Flag Operations

False flag operations (false flag ops for short) have become one of the primary techniques by which governments frighten their populations into obedience and justify outrageous abuses of power. The term "false flag operation" is a military term that has now become widely used due to the increased use of the technique by governments worldwide—and due to the fact that a critical mass of people are now finally beginning to wake up and recognize this technique when they see it.

Whether it be an attack, bombing, shooting, or other act of terrorism, the false flag op involves secretly orchestrating and executing some kind of criminal event (often involving the blowing up of vehicles and buildings and the mass murder of civilians) but blaming it on an innocent person or group. A specific person or group of persons is usually blamed so that the ensuing public reaction and outrage can be channeled onto a patsy (someone designated to take the fall, e.g., Lee Harvey Oswald) or bogeyman (created so there is a new "enemy," e.g., Osama Bin Laden). False flag ops almost always follow a predictable pattern or formula, so you can spot them once you know the game plan. False flag operations are covered in depth in chapter 3.

Secret Black Military Projects

Another telling symptom of our out-of-control world is the unhinged MIC (Military Intelligence Complex), especially in the United States. This sprawling monster dictates the NWO agenda from behind the scenes. Intelligence Agencies such as the NSA (National Security Agency) and CIA (Central Intelligence Agency) in the US, MI5 (Military Intelligence 5), MI6 and GCHQ (Government Communications Headquarters) in the UK, and Mossad in Israel have unprecedented access to everything you email, text, and say on a phone (or even away from a phone for that matter, given how many tiny recording devices now flood our society). This is to help give them "total information awareness" and of course means they can easily blackmail politicians and other frontmen to comply with their agenda—or else.

The MIC has long run secretive programs off the books, which are colloquially known as black military projects, since the trail leading to them goes dark or black once you start getting too close to the truth. Some of these are called USAPs (Unacknowledged Special Access Programs). There are many whistleblowers who have exposed what goes on in some of these programs, including – take a breath – things that are unbelievable to the average person who had been brainwashed and conditioned with a very narrow sense of reality and idea of what is possible. If I mention "UFOs," "ETs," "aliens," "hybrids," and "Reptilians," please don't run out of the room in fear!

Or do so if you like. I care about the ultimate truth and what it means for our freedoms. If that's too much for some people, feel free to put the book down now. I go where the information leads regardless of my preconceptions. I am writing this to alert the public about what is really going on, not to win a popularity contest.

Occasionally we get clues about the extent to which we are completely ruled by the MIC. On September 10, 2001, then US Secretary of Defense Donald Rumsfeld announced the DoD or Pentagon was missing US$2.3 trillion. That's trillion with a "t." But people soon forgot about it given the false flag operation that was 9/11, which occurred the day after. How coincidental that he would just happen to drop that bombshell right before such a momentous event, which would crowd the media's and public's attention for months to come.

There have been more announcements of missing trillions since then. In fact, according to some sources, the DoD could not account for a total of $29 trillion[11]! What is going on? The total US monetary supply (M3) at that time was only supposed to be around $14 trillion, so to say something doesn't add up would be the understatement of the millennium. The Pentagon has never passed an audit in its history. Clearly, this money is being siphoned off to fund secret black military projects about which taxpayers and citizens have no knowledge – some of which I cover in chapter 10.

Conclusion

So, as you can see, our world is deeply imbalanced and out of control in myriad ways. It doesn't work to serve the public. It proceeds along a very sinister and coldly calculated agenda to only serve those at the very top of the pyramid who have the wealth and power to manipulate the world into carrying out their agenda. What this agenda of conspiracy exactly is will be the topic of the next chapter.

After all, we can only hope to confront and defeat the things which enslave us if we actually acknowledge their existence and understand what they are.

---

[11] www.investmentwatchblog.com/29-trillion-dollars-missing-from-pentagon-trump-calls-for-audit/

Chapter 2 – The Conspiracy Revealed

The only people who call conspiracies 'theories' are the conspirators.

– Jay Weidner, researcher and filmmaker

The individual is handicapped by coming face to face with a conspiracy so monstrous he cannot believe it exists.

– J. Edgar Hoover, former FBI head

Men occasionally stumble over the truth, but most of them pick themselves up and hurry off as if nothing ever happened.

The truth is incontrovertible. Malice may attack it, ignorance may deride it, but in the end, there it is.

– Winston Churchill, former British Prime Minister

We are opposed, around the world, by a monolithic and ruthless conspiracy.

– John F. Kennedy, former US President

There is a power somewhere ... so complete, so pervasive, that they (people who knew about it) had better not speak above their breath when they speak in condemnation of it.

– Woodrow Wilson, former US President

There exists a shadowy Government with its own Air Force, its own Navy, its own fundraising mechanism, and the ability to pursue its own ideas ... free from the law itself.

– Daniel Inouye, former US Senator

None are so hopelessly enslaved, as those who falsely believe they are free.

– Johann Wolfgang von Goethe

Fifty years is ample time in which to change a world and its people almost beyond recognition. All that is required for the task are a sound knowledge of social engineering, a clear sight of the intended goal – and power.

– Arthur C. Clarke, famous science fiction author

It must be remembered that the first job of any conspiracy, whether it be in politics, crime or within a business office, is to convince everyone else that no conspiracy exists. The conspirators' success will be determined largely by their ability to do this.

– Gary Allen, author of None Dare Call It Conspiracy

The Kennedy assassination has demonstrated that most of the major events of world significance are masterfully planned and orchestrated by an elite coterie of enormously powerful people who are not of one nation, one ethnic grouping, or one over-ridingly important business group. They are a power unto themselves for whom others work. Neither is the power elite of recent origin.

– Fletcher Prouty

When a well-packaged web of lies has been sold gradually to the masses over generations, the truth will seem utterly preposterous and its speaker a raving lunatic.

– Dresden James[12]

The Council on Foreign Relations (CFR) … the American Branch of a society which originated in England (by the diamond king, Cecil Rhodes) … believes national boundaries should be obliterated and a one-world rule established.

– Professor Carroll Quigley, Tragedy And Hope[13]

*****

So – the world's in a bad state. The question is why. As I said in the previous chapter, it's all too easy to dismiss conspiracy clues as a coincidence. It's easy to mock those trying to research the truth as wacky "conspiracy theorists"; however, those asleep with eyes firmly shut doing the mocking are the theorists, only they are "coincidence theorists", as

---

[12] https://quotes.liberty-tree.ca/quote_blog/Dresden.James.Quote.8B45

[13] https://amzn.to/2FVcljM

they can't see the deeper patterns beyond the seemingly random events of the world. Arrogance and ignorance go hand-in-hand, as they say.

Many of these coincidence theorists suffer from a state of cognitive dissonance where they just can't seem to grasp the truth, even if you politely and respectfully point out fact after fact after fact. They are too invested in their identity, belief system or world view. As the Hoover quote reveals, it is hard for the average person to believe that such a plot could be possible, let alone being carried out so actively.

The term "conspiracy theory" is not accurate anyway when you consider just how many conspiracy theories turned out to be fact. Conspiracy fact would be a better term. This is not to say that every conspiracy theory is correct, because obviously there are many far out ones that are totally wrong, but many have hit the mark, and many of them are far more honest and accurate than the ridiculous official narrative which is trotted out to cover massive governmental crimes, e.g. with the JFK, RFK and MLK assassinations, or with the 7/7 and 9/11 false flag operations.

As a point of fact, declassified document reveal that the CIA weaponized the term "conspiracy theory" and "conspiracy theorist" in the 1960s as a way to discredit genuine truthseekers who were trying to expose what really happened in the JFK assassination. It's a clever way to shut down critical thinking by what has essentially become name-calling and judgement.

The truth is that there is overwhelming evidence for the worldwide conspiracy. We're going to start by taking a look at three key documents or accounts. These three conspiracy documents or accounts which I am about to present, are, in my opinion, the three most chilling conspiracy documents or accounts ever concocted in the mind of man. All of them lay out the groundwork for the implementation of an incredibly evil agenda of a small group of manipulators to rule the world. Indeed, if you have never come across them before, the scale of their evil can quite defy belief and imagination.

However, although these conspiracy documents and accounts may appear as myths, stories or a work of fiction, their content is so compelling and so deadly accurate, it is very difficult to ignore them or sweep them under the mental carpet. It is impossible to see the world in quite the same way after reading them. They describe in minute detail a world of rulers and slaves, where the actions, attitudes, beliefs, thoughts, preferences, ideas and reproduction of the masses are controlled by the elite with the utmost precision. For anyone with a conscience, whose heart yearns for truth, freedom or dignity, the implications of these documents and accounts cannot be overstated. If they are real – which I completely believe they are – everyone of us needs to do whatever we can to ensure we never let them become a reality, if we care even a little about the future of the human race.

Brave New World and 1984

Before getting into these three documents/ accounts, let us quickly review the two most well-known dystopian books in the English language: Aldous Huxley's *Brave New World* and George Orwell's *1984*. Both present a grim version of future life on Earth. Interestingly, the two authors had crossed paths; Huxley was the French teacher of Orwell (whose real name was Eric Blair) during his years at Eton. Huxley was also from an elite family who was very much aware of the NWO agenda (e.g. his brother Julian was a famous eugenicist), so Huxley's and Orwell's vision of the future was not so much purely imaginative but rather based on their insider knowledge of the conspiracy.

Although the books are both brilliant in their own ways, there are some stark differences. The ruling party, government or system in both cases wants indefinite power, however they have different methods for achieving their goals. In *Brave New World*, the emphasis is foremost on stability, and it is achieved scientifically and technologically by precise conditioning. The State controls all reproduction and education (via a Hatchery and Conditioning Center), so it can precisely organize births according to a strict caste system, where everyone has a predetermined role to play in life. The conditioning is mostly done via "brains not fists"; there is so much programming (e.g. "hypnopedic" repetition where people are bombarded with propaganda literally thousands of times when children as they sleep, so that it sinks into their subconscious) that there is not much need for force, and where there is force, it is chemical violence (drug-induced apathy) rather than physical violence. The State deliberately engages people in class identity and warfare (divide and rule), sensual addiction, sexual promiscuity ("everyone belongs to everyone") and drug addiction (via "soma", the drug which takes away all pain but also shortens your life). The State encourages people to be addicted to pleasure and idolizes comfort as the highest good. There is no privacy and it is hard to ever be alone. Instant gratification is pushed ("never put off till to-morrow the fun you can have to-day"). There are seldom negative emotions felt by people in society (and when there are, soma is given out like candy), so there is no thought of rebellion or revolution. The *Brave New World* model is based on collectivism, where the society more important than the individual. This quote from the Director of the "Central London Hatchery and Conditioning Centre" sums it up:

"It is better that one should suffer than that many should be corrupted. Consider the matter dispassionately, Mr. Foster, and you will see that no offence is so heinous as unorthodoxy of behaviour. Murder kills only the individual – and, after all, what is an individual?" With a sweeping gesture he indicated the rows of microscopes, the test-tubes, the incubators. "We can make a new one with the greatest ease – as many as we like. Unorthodoxy threatens more than the life of a mere individual; it strikes at Society itself. Yes, at Society itself," he repeated."

Interestingly, in *Brave New World*, rebellious individuals do have a way out: they can leave "civilization" and go and live on an island where such a system does not exist; however, because that also means giving up comfort, technology and security, many are simply too conditioned and attached to pleasure to do this.

Orwell's *1984* depicts a world of constant surveillance, ruthless control and zero privacy where the State tracks people by monitoring their facial expressions (to try to determine what they are thinking), in order to ensure they remain obedient. People are encouraged to rat on each other. Many of the new terms invented and used by Orwell in *1984* have found their way into the English language, such as "memory hole", "thoughtcrime" and "newspeak", the latter referring to the new language the State is constructing so as to be able to control people's range of thought. Words are deliberately eliminated from the language so as to make it impossible to think of rebellious thoughts, or any thoughts outside of party-approved lines. Orwell once stated that, *"All political language is designed to make lies sound truthful and murder respectable."* Just look at some of our modern day examples: torture is "enhanced interrogation techniques"; murder is "collateral damage"; the aggressive initiation of war is a "pre-emptive strike"; the theft of taxpayers' money is a "bailout". In *1984*, history is constantly rewritten (via editing of historical documents) to align with whatever the ruling class says. The State makes up truth as it goes along; people are expected (and forced) into accepting the State's version of reality by learning to ignore contradictions in their own mind ("doublethink"). Anyone who attempts to step out of line is tortured or killed. The torturing process does not merely aim to make the citizen docile and obedient, but to actually force him to love "Big Brother", an invented face or character of the State, which psychologically functions as a tyrannical father figure for the citizens. Unlike *Brave New World*, in *1984* there is no escape for anyone who does not conform.

Both novels depict a future where a totalitarian State, based on the ideals of collectivism, which exerts a massive amount of control over the average citizen, who has faced a relentless amount of conditioning and propaganda since birth to accept the ways things are, play out his/her role and not to challenge the status quo. In both cases, the rulers tightly censor books and information to control the perception of the ruled. People have very little freedom or independence.

Although they are ostensibly fictional and set in the future, both of these novels provide a great glimpse into the current state of affairs on Earth. Now, let us move into these three accounts/ documents, which go into even greater detail about the New World Order agenda.

#1: The Protocols of the Learned Elders of Zion

The oldest of the 3 conspiracy documents I am presenting here is entitled *The Protocols of the Learned Elders of Zion*[14]. It was written

[14] www.biblebelievers.org.au/przion1.htm

sometime around 1895. Hitler read it, and it may well have escalated his hatred of the Jews; Henry Ford thought the document was so dangerous yet important that he funded printing of 500,000 copies that were distributed throughout the US in the 1920s. It is written from the perspective of the "Elders of Zion" which literally means rich and wise Jewish rulers, and presents a plan for theses rulers to enslave the rest of humanity. Because of this, it has been accused of being antisemitic. However, if you read the text from the viewpoint of Controller vs. Controlled, it all makes sense. If you interpret it through the filter of "Jew=Ruler" vs. "Non-Jew=Goyim=Slave", you realize that the message of it has nothing to do with Jews or Judaism per se. It is rather all about a small cabal of conceited and deluded people, thinking they are inherently superior and that they have the right to rule over all others. The overtly Jewish language is mostly a smokescreen to cover the real (and deadly) intent of the Protocols; I say mostly because there is, at the same time, a strong and undeniable Jewish element to the global conspiracy, centered around the Rothschilds and their creation of Zionism and Israel. However, I must emphasize the NWO conspiracy is not solely a Jewish conspiracy. That is part of it, but the average Jewish man or woman has nothing to do with it and probably knows nothing about it. It would be far more accurate to call it a Satanic conspiracy, and where it does intersect with Jewishness, it does so at a Jewish inner circle or inner cult known as Sabbatean-Frankism. It is grossly unfair to blame ordinary, innocent and well-meaning Jews for the entire conspiracy.

The Protocols promote a way in which a small, power-hungry, cunning and intelligent group can stealthily take over society, by gaining control of banking, the media and Government. It pushes the idea of collectivism to fool people into giving up individual rights "for the greater good" when, in fact, this means allowing the gross centralization of power in Government, regardless of whether that government is "left" (Communist) or "right" (Fascist), which are just labels to confuse people. It shamelessly promotes the exploitation of the weak by the strong, and a society based on hierarchy. It boasts how the "elders" were the force behind the French and other revolutions. It idealizes a world where elite rulers have the right to decide who lives and who dies.

Mr. Henry Ford, in an interview published in the New York WORLD, February 17th, 1921, said:

"The only statement I care to make about the PROTOCOLS is that they fit in with what is going on. They are sixteen years old, and they have fitted the world situation up to this time. THEY FIT IT NOW."

Here are some quotes from it so you can see what it advocates, see how the writers of this conspiracy document regard the rest of humanity, and see how the self-appointed "elders" think of themselves:

"Our right lies in force ... I find a new right – to attack by the right of the strong ... to become the sovereign lord of those who have left to us the rights of their power by laying them down voluntarily.... The

GOYIM are a flock of sheep, and we are their wolves."

"The result justifies the means ... This evil is the one and only means to attain the end, the good. Therefore we must not stop at bribery, deceit and treachery when they should serve towards the attainment of our end. In politics one must know how to seize the property of others without hesitation if by it we secure submission and sovereignty."

"The administrators, whom we shall choose from among the public, with strict regard to their capacities for servile obedience, will not be persons trained in the arts of government, and will therefore easily become pawns in our game in the hands of men of learning and genius who will be their advisers, specialists bred and reared from early childhood to rule the affairs of the whole world."

"It is essential for all to know that OWING TO DIFFERENCE IN THE OBJECTS OF HUMAN ACTIVITY THERE CANNOT BE ANY EQUALITY."

"IT IS INDISPENSABLE FOR US TO UNDERMINE ALL FAITH, TO TEAR OUT OF THE MIND OF THE "GOYIM" THE VERY PRINCIPLE OF GOD-HEAD AND THE SPIRIT, AND TO PUT IN ITS PLACE ARITHMETICAL CALCULATIONS AND MATERIAL NEEDS."

"We shall create an intensified centralization of government in order to grip in our hands all the forces of the community. We shall regulate mechanically all the actions of the political life of our

subjects by new laws. These laws will withdraw one by one all the indulgences and liberties which have been permitted by the GOYIM, and our kingdom will be distinguished by a despotism of such magnificent proportions as to be at any moment and in every place in a position to wipe out any GOYIM who oppose us by deed or word."

"THE PRINCIPLE OBJECT OF OUR DIRECTORATE CONSISTS IN THIS: TO DEBILITATE THE PUBLIC MIND BY CRITICISM; TO LEAD IT AWAY FROM SERIOUS REFLECTIONS CALCULATED TO AROUSE RESISTANCE; TO DISTRACT THE FORCES OF THE MIND TOWARDS A SHAM FIGHT OF EMPTY ELOQUENCE."

"The intensification of armaments, the increase of police forces – are all essential for the completion of the aforementioned plans. What we have to get at is that there should be in all the States of the world, besides ourselves, only the masses of the proletariat, a few millionaires devoted to our interests, police and soldiers."

"NOT A SINGLE ANNOUNCEMENT WILL REACH THE PUBLIC WITHOUT OUR CONTROL ... All our newspapers will be of all possible complexions—aristocratic, republican, revolutionary, even anarchical ... every one of them will have a finger on any one of the public opinions as required."

"We are obliged without hesitation to sacrifice individuals, who commit a breach of established order, for in the exemplary punishment of evil lies a great educational problem."

"WE SHALL SO WEAR DOWN THE "GOYIM" THAT THEY WILL BE COMPELLED TO OFFER US INTERNATIONAL POWER OF A NATURE THAT BY ITS POSITION WILL ENABLE US WITHOUT ANY VIOLENCE GRADUALLY TO ABSORB ALL THE STATE FORCES OF THE WORLD AND TO FORM A SUPER-GOVERNMENT. In place of the rulers of to-day we shall set up a bogey which will be called the Super-Government Administration.

It should also be noted that, in addition to being accused of being antisemitic, the protocols were also accused of being a fraud. The most famous person to have made this accusation was Philip Graves in 3 articles published in *The London Times* (August 16th-18th, 1921). However, his arguments are weak; Graves claims the Protocols are a plagiarism of *Dialogue in Hell Between Machiavelli and Montesquieu* published by Maurice Joly in 1864, however the 2 books are entirely different. Graves relied on the fact that Joly's book was unavailable (confiscated by Napoleon III's police once it was published since it was critical of his rule), but now that it is available, I invite you to read it for for yourself (it's free online here[15]). It's clear the Protocols is a vastly different piece of work. Graves was also a British intelligence agent (and therefore trained in psychical operations). Here David Icke explains the background in this interview[16]:

---

[15] https://archive.org/details/DialogueInHellBetweenMachiavelliAndMontesquieu/page/n2/mode/2up

[16] https://www.youtube.com/watch?v=IV8XA_TBu0s

"Those [London Times] articles were written by a British military intelligence agent called Philip Graves. And he worked with a guy called T. E. Lawrence, the famous "Lawrence of Arabia" of course, the famous movie. And what did Lawrence of Arabia do? He was a British military operative, and his role was to manipulate the Arab people of Palestine during the First World War to join the British in kicking the Ottoman Empire out of those lands. And what Lawrence did to achieve this was promise the ... Palestinians that they would have rights to self-determination on that land once the Ottoman Empire was removed. Now Lawrence of course knew that wasn't true! He knew that they wanted to get rid of the Ottoman Empire, so that the door was open for Israel to be created as it eventually was in 1948. So getting rid of the Ottoman Empire was very, very important, and the guy who produced a Russian emigre which was the Philip Graves' source in those articles, for the fact that the Protocols were a forgery, was Allen Dulles. Allen Dulles! The first head of the CIA (civilian head of the CIA) and a man who was up to his neck in intrigue and mendacity his entire career. And he was operating at that time in a diplomatic role in Turkey, and produced this emigre – never named – and the emigre was given a loan by The Times newspaper which was not expected to be paid back. And this is how those articles came about."

#2: The Secret 1969 Speech of Dr. Richard Day

The 2nd conspiracy document is actually a written account of a speech given by Dr. Richard Day in

1969[17] to a group of pediatric doctors. One of the members in the audience, Dr. Lawrence Dunegan, later recalled the speech. Dr. Day died in 1989 but at the time was a director of Planned Parenthood, a Rockefeller-funded organization that promotes population control through family planning, contraceptives and abortions. Planned Parenthood can be seen as a continuation of the eugenics agenda the elite have been pursuing for centuries, i.e. to reduce the population of "inferior" races.

Dr. Day began his speech by telling everyone to turn off any recording devices, and to not take notes. He then described the changes that would take place in society in the coming decades, from redirecting sex (encouraging promiscuity) to health (suppressing cancer cures and eliminating private doctors) to schools (changing education to indoctrination) to population control (setting up a system to force people to ask permission to have babies). He further declared that the Controllers running the global conspiracy would induce heart attacks as a form of assassination to kill political opponents (or any dissenters resisting their scheme), promote alcohol and drug abuse to weaken the will and mental clarity of the masses, consolidate their grip on the media and restrict the flow of information, obstruct the ability of the ordinary person to travel freely and combine all the world's religions into a One World Religion. Scarily enough, all these plans and more have either become or are about to become a reality. Here are some further points from his speech:

---

17 rense.com/general94/nwoplans.htm

– People will have to get used to change; everything will change, constantly;
– Everything will have 2 goals: the stated goal and the real goal;
– There will be population control; people will have to get permission to have babies. Concomitantly, the controllers will redirect the purpose of sex, so there would be sex without reproduction and reproduction without sex;
– Homosexuality and promiscuous sex would be encouraged;
– The Government will exert planning and control over medicine; private doctors will be eliminated; euthanasia will be encouraged via a "Demise Pill" (i.e. a suicide pill); limiting access to affordable medical care will make eliminating the elderly easier;
– New difficult-to-diagnose and untreatable diseases will emerge (released by government and military-controlled Bioweapons Labs);
– Cancer cures will be suppressed as a means of population control (see chapter 12);
– Food will be controlled by one giant industry;
– Education will be replaced with indoctrination, and will be used as a tool for accelerating the onset of puberty;
– Weather modification will be used by the government against foreign and domestic enemies;
– Undetectable heart attacks will be used as a form of assassination;
– All religions will be blended into a One World Religion;
– The Government will control who has access to information;
– The Government will restrict travel;

– Alcohol and drug abuse (and hedonism and promiscuity in general) will be encouraged.

#3: Silent Weapons for Quiet Wars

The 3rd conspiracy document I am featuring here is called *Silent Weapons for Quiet Wars*[18] (SWFQW). The first people to release it (including researcher and patriot Bill Cooper in 1991) originally claimed the document was found by accident on July 7, 1986 when an employee of Boeing Aircraft Co. bought a surplus IBM copier for scrap parts. However, a man by the name of Hartford Van Dyke has stepped forward and made a claim that he is the author, presenting his case[19]. Van Dyke has written other books. He states he wrote the book as a warning, that SWFQW is not a hoax, and that his great uncle Gerald Mason Van Dyke sent the warning message about the impending Japanese attack on Pearl Harbor on December 4, 1941, 3 days before the actual attack. The message was ignored by Roosevelt who wanted Japan to attack the US so as to give the US a good excuse to enter WWII.

---

[18] www.lawfulpath.com/ref/sw4qw/index.shtml

[19] www.thelivingmoon.com/45jack_files/02archives/Letters_from_the_Author_of_Silent_Weapons_for_Quiet_Wars.html

Regardless of who really authored it, the content and message of SWFQW is chilling. It details how society can be "energetically" controlled by the elite; it looks at people and money as units of electricity or energy that must obey certain laws of physics. It calls for the enslavement of humanity to be brought about quietly and stealthily by the elite using silent weapons, so that people will become gradually confused, distracted, weak and trapped, unable to put their finger on what is happening, why it is happening and who is doing it:

"It is patently impossible to discuss social engineering or the automation of a society, i.e., the engineering of social automation systems (silent weapons) on a national or worldwide scale without implying extensive objectives of social control and destruction of human life, i.e., slavery and genocide. This manual is in itself an analog declaration of intent. Such a writing must be secured from public scrutiny. Otherwise, it might be recognized as a technically formal declaration of domestic war. Furthermore, whenever any person or group of persons in a position of great power and without full knowledge and consent of the public, uses such knowledge and methodologies for economic conquest – it must be understood that a state of domestic warfare exists between said person or group of persons and the public. The solution of today's problems requires an approach which is ruthlessly candid, with no agonizing over religious, moral or cultural values."

"All science is merely a means to an end. The means is knowledge. The end is control. Beyond this

remains only one issue: Who will be the beneficiary?"

"Mr. Rothschild had discovered that currency or deposit loan accounts had the required appearance of power that could be used to induce people (inductance, with people corresponding to a magnetic field) into surrendering their real wealth in exchange for a promise of greater wealth (instead of real compensation) ... Mr. Rothschild loaned his promissory notes to individual and to governments. These would create overconfidence. Then he would make money scarce, tighten control of the system, and collect the collateral through the obligation of contracts. The cycle was then repeated. These pressures could be used to ignite a war. Then he would control the availability of currency to determine who would win the war. That government which agreed to give him control of its economic system got his support. Collection of debts was guaranteed by economic aid to the enemy of the debtor. The profit derived from this economic methodology made Mr. Rothschild all the more able to expand his wealth."

Perhaps the most famous and oft-quoted passage from the document is this:

"Everything that is expected from an ordinary weapon is expected from a silent weapon by its creators, but only in its own manner of functioning. It shoots situations, instead of bullets; propelled by data processing, instead of chemical reaction (explosion); originating from bits of data, instead of grains of gunpowder; from a computer, instead of a gun; operated by a computer programmer, instead of a marksman; under the orders of a banking magnate,

instead of a military general.

It makes no obvious explosive noises, causes no obvious physical or mental injuries, and does not obviously interfere with anyone's daily social life. Yet it makes an unmistakable "noise," causes unmistakable physical and mental damage, and unmistakably interferes with the daily social life, i.e., unmistakable to a trained observer, one who knows what to look for. The public cannot comprehend this weapon, and therefore cannot believe that they are being attacked and subdued by a weapon. The public might instinctively feel that something is wrong, but that is because of the technical nature of the silent weapon, they cannot express their feeling in a rational way, or handle the problem with intelligence. Therefore, they do not know how to cry for help, and do not know how to associate with others to defend themselves against it.

When a silent weapon is applied gradually, the public adjusts/adapts to its presence and learns to tolerate its encroachment on their lives until the pressure (psychological via economic) becomes too great and they crack up.

Therefore, the silent weapon is a type of biological warfare. It attacks the vitality, options, and mobility of the individuals of a society by knowing, understanding, manipulating, and attacking their sources of natural and social energy, and their physical, mental, and emotional strengths and weaknesses."

Distraction of the public is also a key theme

promoted:

"(T)he simplest method of securing a silent weapon and gaining control of the public is to keep the public undisciplined and ignorant of the basic system principles on the one hand, while keeping them confused, disorganized, and distracted with matters of no real importance on the other hand. This is achieved by:

- *disengaging their minds; sabotaging their mental activities; providing a low-quality program of public education in mathematics, logic, systems design and economics; and discouraging technical creativity.*
- *engaging their emotions, increasing their self-indulgence and their indulgence in emotional and physical activities, by:*
    - *unrelenting emotional affrontations and attacks (mental and emotional rape) by way of constant barrage of sex, violence, and wars in the media – especially the T.V. and the newspapers.*
    - *giving them what they desire – in excess – "junk food for thought" – and depriving them of what they really need.*
- *rewriting history and law and subjecting the public to the deviant creation, thus being able to shift their thinking from personal needs to highly fabricated outside priorities.*

These preclude their interest in and discovery of the silent weapons of social automation technology. The general rule is that there is a profit in confusion; the more confusion, the more profit. Therefore, the best approach is to create problems and then offer solutions."

The above three conspiracy documents or accounts have a lot in common. They all share the following themes, which many alternative investigators have come to know as hallmarks of the New World Order:

– Erection of a supra-national World Government based on the idea of collectivism;
– Construction of a highly-segmented, two-tier society of rulers and slaves;
– Centralized control of the key power centers of society: banking, police/military, media, education, industry and government itself;
– Manipulation of the masses through coercion *and* deception: highly efficient mass mind control so refined that its targets are unaware they are being influenced, programmed and controlled.

<u>Quotes from New World Order Insiders</u>

If you're reading any (or all) or those three documents and accounts for the first time, you are probably feeling quite shocked at the extent to which the agenda is being scientifically and meticulously planned out. Further evidence that this plan is in active operation can be found in the words of various NWO ringleaders below:

"We are grateful to the Washington Post, the New York Times, Time Magazine and other great publications whose directors have attended our meetings and respected their promises of discretion for almost 40 years......It would have been impossible for us to develop our plan for the world if we had

been subjected to the lights of publicity during those years. But, the world is more sophisticated and prepared to march towards a world government. The supernational sovereignty of an intellectual elite and world bankers is surely preferable to the national autodetermination practiced in past centuries."

– David Rockefeller[20]

"For more than a century ideological extremists at either end of the political spectrum have seized upon well-publicized incidents such as my encounter with Castro to attack the Rockefeller family for the inordinate influence they claim we wield over American political and economic institutions. Some even believe we are part of a secret cabal working against the best interests of the United States, characterizing my family and me as 'internationalists' and of conspiring with others around the world to build a more integrated global political and economic structure--one world, if you will. If that's the charge, I stand guilty, and I am proud of it."

– David Rockefeller[21]

"The world today has 6.8 billion people. That's heading up to about 9 billion. Now if we do a really great job on new vaccines, health care, reproductive health services, we could lower that [i.e. population growth] by perhaps 10 or 15 percent."

---

20 www.goodreads.com/author/show/9951.David_Rockefeller

21 www.goodreads.com/author/show/9951.David_Rockefeller

– Bill Gates[22], founder of Microsoft and now heavily involved in pushing GMOs, vaccines and microchipping

"A total population of 250-300 million people, a 95% decline from present levels, would be ideal."

– Ted Turner, billionaire and founder of CNN

"If I were reincarnated I would wish to be returned to earth as a killer virus to lower human population levels."

– Prince Phillip, British Royal Family

Here are some quotes from presidents, prime ministers and other leaders who have experienced the nature of the conspiracy firsthand:

"Since I entered politics, I have chiefly had men's views confided to me privately. Some of the biggest men in the United States, in the field of commerce and manufacture, are afraid of somebody, are afraid of something. They know that there is a power somewhere so organized, so subtle, so watchful, so interlocked, so complete, so pervasive, that they had better not speak above their breath when they speak in condemnation of it."

"A great industrial nation is controlled by its system of credit. Our system of credit is privately concentrated. The growth of the nation, therefore, and all our

---

[22] https://www.youtube.com/watch?v=oy6KVKtgL-I

activities are in the hands of a few men ... [W]e have come to be one of the worst ruled, one of the most completely controlled and dominated, governments in the civilized world—no longer a government by free opinion, no longer a government by conviction and the vote of the majority, but a government by the opinion and the duress of small groups of dominant men."

– Woodrow Wilson, President of the US from 1913-1921

"The world is governed by very different personages from what is imagined by those who are not behind the scenes."

– Benjamin Disraeli, Prime Minister of the UK in 1868 and from 1874-1880

"The governments of the present day have to deal not merely with other governments, with emperors, kings and ministers, but also with the secret societies which have everywhere their unscrupulous agents, and can at the last moment upset all the governments' plans."

– Benjamin Disraeli, Prime Minister of the UK in 1868 and from 1874-1880

"Behind the ostensible government sits enthroned an invisible government owing no allegiance and acknowledging no responsibility to the people. To destroy this invisible government, to befoul the unholy alliance between corrupt business and corrupt politics, is the first task of the statesmanship of

today."

– Theodore Roosevelt, President of the US from 1901-1909

"In politics, nothing happens by accident. If it happens, you can bet it was planned that way."

"A financial element in the large centers has owned the government since the days of Andrew Jackson."

– Franklin D. Roosevelt, President of the US from 1933-1945

"From the days of Spartacus-Weishaupt (Illuminati founder Adam Weishaupt) to those of Karl Marx, and down to Trotsky (Russia), Bela Kun (Hungary), Rosa Luxembourg (Germany), and Emma Goldman (United States), this world-wide conspiracy for the overthrow of civilization and for the reconstitution of society on the basis of arrested development, of envious malevolence, and impossible equality, has been steadily growing. It played ... a definitely recognizable part in the tragedy of the French Revolution. It has been the mainspring of every subversive movement during the Nineteenth Century; and now at last this band of extraordinary personalities from the underworld of the great cities of Europe and America have gripped the Russian people by the hair of their heads and have become practically the undisputed masters of that enormous empire."

– Winston Churchill, Prime Minister of the UK from 1940-1945

"There's a government inside the government, and I don't control it."

– Bill Clinton, President of the US from 1993-2001

"The very word "secrecy" is repugnant in a free and open society; and we are as a people inherently and historically opposed to secret societies, to secret oaths and secret proceedings. We decided long ago that the dangers of excessive and unwarranted concealment of pertinent facts far outweighed the dangers which are cited to justify it. Even today, there is little value in opposing the threat of a closed society by imitating its arbitrary restrictions. Even today, there is little value in insuring the survival of our nation if our traditions do not survive with it. And there is very grave danger that an announced need for increased security will be seized upon those anxious to expand its meaning to the very limits of official censorship and concealment. That I do not intend to permit to the extent that it is in my control. And no official of my Administration, whether his rank is high or low, civilian or military, should interpret my words here tonight as an excuse to censor the news, to stifle dissent, to cover up our mistakes or to withhold from the press and the public the facts they deserve to know.

For we are opposed around the world by a monolithic and ruthless conspiracy that relies on covert means for expanding its sphere of influence–on infiltration instead of invasion, on subversion instead of elections, on intimidation instead of free choice, on guerrillas by night instead of armies by day. It is a system which has conscripted vast human and material resources into the building of a tightly knit, highly efficient machine that combines military, diplomatic, intelligence, economic, scientific and political operations. Its preparations are concealed, not published. Its mistakes are buried, not headlined. Its dissenters are silenced, not praised. No expenditure is questioned, no rumor is printed, no secret is revealed."

– John Kennedy, President of the US from 1961-1963

"The real menace of our Republic is the invisible government, which like a giant octopus sprawls its slimy legs over our cities, states and nation ... The little coterie of powerful international bankers virtually run the United States government for their own selfish purposes. They practically control both parties ... [and] control the majority of the newspapers and magazines in this country. They use the columns of these papers to club into submission or drive out of office public officials who refuse to do the bidding of the powerful corrupt cliques which compose the invisible government. It operates under cover of a self-created screen [and] seizes our executive officers, legislative bodies, schools, courts, newspapers and every agency created for the public protection."

– John F. Hylan[23], Mayor of New York City from 1918-1925

---

[23] https://timesmachine.nytimes.com/timesmachine/1922/12/10/109339923.pdf

"A power has risen up in the government greater than the people themselves, consisting of many, and various, and powerful interests, combined into one mass, and held together by the cohesive power of the vast surplus in the banks."

– John Calhoun, former US Vice President from 1825-1832

"[I]nstruments to promote the general welfare, they have become the tools of corrupt interests which use them in martialing to serve their selfish purposes. Behind the ostensible government sits enthroned an invisible government owing no allegiance and acknowledging no responsibility."

– Theodore Roosevelt, former US President

"We have a well-organized political-action group in this country, determined to destroy our Constitution and establish a one-party state ... It operates secretly, silently, continuously to transform our Government ... This ruthless power-seeking elite is a disease of our century... This group ... is answerable neither to the President, the Congress, nor the courts. It is practically irremovable."

– William Jenner, 1954

"[The CIA is a] cult of intelligence ... that held itself to be above the normal processes of society, with its own rationale and justification, beyond the restraints of the Constitution ..."

– William Colby, former CIA Director

"The real rulers in Washington are invisible, and exercise power from behind the scenes."

– Judge Felix Frankfurter

"[The] nation state as a fundamental unit of man's organized life has ceased to be the principal creative force. International banks and multinational corporations are acting and planning in terms that are far in advance of the political concepts of the nation state."

– Zbigniew Brzezinski, former US National Security Advisor, Globalist and Co-Founder of the Trilateral Commission

"*Exitus acta probat*" (The end justifies the means)

– Written on Washington Arch, New York

<u>Testimony and Accounts of 20 Ex-Intelligence Agents</u>

Those quotes capture the essence of the conspiracy. So too does the following collection of testimony of many ex-intelligence officers who have worked in the belly of the beast – the Military Intelligence Complex (MIC). The MIC is an important part of the coming NWO, and forms part of the Deep State, Parallel Government, Shadow Government or Secret Government, depending on what you like to call it. I believe all these terms are basically taking about the same thing: the unelected true power and ruling force that pulls the puppet strings of the politicians and characters you see on TV and in public.

Here are eleven ex-CIA agents who broke out of the cult to tell the public the truth.

1. Edward Snowden: Snowden burst onto the public scene in June 2013 with a story that captured the imagination of billions of people around the world. At only a young 29 years of age, but with a large amount of calmness, confidence and moral integrity, Snowden quit his comfortable life in Hawaii (including leaving his girlfriend and a cushy $100,000+ annual income) and fled to Hong Kong with laptops and thumb drives full of genuine classified NSA documents. There he met with journalists Glenn Greenwald, Laura Poitras and The Guardian's Ewen MacAskill to hand over his total cache.

Ex-CIA employee and ex-NSA contractor Edward Snowden, arguably the most famous whistleblower in the history of the world. His leaks of NSA documents brought the crimes of the Military Intelligence Complex to general public awareness like nothing else before or since.

To protect his life, Snowden gave all the files to several other sources. He instructed them to release all the information in the event of his death. Thanks to Snowden, numerous NSA programs which were only known to avid conspiracy researchers then became public knowledge, since the evidence of warrantless wiretapping was there in black and white for anyone to see. Snowden is especially well know for exposing details on Upstream Collection programs (Blarney, Fairview, Oakstar and Stormbrew), Downstream Collection programs (PRISM) and other projects or programs such as XKeyscore, Echelon, Carnivore, Dishfire, Stoneghost, Tempora, Frenchelon, Fairview, Mystic, DCSN, Boundless Informant, Bullrun, Pinwale, Stingray and SORM. The first Snowden document published by The Guardian was a secret court (a FISA court) order authorizing the NSA to collect the telephone records of millions of US Verizon customers.

The point is that the NSA and MIC forced companies (big or small) to roll over. They then forbade these companies from telling you they rolled over. A massive number of people can access and analyze an obscene amount of data on you. The NSA skirted the law about not spying on Americans through its partnership with Britain's GCHQ (Government Communication Headquarters), because American data can get routed through GCHQ and then become "foreign" data. The GCHQ is the UK version of the NSA and also conducts mass surveillance on its citizens.

Snowden achieved his aim of bringing the topic of

mass surveillance into the public spotlight, in the hopes of provoking discussion and debate. However, despite this success, the NSA remains entrenched in the Deep State and continues its nefarious activities largely undisturbed. In March 2019, Greenwald was part of a disappointing decision made at *The Intercept* (which he co-founded with Poitras) to shut down the Snowden archive completely, despite having released less than 10% of it to the public. The excuses offered by Greenwald (and another *Intercept* co-founder, Jeremy Scahill) that it was shut down for financial reasons don't hold water. Many speculate that PayPal founder and billionaire Pierre Omidyar, sole shareholder of First Look Media that owns *The Intercept*, had planned all along to buy out and "privatize" the Snowden archive as a means of controlling it and preventing future release. Right now, enough of it has been released to scare the public and possibly condition most of them into a state of helplessness. Is the MIC sending a covert message to us all – *"you are being watched, you know you are being watched, we know that you know you are being watched, and there's nothing any of you can do about it?"* If so, it is a trick to reduce resistance to their schemes, just as the Borg in Star Trek would announce that *"resistance is futile."*

2. **Robert Steele:** Former Marine, CIA case officer and US co-founder of the US Marine Corps intelligence activity, the late Robert Steele's mission was to spread the use of Open Source Intelligence (OSINT). He wrote handbooks on OSINT for NATO, the DIA and US Special Operations Forces. He stated that the preconditions for revolution exist in the US, UK and other western countries. He

enumerated[24] such conditions as: *"elite isolation to concentrated wealth to inadequate socialization and education, to concentrated land holdings to loss of authority to repression of new technologies especially in relation to energy, to the atrophy of the public sector and spread of corruption, to media dishonesty, to mass unemployment of young men and on and on and on."*

3. Michael Scheuer: Ex-CIA intelligence Michael Scheuer has been an outspoken critic of US foreign policy for decades. He has been one of the few to have the guts to criticize Israel and cast doubts on why the US would want to ally itself so closely with the Zionist regime (hint: it's because the Rothschilds [richest and most powerful family in the world directing the NWO] control Israel and also the US, thus can dictate how the US spends its money and chooses its allies). Scheuer has also had the intelligence to highlight the dangerous alliance between Israel and Saudi Arabia[25], and expose how that alliance is far, far more dangerous to the US and some surrounding nations than Iran.

In his 2004 book *Imperial Hubris*, he depicted bin Laden as a rational actor who was fighting to undermine the US by weakening its economy, rather than merely combating and killing Americans. Now that doesn't fit too well with the official narrative on

---

[24] https://www.theguardian.com/environment/earth-insight/2014/jun/19/open-source-revolution-conquer-one-percent-cia-spy

[25] thefreedomarticles.com/israel-and-saudi-arabia-best-friends/

terrorism and Islam, as we shall see in the next chapters.

4. Susan Lindauer: Ex-CIA agent Susan Lindauer endured 5 years of unjust imprisonment with no trial under the Patriot Act for the crime of speaking the truth. After 10 years, she broke her silence on 9/11, revealing how George W. Bush, Cheney and Rumsfeld had decided to go to war with Iraq before 9/11 occurred. She also exposed how her CIA handler Richard Fuse made her deliver threatening messages to the Iraqis – even though they possessed no WMDs and had no knowledge of the hijackings. She confirms that the leader of the hijackers, Mohammed Atta, was a CIA asset.

5. John Kiriakou: Kiriakou was one of the most punished whistleblowers in recent times. After being at the CIA for years, he resigned in 2004, then 3 years later in December 2007 he decided to go on television and publicly call out the CIA for its "immoral, unethical and illegal torture programs"[26]. He rightly accused the CIA of lying when the agency falsely claimed that it gained "actionable intelligence" through the torture, which violated many laws and the 8th Amendment in the Bill of Rights (which forbids cruel and unusual punishments). Like Lindauer, Kiriakou was imprisoned for his trouble.

---

[26] thefreedomarticles.com/government-torture-cia-tip-of-iceberg/

6. Kevin Shipp: Ex-CIA agent Kevin Shipp worked as a counter-terrorism agent. He has exposed the corruption of Barack Obama, Eric Holder, Hillary Clinton, George Soros, Susan Rice, John Brennan, Huma Abedin and many more. He has talked on various issues of truth, such as the 9/11 false flag event, the vaccine-autism connection, how mass migration is being deliberately used to destabilize the West and how the MIC has perfected the art of intimidating and destroying whistleblowers.

7. Philip Giraldi: Giraldi is an ex-CIA officer and former director of the Council for the National Interest, a 501c4 nonprofit, non-partisan organization in the US that works for "Middle East policies that serve the American national interest." Giraldi has been outspoken in his criticism of the Deep State, the American war machine and the untoward Israeli influence over US officials. He has exposed the propaganda of the White Helmets in Syria and the War on Terror. Giraldi writes that, *"I would characterize international terrorism as a faux threat at a national level, though one that has been exaggerated through the media and fearmongering to such an extent that it appears much more dangerous than it actually is."*[27] He has said that the idea that Syrian President Assad attacked his own people with chemical weapons is a sham. He has also asked the key question of why the US is targeting Iran when it should be targeting Saudi Arabia.

8. Philip Agee: The late Philip Agee, who died in 2008, was an ex-CIA case officer with a conscience

[27] www.unz.com/pgiraldi/who-is-the-real-enemy/

who blew the whistle on the CIA's dastardly and nefarious activities. He worked in the CIA during the 1950s and finally left in 1968. He became a whistleblower and author of several books exposing the agency. When the US revoked his passport in 1979, he first lived in Grenada in 1980 until Bishop was overthrown by the US, then in Nicaragua until 1990 when the Sandanistas were overthrown by the US, then Germany and Cuba. He knows firsthand the CIA's subversive activities and terrorism of Central and South America. Former CIA Director and later President Bush (senior) called Agee a traitor.

9. John Stockwell: Stockwell worked with the CIA during their covert operations in Angola, Congo and Vietnam. After he left the agency, he exposed how the main activities of the CIA – drug running, assassinating foreign and domestic presidents, installing foreign puppet regimes and destroying the environment – are all interrelated. He boldly stated that the CIA was counterproductive to national security. In 1978 he appeared on *60 Minutes* to expose that then CIA Director William Colby and National Security Advisor Henry Kissinger had systematically lied to Congress about the CIA's operations.

10. Chip Tatum: Ex-CIA agent Chip Tatum worked in Black Operations, in the drug smuggling trade between the US and Central American countries. He personally flew a plane with cargo which, he later discovered, turned out to be cocaine. Tatum was threatened not to speak out but exposed the lurid details of the Mena, Arkansas cocaine smuggling ring, which involved Bill Clinton up to his neck. Additionally, Tatum claims Bush senior had Barry Seal and Manuel Noriega assassinated, and also gave Tatum the order to kill presidential candidate Ross Perot (which he refused to do).

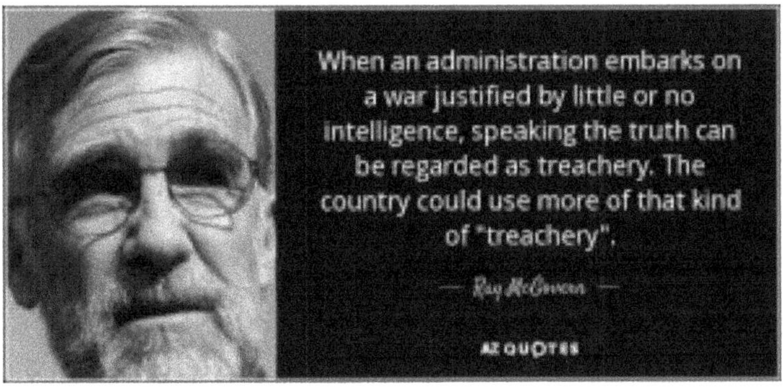

11. Ray McGovern: McGovern is a wonderfully outspoken ex-CIA analyst and co-founder of Veteran Intelligence Professionals for Sanity (VIPs). He has accused the CIA of being a rogue agency many times, stating that the CIA routinely cooks up "intelligence" to justify pre-planned wars (e.g. Iraq, Afghanistan and Libya). It's not bad intelligence; it's fixed intelligence. Furthermore, he has stated that US Presidents are scared of CIA directors, and that Congress hasn't done anything to rein in the CIA before at least 9/11, if not before the time of JFK. In this video[28], McGovern famously challenged the lies of Donald Rumseld to his face. Rumsfeld was a former executive at Searle Pharmaceuticals (that developed the horrible chemical aspartame) and former Secretary of Defense during 9/11 (when they just "lost" $2.3 trillion the day before 9/11). He oversaw the US invade Iraq and other nations post

28 https://www.youtube.com/watch?v=v1FTmuhynaw

9/11.

The following agents didn't work for the CIA but worked for some other agencies such as the NSA.

12. William Binney: William Binney worked at the NSA over 30 years, including time as a director of the NSA's World Geopolitical and Military Analysis Reporting Group. He estimated in 2012 that the NSA had amassed over 20,000,000,000,000 (20 trillion) "transactions" from Americans (in gross violation of the Constitution), where a transaction means a piece of information or communication, such as emails, text messages and scripts of phone calls. This would include every single email sent and received by US residents since 9/11. Binney has been outspoken in his criticism for the NSA, stating how current NSA surveillance far surpasses the capability of the former Soviet KGB and the DDR Stasi agencies. Binney has exposed how we have gone way down the slippery slope towards totalitarianism, while the NSA, the MIC and the National Security State hide behind the ever-present pretext of "national security."

Binney has also pointed out, on many occasions,

the futility of the MIC and NSA collecting so much information. With so much data, the job of trying to find the important stuff becomes extremely difficult or impossible, since 99.99% of what the NSA collects and analyzes is irrelevant (note: irrelevant to the job of counter-terrorism, but not irrelevant to the job of spying on everyone).

To paraphrase Binney: the NSA is suffering from analysis paralysis and data is not intelligence.

13. Thomas Drake: Whistleblower Thomas Drake was not only a senior executive at the NSA, but is also a decorated US Air Force and Navy veteran. Drake exposed another of the NSA's numerous programs, this one called Project Trailblazer. He was charged under the Espionage Act, but in June 2011, all 10 original charges against him were dropped. He is the 2011 recipient of the Ridenhour Prize for Truth-Telling and co-recipient of the Sam Adams Associates for Integrity in Intelligence (SAAII) award.

14. Kirk Wiebe: Ex-NSA whistleblower J. Kirk Wiebe was a senior analyst at the NSA from 1975 to 2001. After the 9/11 false flag op, he stumbled upon secret NSA programs to monitor all Americans. He worked alongside William Binney in exposing these projects, and as with Binney, Wiebe's house was raided by the FBI in 2007 for his whistleblowing efforts. In September 2002, Wiebe, along with Binney, Drake and another NSA agent Ed Loomis, filed a DoD Inspector General report regarding problems at NSA, including Trailblazer. The report was jointly filed with Diane Roark, a staffer for the

Republicans on the House Intelligence Committee of the US Congress who was considered a staff expert on the NSA's budget. The report went nowhere.

15. Russell Tice: Ex-NSA agent Russell Tice came forward in 2004 to expose the NSA's spying invasions. He has revealed shocking details of NSA spying, mentioning some of the specific targets of past NSA wiretapping operations, which included senior Congressional leaders (e.g. Dianne Feinstein), the former White House Press Secretary and high-ranking military generals (e.g. David Petraeus, who was forced to resign as CIA chief because he was caught [by the NSA presumably] having an affair). Tice also revealed that the entire Supreme Court, and even then-Senator from Illinois and future President, Barack Obama, was being tapped.

16. Ted Gunderson: Gunderson is a man who will need little introduction to many investigators in the field of conspiracy research, or to those who have looked into pedophilia, mind control, child trafficking and Satanism. He was a 27-year veteran FBI special agent who worked in the Los Angeles district with over 700 agents under his command. He has worked and done interviews/presentations with various mind control survivors (e.g. Brice Taylor, Paul Bonacci). Towards the end of his career, he stumbled upon the network of occult Secret Societies that rule the world. Through his investigations, he came to understand that we were dealing with a sick Satanic cult that uses mind control over its victims, conducts an international pedophile ring where children were abducted through underground tunnels, and performs dark rituals with human sacrifice and child sex slaves. At these rituals, Satanists get a dark "high" from drinking the blood of their tortured victims, which contains emotional neurochemicals released into the blood at the time of their death. With upwards of 100,000 American children missing every year, Gunderson claimed he knew firsthand that the FBI was fully complicit in the coverup of all this.

17. Sibel Edmonds: ex-FBI agent Sibel Edmonds become a famous whistleblower when she discovered corruption at the FBI and reported it to her supervisors. They retaliated by firing her. She sued for unfair dismissal in July 2002, but as happens so much in this kind of arena, the case was dismissed in July 2004 by Judge Reggie Walton who cited the governmental state secrets privilege (read my article *The Secret Privilege by Which the Military Intelligence Complex Retains Control*[29] to understand the history and significance of the state secrets privilege, which is routinely used by Government to cover up its crimes). In August 2004 Edmonds founded the National Security Whistleblowers Coalition (NSWBC), an organization to help national security whistleblowers. In September 2006 a documentary about Edmonds's case called *Kill the Messenger* (*Une Femme à Abattre*) premiered in France. The film features ex-CIA agent Philip Gerald (whistleblower #8 above) who reveals that Israel was a key player in the illicit activities Edmonds discovered.

Edmonds is also the main source of information about Operation Gladio B. This was a continuation of

---

29 thefreedomarticles.com/state-secrets-privilege-mic/

the Operation Gladio project which the CIA had been running throughout Europe (using right-wing extremes, neo-fascists and arch-nationalists to carry out false flag attacks to frame left-wing communists). According to Edmonds, around 1996-1997, the NATO-CIA-MI5-MI6 alliance decided to switch from using fascists to using Islamic terrorists, as the Cold War had ended. The world was about to be formally introduced into a newer, scarier and more convenient enemy to replace communism – Radical Islamic Terrorism™ – which we will get to in chapter 4.

18. Patrick Lang: Lang is an ex-DIA colonel who spoke up when Trump decided to strike Syria[30] (while eating chocolate cake with the Chinese premier Xi Jinping). Lang compared the attack to the false flag Gulf of Tonkin incident, where then US President LBJ pretended that the North Vietnamese and fired upon US ships (when they were just firing upon empty water – more on this later in this chapter). The Trump Syria strike was likewise based on a pack of lies. Lang said:

"This is Gulf of Tonkin 2. How ironic. Donald Trump correctly castigated George W. Bush for launching an unprovoked, unjustified attack on Iraq in 2003. Now we have President Donald Trump doing the same damn thing ... Here's the good news. The Russians and Syrians were informed, or at least were aware, that the attack was coming. They were able to remove a large number of their assets. The base the United States hit was something of a backwater.

[30] thefreedomarticles.com/trump-syria-strike-same-old-lies/

Donald Trump gets to pretend that he is a tough guy. He is not. He is a fool."

19. Annie Machon: for the last one on the list, we turn to the UK, the staunchest US ally in the world and the erstwhile World Empire from which the US learnt its tricks. The UK, like the US, has a sprawling Military Intelligence Complex, composed of various agencies such as the aforementioned GCHQ, MI5 (Military Intelligence 5, responsible for domestic counterintelligence and security) and MI6 (Military Intelligence 6, responsible for domestic counterintelligence and security). Machon resigned in 1996 to blow the whistle on all the incompetence and crimes she witnessed. She has spoken on topics such as 9/11, 7/7, false flag ops, Secret Societies and the Bilderberg Group. In earlier interviews and films, she appeared alongside another ex-MI5 agent, David Shayler, her former partner.

There is one more whistleblower I am including to round out the twenty called Robert Duncan. He is featured later in chapter 11 relating to mind control.

Declassified Governmental Documents

So far, we have looked at reports, accounts and testimonies. While they offer valuable evidence of the New World Order conspiracy, they have certain shortcomings. People may have false memories. People may be deliberately lying. The conspirators rely on a concept known as "plausible deniability", which is a fancy way of saying that they try to prevent enough details and solid, forensic evidence from coming out, so that they may plausibly deny things and escape legal liability. Some accounts and testimonies are too vague and unprovable to convict someone in a court of law.

However, to counter this, below I present even more evidence of the conspiracy, this time in actual declassified governmental documents. This is only a small snippet of the available range of declassified files out in the public for all to see – and will hopefully satisfy those skeptics who require black-and-white proof.

The handy thing about declassified docs is that they are genuine pieces of evidence that prove governmental criminality. It's hard for naysayers and censors to deny the authenticity of governmental declassified files which show that our history is full of conspiracy fact, not conspiracy theory. These declassified files (most from the US Government) prove the real crimes it has been engaged in, spanning areas including forced sterilization, mind control, weather modification, false flag operations and igniting war. The documents speak for themselves.

Operation Mockingbird

Operation Mockingbird was a CIA project to infiltrate and covertly control the media. It began in the 1950s under then CIA director Allen Dulles. The declassified files (most are classified and secret, but you can find a tiny fraction here[31]) show how the CIA

[31] documents.theblackvault.com/documents/cia/operationmockingbirdCIA.pdf

infiltrated the mainstream media and had its pieces inserted into TV, newspapers and journals everywhere as "news" when they were nothing more than lies and propaganda. Richard Salant, former President of CBS News, once said that *"our job is to give people not what they want, but what we decide they ought to have."* Mockingbird was famously exposed in the 1975 Church Committee hearings (see a video excerpt here[32]). Nothing much has changed today. Journalists worldwide are still on the payroll, and some were brave enough to talk about it, such as the late Udo Ulfkotte[33].

Operation Paperclip

Think that World War II ended with the defeat of the Nazis? Think again. They didn't get defeated; they just went south (Argentina) and joined the ranks of their conquerors (US, UK, Russia) in a dirty deal of legal immunity for inside information. The German scientists, technicians and engineers had made brilliant and groundbreaking advances in many fields in the leadup to and during the war, and the victors didn't have a moral problem with the Nazi weapons of destruction ... the only problem was that the brilliant scientists were on the wrong side. The US got a sizeable portion of these Nazi scientists (around 1500) and smuggled them into NASA and the CIA, where some of them such as Wernher von Braun went on to make a name for themselves. Thus, the US willingly allowed its military and intelligence agencies to be infected with Nazi

[32] https://www.youtube.com/watch?v=cDCfTlapds0

[33] https://www.youtube.com/watch?v=alaFkR9uriU

ideology, which continues to this day. You can read the declassified docs relating to Project Paperclip or Operation Paperclip at this footnote[34].

Some of the many Nazis smuggled into the US under Operation Paperclip.

The Escape of Hitler and Other Nazis to Argentina

The mainstream narrative is that at the end of WWII, Hitler committed suicide in Berlin in a bunker. It's a nice story, but apparently, that's all it is – a story. In his book *Hitler in Argentina: The Documented Truth of Hitler's Escape from Berlin*, author Harry Cooper produced a slew of astounding evidence that Hitler and other top Nazis such as Martin Bormann traveled in German submarines all the way to Argentina. Some of the evidence that this astonishing

[34] documents.theblackvault.com/documents/wwii/paperclipcia.pdf

claim is true are these FBI declassified docs[35].

The article *FBI Quietly Declassified Secret Files Attesting Hitler Fled to Argentina in 1945*[36] contains further information:

"Along with the FBI documents detailing an eye witness account of Hitler's whereabouts in Argentina, more evidence is coming to light to help prove that Adolf Hitler and Eva Braun did not die in that bunker. In 1945, the Naval Attaché in Buenos Aires informed Washington there was a high probability that Hitler and Eva Braun had just arrived in Argentina. This coincides with the sightings of the submarine U-530. Added proof comes in the form of newspaper articles detailing the construction of a Bavarian styled mansion in the foothills of the Andes Mountains. Further proof comes in the form of architect Alejandro Bustillo who wrote about his design and construction of Hitler's new home[37] *which was financed by earlier wealthy German immigrants … [An] archeologist from Connecticut State, Nicholas Bellatoni was allowed to perform DNA testing on one of the skull fragments recovered. What he discovered set off a reaction through the intelligence and scholarly communities. Not only did the DNA not match any recorded samples thought to be Hitler's, they did not match Eva Braun's familiar DNA either."*

---

35 https://vault.fbi.gov/adolf-hitler/adolf-hitler-part-01-of-04/view

36 humansarefree.com/2015/02/fbi-quietly-declassified-secret-files.html

37 https://books.google.com/books?id=OBFNCAAAQBAJ&pg=PA243#v=onepage

Operation Northwoods

This is a great one for all those who think that the government would never hurt its own citizens. Operation Northwoods was the outrageous plan for the US military to attack its own people and cities (Washington DC and Miami) as a false flag operation to frame Cuba. The plans detailed in the document included the possible assassination of Cuban émigrés, sinking boats of Cuban refugees on the high seas, hijacking planes, blowing up a US ship and carrying out acts of terrorism on US soil – all done secretly by the US military as a pretext to gain sympathy and support to invade Cuba.

The 1962 declassified US Joint Chiefs of Staff Memo was entitled *"Operation Northwoods – Justification for US Military Intervention in Cuba."* In its own words, the document states that a *"series of well coordinated incidents will be planned to take place in and around Guantanamo to give genuine appearance of being done by hostile Cuban forces."* Luckily JFK had the nous to reject the plan; by 1962 he had discerned the insidious influence of

Military Intelligence Complex upon his presidency. You can find some of the declassified docs for Operation Northwoods at this footnote[38].

ColntelPro

ColntelPro has become a famous word of its own, derived from the full operational name Counter Intelligence Program. This was a program run by the FBI under Hoover which started in 1956. ColntelPro was a series of undercover operations that targeted people and groups the US Government deemed were a problem, such as the communist party, other far left groups, civil rights groups, far right groups (e.g. the KKK) and individuals activists such as Martin Luther King. The scope of ColntelPro was broad: it involved monitoring, surveilling, infiltrating, discrediting and disrupting. Although then Attorney General Robert Kennedy authorized some spying, the FBI was given an inch and took a mile (much like today's spy agencies), clearly overstepping the bounds of legality. It became a way for the government to intimidate and stifle dissidents. You can read declassified docs on ColntelPro at this footnote[39].

CIA Drug Smuggling

The CIA has long used illegal drugs to fund its illegal operations. Drugs are often one of the secret motivation behind wars. Vietnam is part of the Golden Triangle of heroin-producing opium poppies,

---

38 nsarchive2.gwu.edu//news/20010430/doc1.pdf

39 https://vault.fbi.gov/cointel-pro

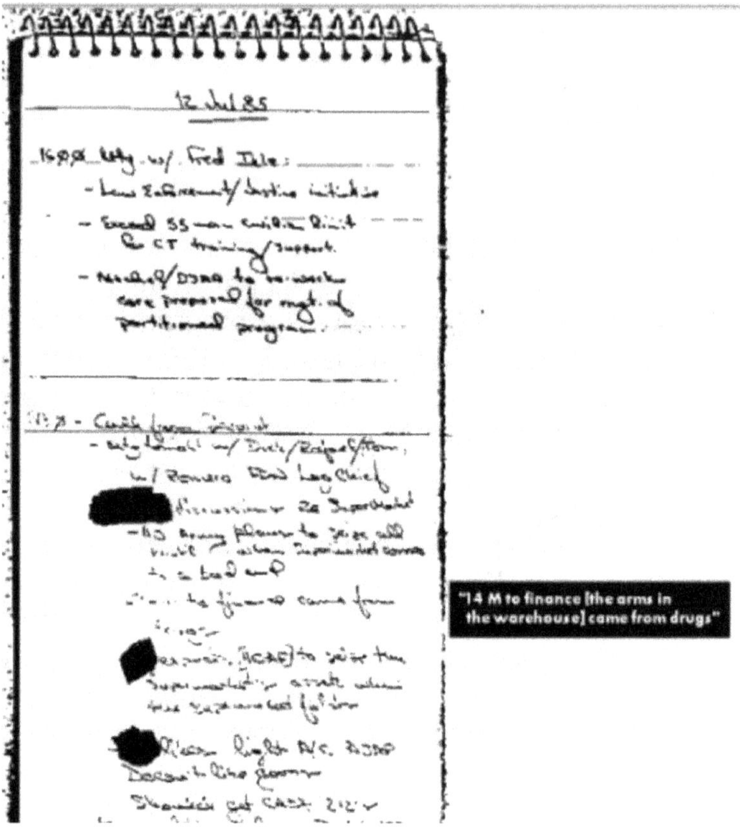
"14 M to finance [the arms in the warehouse] came from drugs"

Afghanistan is also home to huge swathes of opium poppies and after the US invaded many Central and South American countries, it took control of the cocaine production there. In 1996, journalist Gary Webb exposed the connection between the CIA, cocaine and the Nicaraguan contras. In the early 1980s the CIA pushed the sale of cocaine in Los Angeles to help finance their covert war against the Sandinistas in Nicaragua. You can read some of the declassified files on this at this footnote[40], including

[40] https://nsarchive.wordpress.com/2015/04/07/the-dark-alliance-declassified/

excerpts from Oliver North's notebook obtained under the FOIA. North writes that Air Force General Richard Secord told him (North) that *"14 M to finance [the arms in the warehouse] came from drugs."*

Operation Gladio

Operation Gladio, which still continues to this day, is the codename for a clandestine NATO "stay-behind" operation in Italy during the Cold War. The CIA spearheaded Gladio under the pretext of preventing the spread of Soviet communism in Europe. The name *gladio* is the Italian form of *gladius*, a type of Roman shortsword. Gladio came to refer to a whole range of stay-behind cells and groups in Europe, although originally, Operation Gladio was the Italian branch. Gladio became famous when then Italian Prime Minister Giulio Andreotti talked about it. Gladio involved the Freemasons, Mafia members and the Vatican, who all united with the CIA and NATO in a holy war against communism. Operation Gladio was responsible for some horrible atrocities and false flag attacks in Italy, such as the bombing of Bologna train station in 1980. Today, even the Western-backed fighters in Nazi Ukraine and Syria are basically Gladio fighters. Declassified files on Gladio can be found at this footnote[41].

Forced Sterilization Programs

The United States Government has a long and

---

[41] www.theblackvault.com/documentarchive/operation-gladio/

sordid history of using its own people as guinea pigs and unwitting subjects for experimentation, much of which was done without their knowledge or consent. Some of this came in the form of forced sterilization programs. You can read the declassified files at this footnote[42]. This article[43] describes a particular program aimed at Native American Indian women:

"During the late 1960s and the early 1970s, a policy of involuntary surgical sterilization was imposed upon Native American women in the United States, usually without their knowledge or consent, by the federally funded Indian Health Service (IHS), then run by the Bureau of Indian Affairs (BIA). It is alleged that the existence of the sterilization program was discovered by members of the American Indian Movement (AIM) during its occupation of the BIA headquarters in 1972. A 1974 study by Women of All Red Nations (WARN), concluded that as many as 42 percent of all American Indian women of childbearing age had, by that point, been sterilized without their consent. A subsequent investigation was conducted by the U.S. General Accounting Office (GAO), though it was restricted to only four of the many IHS facilities nationwide and examined only the years 1973 to 1976. The GAO study showed that 3,406 involuntary sterilizations were performed in these four IHS hospitals during this three-year period. Consequently, the IHS was transferred to the Department of Health and Human Services in 1978."

---

[42] www.gao.gov/assets/120/117355.pdf

[43] https://www.encyclopedia.com/social-sciences/encyclopedias-almanacs-transcripts-and-maps/forced-sterilization-native-americans

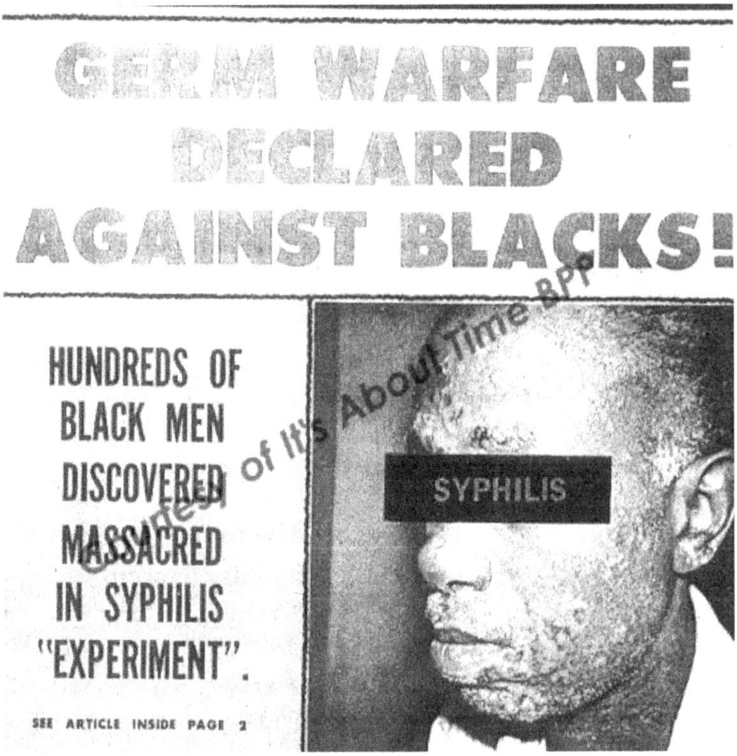

GERM WARFARE DECLARED AGAINST BLACKS!

HUNDREDS OF BLACK MEN DISCOVERED MASSACRED IN SYPHILIS "EXPERIMENT".

SEE ARTICLE INSIDE PAGE 2

Tuskegee Syphilis Experiment

One of the darkest episodes in the history of the US Government, the Tuskegee syphilis experiment was a nefarious clinical study conducted by the US Public Health Service which began in 1932 and lasted all the way to 1972. The point was to study the natural progression of untreated syphilis in rural African American men who thought they were receiving free health care from the government. It involved knowingly giving the men syphilis without their knowledge, telling them they just had "bad blood", then watching them as the disease progressed. The researchers (or perhaps better put, sadists) deliberately didn't treat the men with penicillin which was found in the 1940s to be an effective cure for syphilis. Meanwhile, numerous men in the study died of syphilis, 40 of their wives contracted the disease and subsequently 19 children were born with congenital syphilis. If you feel angry reading about this, or shake your head in disbelief at the sheer level of evil involved, I don't blame you.

You can read the declassified files at this footnote[44].

Operation LAC and Operation Dew

Human experimentation has not just been limited to the injection of diseases and sterilization. There have also been tests upon the population which have involved spraying entire areas with pathological agents (sometimes natural, sometimes manmade biological warfare agents). Two examples of this are Operation LAC (Large Area Coverage) and Operation Dew, both carried out by the US Army Chemical Corps in the 1950s, both of which involved dispersing tiny zinc cadmium sulfide (ZnCdS) particles (which were fluorescent) and plant spores (*lycopodium*) from an aircraft over much of the country. The goal was to ascertain the dispersion and geographic range of the sprayed agents. The Government said it was safe at first, but Wikipedia states that *"according to the National Library of Medicine's TOXNET database, the EPA reported that Cadmium-sulfide was classified as a probable human carcinogen."*

---

[44] https://catalog.archives.gov/id/281643

You can read some of the declassified files at this footnote[45].

Project Sunshine

Body snatching and experimentation upon dead bodies (cadavers) is also a documented fact when it comes to governmental crimes. During the 1950s, the US AEC (Atomic Energy Commission) and US Air Force conducted a study on the global health effects of fallout from nuclear weapons testing. The AEC wanted to learn more about how strontium-90 (a radioactive isotope of strontium) affected human tissue and bones, so they secretly collected (stole) over 1500 tissue samples from the bodies of dead babies and young children from around the globe – without consent. Project Sunshine was declassified[46] in 1959.

Operation Popeye

All those who are still in denial over the reality of chemtrails, cloud seeding and geoengineering programs may want to take a look at this. Operation Popeye was a weather modification program in Southeast Asia (mainly Laos and Vietnam) from 1967 to 1972. The purpose was to aid US efforts in the Vietnam War. Specifically, it was a cloud seeding operation which aimed to extend the monsoon season (targeted over areas of the Ho Chi Minh Trail) by inducing rain over the *"infiltration routes in North*

[45] data2.archives.ca/e/e443/e011063033.pdf

[46] https://www.rand.org/content/dam/rand/pubs/reports/2008/R251.pdf

Vietnam and southern Laos" and therefore to *"interdict or at least interfere with truck traffic between North and South Vietnam"* – as written in this memo[47] from the Deputy Under Secretary of State for Political Affairs (Kohler) to Secretary of State Rusk. Remember, this was the 1960s. Imagine what they can do today with HAARP and geoengineering.

Iran Flight 655

The US and Iran have been on tense terms for a long time. In 1953, the US decided to target Iran with one of its now famous regime change programs to overthrow the democratically elected Mohammad Mosaddegh and replace him the puppet dictator Shah who was happy to give the US and UK a cut of the Iranian oil profits. Then, during the Iraq-Iran War of the 1980s, the US took the side of Iraq against Iran. Towards the end of the 1980s (July 3rd, 1988 to be exact), Iran Air Flight 655 (a commercial flight) was flying along a standard flight path through Iranian airspace on the way to Dubai. Just a few minutes after taking off, it was shot down by the US Navy, killing all 290 people on board.

The Navy lied and stated they thought Flight 655 was an attacking fighter plane, and that they had attempted radio contact but received no response. However, declassified documents[48] reveal a different

---

[47] https://history.state.gov/historicaldocuments/frus1964-68v28/d274

[48] documents.theblackvault.com/documents/dtic/ADA260260.pdf

story. The truth was that the US only used emergency radio frequencies but not air traffic control frequencies, and also that the Navy cruiser registered the plane was climbing at the time, not descending as an attacking plane would be. Some of the files were declassified in 1988 and others in 1993. Serial rapist and war criminal George H. W. Bush refused to apologize to the Iranian people for this incident.

Unit 731

This one is another shocking event in the annals of governmental crime, although in the case the perpetrator was the Japanese Government. Unit 731 refers to a covert biological and chemical warfare research and development unit of the Japanese Army located in China during World War II. Under the command of General Ishii, the Japanese committed war crimes and lethal human experimentation upon around 300 people, mostly Chinese victims (though there were some Mongolian, Russian, Korean and Allied POWs too).

At the end of the war, the Japanese were caught, but in a familiar tale, the US traded immunity for data (a common theme which also happened with Project Paperclip). The Unit 731 researchers were secretly given immunity by the US in exchange for the data they gathered through human experimentation. You can read some of the declassified files at this footnote[49].

[49] https://www.archives.gov/files/iwg/japanese-war-crimes/select-documents.pdf

The Gulf of Tonkin Incident

It was the war of a generation. It was a war of failure. It was a war that should never have been. It was a war that awoke a mass of peace activists across the US and the world. It was a war that produced swathes of soldiers suffering from PTSD. It was a war that killed millions.

The Vietnam War was brutal, and so was the deception that started it. LBJ, fresh from his role in the Kennedy assassination[50], decide to plunge the US into war in 1964 by "making shit up." He claimed that the US ships were being fired upon in the Gulf of Tonkin, but it was an utter lie. In 2005 and 2006, NSA documents were declassified[51] showing that the second Gulf of Tonkin incident, which was used as a

---

[50] thefreedomarticles.com/jfk-assassination-who-how-why-part-1/

[51] https://www.nsa.gov/news-features/declassified-documents/gulf-of-tonkin/

justification for the Gulf of Tonkin Resolution (which led to the Vietnam War), never happened. The Gulf of Tonkin incident is in many ways the epitome of government crime. The whole thing was entirely fabricated (lying, deceit). Although there was no enemy ship, it was designed to frame the enemy (false flag operation). It was only invented to start a war the New World Order already wanted (pretext for war). Then, the truth was hidden afterwards for decades and decades until finally it was decided that enough of the people involved were old, well out of office/power and dead, so that the truth could finally be revealed in 2005 (classifying the truth for 40+ years). The same is going on with other great crimes such as the JFK assassination and 9/11, although perhaps we will have to wait 100 years for all the files to be released with those events.

Project Stargate

So much for human experimentation, war crimes and weather modification. For the last 3 declassified projects, we delve deeper down the rabbit hole into strange and mysterious operations, which although far out, are nonetheless proven to have taken place. Project Stargate was the codename for a secret US Army unit established in 1978 at Fort Meade, Maryland, by the Defense Intelligence Agency (DIA) and SRI International (a California contractor). The goal was analyze psychic phenomena (remote viewing, ESP, clairvoyance, astral travel, etc.) and see if they could be weaponized for military and intelligence purposes. The original founders of the program were Russell Targ, Hal Puthoff and Ingo Swann – nicknamed the "Psi Spies" by the late Jim

Marrs. The Project had various predecessors and offshoots (such as Gondola Wish, Grill Flame, Center Lane, Sun Streak and Scanate) until 1991 when they were consolidated and renamed under the umbrella term Stargate Project. At one point, the late Major General Albert Stubblebine was in charge, the same one who was outspoken in exposing the 9/11 false flag op, and who was the husband of health and nutrition activist Dr. Rima Laibow. The CIA terminated Project Stargate in 1995, deeming that it had provided no use. You can read the declassified files at this footnote[52].

Project 1794

There are some who can accept many parts of the worldwide conspiracy, but simply "can't go there" when it comes to UFOs and ETs. If you or someone you know is such a person, take a look at this. Project 1794 is black-and-white proof that the US military, specifically the USAF (US Air Force), was developing UFOs or flying saucers. In 2012, the USAF revealed that its Aeronautical Systems Division had plans to produce a UFO craft in the 1950s. The craft vehicle was designed to reach speeds of Mach 4, an altitude of 100,000 feet and have a range of over 1,000 nautical miles. The project was

---

[52] https://www.cia.gov/library/readingroom/collection/stargate

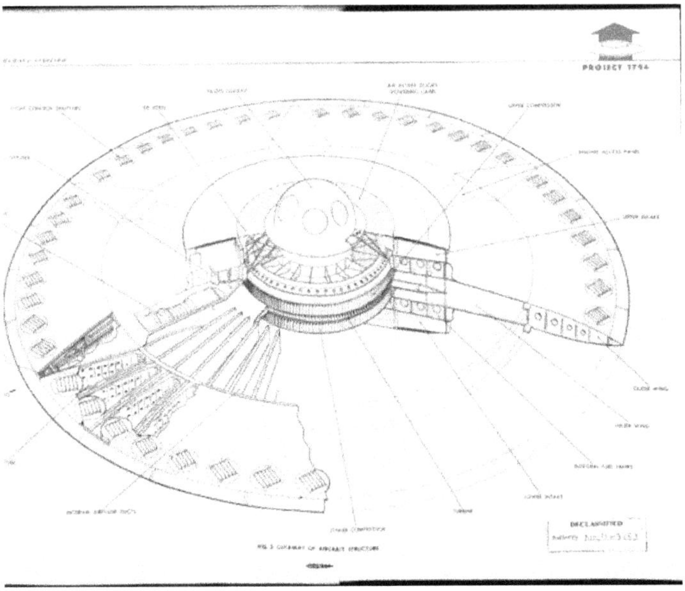

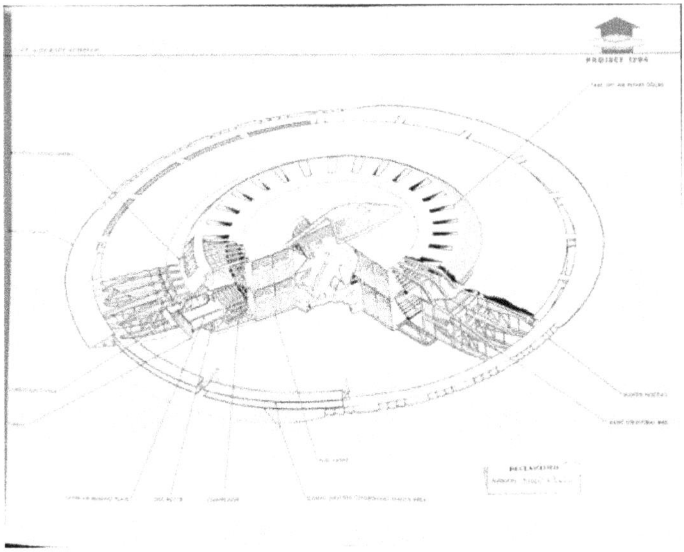

Project 1794: USAF declassified plans for a supersonic saucer.
Image credit: National Archives

abandoned in 1961. You can read some of the declassified files at this footnote[53].

Majestic 12 aka MJ 12

One of the biggest and most exciting collection of declassified documents are those of Majestic 12, also known as MJ-12 or MJ 12. This shadowy group was allegedly given the task of overseeing the "alien question" during the aftermath of WWII, the start of the Cold War and the aftermath of the 1947 UFO Roswell crash. Many researchers and whistleblowers have drawn the conclusion that MJ 12 was the core group within other groups that controlled access to extraterrestrial technology. Some of its members included famous people such as Vannevar Bush, who was also instrumental in the development of weather manipulation programs (as exposed by Peter Kirby in his research on what he calls *The New Manhattan Project*[54]).

Respected UFO researcher Bob Wood (together with his team including son Ryan Wood, UFO researcher Nick Redfern, UFO researcher Stanton Friedman, Timothy Cooper, Jim Clarkson and the late Jim Marrs) has made a website with many Majestic docs available. You can read these MJ12 files here[55]. They have they own system of rating the documents

---

[53] https://catalog.archives.gov/id/6920770

[54] www.activistpost.com/2017/03/chemtrails-exposed-truly-a-new-manhattan-project.html

[55] www.majesticdocuments.com/

for authenticity. I will expand more upon the topic of UFOs, ETs and the alien agenda in chapter 10.

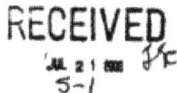

RECEIVED
JUL 21 [illegible]
5-1

TOP SECRET

SENSITIVE

5 November 1961

Operations Review
by Allen W. Dulles

THE MJ-12 PROJECT

The Overview. In pursuant to the Presidential National Security Memorandum of June 28, 1961, the U.S. intelligence operations against the Soviet Union are currently active in two broad areas; aircraft launch vehicles incorporating ELINT and SIGINT capabilities; and balloon borne decoys with ECM equipment.

The Situation. The overall effectiveness about the actual Soviet response and alert status is not documented to the point where U.S. intelligence can provide a true picture of how Soviet air defenses perceive unidentified flying objects.

Informational sources have provided some detail on coded transmissions and tactical plans whose reliability is uncertain, and thus, do not give us precise knowledge of Soviet Order of Battle. Current estimates place Soviet air and rocket defenses on a maximum alert footing with air operations centered on radar and visual verification much the same as ours.

Future psychological warfare plans are in the making for more sophisticated vehicles whose characteristics come very close to phenomena collected by Air Force and NSA elements authorized for operations in this area of intelligence.

Basis for Action. Earlier studies indicated that Americans perceived U.F.O. sightings as the work of Soviet propaganda designed to convince U.S. intelligence of their technical superiority and to spread distrust of the government. CIA conducted three reviews of the situation utilizing all available information and concluded that 80% of the sighting reports investigated by the Air Force's Project Blue Book were explainable and posed no immediate threat to national security. The remaining cases have been classified for security reasons and are under review. While the possibility remains that true U.F.O. cases are of non-terrestrial origin, U.S. intelligence is of the opinion that they do not constitute a physical threat to national defense. For reasons of security, I cannot divulge pertinent data on some of the more sensitive aspects of MJ-12 activities which have been deemed properly classified under the 1954 Atomic En[illegible] of 1954.

I hope this clarifies the necessity to keep current operations w[illegible]A activities in sensitive areas from becoming official disclosure. From time to time, updates will be provided through NIE as more information becomes available.

(Signed) Allen W. Dulles

This document contains information affecting
the national defense of the United States within
of the Espionage Laws, Title 18,
U. S. C., Section 793 and 794. The transmission
or the revelation of its contents in any manner
to an unauthorized person is prohibited by law.
Exempted from automatic regrading: DoD 5200.10

This document contains ____ pages
Copy No. of copies

Mind Control – Operation MK Ultra

Lastly, we will end with one of the most manipulative operations that the USG orchestrated, and which has been declassified for a long time now, so is proven beyond all doubt: mind control. Operation MK Ultra has become so infamous that the term is basically synonymous with mind control. The "MK" of MK Ultra stands for *mind kontrolle* (German spelling of control), with a nod to the German Nazi scientists who developed it for the CIA who were brought in under Paperclip. In 1953, CIA agent Richard Helms (later CIA director in 1966) chose Dr. Sidney Gottlieb to run the TSS (Technical Service Staff) to develop truth serum drugs, hypnotic techniques and mind control techniques, with the purpose of creating spies, couriers and assassins. Eisenhower approved using Nazi scientists and Jewish victims as guinea pigs. MK Ultra was so large it had 149 sub-projects. By 1953, the emphasis of MK Ultra was LSD (see below), but by the 1960s, this had changed into biological radio communications. Helms later destroyed much of the MK Ultra archive when he left in 1972, but some declassified files remain[56].

Operation Midnight Climax, one of many MK Ultra sub-projects, used paid prostitutes to lure people into CIA safe houses in San Francisco, Marin and New York. There, they were surreptitiously given a wide range of substances, including LSD, and monitored behind one-way glass. This was not the first time, nor

[56] https://www.cia.gov/library/readingroom/docs/DOC_0000707674.pdf

the last, that the US Government used drugs and other substances with which to experiment upon unsuspecting individuals. The point was to study the effects of LSD and gain research on the potential military and intelligence uses of sexual blackmail, surveillance technology and mind-altering drugs. Some of the declassified files are here[57].

Scientist and mind control researcher Dr. Jose Delgado, famous for his 134 publications within two decades (1950-1970) on electrical stimulation on animals and humans, and author of *Physical Control of the Mind: Toward a Psychocivilized Society*, once stated[58]:

"We need a program of psychosurgery for political control of our society. The purpose is physical control of the mind. Everyone who deviates from the given norm can be surgically mutilated. ... The individual may think that the most important reality is his own existence, but this is only his personal point of view. This lacks historical perspective. Man does not have the right to develop his own mind. This kind of liberal orientation has great appeal. We must electronically control the brain. Someday armies and generals will be controlled by electric stimulation of the brain."

Mind control, of course, has been going on a lot longer than the CIA and the Nazis. It has roots all the way back to an 11th century Arabian cult of assassins. The word assassin has Arabic roots; the

---

57 https://www.cia.gov/library/readingroom/docs/CIA-RDP88-01315R000200070024-3.pdf

58 libertytree.ca/quotes_by/dr.+jose+delgado

Arabic word *hashshaseen* means "hashish smoker" and the Arabic word *assasseen* translates to "guardians of the secrets." The group was founded in 1094 by Hasan bin Sabah, who was a Secret Society adept (he studied at the Grand Lodge of Cairo). Apparently, this cult had sufficiently mastered the techniques of mind control to create mind-controlled assassins who they used to carry out assassinations.

There is a connection among the USG, the Nazis and this ancient cult. In the 1920s a young Egyptian named Hassan Al-Banna revived the Muslim Brotherhood, which had its origins in the same Grand Lodge of Cairo that also spawned Freemasonry and the Knights Templar. Al-Banna was an admirer of Adolf Hitler. At some point in the 1930s his group became a secret arm of Nazi Intelligence. During WWII the Palestine-based Grand Mufti went to Germany as a Muslim Brotherhood representative to recruit an international SS division of Arab Nazis. Based in Croatia, the group was known as the Handzar Muslim Division.

WWII ended with the USG already setting itself up against its future opponent, Soviet Russia, by gathering the spoils of war before the USSR could. The US tried to get its hands on as many Nazis and as much Nazi technology lest it fall into the hands of the Russians. The USG formed a new relationship with the Muslim Brotherhood in order to use them to achieve its geopolitical objectives, including countering the USSR and Soviet-aligned nations. The Cold War had begun. The newly formed CIA ended up hiring these Muslim Brotherhood mercenaries. They were used to infiltrate and attack a burgeoning left-wing Arab nationalist movement led by Egyptian President Gamel Nasser, who was aligned with the USSR. Nasser brought in Soviet advisors and banned the Muslim Brotherhood from Egypt, but the leader of the Egyptian Muslim Brotherhood Sayed Kuttub received payments from Saudi King Faisal to undermine Nasser. The US continued to promote the Muslim Brotherhood, fanatical Islam, Saudi Wahhabism (the basis for groups like ISIS) and the Saudi-based spread of Islamic schools (madrasses) all over the Middle East. Fascistic Wahhabism was also encouraged by Britain's MI6 and Israel's Mossad. Brotherhood leader Sayed Kuttub stated that during the 1960s that *"America made Islam."* One-time CIA Director Allen Dulles (who had been a lawyer for Nazi conglomerate IG Farben, forerunner to today's Big Pharma cabal) actively worked with the Nazis during WWII. In 1952 he founded Banque Commerciale Arabe in Lausanne, Switzerland, which represented a pact between the CIA and the Muslim Brotherhood. Saudi royal family members were involved. Part of the deal was that the House of Saud (itself installed in power in Saudi Arabia with the help of the British during WWI) would provide information to US intelligence on how to create mind-controlled assassins. As soon as Dulles became CIA Director in 1953, the CIA began MK Ultra.

Mind control has advanced far beyond the days of MK Ultra, as you are about to find out. However, for now, we will end with this. Here is some more hard proof. Go to a computer and do a search for a US patent number 5159703. It will bring up the result of a patent belonging to Dr. Oliver Lowery, granted October 27th, 1992, for a system he had developed known as SSSS (Silent Sound Spread Spectrum). What does it do? It beams transmissions subliminally ("below the conscious threshold") into your mind. Here's what the patent says:

"A silent communications system in which nonaural carriers, in the very low or very high audio frequency range or in the adjacent ultrasonic frequency spectrum, are amplitude or frequency modulated with the desired intelligence and propagated acoustically or vibrationally, for inducement into the brain ... The modulated carriers may be transmitted directly in real time or may be conveniently recorded and stored on mechanical, magnetic or optical media for delayed or repeated transmission to the listener ... "

<u>Cognitive Dissonance vs. the Overwhelming Evidence of the Existence of the Conspiracy</u>

Whether it's overarching accounts, prophetical works (disguised as fiction), former insiders, whistleblowers or declassified files, the evidence is truly mindblowing and overwhelming that there is indeed a grand conspiracy being orchestrated to control the world. Some governmental crimes are difficult to prove conclusively. We have a pretty good idea of what happened in the JFK assassination[59] and on 9/11[60], but it's difficult to prove every detail, since so many agents were involved and so many

---

[59] https://thefreedomarticles.com/jfk-assassination-who-how-why-part-1/

[60] thefreedomarticles.com/category/911-inside-job/

docs are still classified. However, there is little arguing with the declassified docs presented above. They are part of the record of historical fact. Therefore, they are a great thing to show skeptics and those stuck in denial. They are also very important pieces of evidence for those mysteries we are still yet to uncover. They function as clues pointing us in the right direction. If the Government was willing to kill its own innocent citizens to start a war with Cuba (Northwoods), to entirely fabricate an incident that never happened to start a war with Vietnam (Gulf of Tonkin) and to experiment on its own citizens no matter what harmed it caused them (MK Ultra, Midnight Climax, Tuskegee, forced sterilization, etc.), what lengths is it not willing to go to? Are there any limits at all on its behavior or capacity to harm?

As I said, these examples are just a tiny fraction of what's out there. There are also declassified files documenting the Israeli attack on the USS Liberty in 1967, the My Lai Massacre in Vietnam in 1968 and the chemical experimentation programs in the NYC subway. Additionally, there are all the genuine governmental files that have been leaked over the years by WikiLeaks (led by Australian Julian Assange) and Edward Snowden (mentioned earlier in the chapter), which cover a breathtaking array of governmental crime, including illegal hacking of (and surveillance through) people's private electronic devices.

The evidence presented in this chapter is overwhelming by itself, however we have only just begun. Now that your mind has been opened to the factual and provable crimes and conspiracies that have been occurring, let's journey deeper into the rabbit hole, for there is much more to uncover.

Chapter 3 – False Flag Operations

False flag operations, or "false flag ops" for short, have become one of the primary techniques by which governments scare their populations and justify outrageous abuses of power. The term "false flag operation" is a military term that has now become broadly known due to the increasingly widespread use of the technique by governments all over the world – and because a critical mass of people are finally beginning to identify said technique when it is used.

The false flag op – whether it be an attack, bombing, shooting or other act of terrorism – involves secretly orchestrating and executing some kind of criminal event (often involving the destruction of vehicles and buildings and the mass murder of civilians) while cleverly framing an innocent person or group. A person is usually blamed so that the ensuing public reaction and outrage can be directed toward a patsy (designated to take the fall, e.g., Lee Oswald) or bogeyman (a created "enemy" who was often a prior CIA asset, e.g., Osama bin Laden); however, the official narrative parroted by the MSM almost always includes some new group that the government wants you to fear and hate. Today in the West, ever since 9/11, Muslims have become the new enemy and, more recently, the Russians and Chinese. Islamophobia, Russophobia and Sinophobia are the trends. Many Westerners have been whipped into a frenzy of judgment, prejudice and fear, not because of their personal experience and interaction with Muslims but rather because of what the MSM and politicians tell them to believe. Yes, some Muslims have done some horrible things, but if you fear and hate an entire race, culture or religion just because of the actions of a tiny minority of its members you have been conned.

False flag events have a long history. If we go back over 120 years, we can see how false flag ops have been systemically used to trigger wars. The Spanish-American War of 1898 was triggered by a suspicious explosion that sank the USS Maine; the US entry into WWI was justified on the basis that the *USS Lusitania* was sunk by German U-Boats (even though the US let it happen); the US entry into WWII was prompted by a "surprise" attack on Pearl Harbor (with US foreknowledge); the Vietnam War was justified by the nonexistent Gulf of Tonkin incident; the First Gulf War (which began under George Bush Sr. in 1991) was justified by lies a Kuwaiti girl told (really the daughter of the Kuwaiti Ambassador to the US) who falsely claimed Iraqi soldiers were killing Kuwaiti babies in incubators; and the US/UK-led War on Terror™ (see chapter 4) was vindicated and justified due to the horrible attacks of 9/11 and 7/7 respectively. None of the incidents are what they seem; in all cases, a massive dose of trickery and deception was used.

Books could be written (and they have) about all the deception that was used to engineer these events to start wars; however, in this chapter, I will focus on false flag ops in around the last two decades since the year 2001. My reason in doing so is to point out the pattern – the false flag formula – which is used as template or blueprint by the NWO controllers to orchestrate these events. Events which fit the false flag formula include the 9/11 attacks on the World Trade Center in New York and on the Pentagon in Washington, DC; the 7/7 attacks on the London Underground, the 2011 Norway shooting; the 2012 Aurora Colorado shooting; the 2012 Sandy Hook school shooting; the 2013 Boston Marathon bombing; the 2015 Charleston, South Carolina shooting; the 2015 San Bernardino, California shooting; the two attacks in Paris in 2015 (Charlie Hebdo); the 2017 Las Vegas shooting; the 2018 Parkland, Florida shooting; and many more.

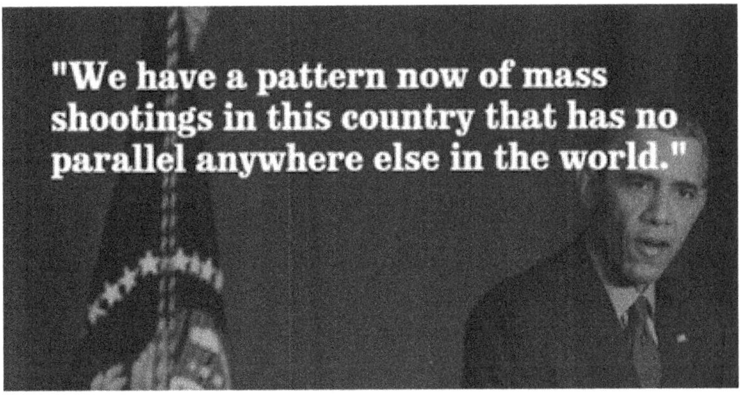

During the Obama presidency, especially 2012 to 2016, there was an unprecedented amount of mass shootings in the USA; Obama himself revealed that there was a "pattern" to all this – the false flag formula.

While each false flag op may not have every single feature listed below, they tend to have the following structure:

1. **Foreknowledge:** evidence of foreknowledge

shows the attack was planned beforehand. There was foreknowledge of the Pearl Harbor attack[61] of 1941 that justified the United States' entrance into World War II. There were many aspects of foreknowledge concerning 9/11, including the BBC reporting WTC7 falling before it actually did[62], and mysterious calls to people before the event like author Salman Rushdie and San Francisco Mayor Willie Brown advising them not to fly to NYC on September 11, 2001. Sandy Hook had blatant foreknowledge (with various webpages put up days before the event), as did the Boston Marathon.

2. Drill at the Same or Nearby Time and Place: the exercise or drill – at the same (or nearby) time, at the same (or nearby) place – has become the sine qua non (i.e., indispensable element) of recent false flag ops. There are slight variations on this when the government plans a drill nearby (a few miles away) rather than at the exact place, or plans a drill earlier on in the day so it can just coincidentally "go live". There was a twist in the case of the 2015 San Bernardino shooting: the government planned regular drills in the building where the shooting took place every month[63]! (Think about it – what are the chances of a real mass shooting occurring in a building used for mass shooting drills?)

As Captain Eric H. May, a former US Army

---

[61] https://www.youtube.com/watch?v=u7-QDfq4opU

[62] https://www.youtube.com/watch?v=6mxFRigYD3s

[63] www.naturalnews.com/052196_active_shooter_drills_San_Bernardino_shooting_Inland_Regional_Center.html

military intelligence officer, stated:

The easiest way to carry out a false flag attack is by setting up a military exercise that simulates the very attack you want to carry out.

In the case of 9/11, there were no less than forty-six drills occurring simultaneously during the event[64], according to Webster Tarpley, author of *Synthetic Terror: Made in USA*. In the case of the London 7/7 bombings, Peter Power admitted on radio that he was leading a team who were training for that exact scenario when it unfolded[65]. There were active shooter drills in all of the false flag attacks of Norway[66], Sandy Hook[67], Boston[68], Charleston[69], San Bernardino[70],

64 https://www.youtube.com/watch?v=q41nZpGTm74

65 https://www.youtube.com/watch?v=JKvkhe3rqtc

66 www.infowars.com/norwegian-police-confirm-drill-identical-to-breiviks-attack/

67 thefreedomarticles.com/sandy-hook-conspiracy-shooting-drill/

68 www.shtfplan.com/headline-news/shock-report-police-were-engaged-in-active-shooter-drill-just-before-san-bernardino-massacre_12022015

69 www.localterror.com/false-flag-charleston-shooting-happened-during-federal-active-shooter-drill/

70 thefreedomarticles.com/san-bernardino-mass-shooting-shooter-drill/

the second Paris attack of 2015[71] and many more.

What's the point of having a drill at the same time and place? Here are a few reasons:

1. Distract and remove key personnel who would otherwise be at the scene to contain and investigate it.
2. Confuse other personnel who will treat the whole event in a different way if they think it is a drill rather than a real event.
3. Slow down, reduce or eliminate an effective response, especially of police and other law enforcement, given the removal and confusion of personnel.
4. Distract and confuse witnesses, the media and the public in general.
5. Provide a great cover and period of lower defenses and security to carry out an attack, which would otherwise be difficult or impossible if defenses were at their usual or optimal operating level.

3. MSM Quickly Name and Demonize the Patsy: Have you ever wondered how quickly the MSM (Mainstream Media) discovers the name of the patsy? They had somehow deduced that Osama bin Laden was responsible for 9/11 just hours after the attacks. Have you ever wondered why the government is so good at telling us who supposedly executed these attacks right after they happen, with almost no time to investigate, yet can't seem to

[71] thefreedomarticles.com/paris-shooting-10-signs-false-flag/

manage to actually stop these alleged terror attacks? Without any evidence, the MSM endlessly repeated "bin Laden" like a crazy mantra after 9/11, despite the fact bin Laden himself denied involvement in the attacks and that in the end he was never formally charged by the FBI.

Sometimes the patsy is a small, thin guy who somehow has the strength to carry lots of ammo and shoot incredibly accurately under stress without obvious military training.

4. Patsy Has No Military Training, Yet Shoots Extremely Fast and Accurately: Another element of the false flag formula is the skilled and lethal patsy. According to the official narrative of false flag ops like Sandy Hook and Aurora, we are supposed to believe that frail youths, without any discernible military training, were able to acquire expensive military gear (including armor, guns, ammunition and more), wear that gear without slowing their movements, and shoot incredibly fast and accurately. In San Bernardino, we are supposed to believe that a young mother was strong and skilled enough to participate in killing fourteen and injuring seventeen people while she was strapped up with body armor and holding heavy weaponry! In these cases and more, the official story would have you believe that it's no big deal or just a coincidence that the patsy can acquire all this high-end gear and the incredible physical abilities to use it. In this version, it is much more likely the actual shooting was done by others at the scene (who escape and are never identified – the real killers) while the patsy is just the fall guy who is actually innocent.

5. Patsy Has History of Mental Illness or Strange Ties to the Military: This point contradicts the one just made in point 4 above, but there are two versions at play here. In this version, the patsy has military ties (he may be a disaffected vet) which explains his access to weapons and good shooting skills. In some cases, he has a history of mental illness and was or is being prescribed psychiatric drugs; in other cases, he gives clues that he is being mind-controlled. James Holmes (Aurora Colorado shooting 2012) and Dylan Roof (Charleston shooting 2015) were confirmed to be on psychiatric drugs in the lead up to their mass shootings. Aaron Alexis (Washington Naval Yard shooting 2013) claimed he heard voices in his head[72] before his shooting spree – voices telling him to do it.

5. Eyewitnesses Have Conflicting Accounts: You can also spot a likely false flag operation when you see or hear of multiple conflicting witness

---

[72] https://exposinginfragard.blogspot.com/2014/05/aaron-alexisffchs-timeline-and-analysis.html

accounts. In the case of the Aurora, Colorado "Batman" mass shooting, eyewitnesses_claimed they saw an entire team of shooters[73], rather than the single shooter James Holmes of the official narrative. With Sandy Hook, we saw multiple scenes of law enforcement chasing men into the surrounding forest, yet the official narrative declares the only shooter was Adam Lanza. In San Bernardino, too, witnesses stated they saw three white athletic men[74], not the Hispanic husband-and-wife team we were told did the shooting. In many cases, there are many eyewitness accounts of multiple shooters, yet the MSM zeroes in on one patsy who is destined to be the scapegoat.

Conflicting eyewitness accounts can destroy the official narrative no matter what the details are. On 9/11, various firemen told us there were bombs in the building[75], contradicting the official story that planes alone took down the Twin Towers. With Sandy Hook, Gene Rosen's testimony itself was full of holes and was contradicted by that of the school bus driver

---

[73] nodisinfo.com/lies-inconsistencies-aurora-theater-james/

[74] thefreethoughtproject.com/media-refusing-cover-police-witness-accounts-3-white-male-shooters-san-bernardino/

[75] https://www.youtube.com/watch?v=G1zED8dy63w

and the official report.

6. Patsy Gets Killed, Drugged or "Suicided": It is also part of the false flag formula to ensure that the patsy, who is earmarked before the event to take the fall, cannot speak out to rationally defend himself. This is achieved in a number of ways. The simplest is to have the patsy kill himself or herself by committing "suicide". A second way is to take the patsy out in a thrilling high-speed chase, which has the added benefit of drawing clueless people in through the MSM and gushingly promoting the police state. Sometimes a patsy is killed in plain sight, especially when it's crucial to suppress his testimony (e.g., Lee Oswald in the JFK assassination). A third way is to mind control and drug the patsy to such an extent that they become a zombie vegetable unable to articulate anything, as was the case with James Holmes (pictured above).

Many cases feature a patsy with a strange, expressionless look on his/her face during the rampage and an inability to remember the act afterward – a clear indication of mind control. Also, on some occasions the patsy just happens to be from a particular ethnicity, race, religion or socioeconomic class, which has the effect of influencing people's perception of that entire group – think of the now classic "radicalized Islamist" type. This will be explored more in chapter 4. Sometimes, the patsy is a veteran. Vets are obviously trained militarily and know how to use guns (which contradicts point 4 above), however sometimes because they've experienced the horrors of war firsthand, they suffer from mental illnesses like PTSD (Post Traumatic Stress Disorder), flashbacks, chronic depression and anxiety, etc., so are ripe targets for mind control operations.

7. Shooter Leaves Manifesto: These days, writing a manifesto is a strange and anachronistic thing to do. Yet, for some strange reason, shooter's manifestos seem to crop up an awful lot after mass shootings. Conveniently for the controllers, these manifestos provide a perfect explanation for the official narrative and help fill in the missing (nonexistent) motive for the attack – which probably pushes those on the fence over into believing the government's version of the event. While the manifesto is not an element in every false flag operation, it is present in enough of them to be regarded as part of the false flag formula.

8. (Real) Evidence Gets Conveniently Destroyed: Another element of the false flag formula is the deliberate destruction of evidence, so that the

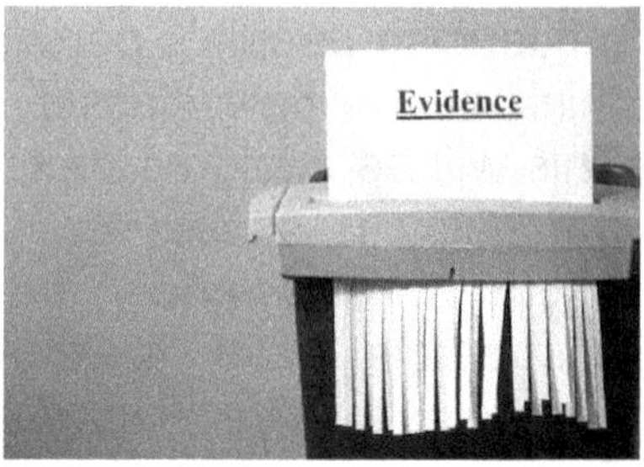

controllers can cover their tracks. In 9/11, the scrap metal (in the smoldering ruins of the WTC towers) was immediately shipped off to China[76]; with Sandy Hook, the entire school was demolished[77]; in San Bernardino, the purported landlord of the supposed shooters actually allowed MSM reporters into the suspects' house[78] to poke around and touch all their stuff, in complete disregard for what could be a possible crime scene! In many cases, the investigation is immediately taken over by the Feds, as represented in the US by the FBI or ATF, so that the coverup can be centrally coordinated.

9. Planted (Fake) Evidence: The NWO in many ways is all about supplanting the real with the fake. Just as real evidence is destroyed (as in the point above), fake evidence is injected into the situation to deceive. Even in normal crimes, cops have been known to plant evidence on the person, in the car or at the house of suspects to make them look guilty. Why do so many false flag events feature extra guns and ammunition at the home of the shooter? In many cases there is a ridiculous array of extra weapons

76 911research.wtc7.net/wtc/groundzero/cleanup.html

77 www.msnbc.com/msnbc/sandy-hook-demolished-winterized

78 www.huffingtonpost.com/entry/san-bernardino-shooters-home_5661d125e4b08e945fef418b

and ammo found at the home of the patsy. In the 2017 Las Vegas shooting, we were told by the MSM that patsy Stephen Paddock had ten, then twenty-four, and then finally twenty-seven extra guns. Why? Even if someone had a sufficient motive to open fire on hundreds of random people, why would they risk bringing all that firepower into a hotel room, when it drastically increased their odds of being seen or getting caught – and they couldn't use it anyway? Could this be anything other than a ploy to make these mind-controlled shooters look like psychotic madmen in order to sufficiently frighten the public?

10. The Miraculous Passport: In some false flag ops such as 9/11 and the Paris attacks, we were told by the MSM that they had, somehow, found the passports of the alleged shooter. Sometimes the patsies leave their passports in their hotel rooms or even in the getaway vehicles; sometimes they just leave a copy of the Quran lying around. Are we supposed to believe that Islamic terrorists are so pious that right before committing an act of terrorism, they conveniently leave behind a copy of the Quran in their rental car for police to find? On 9/11, the FBI claimed it miraculously found a passport of the alleged hijacker, which we are told survived the fire and heat to make it safely to the ground when not many other things could.

11. All Shooters Have the Same "Uniform": So many shooters (from different times and places) seem to have the same uniform – a black trenchcoat. Coincidence?

12. Early Start Time to the Attack: Is it just a

coincidence that so many of these events start very early in the day, so that the story dominates the day's headlines?

13. No Obvious Motive for the Mass Attack: Have you ever wondered why there is no obvious motive in any of these mass shootings? Crimes are supposed to be solved on the merit of motive and opportunity, yet to hide the reality of a false flag op, the MSM just lies about the motive part and chalks it up to a deranged shooter. Other times we are offered the flimsiest of motives, such as people going on an all-out rampage because they had a grievance with a coworker. In San Bernardino, we were told the young mother, with a one-year-old child, was aggressive and psychotic enough to help kill fourteen and injure seventeen people – at the risk of never seeing her child again! Meanwhile, the real purveyors of these operations profit immensely from the ensuing fear, yet somehow the majority of people don't seem to see that motive.

14. Immediate Calls for Gun Control: Gun control is obviously one of the key agendas behind all of these false flag mass shootings since a disarmed population is far easier to exploit and manipulate than an armed one. It is an obvious aspect of the false flag formula. Sometimes gun control is even pushed in the immediate aftermath of the event when people are still in a highly emotional and suggestible state.

Take a look at the behavior of Andy Parker, who we were told was the father of a victim killed in the Virginia mass shooting of 2015. Within hours of hearing the news of the death of his child, Parker had already contacted and talked with the governor of Virginia and then appeared on TV saying he would be devoting his entire life to gun control. In a similar fashion, Richard Martinez, the alleged father of a Santa Barbara mass shooting victim, appeared on TV right after the death angrily pleading for more gun control. In both cases, the political agenda of gun control angrily dominated their reactions rather than grief or other emotions.

The false flag hoax with fake victims and crisis actors. Image credit: David Dees

The False Flag Hoax

The preceding fourteen points are a useful outline of the false flag formula as it pertains to mass shootings with real victims (i.e., where real people die). However, ever since the surreal Sandy Hook event, which still contains many unanswered questions, we have entered the twilight zone of the false flag hoax. This is a term used to describe the false flag mass attacks where no one dies – where fake bodies, fake blood and fake victims are used instead. In this way, the entire operation is more tightly controlled and less messy. A hallmark of the false flag hoax is that the authorities never produce a credible piece of evidence showing an actual dead body of a victim.

We live in a world of such immense fakery that we have to question everything, because unfortunately our eyes and senses are easy to deceive. This is only going to become even worse as technology develops. Face fakery/invention is easy; video fakery is easy[79]; holograms are now so good that it's hard to tell the difference between them and reality.

Sandy Hook[80] was a watershed event in the history of mass shootings because, for the first time, awakened individuals had to ask whether there were actually real victims: in other words, whether it was a false flag (with real victims) or a "false flag hoax"

---

79 thefreedomarticles.com/video-photo-evidence-faked-fabricated/

80 thefreedomarticles.com/sandy-hook-3rd-anniversary-hoodwinked/

(with no real victims). Fake blood, fake injuries and smiling and laughing crisis actors are strong evidence that these events were *at least partially* (and perhaps fully) staged. Despite the conclusion of the various Alex Jones show trials in 2022, where Jones was fined in excess of US $1 billion (most of which was punitive damages claiming he profited off saying the whole event was staged), a great many questions are left unanswered, and a great many holes in the official narrative still remain. The trials were clearly a warning to free-thinking individuals to back off and self-censor. However, the truth is still the truth. It would not be that difficult for the CIA or the Deep State agencies to construct entirely fake families, then wheel them out after the event to the media and even to the courtroom to testify. Such is the level of deception by which we are currently plagued. Many independent researchers have done great work on this (e.g. see the work of Wolfgang Halbig and Sofia Smallstorm). As always, take a look at the evidence and make up your own mind.

From the perspective of the controllers, having an entirely staged event with no real victims is "cleaner", because you can control everything down to the last detail (exactly who gets shot, who "dies", etc.) without worrying about a situation getting out of hand or possible lawsuits in the future. If there are no real victims or real dead kids, there are no parents to sue the government, right?

The NWO manipulators who orchestrate these events are very cunning. They have deliberately targeted schools as the object of many false flag mass shootings so as to inspire the maximum amount of fear and chaos, which is their life-force energy. There is even a mass shooting simulator[81] to program children!

Another benefit for them is that anyone who suggests these events are not merely false flags but actually false flag hoaxes, is immediately ridiculed and/or censored in many ways, including being viciously attacked for being insensitive to the "dead" kids. This adds to the atmosphere of self-censorship where there are certain "no go" zones for researchers (and ultimately "no think") zones, which is the exact goal, of course, of political correctness (see chapter 7).

The following five points relate to false flag hoaxes, and specifically to the people employed to pull them off: crisis actors.

The same woman was a friend of the Sandy Hook shooter's mother,
and an eyewitness of BOTH the Boston bombing and Watertown shooting?
WOW, WHAT A COINCIDENCE!

1. Fake "Victims" = Crisis Actors: It is truly a testament to just how utterly fake our normal world is (the matrix) that false flag ops have now

---

[81] https://www.youtube.com/watch?v=A_9k4lnq2V4

descended to the level where we have to question *whether the event even happened at all*. There are organizations of crisis actors in the US (such as the IIF[82]), and there is clear evidence crisis actors were used at Sandy Hook, the Boston Marathon, and many other events. Government officials have been caught using the word "actor" to describe various players in these dramas; the MSM has even resorted to calling them actors, too.

2. "Victims" Get Killed Twice: The surreal quality of the false flag hoax reached the point of absurdity when it was discovered that one of the "victims" was reportedly killed twice! We were told that Noah Pozner was one of the victims of the Sandy Hook shooting, yet his picture was also among those killed in a Pakistan Taliban attack. Apparently the recycling of fake victims is another part of the false flag formula.

3. Families of "Victims" Have Elite or Acting Backgrounds: Is it just a coincidence that the families of mass shooting "victims" have either elite or acting backgrounds? At the Sandy Hook event, local CEO of the Newtown bank John Trentacosta[83] (whose house was next to the Lanzas and had a lot of unusual activity occurring there the day of Sandy Hook) was connected to the New York Federal Reserve (and thus the international banking

---

[82] www.iifdata.com/rpss-exercises/first-military-response-to-natural-disaster-al-2/

[83] www.insanemedia.net/sandy-hook-trentacostas-and-the-united-way/4645

elite). Francine Wheeler[84] was formerly the personal assistant of former chief Democratic National Committee fundraiser Maureen White whose husband Steven Rattner is a Wall Street investment banker and member of the Rockefeller CFR (Council on Foreign Relations)! It was also noteworthy at Sandy Hook how acting showed up in the résumés of so many of the key players there. Gene Rosen, David and Francine Wheeler (both professional actors) and others all had a background in acting. Father of Virginia mass shooting "victim" Andy Parker is an actor (and a politician, too). This fact supports the idea that another element of the false flag formula is to watch for people with elite connections and acting backgrounds.

False flag formula giggles: laughing crisis actor Richard Martinez apparently thinks it's pretty funny that his son was murdered.

4. Families of "Victims" Show Little to No Emotion, and Even Snigger and Laugh: Luckily for truthseekers, the majority of crisis actors used in

---

[84] memoryholeblog.com/2013/10/13/sandy-hook-actors-elite-political-connections/

these false flag events are poor actors who are utterly unconvincing in the roles they play. The majority displays little or no emotion after an alleged tragedy like losing a family member child to a random and violent mass shooting. It is true that humans do vary widely when it comes to emotional response and expression. However, judging by the reactions of many crisis actors, it simply strains credibility too much to believe that they have just been through a harrowing and traumatic ordeal. Given the range of possible reaction to a tragedy like losing a loved one in a mass shooting, what are the chances that many of the "victims'" family members are so nonemotional, so understanding, or so quick to forgive?

It's shameful enough that the crisis actors playing these roles are perpetrating a monumental deception on the public, tugging at the average person's heartstrings solely to trick them. However, on top of that, these actors have the gall to actually laugh – to smile, snigger and giggle – while pulling off their atrocious stunts. The conclusion to draw from this is that it must be pretty funny to get a paid gig like this fooling millions of people.

5. Families of "Victims" Receive Millions in Federal Payoffs: In the US, the land of the lawsuit, people are generally pretty quick to initiate a lawsuit if they feel they have been wronged. It is highly strange, therefore, that none of the alleged parents of the Sandy Hook event decided to sue the government for negligence or to demand redress for any other grievance. Additionally, many of the alleged parents received millions in unsolicited federal payouts (check out the free houses they magically got on Christmas Day 2009). The Federal Government just gave it over to them without asking! Ask yourself: is it more likely the government would just do this out of the goodness of its heart, or that the money was more like a bribe/blackmail/payout all rolled into one, awarded to actors playing a part in a role and being sworn to silence?

Stages of Awakening

There is an undeniable pattern to the false flag operations you see many times a year on TV. While not every single element listed above fits the false flag formula, many do. Overall, they form a profile of an operation which is intended to deceive. False flag mass shootings continue to be a favored strategy used by the NWO controllers to further their agenda of fear and domination. It seems that every time a gap of time opens up since the last one, the US public is again hit with another incident. This shows that these events must be working to achieve the intended objectives of their orchestrators. For those who wonder when false flag mass shootings will become an ineffective social engineering tool, the answer is simple: only once enough people awaken to the deception, bring consciousness to their reactions to these events, and intentionally respond in new ways. Having said that, there are various stages of awakening to pass through regarding these events. It is only from a broader perspective that we can truly hope to stop the effectiveness of these events, designed to play with and exploit the emotions of the average person.

Awakening Stage One: It's the Gun

The first stage is the knee-jerk reaction: *"Something has to be done! Let's get rid of all the guns!"* However well-meaning these sentiments are, they lack the basic recognition that guns in and of themselves are a tool, which can be used constructively or destructively. Yes, guns are designed to shoot bullets to injure or kill, but nonetheless, they can be used as a deterrent or for other defensive purposes. For those who hunt, or simply defend their livestock from other predatory animals, guns serve a constructive purpose. To focus on the tool or instrument, rather than the intent and mindset of the person that uses them, is only approaching the issue from a very shallow perspective.

I am not a typical gun rights advocate; I don't like guns. I recently read a bumper sticker that stated, *"If guns cause crime, pencils cause misspellings."* It's humorous, yet at the same time, it's undeniable that guns are a tool of violence. I understand that violence begets more violence. By owning and carrying a gun, you may be attracting or drawing in situations where gun use will be likely or required. However, I am a firm believer in gun rights, the Second Amendment and the decentralization of power in all its aspects. I trust that the overwhelming majority of gun owners are sensible, moral people who exercise extreme care in handling a gun, which is more than we can say for the US government, whose agents are trained to kill foreigners (US military) or to kill its own citizens (trigger-happy US cops). US police killings account for far more annual American deaths than false flag mass shootings.

Here are seven reasons that gun control is short-sighted, reactionary and fails to achieve the objectives that people want:

– gun control doesn't guarantee that criminals won't get guns. Criminals will break the law and find a way to acquire them illegally. It only limits gun ownership by law-abiding citizens;

– gun control punishes the respectful, decent majority of gun owners for the alleged actions of a tiny few crazies;

– gun control centralizes power. It puts exclusive rights of gun ownership in the hands of the government, which people already know to be extremely untrustworthy. Why is the corrupt, deceitful and violent government somehow more likely to protect you, or do you less harm, than your average fellow citizen?

– it plays into the broader scheme of citizen disarmament which was carried out by past tyrants (Hitler, Stalin, Mao). History shows that this mostly served to solidify their power, thus making people in those nations less safe;

– gun control emboldens burglars and other criminals who, knowing that guns will be illegal and obtain some for themselves anyway, can carry out more attacks since their victims are less able to defend themselves;

– it abandons a right that our forefathers had the wisdom to instate in the Bill of Rights. The real reason for the Second Amendment was not to protect those who wanted guns for hunting but rather as a last recourse for citizens to overthrow an out-of-control government that no longer served them; and

– gun control is a key plank of the overarching NWO agenda known as Agenda 21 or Agenda 2030. The idea is to force people into human habitats like smart cities where they will be monitored 24/7, dependent on government for everything and without the rights they currently have today.

Awakening Stage Two: Pharmaceutical, Psychiatric and Psychotropic Drugs

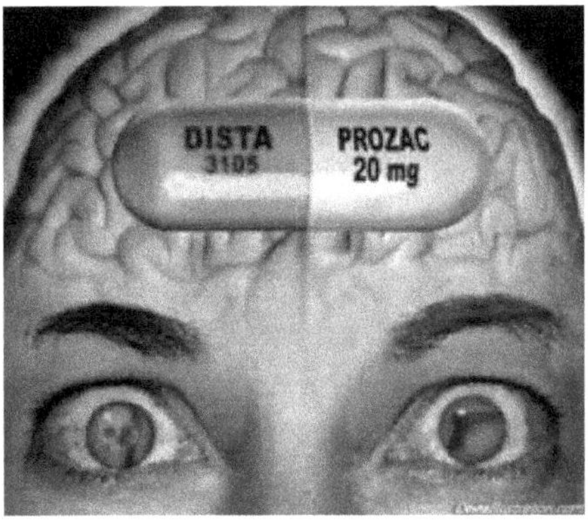

The next stage of awakening around false flag mass shootings is to look more closely at the mindset of the alleged shooter. More and more people are starting to recognize the obvious connection between pharmaceuticals – often psychiatric and psychotropic drugs – and mass shootings. These drugs are designed to numb you out, detach you from reality and kill your ability to feel emotion – including empathy. With empathy gone, it's anything goes.

There is much evidence of the psych drug-mass shooter connection. I wrote the following in a 2013 article *Psychiatric Drugs and Mass Shootings: The Definitive Connection*[85]:

The link between violence (especially gun murder) and pharmaceutical drugs has been well established. [The former website www.ssristories.com] contain [ed] a long list of documented instances where hundreds of people have been wounded or killed by gunshot at the hands of someone who was under the influence of SSRI antidepressant psychiatric medication – Prozac, Celexa, Paxil and Zoloft being the most common. The list (which is not exhaustive) shows that psychiatric drugs are not only connected to gun violence – they have also been implicated in numerous instances of knife attacks, bomb threats, bizarre behavior, assault and hitting victims with a car. According to CCHR[86]*, between 2004 and 2011, there have been more than 11,000 reports placed via the U.S. FDA's MedWatch system of psychiatric drug side effects related to violence, including 300 cases of homicide, close to 3,000 cases of mania and more than 7,000 cases of aggression. There is evidence that psychiatric drugs were involved in all of the* ***mass shootings*** *at Columbine (1999), Virginia (2007), Aurora (2012) and Sandy Hook (2012).*

Jon Rappoport[87] quotes psychiatrist and author Dr. Peter Breggin:

---

85 thefreedomarticles.com/psychiatric-drugs-mass-shootings-definitive-connection/

86 www.cchrint.org/school-shooters/

87 https://jonrappoport.wordpress.com/2018/02/22/mass-shootings-and-psychiatric-drugs-the-connection/

With Luvox there is some evidence of a four-percent rate for mania in adolescents. Mania, for certain individuals, could be a component in grandiose plans to destroy large numbers of other people. Mania can go over the hill to psychosis.

In his book, Toxic Psychiatry, Dr. Breggin discusses the subject of drug combinations: "Combining antidepressants [e.g., Prozac, Luvox, Paxil] and psychostimulants [e.g., Ritalin] increases the risk of cardiovascular catastrophe, seizures, sedation, euphoria, and psychosis. Withdrawal from the combination can cause a severe reaction that includes confusion, emotional instability, agitation, and aggression." Children are frequently medicated with this combination, and when we highlight such effects as aggression, psychosis, and emotional instability, it is obvious that the result is pointing toward the very real possibility of violence.

In true problem-reaction-solution style, some are now advocating more authority for mental health agencies[88].

Awakening Stage Three: Mental Health and the Culture of Violence

Moving beyond blaming just the weapon, or even just the shooter, some people now believe that the deepest cause for these false flag mass shootings is the culture of violence. We are inundated with violence, especially in the form of Hollywood movies

[88] https://www.naturalblaze.com/2018/02/authority-mental-health-agencies-not-solution-mass-shootings-dangerous-course.html

and video games which are now becoming so realistic it is easy for the brain to confuse the two. We are the imagination of ourselves; we become what stories we tell to ourselves and our children. As long as our hall of heroes is full of men (and women) shooting others with guns, we will worship and emulate these "heroes."

This culture of violence creates a mindset of "might is right", "force is justified" and "peace through strength." This last phrase was adopted by the US government/military (e.g., Ronald Reagan) but is very old. It was even used by leaders such as the Roman Emperor Hadrian in the first century AD. The idea is that you have to be strong, tough, macho and aggressive to deter anyone else from attacking you, and that this translates into peace. This is another shallow idea which fails to understand that genuine peace can only be created through a win/win scenario, not through a situation where others harbor feelings of fear, resentment and hate towards you, for that is a powder keg waiting to blow.

This culture of violence also affects people's mental health on an individual level, which is exacerbated by psych drugs as pointed out in point 2 above. This leads on to the next stage of awakening around false flag mass shootings: mind control.

Awakening Stage Four: Mind Control

Mind control is a massive topic that is directly relevant to false flag mass shootings because so many of these patsy shooters show evidence of being mentally influenced and tampered with. Mind-controlled assassins can be traced way back to the

Cult of the Assassins in the Middle East during the Middle Ages. In more recent history, as discussed in chapter 2, the CIA, using Nazi research and scientists under Project Paperclip, developed MK Ultra starting in 1953, which was so large it had 149 subprojects. The fruits of this operation began to pay off in the 1960s, when the CIA used their mind-control techniques to cultivate assassins such as those used in the murders of JFK, RFK, MLK and John Lennon.

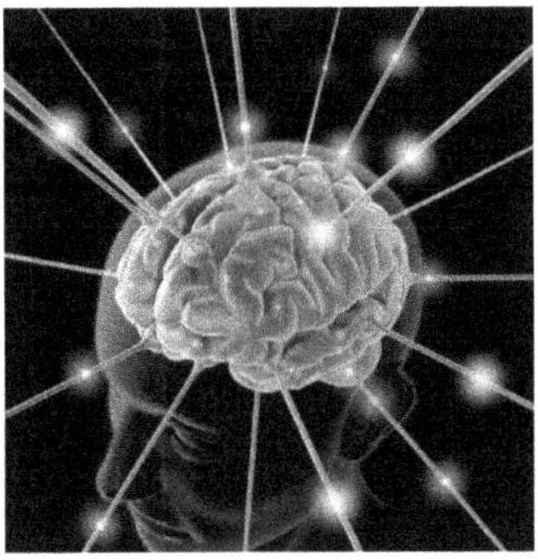

These days the techniques have no doubt been perfected. I have already mentioned the cases of James Holmes and Aaron Alexis. Holmes looked incredibly drugged up and mind controlled during his time in court. There are also links among James Holmes' family, DARPA and mind control[89]. As mentioned earlier, Alexis said in a statement that "he heard voices in his head" which may well be a reference to the electronic and psychotronic weaponry deployed by the Intelligence Agencies to mind control the shooters. Alexis reported[90] that *"individuals were speaking to him through the floor and ceiling"* and using *"some sort of microwave machine to send vibrations through the*

89 https://www.sott.net/article/248803-Wayne-Madsen-James-Holmes-Family-Tied-To-DARPA-And-Mind-Manipulation-Work

90 www.newportthisweek.com/pageview/view/1001

ceiling … penetrating his body so he could not fall asleep." It is worth revisiting the testimony of TIs (Targeted Individuals) such as Bryan Kofron, whose account I wrote about in *Total Individual Control Technology: Insider Exposes How You & Your DNA Are Being Targeted*[91]. Based on the experiences he suffered through and evidence he saw, Kofron believes the technology is at the point where it can target not only an individual's thoughts but also their very DNA.

When you understand the scale on which these events operate, a knee-jerk reaction advocating gun control seems absurd. The evidence shows that the government is literally mind controlling people to commit heinous acts without being fully conscious of it. Why are we wasting our energy and attention on the type of weapon used when this type and scale of evil is being perpetrated?

Conclusion

False flag mass shootings are all about fear, chaos and control. They are designed to usher in the NWO. They induce an enormous amount of fear in people who worry that they or their children could be struck at any time; they create huge emotional upheaval and chaos to shake people out of their grounded or rational way of seeing the world to create a skewed perspective; they aim to deceive people into giving up control.

---

91 thefreedomarticles.com/total-individual-control-technology/

Tying it all together, when you see the historical pattern of false flag operations – bombings, shootings, attacks or other events, regardless of which government or group orchestrates and executes them – you can see they have been around for a long time. They are a classic and effective way to manipulate the human mind, to hack the weakness in human perception, if you will, exploiting people's belief in authority, overreliance on believing their own eyes, overdependence on believing whatever they see in the media and the natural tendency to have compassion and empathy during a tragedy. From this larger perspective, you can see that there is a large force directing events that allows us to see the gun control debate in a completely new light. Why are we so focused on supposedly protecting our safety by advocating giving more control and weaponry to the very same government, which then has the effect of disempowering us further and thus doing the exact opposite of what we want?

False flag mass shootings will continue to be rolled out against a bamboozled and unsuspecting public as long as the deception remains profitable and effective in achieving its intended goals, be it promoting gun control or justifying the launching of a new war. However, as more and more people awaken to the game and begin to see the bigger picture, these events will become less effective. I see signs that people are beginning to question more, for example, in the case of the February 14, 2018 Florida high school shooting, people were asking questions about the psych drug-shooter connection in the immediate aftermath. Hopefully the awakening will quickly continue to the next stages en masse.

It's important to use the knowledge you have of the false flag formula to become more aware of the deception. The next time it unfolds (as it surely will), hopefully you will be among those that spot the fakery, rather than among those too scared and gullible to do anything other than buy the official narrative.

Chapter 4 – The War on Terror™

In the mid-'80s, if you remember... Saudi Arabia and the United States were supporting the Mujahideen to liberate Afghanistan from the Soviets. He [Osama bin Laden] came to thank me for my efforts to bring the Americans, our friends, to help us against the atheists, he said the communists. Isn't it ironic?

– Prince Bandar bin Sultan of Saudi Arabia, on Larry King Live

Bin Laden was, though, a product of a monumental miscalculation by western security agencies. Throughout the '80s he was armed by the CIA and funded by the Saudis to wage jihad against the Russian occupation of Afghanistan. Al-Qaida, literally "the base[92]", was originally the computer data-base of the thousands of mujahideen who were recruited and trained with help from the CIA to defeat the Russians. Inexplicably, and with disastrous consequences, it never appears to have occurred to Washington that once Russia was out of the way, Bin Laden's organization would turn its attention to the west.

– Robin Cook, former UK Foreign Secretary

We didn't push the Russians to intervene, but we

92 www.theguardian.com/books/2002/aug/24/alqaida.sciencefictionfantasyandhorror

knowingly increased the probability that they would... That secret operation was an excellent idea. It had the effect of drawing the Soviets into the Afghan trap. The day that the Soviets officially crossed the border I wrote to President Carter, "We now have the opportunity of giving the Soviet Union its Vietnam War."

– Zbigniew Brzezinski, President Carter's National Security Advisor

The Muslim terrorist apparatus was created by US Intelligence as a geopolitical weapon.

– Zbigniew Brzezinski, Interview by *Le Nouvel Observateur*, published January 15-21, 1998

If you were a US leader, or an official of the National Security State, or a beneficiary of the private military and surveillance industries, why would you possibly want the war on terror to end? That would be the worst thing that could happen. It's that war that generates limitless power, impenetrable secrecy, an unquestioning citizenry, and massive profit.

– Glenn Greenwald, writing for *The Guardian*

In times of war, the law falls silent.

– Cicero, 2000 years ago

The War on Terror™ and Its Franchises: Terrorism™, Domestic Terrorism™ Radical Islamic Terrorism™ and Zio-Islamic Terrorism™

It's funny how our misleaders like to declare war on things as part of their modus operandi. Perhaps it makes them feel strong and powerful. US President Lyndon Johnson declared the "War on Poverty" in the 1960s, followed by Richard Nixon in the 1970s who declared both a "War on Cancer" and a "War on Drugs". We have had many more figurative wars since then, all against a constant backdrop of real war, which has basically never stopped ever since the US became a nation in 1789. All this talk and declaration of war shows a divisive mindset that has to make problems into martial enemies in order to solve them.

Ask yourself: have the issues of poverty, cancer or drug abuse improved since these "wars" against them began? Doesn't look like it. If anything, these problems are getting worse. In 2012, 52.2 million people (21.3 percent of the US population) were on some form of governmental welfare per the US Census Bureau[93]. The COVID 'pandemic' (Operation Coronavirus as I call it – see chapter 8) has exacerbated that. In 2016, cancer was the second leading cause of death in the US, accounting for six hundred thousand and close to 40 percent of total American deaths that year according to the CDC[94]. In 2017 and up until the present day, the US was in the grips of a horrible wave of opioid addiction (declared a national emergency), which includes both opioid street drugs like heroin and prescription drugs like

---

93 https://www.census.gov/newsroom/press-releases/2015/cb15-97.html

94 https://www.cdc.gov/nchs/fastats/leading-causes-of-death.htm

fentanyl. Most of the world's opium comes from places like the closely guarded poppy fields in Afghanistan, which up until August 2021 had been under the watchful eye of the US and UK militaries for decades. Drug overdose is now the leading cause of death for Americans[95] under the age of fifty.

Amidst all this war, something happened in late 2001 which changed the game forever. I am referring to the introduction and launching of the most cunning war of all: the War on Terror, or to be more accurate, the War on Terror™. So what is this now-ubiquitous War on Terror™? It is a means by which humanity can be kept in a constant state of literal war against a nameless, faceless, formless, homeless and ultimately undefinable enemy. And since there's no definable enemy, there's no real accountability or method of keeping politicians honest on the supposed progress they are making. The War on Terror™ can be invoked at any time and at any place against any enemy whom the aggressor nation deems to be a threat. It's a carte blanche, open-book kind of deal that allows unlimited military missions, all in the name of vague concepts like freedom, peace and the spread of democracy. Some have even suggested the brainwashing surrounding the War on Terror™ goes beyond the conscious and into the subconscious. Is it a war on terror or a war on "terra" (as is often pronounced), with "terra" the Latin word meaning "earth"? Are we allowing our misleaders to declare war on the earth itself?

---

95 www.breitbart.com/big-government/2017/06/07/doj-drug-overdose-now-leading-cause-of-death-for-americans-under-50/

The granddaddy false flag operation of 9/11 was the excuse for the War on Terror™. Terrorism was around before 9/11, but that incident catapulted the concept into mass consciousness. The 9/11 attacks became an all-pervading political pretext under which it seems literally anything can be done: from trampling human rights, quashing civil liberties, spying on the public, passing draconian laws, funding massive military intelligence budgets, invading foreign nations, starting wars and declaring states of emergency (which start off as temporary but end up becoming permanent). Broadly speaking, terrorism is the authoritarian's wet dream because it allows for equal domination both domestically and abroad. For domestic policy, the authoritarian uses terrorism to surveil, monitor, spy, track, collect, record and denounce those not going along with the agenda as unpatriotic. For foreign policy, the authoritarian uses terrorism to justify any type and number of wars anywhere in the world – because there are terrorists everywhere, remember?

If you are thinking that the term and concept itself "War on Terror" has all the hallmarks of a New World Order scheme, you're right. Former Israeli Prime Minister Benjamin Netanyahu, who has been behind the horrible exploitation, theft and even genocide of the Palestinian people at the hands of Israeli settlers and military, is credited with inventing the War on Terror™, as this article by Christopher Bollyn[96] states:

---

[96] tapnewswire.com/2016/05/how-israel-created-the-fiend-for-the-war-on-terror/

The War on Terror is essentially an Israeli war strategy. It was first promoted on the world stage by Benjamin Netanyahu and Menachem Begin (of the terrorist Likud party) at the Jerusalem Conference hosted by the Netanyahu Institute in July 1979.

According to the War on Terror doctrine advocated by Netanyahu, "Islamic terrorists" attack Israel because it is a Western state with Western values. The West, Netanyahu says, is the real target so the U.S. must lead the West in waging a global War on Terror to destroy Islamic terrorists and the regimes that support them. This is exactly what the United States has done since 9/11, at incredible expense to its own population, leaving a trail of devastated nations in its wake.

The Israeli construct was designed to get the U.S. to destroy the enemies of the Zionist state. The Israelis developed the War on Terror construct and then created the Islamic opponent, al Qaida, to serve as the antithesis – the virulent enemy of the West. The real purpose of al Qaida, and its subsequent iterations like ISIS, is to be a moving target used to destabilize and destroy sovereign countries, like Syria, while sustaining the illusion of an Islamic antithesis, posing a mortal threat to the security of the West. The Zionist-controlled media is the essential element in selling the fraudulent War on Terror to the public.

Netanyahu is more than just an Israeli politician. He has been a key driver of world events. As mentioned above, he was already talking about terrorism in 1979 when he wrote the book

International Terrorism: Challenge and Response in that year. He wrote another book on terrorism in 1995, a major work entitled *Fighting Terrorism: How Democracies Can Defeat Domestic and International Terrorism*. The book explains all sorts of themes that have now become public knowledge and household ideas: terrorism, radical Islamic suicide attacks and Iran pursuing a nuclear program, for example. He repeatedly uses the phrase "Weapons of Mass Annihilation" throughout the book (now you know where the term "WMD" (Weapons of Mass Destruction) originated from!). Netanyahu is not a prophet but rather a driver of these agendas. Using the immense power of Zionism, Jewish lobbies in America and the Jewish international banking cabal, he persuaded the US to align itself with Israel and view Islam as the next great enemy.

According to this source[97], Netanyahu made a speech in Israel at the Jewish Agency Assembly Plenary meetings held in Israel on June 24, 2001 (two to three months before 9/11) where he made these points:

1. *The Palestinians are to blame for the conflict in the Middle East, and specifically Yasser Arafat.*
2. *It is legitimate for established states to engage in wars, because the societies are imperfect.*
3. *Palestinians are not waging a legitimate war (like established states using regular armies) and are terrorists.*
4. *The Palestinian terrorists deliberately attack*

[97] www.truth-and-justice.info/origwat.html

civilians.

5. *The Israelis are responding in self-defense.*
6. *When the Israelis respond, they respond against combatants.*
7. *Arafat and the Palestinian Authority are committed to the destruction of the State of Israel.*
8. *Arafat and the Palestinian Authority are using the illegitimate and criminal means of terrorism.*
9. *The Palestinian are wrong and the Israelis are right.*
10. *Terrorism invariably comes from terrorist regimes.*
11. *Terror is useful, only if the cost of waging terrorism, the cost of that regime is lower than the benefits of waging terrorism.*
12. *To stop terrorism, one must make the terrorist regime pay very very heavily.*
13. *The root core of the Middle East conflict is the existential opposition by a great many in the Arab world still, and certainly by the Palestinian leadership to Israel's very existence.*
14. *The first way of ensuring Israel's existence is that the Arabs simply understand that Israel is so powerful, so permanent, so unconquerable in every way that they will simply abandon by the force of the inertia of Israel's permanence all opposition to Israel.*
15. *The second way [of ensuring Israel's existence] is for the forces of democratization get to the Arab regimes.*
16. *Using propaganda techniques, like broadcasting American television serials*

(which Netanyahu sees as subversive material) will ultimately bring down regimes like the Ayatollah regime and the Khoumenei regime in Iran.

17. *In the 21st century, you cannot achieve a military victory unless you achieve a political victory to accompany it; and you cannot achieve a political victory unless you achieve a victory in public opinion; and you cannot achieve a victory in public opinion unless you persuade that public that your cause is just.*
18. *It doesn't make any difference if you are on the side of the angels or on the side of the devil. Anyone fighting in the international arena for public opinion must argue the justice of his cause. Hitler argued for the justice of his cause and Stalin argued for the justice of his cause. They all had propaganda machines. Whether you are right or you are wrong you must argue the justice of your cause.*

Note how he was already setting up a distinction between “legitimate” war and “illegitimate” war, thus trying to provide a legal and moral justification for war (which is legalized violence and mass murder) that would be initiated by Israel, the US and allies in the years to come against the Palestinians and other Muslim-majority nations. He made the point that states using regular armies can engage in legitimate war but not the loose bands of fighters which he brands terrorists.

It wasn’t long after until George W. Bush (Bush Jr.

or "Dubya") declared[98] the Netanyahu doctrine of War on Terror as official US policy on September 20, 2001:

We will pursue nations that provide aid or safe haven to terrorism. Every nation, in every region, now has a decision to make. Either you are with us, or you are with the terrorists. From this day forward, any nation that continues to harbor or support terrorism will be regarded by the United States as a hostile regime . . . the civilized world is rallying to America's side. They understand that if this terror goes unpunished, their own cities, their own citizens may be next. Terror, unanswered, can not only bring down buildings, it can threaten the stability of legitimate governments.

This speech included the famous "you're either with us or with the terrorists" ultimatum, a manipulative way to force other nations to take sides and to make a complex issue black and white. It also echoed Netanyahu's concept of "legitimate" nations, "legitimate" war and "legitimate" government. In this way, the US tried to claim the moral high ground and granted itself the tyrannical power of being able to list any individual or group as "terrorists" and justify killing them on those grounds, as well as branding any nation as a "terrorist haven" and justify invading them on those grounds – both in stark violation of international law.

It also wasn't long before Netanyahu expanded this now official War on Terror doctrine to include Israel. Netanyahu now expanded upon the childish

---

98 https://www.youtube.com/watch?v=G5hYwdQn1z8

"us vs. them" demarcation set up by Dubya to make it "US, Israel and the civilized democracies of the world" vs. "Iraq, Iran, Afghanistan and other Arab and Muslim dictatorships of the world." Here are the main points of his speech on April 10, 2002 in front of the US Senate, from the same source[99]:

1. *The American victory against terror in Afghanistan is only the first step in dismantling the global terrorist network. The other terrorist regimes must now be rapidly dealt with in similar fashion.*
2. *Israel, a democratic government that is defending itself against terror should not be equated with the Palestinian dictatorship that is perpetrating it.*
3. *Israel should not be asked to stop fighting terror and return to negotiating table with a regime that is committed to the destruction of the Jewish State and openly embraces terror.*
4. *Israel has the right to defend itself.*
5. *The government of Israel must fight not only to defend its people, restore a dangerously eroded deterrence and secure the Jewish State, but also to ensure that the free world wins the war against terror in this pivotal arena in the heart of the Middle East.*
6. *Israel must dismantle Arafat's terrorist regime and expel Arafat from the region.*
7. *Israel must clean out terrorists, weapons, and explosives from all Palestinian*

[99] www.truth-and-justice.info/origwat.html

controlled areas.

8. *Israel must establish physical barriers separating the main Palestinian population centers from Israeli towns and cities to prevent any residual terrorists from reaching Israel.*
9. *There can never be a political solution for terror. The grievance of terrorists can never be redressed through diplomacy. That will only encourage more terror. Yasser Arafat's terrorist regime must be toppled, not courted. The Oslo agreements are dead. Yasser Arafat killed them.*
10. *A political process can only begin when this terrorist regime is dismantled.*
11. *The urgent need to topple Saddam is paramount. The commitment of America and Britain to dismantle this terrorist dictatorship before it obtains nuclear weapons deserves the unconditional support of all sane governments.*
12. *America must show that it will not heed the international call to stop Israel from exercising its right to defend itself. If America compromises its principles and joins in the chorus of those who demand that Israel disengage, the war on terror will be undermined.*
13. *For if the world begins to believe that America may deviate from its principles, terrorist regimes that might have otherwise been deterred will not be deterred. Those that might have crumbled under the weight of American resolve will not crumble. As a result, winning the war will prove far more*

difficult, perhaps impossible.

14. *To assure that the evil of terrorism does not reemerge a decade or two from now, we must not merely uproot terror, but also plant the seeds of freedom.*
15. *It is imperative that once the terrorist regimes in the Middle East are swept away, the free world, led by America, must begin to build democracy in their place.*
16. *We simply can no longer afford to allow this region to remain cloistered by a fanatic militancy. We must let the winds of freedom and independence finally penetrate the one region in the world that clings to unreformed tyranny.*

Those who follow Middle Eastern and Zionist affairs will notice some key themes introduced here. Firstly, Netanyahu pushes for the US to invade Iraq, a wish that was soon fulfilled. Secondly, Netanyahu pushes back against calls for Israel to stop its harsh and barbaric treatment of the Palestinians, by simply declaring that Israel has a right to defend itself – even if Israel attacks first and uses missiles and bombs against Palestinian Arabs who retaliate by throwing sticks and stones. Thirdly, diplomacy doesn't work with terrorists, so Israel must keep killing its enemies (note the dehumanization of the word "terrorist" and the big lie that there's no point talking or negotiating). Lastly, Netanyahu even promotes the idea of US seeding "democracy" (which is a big con in this context) in other nations after the invasions (i.e., more permanent US occupation and military bases abroad), which only serve to expand the US (NWO) Empire!

ISIS in the Philippines, radical Islamic terrorists in Myanmar ... just a coincidence?
Image credit: DavidIcke.com

Radical Islamic Terrorism™

Radical Islamic terrorism is yet another manifestation of the War on Terror™. It would seem that radical Islamic terrorists are everywhere. They're all over Syria and Iraq. They're in Libya and Nigeria, too. They attacked the former Soviet Union from Afghanistan and modern-day Russia from Chechnya. We've seen them in the Philippines. They attacked an Australian café in Sydney, so we were told. They've been in Myanmar (Burma). They've infiltrated Europe and are behind various attacks in London, Paris, Berlin and Barcelona, so we were told. They're even in China (Uyghur/Xinjiang). And of course, they paid a grand visit to the US on 9/11 in 2001, right?

While I understand people's desire for border control and limited immigration policies, some who gravitate towards the right of the political spectrum are quick to demonize all immigrants, find fault with Islam as a religion and blame all Muslims for the world's evils. They point to radical Islamic terrorists as proof that anything Islamic has to be feared and hated. Aside from the obvious problems with this position – gross generalization, guilt by association, assigning collective guilt to individuals, judging that which you don't know or understand, etc. – it's only looking at the situation from a very superficial perspective. The game is being played at much deeper levels. We need to expand our perceptions if we're going to see it.

The real issue is this: are radical Islamic terrorists the cause of all the world's ills – or are they just the symptom? What's behind radical Islamic terrorism? Who created it? Who keeps creating it? Who trains these radical Islamic terrorists? Who funds them? Who arms them? Who controls them? Answers to these questions will help shed light on the whole situation.

You don't have to dig very deep to discover that Saudi Arabia is the veritable marble fountainhead of radical Islamic terrorism. Saudi Arabia is such a wellspring of radical Islamic terrorism that the terms *Saudi Arabia* and *radical Islamic terrorism* may as well be synonymous. Events really descended into the pit of absurdity when in June 2017 Saudi Arabia had the gall to accuse Qatar of funding terrorism, claiming that was their reason for cutting all Qatari ties! No less absurd were Donald Trump's claims that he was fighting radical Islamic terrorists while sucking up to and cutting deals with the Saudis. Last time I checked, funding something and selling it your weapons is not a very effective way of fighting it. Iran, one of the few Middle Eastern nations that is genuinely committed to fighting terrorism, is constantly accused of being the biggest state sponsor of terrorism in the world, but it's all a game of distraction and smoke and mirrors. Until China brokered a game-changing peace deal and rapprochement between Saudi Arabia and Iran in 2023, the Saudis and Iranians considered each other mortal enemies, which suited Israel and the US very well, who took the Saudi's side and kept threatening Iran militarily. Things are finally starting to change now, however Saudi Arabia is still the source of Islamic terrorism.

Saudi Arabia has entire networks of madrassas or schools that train jihadi terrorists and teach a militant form of Islam known as Wahhabism. Other terms used to describe radical Islamic terrorists are Salafists (fundamentalist and strict Muslims who claim to follow the exact teachings of Mohammad and support Sharia law) and Takfiris (literally an apostate or an unbeliever [i.e. worthy of being killed]). The depth and breadth of Saudi funding of radical Islamic terrorists are truly staggering, as this article[100] explains:

How does Saudi Arabia go about spreading

---

100 www.huffingtonpost.com/dr-yousaf-butt-/saudi-wahhabism-islam-terrorism_b_6501916.html

extremism? The extremist agenda is not always clearly government-sanctioned, but in monarchies where the government money is spread around to various princes, there is little accountability for what the royal family does with their government funds. Much of the funding is via charitable organizations and is not military-related.

The money goes to constructing and operating mosques and madrassas that preach radical Wahhabism. The money also goes to training imams; media outreach and publishing; distribution of Wahhabi textbooks, and endowments to universities and cultural centers ... Although the Wahhabi curriculum was modified after the 9/11 attacks, it remains backward and intolerant. Freedom House published a report on the revised curriculum, concluding that it "continues to propagate an ideology of hate toward the 'unbeliever,' which include Christians, Jews, Shiites, Sufis, Sunni Muslims who do not follow Wahhabi doctrine, Hindus, atheists and others." This is taught not only domestically but also enthusiastically exported abroad.

Get 'em while they're young: young boys being trained to become the next generation of radical Islamic terrorists. Image credit: WorldAffairs.blog

WikiLeaks has exposed cables where Hillary Clinton admitted the Saudi–radical Islamic terrorism connection, as well as cables discussing Saudi front companies:

For instance, a Wikileaks cable clearly quotes then-Secretary of State Hillary Clinton[101] saying "donors in Saudi Arabia constitute the most significant source of funding to Sunni terrorist groups worldwide." She continues: "More needs to be done since Saudi Arabia remains a critical financial support base for al-Qaeda, the Taliban, LeT and other terrorist groups." ... Other cables released by Wikileaks outline how Saudi front companies[102] are also used to fund terrorism abroad.

This article[103] states:

... out of the 61 groups that are designated as terrorist organizations[104] by the U.S. State Department, the overwhelming majority are Wahhabi-inspired and Saudi-funded groups, with a focus on the West and Iran as their primary enemy. Only two are Shi'a—Hezbollah and Kataib Hezbollah, and only four have ever claimed to receive support from Iran.

---

101 https://wikileaks.org/plusd/cables/09STATE131801_a.html

102 https://wikileaks.org/plusd/cables/09STATE83026_a.html

103 www.huffingtonpost.com/entry/the-real-largest-state-sponsor-of-terrorism_us_58cafc26e4b00705db4da8aa

104 https://www.state.gov/j/ct/rls/other/des/123085.htm

Nearly all of the Sunni militant groups listed receive significant support from either the Saudi government or Saudi citizens.

It is important to understand that mainstream Sunni Islam rejects all types of militant Islam, as can be seen in the declarations and discussions of leading Islamic imams and scholars at this international Islamic Conference in 2016[105].
So there is a mountain of evidence that Saudi Arabia funds radical Islamic terrorists and exports its brand of militant Islam to Pakistan, Afghanistan and many other parts of the world. However, the story is much deeper than this, so let's peel back another layer of the onion.

[105] thefreedomarticles.com/sunnis-denounce-salafist-takfiri-terror/

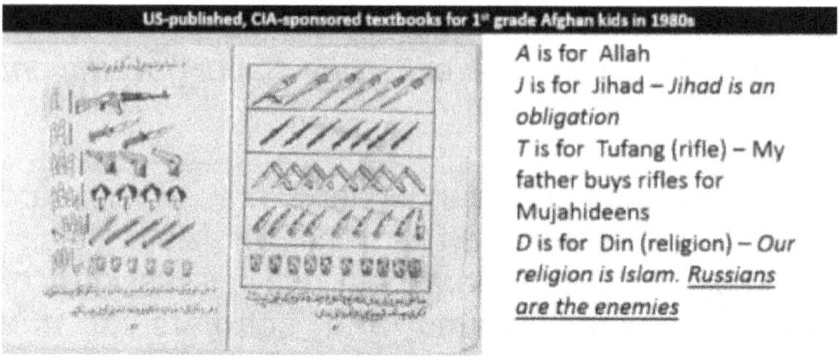
US-published, CIA-sponsored textbooks for 1st grade Afghan kids in 1980s
A is for Allah
J is for Jihad – Jihad is an obligation
T is for Tufang (rifle) – My father buys rifles for Mujahideens
D is for Din (religion) – Our religion is Islam. Russians are the enemies

From the Anglo-American-Zionist New World Order point of view, radical Islamic terrorists are cheap, expendable, easy to arm and easy to fool (e.g., by using religion to trick them as Zbigniew Brzezinski did in this video[106]). Yes, sometimes there is blowback when you train an asset like Saddam Hussein or Osama bin Laden and then lose control of him, but as long as you still retain control, the results can be fantastic. It works like a charm.

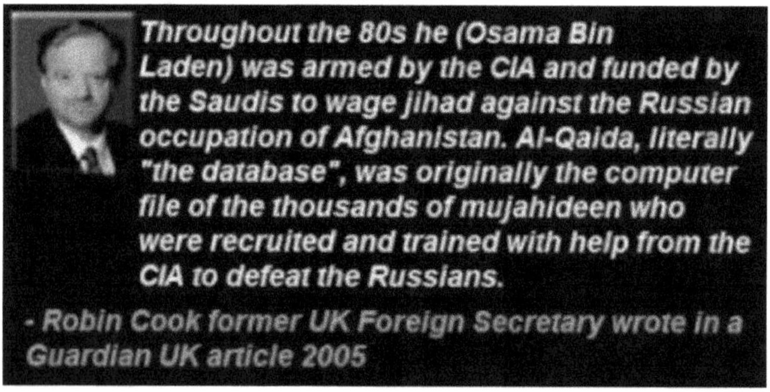
Throughout the 80s he (Osama Bin Laden) was armed by the CIA and funded by the Saudis to wage jihad against the Russian occupation of Afghanistan. Al-Qaida, literally "the database", was originally the computer file of the thousands of mujahideen who were recruited and trained with help from the CIA to defeat the Russians.
- Robin Cook former UK Foreign Secretary wrote in a Guardian UK article 2005

Take a look at Afghanistan in the 1980s. The US, expanding its empire on behalf of the NWO, was working on *containment* of Russia. They recruited

[106] https://www.youtube.com/watch?v=A9RCFZnWGE0

Afghanis and turned them against the then Soviet Union by using religion as a weapon – where the narrative was holy righteous Islam against the godless Communist USSR. These fighters became the Mujahideen – a proxy US army – and the whole Soviet-Afghan war served as a template for how the US could use radical Islamic terrorists to achieve its geopolitical goals. The deployment of Islamic terrorism continued on into the 1990s, 2000s and beyond, as Chris Kanthan[107] explains:

When the Afghan war was about to be won, it dawned on us that the Mujahideen project was a brilliant playbook that could be replicated in other parts of the world. That's when Al Qaeda was formed … Without the knowledge of the American public, the Mujahideen were very active all throughout the 1990s in Bosnia, Kosovo, Azerbaijan, Uzbekistan, Dagestan, Chechnya etc. These fighters were used for three major purposes:

- *throw out pro-Russia dictators*
- *install pro-West leaders who would help us build oil/gas pipelines and agree to host US military bases, and*
- *disrupt Russian pipelines and other interests*

Azerbaijan was an easy one and we got our man in 1993. Georgia took a long time, but George Soros and his color revolution finally installed our guy in 2005. Within a year, we had a 1000-mile pipeline that linked Azerbaijan (Caspian Sea), Georgia and

[107] https://worldaffairs.blog/2017/05/28/embracing-islamic-terrorism/

Turkey! Chechnya was a partial success. They were struggling for independence from Russia and thus gladly welcomed the Mujahideen who also had plenty of Saudi money and US weapons. Within a short time, the non-violent and mystical Sufism of Chechnya was taken over by Saudi Wahhabism.

Through agencies like the CIA, the US has continued to use radical Islamic terrorists to do its dirty work throughout the world, especially in places like Libya and Syria.

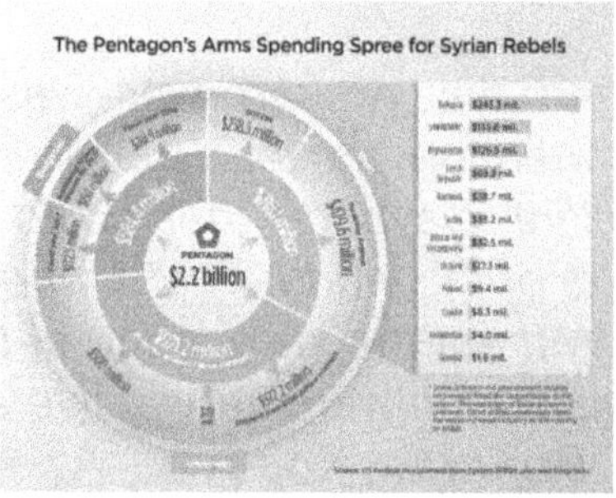

Al-Qaeda (Al-CIA-da) has been great, but ISIS (I-CIA-SIS) even better. We know that the CIA spent $2.2 billion on getting arms to radical Islamic terrorists in Syria[108] (the so-called moderate rebels) – though this is just the tip of the iceberg. Although it's not about Islamic terrorism, the US has also poured well over $100 billion thus far into Ukraine in an attempt to "weaken Russia" (see chapter 5 for more on this.)

Zio-Islamic Terrorism™: Islamic Terrorism Made in Israel

All of these ideas are disgusting and destructive enough on their own – but they are beyond reprehensible given the major role played by the Mossad (the Israeli Secret Intelligence Service, like

[108] www.collective-evolution.com/2017/09/14/the-pentagon-is-spending-2-2-billion-to-arm-syrian-rebels-falsifying-paperwork/

an Israeli CIA) in the 9/11 false flag operation. It is beyond the scope of this book to go deep into the details of that event; however, it is one of many such events in a long history that have been orchestrated and executed by Israel in order to frame Arabs or Muslims (or both) and incite hatred against them. It's literally creating an enemy. Such Radical Islamic Terrorism™ would be better called Zio-Islamic Terrorism™ or simply Zio-Terrorism™. Make no mistake about it: Israel loves radical Islamic terrorists just as much as the West. The connections between Israel and ISIS, Nusra, FSA, Syrian rebels and other radical Islamic terrorists[109] are undeniable. Israel has a long history of framing Arab and Muslim patsies for Mossad-orchestrated crimes, the grandest of which to date is the 9/11 false flag op. The Mossad routinely uses fake passports and other tricks to implicate Arabs in their false flag terror operations. There are many examples, but a revealing one is Operation Trojan in 1986. Israel deliberately created false evidence of Arab terrorism in order to trick the US into going to war against an innocent nation (Libya). Ex-Mossad agent Victor Ostrovsky admitted the plot in his book *The Other Side of Deception*, an excerpt of which is here[110]:

A Trojan was a special communication device that could be planted by naval commandos deep inside enemy territory. The device would act as a relay station for misleading transmissions made by the

---

[109] thefreedomarticles.com/israeli-islamic-terrorism-11-clues/

[110] www.whatreallyhappened.com/WRHARTICLES/deception.html

disinformation unit in the Mossad, called LAP, and intended to be received by American and British listening stations. Originating from an IDF navy ship out at sea, the prerecorded digital transmissions could be picked up only by the Trojan. The device would then rebroadcast the transmission on another frequency, one used for official business in the enemy country, at which point the transmission would finally be picked up by American ears in Britain. The listeners would have no doubt they had intercepted a genuine communication, hence the name Trojan, reminiscent of the mythical Trojan horse

. . .

By the end of March, the Americans were already intercepting messages broadcast by the Trojan, which was only activated during heavy communication traffic hours. Using the Trojan, the Mossad tried to make it appear that a long series of terrorist orders were being transmitted to various Libyan embassies around the world (or, as they were called by the Libyans, Peoples' Bureaus). As the Mossad had hoped, the transmissions were deciphered by the Americans and construed as ample proof that the Libyans were active sponsors of terrorism. What's more, the Americans pointed out, Mossad reports confirmed it.

The Trojan transmitter planed in Tripoli Libya fooled the West into thinking that Libya was responsible for the killing of 2 Americans in the bombing of the La Belle discothèque in Germany. It was later proven that Libya had nothing to do with the bombing. Israel induced the American bombing of

Libya by using radical Islamic terrorists as the pretext. More Zio-Islamic Terrorism™ which killed innocent civilians.

Much of the general Islamophobia in the West has been generated by Zionist organizations to distract people away from Zionist crimes. The Mossad motto is, "By way of deception, thou shalt do war". In so many ways, Israel is behind the invention and creation of radical Islam, Islamic terrorism, Islamophobia and the demonization of Islam. It's behind the creation of the latest boogeyman group ISIS, including making and releasing fake footage of supposed beheadings via its front group SITE. The Pentagon was caught paying a British PR firm $540 million to make fraudulent Islamic terrorist videos[111]. Zander Fuerza writes in a chapter entitled *The Myth of Osama bin Laden & the Nineteen Arab*

[111] https://www.rt.com/usa/361385-pentagon-pr-firm-terrorist-videos/

Oswalds[112] from his book *Masters of Deception*:

It is the Mossad's specialty to frame Arabs and Muslims for acts of terror that they commit themselves ... on 9/11 the Mossad tried to trick the NYPD into thinking Palestinians were going to bomb the Holland tunnel when in reality two Israelis attempted to explode a truck bomb on the George Washington Bridge. We also witnessed the Jewish-owned news media promulgate a fraudulent video clip purporting to show Palestinians celebrating the 9/11 attacks in the West Bank, when five Israelis were actually celebrating the attacks in New Jersey, right across the Hudson river! ... the myth of Osama bin Laden and Al-Qaeda has been used to hoodwink the American public into supporting the imperial schemes of Zionism.

He's referring to the incident that Trump got wrong: the dancing Israelis celebrating the destruction of the WTC. The brainwashing is so heavy that people can't even remember who the supposed terrorists are.

In the weeks after 9/11, evidence suggested it was Israel that framed Muslims in the anthrax murders[113]. Israel's fingerprints were over the 2015 Paris "Charlie Hebdo" attacks[114] and the 2016

---

[112] https://mastersofdeception.wordpress.com/2013/07/16/masters-of-deception-chapter-seven/

[113] www.abeldanger.net/2015/08/israeli-intelligence-frames-muslims-for.html

[114] thefreedomarticles.com/another-day-another-false-flag/

Brussels bombing[115] which we were told was committed by two Arabs. In so many of these cases, Israel controls the security before the event and thus can dismantle cameras, weaken vigilance and order stand-downs to secretly allow the event to happen, when under normal security conditions it would be impossible.

Domestic Terrorism™ and Domestic Extremism™: Coming for the Average Western Citizen, Too

So far this discussion has just been limited to terrorism as a concept fueling foreign policy and international war. However, if you're an American, Brit, Australian, Canadian, New Zealander, European or living anywhere else in the West, don't feel that you're excluded from the danger of this concept. All the governments of these nations and more have been systemically using the concept against their own citizens, too. The language in this case changes to "domestic terrorism", "domestic terrorist" and even "extremist" – language so broad it can be used to impute and accuse virtually anyone of anything. After all, we live in a yin-yang universe where any action falls along a spectrum with two poles, and thus any behavior towards the end of those spectra can be regarded as extreme. That's the base idea of the War on Terror™ – come up with a totally vague, abstract ideology to bypass natural human rights, established legal principles (e.g. innocent until proven guilty) and give the government the powers to get rid of literally anyone they don't like. The COVID operation

[115] thefreedomarticles.com/israeli-brussels-connection-made-in-israel/

(chapter 8) works on the same principle.

To get an idea of how this is playing out, let's look at what's happening inside of the US. The DHS (Department of Homeland Security) was created in the aftermath of the 9/11 false flag op, so you could say it owes its very existence to Terrorism™. As an aside, the DHS is a truly wonderful Orwellian title; it's yet another governmental agency or department doing the exact opposite of its name: it's making us *less secure*. The only people it's making safer are those in the ruling class.

The People Are "The Enemy"

The DHS (Department of Homeland Security), Office of Intelligence and Analysis, "Rightwing Extremism" Report (March 09), with supplementary "Domestic Extremism" Lexicon (April 09) classifies individuals as "extremists" if they identify/ are identified with one or more of the following criteria—among many others—each of which is described as "violent:"

- **Military Veterans** who have fought in foreign wars and are "disgruntled" about the takeover of the US (*see Operation Vigilant Eagle*).
- **Anti-War Individuals/ Groups**.
- **Tax Resistance Movement**: "Groups or individuals who vehemently believe taxes violate their constitutional rights... and that the 16th Amendment to the U.S. Constitution, which allowed Congress to levy taxes on income, was not properly ratified... (also: tax protest movement, tax freedom movement, anti-tax movement)."
- **Militia:** "Members oppose most federal and state laws, regulations, and authority (particularly firearms laws and regulations)."
- **Alternative Media** which provide "interpretations of events and issues that differ radically from those presented in mass media outlets."
- **Opponents of Open Border Policies**, defined as "highly critical of the U.S. Government's response to illegal immigration and [who] oppose government programs that are designed to extend 'rights' to illegal aliens, such as issuing driver's licenses or national identification cards and providing in-state tuition, medical benefits, or public education."
- **Single-Issue:** "Groups or individuals who focus on a single issue or cause—such as **animal rights, environmental** or **anti-abortion**... Group members may be associated with more than one issue (also: special interest extremists)."
- **Patriot Movement**: "A term used by rightwing extremists to link their beliefs to those commonly associated with the American Revolution... (also: Christian patriots, patriot groups, Constitutionalists)."

The DHS has established dozens of "**Fusion Centers**" in cities and states across the country to monitor domestic activity. Local, state, and federal agents from DHS, CIA, and DOJ share information concerning the activities of citizens.

Activities monitored by Fusion Centers overlap with those stated in the DHS Report/ Lexicon (above) and further include the following (which tend to vary state-to-state):

- Frequent references to the **Constitution**
- Support of **third-party** candidates
- Support for an audit of the **Federal Reserve**
- Opposition to a **carbon tax** to be paid to a world bank
- Opposition to US submission to the **United Nations** and/or the **World Health Organization**

The FBI's "**InfraGard**" program: In addition to collecting data internally, FBI agents work within the private sector with businesses which report on citizens' "suspicious" activities.

The **US Department of Defense**'s current training manual (introduced at *Antiterrorism and Force Protection Annual Refresher Training Course*, 2009) advises personnel that political protest (admittedly protected under the First Amendment) is to be regarded as "low-level terrorism".

The image on the left, taken from a DHS manual, details what kind of people the NWO, via the US government, is now targeting. This is nothing more than a blatant attempt to criminalize ordinary people engaged in perfectly normal, lawful activities – the kind of people that are hard to rule because they have principles and think for themselves rather than being swept along with MSM propaganda or blind nationalism.

This list shows how inverted things are. To any rational person, being antiwar is a sign of being lawful and nonextreme, as war is rarely (if ever) lawful. And it's the most extreme version of violence in existence since it often involves the deaths of millions of people. Yet, according to the DHS, if you are antiwar, you are an extremist that needs to be monitored. Apart from the listed groups (veterans, citizens for lawful taxation, militia members, alternative media journalists, border control advocates and patriots), look also at the bottom section where the DHS classifies as extremists those opposed to a worldwide carbon tax and the subjugation of the US by the UN (United Nations). Could it be any more blatant? The carbon tax and the UN are, of course, brainchilds of the Rothschilds and Rockefellers and necessary stepping-stones in their plan to unite all nations under a One World Government ruled by the international banking cartel. These two schemes are the very essence of the NWO, so it's unsurprising that opponents to them have been singled out.

Everything is backwards here. Consider: who's

insane in this case? If I run around trying to silence dissent and shut people up who disagree with me, even if 99.9 percent are completely nonviolent and pose no threat to me or society, wouldn't I be worthy of a psychological examination? Wouldn't that examination possibly find sociopathic or psychopathic tendencies in my character? Wouldn't I perhaps be regarded, in colloquial terms, as a kind of "control freak" that can't stand not being in control of everything? Wouldn't it make more sense to call me an "extremist", since it's pretty extreme to condemn, criminalize and harm others just because I don't like their views?

So who's the *real* extremist?

Chapter 5 – We Are Already in World War III

From the very beginning, the United States coalition, while fighting Daesh more or less actively (sometimes more, sometimes less), has been sparing Jabhat al-Nusra (Nusra Front). Obviously, all facts indicate in this direction.

– Sergei Lavrov[116], Russian Foreign Minister

We'll give $20 million.

– Mike Pompeo[117], US Secretary of State, pledges money to the Venezuelan opposition to help them overthrow the legitimately elected Maduro Government

War is the health of the state.

– Randolph Bourne, author

America has no permanent friends or enemies, only interests.

– Henry Kissinger, Globalist and NWO insider, US Secretary of State 1973-1977

---

[116] presstv.com/Detail/2017/07/22/529282/Russia-Lavrov-Syria-Nusra-terrorists-US-refusal

[117] https://www.cbsnews.com/news/mike-pompeo-venezuela-aid-pompeo-pledges-20-million-in-venezuela-aid-at-request-of-u-s-backed-opposition-leader-today/

*****

In the previous two chapters, I've laid out how the world is in a precarious state – and how this has come about not through random events or through purely self-interested human motivations like greed but rather according to a coldly calculated overarching agenda which has been in place for decades if not centuries. In this chapter we will explore how this plan for worldwide domination is playing out – in the area of war, which is after all a manifestation of the brutality, lawlessness and lust for control of the NWO agenda itself. We have already been living through World War III (WWIII) for quite awhile now; it just looks different to a traditional war that is limited to trenches, tanks and bombs. Nations like Syria, North Korea, Venezuela, Iran, Ukraine and Taiwan are all flashpoints or gateways to making WWIII hotter.

Many fictional works, including modern movies such as *Wag the Dog* and books like the aforementioned *1984*, have pointed out the truth that the state seems to thrive on war and even needs war, in the end, to survive and to justify its own existence. Why? Because war distracts, justifies and creates the chaos from which order can be arranged. War distracts people from difficult issues that society needs to solve, as well as from focusing too much on the corruption and crime of the political class. War justifies so many things that cannot be otherwise justified – it's an emergency which puts people into a reactionary, emotional fight-or-flight state (controlled by the amygdala or the reptilian brain) rather than a calm, logical, reasonable state (controlled by the neocortex or mammalian brain). War also neatly contributes (from the psychopathic point of view) to the (imaginary) problem of overpopulation by providing an acceptable avenue for mass murder. *Wag the Dog* features a president actually going to war just to boost his popularity ratings. Fiction or fact? In *1984*, Winston's society is part of a grander coalition (Oceania) that is literally always at war with someone: it doesn't matter who the opponent is. Oceana goes from being at war with Eastasia to war with Eurasia, and the history books are rapidly rewritten so that the public is brainwashed to believe that *"we were always at war with Eurasia."* In this dystopic world (which is basically our reality), Orwell hints that war is the lifeblood of the state, not because there are actual dangerous enemies out there but rather to keep people busy, distracted, stressed and (most importantly) afraid – to justify the draconian regulation of life. War is the sine qua non of life in *1984*. Is the same true today?

In our world today, we find war is constant, incessant and all-pervasive. Peace has not prevailed. While it may have been seventy-two years since the end of the last official world war, the world has nonetheless been embroiled in war ever since. We've had the Korean War, Vietnam War and numerous wars in the Middle East, which have escalated since the 9/11 false flag event. The alternative media site WashingtonsBlog.com calculated that as of 2015, the US itself had been involved in war in 222 out of the 239 years[118] of its existence, which is 93 percent of

---

[118] www.washingtonsblog.com/2015/02/america-war-93-time-222-239-years-since-1776.html

the time. Now in 2023, this statistic stands at 230 out of 247 years. Trump continued many wars, despite rhetoric about pullouts, and Biden bombed Syria in February 2021 in "self-defense" before overseeing the continued catastrophic provocation of Russia in Ukraine, leading WWIII to turn from cold to hot. It matters not which puppet sits upon the US presidential throne; the agenda continues unabated.

Many regional wars are proxy wars fought between the world's superpowers, so they are world wars in essence, just not in name. This was the case with the US funding the mujahideen (radical Islamic terrorists) to fight the Soviets in Afghanistan in the 1980s. It was again the case with the US funding groups like Al-Qaeda, FSA [Free Syrian Army] and Jahbat Al Nusra (overtly) and ISIS (covertly) to the fight the Russians in Syria, a "third party" country. And, it is most assuredly the case in the current Russo-Ukraine war that officially began on February 24th 2022, but which in reality had been going on a long time.

Before we get to Ukraine, we're going to look at other examples of regional conflict from the last decade or so. Syria is a pertinent example. The conflict is still ongoing there, however for now, it has died down. While the lying MSM tried to paint the Syrian conflict as a civil war, it was anything but that. There were/are various internal rebel and terrorist groups vying for power but even more outside forces creating, funding, directing and controlling them. We have had the US, UK, France, Germany, Turkey, Saudi Arabia, Israel and NATO (North Atlantic Treaty Organization, a military alliance controlled by the US) intervening on one side (often helping the so-called moderate rebels) against the SAA or Syrian Arab Army (the forces of the legitimate government of Syrian President Bashar Al-Assad), supported by Iran, Russia and China on the other. Meanwhile, insane homicidal groups like ISIS have been running around killing and beheading people – with money, vehicles and weapons courteously supplied by the US. Syria is a powder keg, a recipe for disaster which luckily as of now has not erupted into an official WWIII scenario. (It should be noted that Israel is trying to play both sides since it also has a close relationship with Russia.)

It is worthwhile noting what US General Wesley Clark confessed in 2011 during an interview on *Democracy Now!*. He let the cat out of the bag by admitting that a plan was drawn up by the Pentagon to go to war with seven countries in the first five years after 9/11, despite the fact that these nations had not attacked or harmed the US. Clark said[119]:

I had been through the Pentagon right after 9/11. About ten days after 9/11, I went through the Pentagon and I saw Secretary Rumsfeld and Deputy Secretary Wolfowitz. I went downstairs just to say hello to some of the people on the Joint Staff who used to work for me, and one of the generals called me in. He said, "Sir, you've got to come in and talk to me a second." I said, "Well, you're too busy." He said, "No, no." He says, "We've made the decision we're going to war with Iraq." This was on or about the 20th of September. I said, "We're going to war with Iraq?

119 https://www.youtube.com/watch?v=9RC1Mepk_Sw

Why?" He said, "I don't know." He said, "I guess they don't know what else to do." So I said, "Well, did they find some information connecting Saddam to al-Qaeda?" He said, "No, no." He says, "There's nothing new that way. They just made the decision to go to war with Iraq." He said, "I guess it's like we don't know what to do about terrorists, but we've got a good military and we can take down governments." And he said, "I guess if the only tool you have is a hammer, every problem has to look like a nail."

So I came back to see him a few weeks later, and by that time we were bombing in Afghanistan. I said, "Are we still going to war with Iraq?" And he said, "Oh, it's worse than that." He reached over on his desk. He picked up a piece of paper. And he said, "I just got this down from upstairs" -- meaning the Secretary of Defense's office -- "today." And he said, "This is a memo that describes how we're going to take out seven countries in five years, starting with Iraq, and then Syria, Lebanon, Libya, Somalia, Sudan and, finishing off, Iran." I said, "Is it classified?" He said, "Yes, sir." I said, "Well, don't show it to me." And I saw him a year or so ago, and I said, "You remember that?" He said, "Sir, I didn't show you that memo! I didn't show it to you!"

Knowingly or not, Clark had just revealed more of the game plan – constant war. At the highest levels, the US military is a tool in the hands of the New World Order. What we find here is a pattern of constant subjugation for grand geopolitical objectives. It has nothing to do with defense, duty or patriotism. It is all-out conquest, barely veiled under the flimsy pretext of fighting terrorism.

George W. Bush further affirmed the NWO agenda of encircling China and Russia by coming out right after 9/11, in early 2002, to declare a new "Axis of Evil" which comprised Iran, Iraq and North Korea. Later in May 2002, neocon hawk and then Undersecretary of State John Bolton gave a speech entitled "Beyond the Axis of Evil" where he nominated three more so-called "rogue nations": Cuba, Libya, and Syria. In reality, the USA is the rogue state of the world. Interestingly, now, over eighteen years later, we have witnessed the illegal invasion and conquest of Iraq and Libya and the attempted but thus far unsuccessful conquest of Syria. North Korea has been constantly provoked. Iran has not only been sanctioned to the hilt, but the US also struck by assassinating its top general, Qassem Soleimani, at the start of 2020. It should be noted that all of these nations – whether you take Wesley's Clark list of seven, or the Bush-Bolton list of six (and some of them are on both lists) – are nations which surround the two giants of Eurasia, Russia and China, who are the ultimate targets of the US.

North Korea and the US – Who's Provoking Whom?

One prominent characteristic of conflicts and wars in the last century has been the use of provocation – goading an enemy into attacking, then playing the victim and assaulting them ruthlessly white claiming self-defense. Sometimes this is done with false flag attacks, but other times simply by encroaching on another nations' territory, treating them with disrespect and putting pressure on them so they feel they have no choice but to attack.

In the first two years of the Trump Administration (2017–2018), there was once again a lot of focus on North Korea. Predictably, the media painted the North Korean leader Kim Jong-un as crazy and his regime as hostile and dictatorial. While I have no desire to live under such a regime, such a characterization of Kim was exactly in alignment with what the MSM does before a war: paints the future target as crazy, barbaric, hostile and murderous. In short, they make them an enemy so the Western and American public can feel better when their combined militaries (paid killers) invade and destroy that country.

The MSM goes to great lengths to present people like Osama Bin Laden (former CIA asset and leader of the supposed "Al-Qaeda" [database] terrorist group), Saddam Hussein (Iraq), Muammar Gaddafi (Libya), Bashar Al-Assad (Syria) and Kim Jong-un (North Korea) as cruel dictators who oppress their own people, and more importantly, as crazy. The idea is to stop you from thinking that these people are actually acting rationally in the face of the US Empire.

But think about it: if you were Kim Jong-un, and you saw how Hussein and Gaddafi had been brutally murdered by American soldiers and their nations brutally invaded, would you give up your nukes, which are the ultimate self-defense weapons? Not if you were interested in your own survival. The truth is that to retain nukes purely for self-defense is a rational decision in the face of a global superbully like the US – still the only nation to have ever dropped atomic bombs on another nation. We were told that North Korea was provoking the US. While that might be true, who is engaging in the greater provocation? To answer that, you have to understand the history, background and context of Korea, particularly since the end of World War II. Are you aware that:

– the US entered the Korean War and proceeded to bomb North Korea to smithereens under the leadership of bloodthirsty generals like Douglas MacArthur (who led the United Nations Command) and Curtis LeMay?

– the US used 635,000 tons of bombs and 32,557 tons of napalm against North Korea, more than they used in the entire Pacific War against the Japanese during World War II?

– LeMay stated, *"We killed off ... 20 percent of the population"* and *"We went over there and fought the war and eventually burned down every town in North Korea"*?

– That MacArthur's MAD plan[120] was to try to win the war against North Korea in 10 days by dropping *"between 30 and 50 atomic bombs ... strung across the neck of Manchuria"* that would have *"spread behind ... a belt of radioactive cobalt"*?

– That the Korean War ended in 1953 only with an armistice, not a Peace Treaty? That this technically means the war is still going? That this gives the US the excuse to continue treating South Korea as its vassal state (as it treats Japan, Australia, Germany,

[120] www.nytimes.com/1964/04/09/texts-of-accounts-by-lucas-and-considine-on-interviews-with-macarthur-in-1954.html?_r=0

France and many, many nations in the world), because if there were a formal Korean Peace Treaty in existence, the US would have no legal basis for the occupation of South Korea with American military bases and troops?

North Korea provocation: the US is provoking North Korea by installing the THAAD missile “defense” system (i.e. offense system) in South Korea right near North Korea’s border, but there are some South Koreans protesting it.

If you knew all of the above, did you also know that:

– Many South Koreans are tired of South Korea being a US puppet state? The opposition party and the other forces who were behind the impeachment of the South Korean president wanted the US out of South Korea? They also want the THAAD missile system recently installed by the US dismantled?

– George Bush Jr. (you know, the same one who

proved that evolution goes in reverse) stated that the US would grant itself the right of striking first by way of a preemptive attack? That because of this American policy, North Korea left the nuclear NPT (Non-Proliferation Treaty) since the US wasn't following its own rules?

The Korea reunification monument (located south of Pyongyang and opened in 2001 to commemorate Korean reunification proposals put forward by Kim Il-sung).

– The Koreans tried reuniting despite all the forces against them wanting to keep them separated? It was called the Sunshine Policy.

Sadly, reunification has yet to happen in Korea due to the divide-and-conquer strategies of the NWO. The Sunshine Policy (from 1998 to 2008) was a time when South Korea and North Korea were moving closer towards reunification when the Bush-Cheney administration, a hotbed of traitors, globalists, Zionists and neocons, moved to demonize and isolate North Korea. Stuart Bramhall[121] wrote:

In 1998 South Korean president Kim Dae Jung began his Sunshine Policy aimed at lessening tensions and building reconciliation between North and South Korea. In June 2000, leaders of the two countries held a historic three-day summit in Pyongyang (the first in 50 years) and signed a pact in which they agreed to work towards reunification. Among other provisions, the agreement included substantial South Korean humanitarian aid to address North Korea's chronic food shortages, loosening of restrictions on South Korean investment in North Korea, the opening of North Korea's Kumgang Tourist Region to South Korean visitors, the establishment of a family reunification program, the opening of rail links through the Demilitarized Zone (DMZ) and a worker exchange program permitting South Korean workers to work at North Korea's Kaesang Industrial Park.

In 2000, Kim Dae Jung won the Nobel Peace Prize for his successful implementation of the Sunshine Policy.

Unfortunately George W Bush, who took office in 2001, had very different plans for the Korean peninsula. In his view, a paranoid militarist North Korean threatening US allies South Korea and Japan was the most potent argument he had to justify his obsession with building a missile defense system ... the immediate trigger for these moves was a visit

---

[121] www.globalresearch.ca/koreas-sunshine-policythe-reunification-of-north-and-south-korea/5585282

by Japanese prime minister Junichiro Koizumi to North Korea in a first effort to normalize relations between the two countries. In the view of the Bush administration, an independent economic-political block consisting of Japan and a unified Korea posed a serious strategic threat to US dominance in Asia and had to be stopped.

If you knew all of that, you should also know the following:

– The US and South Korea have been conducting joint annual military drills and war games for decades (now called Foal Eagle) which simulate a war with North Korea. The games were given the name Operation Decapitation and simulated the attack and overthrow of North Korea.

– North Korea agreed to suspend its nuclear tests if the US agreed to end these annual war games along the North Korean border.

– The entire military budget of North Korea is around US$6 to 7 billion[122] per year, compared to the US military budget which has been consistently above US$400 billion per year since 2000, and in 2019 was over US$900 billion?

– As Joe Clifford wrote in his article *What The Corporate Media Never Tells You About North*

---

122 www.globalfirepower.com/country-military-strength-detail.asp?country_id=north-korea

Korea[123]*: "North Korea, China, and India are the only three nations who have committed to a "no nuclear first" policy? They have pledged never to use nuclear weapons first, but of course reserve the right to use them if attacked."*

Funny, but Theresa May, former PM of staunch US ally Great Britain, shocked many people by declaring that the UK would be willing to use nuclear weapons in a first strike[124] (just as the intellectually challenged Dubya had claimed). Why are the US and UK allowed to openly and brazenly claim the right to attack (and not be dismissed as aggressive, mad and irrational), but other countries' leaders cannot? Who's threatening whom? Who's provoking whom? What's the reality? Is the North Korea provocation about North Korea provoking the US or the US provocation of North Korea?

Again, I would not like to live in North Korea, nor live under Kim Jong-un. That said, do you really think the complicit Anglo-American-Zionist MSM is demonizing him because they care so deeply about the plight of the average North Korean? North Korea has repeatedly asked the US to engage in bilateral talks to decrease the tension. They have promised not to fire any more test missiles in exchange for the US promising not to continue its military drills with South Korea which simulate the invasion of North

123 www.globalresearch.ca/what-the-corporate-media-never-tells-you-about-north-korea/5587728

124 www.independent.co.uk/news/uk/politics/theresa-may-nuclear-weapons-first-strike-michael-fallon-general-election-jeremy-corbyn-trident-a7698621.html

Korea and the destruction of its regime. At different points during the height of US–North Korean tensions during 2017–2018, Trump acknowledged how the US was provoking North Korea; however, his insight wasn't enough to actually change US policy, which is largely dictated by those in the shadows, not presidential frontmen on stage.

The US mercilessly obliterated and decimated North Korea in 1953. Since then, the US has gone on to bomb, invade and attack over forty-four countries, while North Korea has invaded no one. Experts suggest North Korea has around eight to ten nuclear weapons (with no effective delivery system), while it is a fact that the US has 6,800[125] (of which a large number are deployed against North Korea). And yet we are supposed to believe that North Korea is a dangerous rogue state that is posing a genuine threat to the US?

Venezuela – Another Country Not Playing Ball with US Multinationals Over Oil

The attempted 2019 Venezuela coup orchestrated by the US was utterly blatant, even by American standards. Venezuela is not a black-and-white issue. Yes, extreme socialism can lead to instability and disaster. No, Maduro is not the greatest leader. And yes, the people of Venezuela are suffering under massive hyperinflation. However, by far the largest factor affecting Venezuela now is not Maduro or

---

[125] https://www.armscontrol.org/factsheets/Nuclearweaponswhohaswhat

socialism but rather US foreign intervention[126]. Juan Guaido, the latest Washington puppet and fraudulent nonpresident, has a background steeped in US-trained provocation. He's a trained agent provocateur or "opposition leader" who was carefully groomed to play a pivotal role in the Venezuelan coup. Former US Vice President Mike Pence phoned Guaido the night before he proclaimed himself "president" to give the green light to the coup, and former US Secretary of State Mike Pompeo openly proclaimed the US would be giving the Venezuelan opposition US$20 million. Guaido's job was to claim he was the interim president of Venezuela (under Article 233 of the Venezuelan Constitution) because Maduro somehow didn't hold fair elections. However, that argument held no legal water as this *Global Research* article *The Failure of Guaido's Constitutional Claim to the Presidency of Venezuela*[127] explains:

The opening paragraph envisions six scenarios whereby a President might no longer serve … Of the six scenarios envisioned (death, resignation etc.) Guaido relies on "abandonment of his position." This clearly never happened. Maduro isn't gone. He's still there … Guaido, as head of the National Assembly, only becomes involved when the vacancy occurs in the twilight zone between election and inauguration. This definitely did not happen here. Moreover, by citing Article 233 Guaido implies there was a recent (lawful) election. Finally, Guaido's January 23 self-

---

[126] https://thefreedomarticles.com/venezuelan-economic-crisis-cause-not-socialism/

[127] https://www.globalresearch.ca/failure-guaidos-constitutional-claim-presidency/5666847

anointment occurred 13 days after Maduro's January 10 inauguration. He missed the boat.

Here's the deal: the US funds opposition in countries whose leaders and governments are hostile to it, i.e. are strongly nationalist, isolationist, refuse to let US corporations access their resources or refuse to toe the US line in other ways. If its controlled opposition is too unpopular to win free and open elections, the US will proceed with its agenda of sabotage by making them not run in the elections, then afterwards claiming the elections were rigged. A usual line in the script is that the US "cares so much"

about the people of that country (Libya, Syria, Iran, Venezuela, etc. as opposed to the government of that country) and just wants to spread "freedom and democracy." Pompeo revealed the brazen duplicity in this quote as reported by Reuters:

We in the Trump Administration continue to support countries trying to prevent Cuba and Venezuela from hijacking those protests and we'll work with legitimate (governments) to prevent protests from morphing into riots and violence that don't reflect the democratic will of the people.

The quote is rather shocking in its two-faced arrogance but this is the mindset of those that run the world. When you pass it through the Orwellian translation unit, strip it of its PR and propaganda surface sheen and translate it into plain English, this is what it means:

The USA will sometimes support the government of a particular country and sometimes support the opposition party, protestors or rioters of a particular country. When we want to support the government, we'll call it legitimate and the protests illegitimate. When we want to support the opposition, we'll call it legitimate and the government illegitimate. Whichever side we support, we'll say we are doing that because it reflects the democratic will of the people.

Again, as Kissinger said, it's all about interests – not fundamental values or principles. As interests shift, so does US policy. The NWO controllers wouldn't know a healthy value or principle if it kicked them in the face.

Another aspect to this same agenda is an idea put forward by NWO insider and mastermind George Soros[128]. He proposed that sovereignty lies with the people, not with the leaders or government of a nation. It sounds just, fair and in alignment with libertarian principles, but Soros and his cronies have something else in mind. By promoting this notion, the US-led NWO (and US-controlled organizations like the UN, NATO, WTO, etc.) can now claim that a particular leader not toeing the line with the US does not represent the sovereignty of the people – and therefore needs to be toppled with a "humanitarian intervention." It has basically become an excuse to overthrow legitimately elected governments anywhere in the world.

The US has sanctioned nations like Venezuela and Iran to the hilt, since sanctions are another means of warfare. They can cripple, destroy and paralyze. The USG and lapdog MSM may pass off sanctions as soft, but the US has been attacking Venezuela with economic warfare for a long time. This *Activist Post* article[129] refers to the work of former special rapporteur for the United Nations Human Rights Council Alfred de Zayas:

De Zayas also called for the International Criminal

---

128 https://thefreedomarticles.com/soros-hack-top-10-machinations/

129 https://www.activistpost.com/2019/01/medieval-siege-in-buried-report-un-official-slams-venezuela-sanctions-as-criminal.html

Court to investigate the anti-Venezuela sanctions as a possible crime against humanity under Article Seven of the ICC's Rome Statute, powerfully stating: "Modern-day economic sanctions and blockades are comparable with medieval sieges of towns with the intention of forcing them to surrender. Twenty-first century sanctions attempt to bring not just a town, but sovereign countries to their knees.

Neocon Zionist and mad warmonger John Bolton announced US$7 billion of PDVSA (Petróleos de Venezuela, S.A., the Venezuelan state-owned oil and natural gas company) assets would be immediately blocked as a result of US sanctions while the company would also lose an estimated US$11 billion in export proceeds over the coming year. Many US officials began to repeat the mantra *"Maduro must go"*[130] just as so many of them said "Assad must go" about Syria. John Bolton even admitted[131] that *"it will make a big difference to the United States economically if we could have American oil companies invest in and produce the oil capabilities in Venezuela."* This is not to say NWO conquests are just about hydrocarbons and natural resources (they're more about power, control and bringing all nations under the heel of the NWO) however oil is part of it – and certainly the sovereignty and democratic will of the people has absolutely *nothing* to do with it.

US coups, often led by the notorious CIA ever since the end of WWII, have become commonplace

---

130 https://www.youtube.com/watch?v=C3j1hHNz6aE

131 https://www.youtube.com/watch?v=6fkBORwhZgo

all over the world, and especially so in Venezuela. During the Dutch-Venezuelan crisis of 1908, the US Navy assisted in a coup whereby Venezuelan VP Juan Vicente Gómez seized power. During his brutal authoritarian rule, he granted lucrative concessions to foreign oil companies including Standard Oil (ExxonMobil today) and Royal Dutch Shell. Decades later the US-backed dictator Marcos Jimenez from 1948 to 1958, who gave the oil companies a similar deal.

The Bolivarian Revolution in 1998 led by Hugo Chavez upended the apple cart. Chavez was not afraid to spit at the US and did things such as openly insult George Bush at the UN, calling him the Devil himself. In 2002, the US was behind a Venezuelan coup which temporarily removed Chavez from power for two days; however, the Venezuelan military soon restored him to power. That particular 2002 Venezuela coup was led by neocon Elliott Abrams, the very same man Trump appointed to get the job done again apparently. You can watch the story of this coup in the documentary *The Revolution Will Not Be Televised*[132]. Fast forward to 2015, and Nicolas Maduro has replaced Chavez as president, but the coups continue. On February 23, 2015, Maduro had this to say[133] about another US-backed Venezuela coup which was foiled:

It is the government of the United States that is behind the plans of destabilization and coups against Venezuela. I have come here to denounce it. ... We have dismantled a coup attempt against democracy, against the stability of our homeland ... It was an attempt to use a group of officials from the air force to provoke a violent act, an attack.

The fact is that the US has embarked upon a steady campaign of warfare against Venezuela. 4th Generation Warfare (fourth-generation warfare or 4GW) is a term used to define the kind of war often waged in the 21st century by (mostly) the US. It blurs the lines between war and politics, and soldiers and civilians. It includes new forms of attacks such as cyber attacks, electromagnetic attacks, infrastructure attacks and propaganda, which can effectively "win" a war for the aggressor without it ever needing to deploy its own troops in the attacked country.

The plan has never changed. A SOUTHCOM (US southern command, one of eleven command units

---

[132] https://www.youtube.com/watch?v=Id--ZFtjR5c

[133] https://www.cnn.com/2015/02/12/americas/venezuela-coup-attempt-foiled/index.html

assigned to operate worldwide; this one in Central America, South America and the Caribbean) document[134] dated February 23, 2018 is entitled *"Plan to overthrow the Venezuelan Dictatorship – 'Masterstroke'"* and was signed by Kurt W. Tidd, then admiral and commander of SOUTHCOM. The document starts with propaganda against Venezuela's existing government (ignoring the extent to which preexisting US economic sanctions against Venezuela had actually caused these problems) then presents the plan to overthrow the so-called dictatorship. Tidd calls Maduro "the Dictator" throughout virtually the entire document.

In March 2019, the US was behind a cyberattack that took down Venezuela's power grid and another so-called terrorist attack that ruptured storage tanks at a heavy oil processing plant in eastern Venezuela. The power outages had a grave effect on Venezuela. The Caracas subway came to a halt. Around 70 percent of the nation was without electricity for at least a day. Food went rotten in fridges. Many people who depended on electric pumps had to resort to getting water from drainpipes and dirty streams. Looting and vandalism increased. Some people who depended on dialysis machines or electricity-operated living units just to stay alive died. Luckily the Venezuelan government was able to get the power back to some or most of the country within a day. China also stepped in to assist. USG officials, predictably, blamed Maduro and his mismanagement and corruption for the problem. But of course they

---

[134] https://web.archive.org/web/20180514190031/https://www.voltairenet.org/article201100.html

would do this, since that's the appeal of 4GW: destroy a country's infrastructure and make it look like ineptitude so the leader has less support from his own people. This is not to say that Maduro is perfect, or that he hasn't mismanaged things. The point is that the US blatantly attacks other nations like this just because they don't bow down to the Empire. When it comes to 4GW, history repeats itself, and for those who look closely and study the patterns, there are almost always clues in past events. Here are two cases in point. The US famously overthrew democratically elected Chilean President Salvador Allende in order to install puppet dictator Pinochet in a 1973 coup. Guess what? They also cut the electricity there, too, before the actual coup that ousted Allende, as this *New York Times* article[135] reported. Meanwhile, the US-Israeli alliance in a joint operation (Operation Olympic Games) pulled off a damaging cyberattack against Iran's nuclear facility in Natanz using the Stuxnet virus, widely believed to have been created in a collaboration between the NSA and Israel's elite cyberwarfare unit named Unit 8200.

By the way, did you hear that the US deeply cares about the Venezuelan people (just as it cares about the North Korean people, the Syrian people, the Libyan people, the Iranian people and so on)? I'm sure at some point US leaders said they cared about the Iraqi people; however, they have killed over a million Iraqis since 2003 when the US illegally invaded Iraq to supposedly overthrow the cruel

---

[135] https://www.nytimes.com/1973/08/14/archives/blackout-interrupts-address-by-allende.html?smid=tw-share

dictator Saddam Hussein and set the Iraqi people free. The US still refuses to stop its occupation and leave Iraq despite the Iraqi Parliament in late 2019 telling them to get out. I guess the US is generous enough to grant sovereignty to the conquered, as long as their sovereignty lines up with US wishes. It is a page straight from the songbook when the US government claims it "cares about the people" of the nation it is overthrowing, while simultaneously sanctioning that nation to the point where it can no longer import essential life products such as medicines, food staples and sanitation items. It's like a psychopath that feigns empathy with you while plotting to rob you. It is a pathetic attempt to sugarcoat flagrant and highly illegal interference, meddling and theft. If the US cared about the Venezuelan people, it would lift the crippling sanctions which have tied up literally billions and billions of Venezuelan money in banks which it cannot access. If the US cared about freedom, it would respect the legitimacy of the elections and the Maduro administration and keep its nose out of foreign affairs.

Pigs might fly, too.

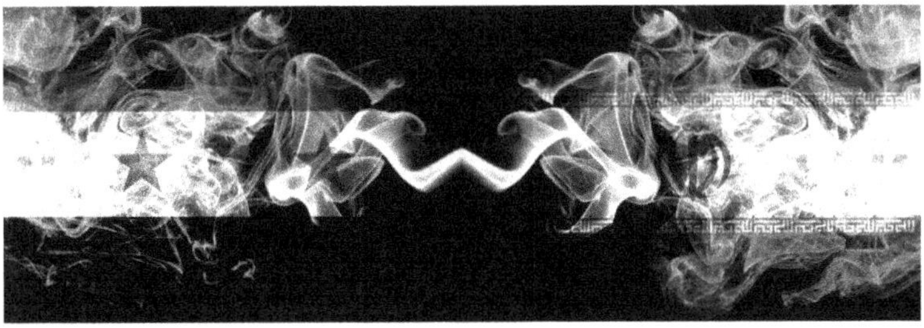

What's Different about Syria and Iran

Despite all the destruction that has been wrought there since 2011, you can look at Syria in a positive way because it's the only example in the last two decades of a nation that fought back successfully (two some degree) against the US-led NWO after being invaded and occupied (like Vietnam). At the time of writing, Syria still has US forces illegally occupying its land and stealing its oil, which is quite horrific, however it Bashar Al-Assad did manage to stay in power and prevent his nation from being totally destroyed and balkanized. Syria has proven not to be a pushover like some of the other nations around it. Take Libya for instance. In 2011, the US-led coalition (NATO, UK, France and the usual partners in crime) decided to take out Muammar Gaddafi, leader of Libya. The usual pack of lies were spread to justify the invasion: here was a horrible dictator, killing his own people and even giving Viagra to his soldiers so they could rape more women (a creative but bald-faced lie). As leaked Hillary Clinton emails show, such as one from Sidney Blumenthal (Clinton advisor) to then Secretary of State Hillary Clinton entitled *France's client and Qaddafi's gold*[136], the real reason Gaddafi was targeted was that he was bringing Libyans out of poverty, sharing the oil wealth with the people of his nation, rapidly improving the standard of living for the average Libyan (which became the highest in the entire continent of Africa) and importantly was developing plans to start a new pan-Africa currency backed by Libyan silver and gold reserves. The West ratcheted up all its military and nonmilitary resources, the latter of which included its vast propaganda machine of NGOs, who kept

136 https://wikileaks.org/clinton-emails/emailid/12659

pushing the agenda that we must have a "No Fly Zone" over Libya. Meanwhile, the UN (largely controlled by the West) declared its new doctrine of R2P (Responsibility to Protect) and MSM outlets proudly declared that the US was conducting a "humanitarian intervention" – a grotesque oxymoron and inversion of reality. There is no such thing as humanitarian intervention, since all interventions are military invasions including bombing a country and killing its people. Libya has been in a sorry state ever since then. The US-led forces created a power vacuum, and now the nation is besieged by constant infighting.

Undoubtedly the NWO thought they could knock off Syria just like they had knocked off Libya. However, not everything has gone according to the game plan. Syria has proven to be a difficult nut to crack. The main reason is that Syria has powerful allies who are prepared to step in to defend it – Iran and Russia (and by proxy China, since China and Russia are bound closely together in military agreements and cooperation). Iran is a dominant nation in the region and vies with Saudi Arabia (its chief Muslim rival) to be the most powerful country in the Middle East. Islam has two main sects – Sunni Islam and Shia Islam. To oversimplify things, Saudi Arabia is predominantly Sunni, and Iran is predominantly Shia (although Saudi Arabia is also home to fanatical and extremist forms of Islam such as Wahhabism which promote the idea of violence against infidels or unbelievers). The Saudi Arabia–Iran rivalry was until March 2023 characterized by intense hatred, and Iran has used its power and influence to protect other Shia Muslim–majority nations in the region, such as Iraq and Syria. Russia is a nuclear power (officially owning more nuclear weapons than any other country on Earth) and was the central nerve center of the Soviet Union, a massive sprawling empire engaged in the Cold War against the US for decades. Under the leadership of President Vladimir Putin, Russia has shown that it will not back down as the US-NATO coalition creeps closer and closer to its borders, including overtaking nations that were either formerly part of the USSR (Ukraine) or overtaking nations that are vital to its trading, geopolitical and national interests (as Syria is). Quite simply, Russia will not allow the US to edge any closer to its national borders (and set up bases and missile systems on Russia's doorstep).

The Syrian War has decreased in intensity, having at one point contained the massive potential to ignite a hot WWIII, given the fact it has involved over ten very powerful nations to varying degrees, plus the proxy armies that were laughingly called "moderate rebels" (e.g., ISIS/Daesh, Al-Qaeda, Al Nusra and others). The fight continues in other ways, however. The US-NATO Plan B scenario all along has been the balkanization of the Middle East (i.e., the fracturing of the Arab nation-states along ethnic and sectarian lines to create a number of smaller mini-states or micro-states). The idea of this is to weaken nations like Syria. Smaller nations would not be able to defend themselves as well against the inevitable US corporate and military invasion. Israel is a big fan of this plan, since it falls in line exactly with the Zionist vision of Israel being the strongest nation in the region. It also synchronizes with the 1982 Oded Yinon plan for "Greater Israel" which outlines the goal to expand Israel's territory to extend from the Nile (Egypt) to the Euphrates (Syria/Iraq). In order to achieve this vision, however, Israel would necessarily have to annex more land (in addition to the land it has already stolen), a task which would be much easier if the nations surrounding it were smaller and weaker.

From the NWO perspective, Trump was a blabbermouth about what the US was doing in Syria. While other US presidents and other Western leaders pushed the same rapacious and aggressive agenda of invading Syria but gave it the lip service of saying that it was a humanitarian intervention (like Obama), Trump didn't bother with PR fluff; he just blurted out that the US was still illegally occupying Syria to steal its oil. This was an open admission of theft and a war crime, but the US will go unpunished as it always has because there is one set of rules for the strong and another set of rules for the weak. Meanwhile, as covered in chapter 4, the US has all along been covertly using radical Ismaic terrorists in the form of the head-chopping ISIS as major destabilizing tool by secretly creating, arming and funding them to do its dirty work, while overtly claiming to fight them so as to justify US presence in Syria. ISIS has been caught collaborating with all sorts of US allies in the region, including Israel (they treated wounded ISIS soldiers in its hospitals) and Turkey (they were caught on Russian satellite imagery trading oil with ISIS).

I first mentioned Iran in this book in chapter 2 when referring to the overthrow of Mosaddegh and Iran Flight 655. Iran has been in the NWO crosshairs for challenging Zionist expansions and crimes in the

Middle East. There are many ways "Mr. Hope and Change" Obama dutifully served the NWO, but to his credit, he did negotiate the nuclear deal with Iran called the JCPOA (Joint Comprehensive Plan of Action). Trump, completely owned by Israel down to a cellular level, bent over backwards to give Israel everything it wanted, including tearing up the Iran deal that his predecessor constructed. Israel has been able to effectively dominate its other neighbors, but Iran has refused to back down. Current US President Biden, who with advanced cognitive decline is the quintessential presidential puppet, is another self-proclaimed Zionist who once made a point of proudly saying that one can still be a Zionist even if one is not Jewish.

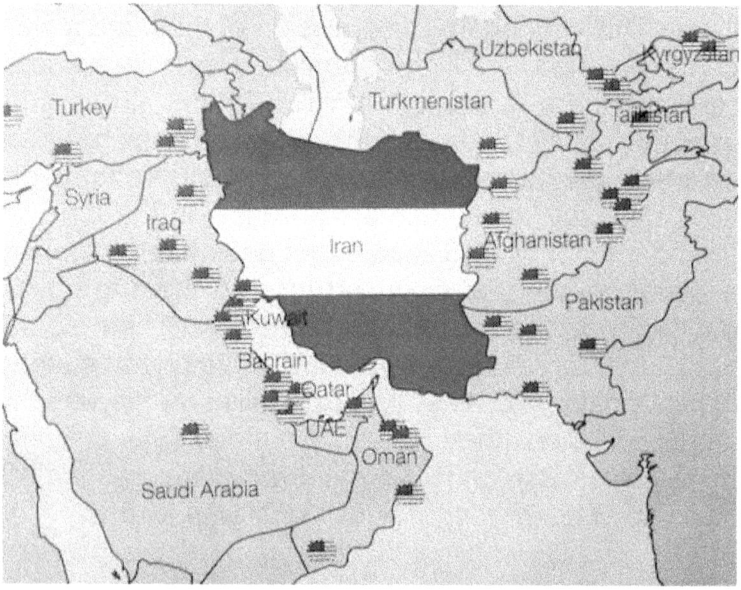

The US has been chafing at the bit to start a war with Iran. Various think tanks have been pushing this over the years. A speaker from the influential neocon

Washington Institute for Near East Studies, Patrick Clawson, openly suggested in this video[137] that the US provoke Iran into taking the first shot. Other neocon think tanks such as the Brookings Institute released *Which Path to Persia?*[138] which pondered the best way to get the US into a war with Iran, without the US appearing to be the aggressor (which they obviously are – see the US bases in the image below which surround Iran, a peaceful nation with no history of starting wars). Trump took a highly illegal, immoral step in January 2020 when he ordered the assassination of General Qassem Soleimani, who was head of Iran's elite Quds Force and part of the IRGC (the Iranian Revolutionary Guard Corps). Soleimani was considered the second most important military man in Iran and the key architect in the region of the resistance to radical Islamic terrorists like ISIS (sprung from Saudi Arabia and helped by Israel/US, as covered in chapter 4). Iran has been a strong force against the spread of radical Islamic terrorism (ISIS attacked Iran at some points including an attack in Iran's capital Tehran) but don't let that fact worry you – the Trump administration (and Biden is no different) was eager to spread the lie that Iran is the "biggest state sponsor of terror in the world" (a dubious honor that actually belongs to the US, Israel and Saudi Arabia). The Soleimani assassination was an outright, aggressive and unbridled act of war committed by the US against Iran. Trump initially lied about it by claiming he killed Soleimani because of supposed "imminent attacks" against four US

---

137 https://www.youtube.com/watch?v=PfoaLbbAix0

138 https://www.brookings.edu/wp-content/uploads/2016/06/06_iran_strategy.pdf

embassies in the area, but he later flip-flopped and gave other reasons for the assassination. He was also contradicted by his Secretary of Defense Mark Esper who acknowledged that he didn't see any specific evidence that the four US embassies were about to be attacked. In a very calculated act of retaliation, Iran hit US bases in Iraq with pinpoint accuracy, notifying various governments (such as Iraq's) first so as to reduce or eliminate human casualties. Iran did just enough to let the US know not to mess with it, but not so much that Trump would look foolish. Luckily, for now, regional war was averted, but Iran is very much still in the crosshairs. However, it must be noted that the March 2023 deal brokered by China to reunite the two Muslim powerhouses, Saudi Arabia and Iran, has the changed the geopolitical landscape significantly.

The US-NATO-led army is the cornerstone of the NWO military, and the NWO doesn't accept the answer "no." For them, to be stymied in Syria like this is unacceptable, just as Iran's recalcitrance is in opposing Zionist and US interests. It prevents them from carrying out their major game plan of conquering the entire region, moving on to Russia and China. So what has been their response? Why, demonizing Russia of course, and bringing back the Cold War.

Rampant Russophobia – and Ukraine as the Flashpoint Powder Keg

The Cold War 2.0 has become hot. Former

Russian Prime Minister Dmitry Medvedev[139], speaking in 2016, said the following:

NATO's political stance toward Russia remains unfriendly and isolated ... One can say even more harshly, we have slid into the times of a new Cold War ... I sometimes wonder whether we are in 1962 not 2016.

The Russians are coming! The Russians are coming! Funny how everything that's happening seems to be blamed on the Russians. Yes, Islamophobia has been big in the West as the mass public has been whipped into shape through constant conditioning to assume every Muslim is a terrorist. However more recently bigger efforts have been made by the Western MSM to frame the Russians (and by extension the Chinese) as the ultimate enemy that must be contained and destroyed.

Russophobia is truly out of control. Russia has fast become the scapegoat of choice upon which the US can place blame for all its failures. No victory in Syria? It's the Russians' fault. Assad using chemical weapons on his own people? It's the Russians' fault. Rigged elections in America? It's those dirty Russian hackers. Hillary Clinton lost the election? It's the Russians' fault for colluding with Trump. And on and on it goes, mindlessly repeating lie after lie, making accusation after accusation with nothing to back it up. Donald Trump, for all his faults (and he has many) was crucified in the media for simply wanting to have

---

[139] https://www.latimes.com/world/europe/la-fg-russia-nato-20160213-story.html

peaceful and friendly relations with Russia! After all, what could be worse for world peace than to have the prospect of war between the two strongest militaries on the planet? It is a sign that the "normal" way of thinking as dictated by the MSM is utterly insane. The MSM even went so far as to concoct a wild conspiracy theory that it was really Russia who had orchestrated the JFK assassination!

Blaming the Russians for everything has become a knee-jerk reaction for MSM journalists too intellectually weak or lazy to do any real research. Calling them journalists at all is an insult to the profession. I prefer the word "presstitutes", an elegant portmanteau of press and prostitutes. The source of much of the rampant Russophobia seems to be Hillary Clinton and the DNC, sore losers who needed a scapegoat after losing to Trump in 2016. Russia became an external victim of what was and is essentially an internal fight between the Left/ Democrats and the Right/Republicans inside the US.

The Russian hacking hoax is the story that just never seems to die. Amazingly, despite lacking any substance and the conclusion of the Mueller Report (no collusion), it keeps on going. Yet, if you pause a moment to take a critical look at the story, it doesn't hold water. Firstly, how do we know the supposed hackers were Russian? It's the easiest thing in the world for any good hacker worth his salt to cover his tracks and make it look like the hack originated elsewhere. In fact, in June 2017 WikiLeaks brought out new information (as part of their CIA Vault 7 series) with the exact CIA documents showing how they have developed the tools to mask hacking attacks (Marble). Marble exposes CIA source code files along with decoy languages that can be used to disguise the CIA's own hacks – and make them appear as if they were Russian. Secondly, it has been confirmed that the leaks that incriminated the DNC (Democratic National Committee) did not originate from Russia but rather from inside the DNC, specifically with a staffer called Seth Rich (who was later murdered). Hillary Clinton and the DNC were poor losers who would rather stoke tension with another superpower than take responsibility for their loss. Thirdly, even if Russia had the capability and prowess to hack the US elections, what is their motive for doing so? Putin himself said in a 2017 interview[140] that he has met many US Presidents, and they seem to come and go, but the policy never changes. This is because presidents are puppets, and the really important decisions are being made at levels higher than them. Why would Russia risk straining relations with the US – and giving the US a case for war – to rig the presidential elections when it matters not which puppet president sits in the White House? *"Dark suits rule the US,"* said Putin, referring to the entrenched "Deep State" or Military Intelligence Complex which stays in power no matter who gets voted in. Fourthly, free speech champion Julian Assange, the Australian citizen who founded WikiLeaks, hinted Seth Rich was his source but has categorically stated many times that the DNC documents were leaked not hacked and that the source was not Russia nor any "state actor." Sadly, Assange is being tortured in an English prison as I write these words, with Ecuador and the UK

---

[140] https://www.youtube.com/watch?v=XP3D1sUSuzg

kowtowing to the US to hand over a man who is not even a US citizen to be tried under US jurisdiction and US law. Go figure. Such cowardice is a disgrace to the supposed free West which once upon a time actually valued freedom of speech and freedom of the press.

Besides, the myth of Russian collusion is a cover for the real story: Israeli collusion. As exposed in the previous chapter, Israel has a massive grip on the governments of Western nations like the US and UK, who basically do its bidding in every situation. Israel has cleverly manipulated and weaponized the definition of anti-Semitism, changing its meaning (as Gilad Atzmon so eloquently says) from someone who hates Jews to someone whom Jews hate. Israel has bribed, bullied and blackmailed laws into existence in the US, UK and beyond which make it illegal to criticize the Israeli government for its policies! What other government in the world enjoys such as extraordinary privilege?

So, Russophobia is unfortunately alive and well, and as long as the US needs enemies to justify its military, it's here to stay. A French security expert by the name of Paul Barril revealed that there was a covert Western intelligence scheme intended to destabilize Russia and to discredit its leaders: Operation Beluga. Everywhere you look, Russia is being undermined. This is not to say that Russia is perfect and without fault, but what is happening clearly fits the pattern. The US has a range of tactics with which it fights to get its way: using lies, unfounded accusations and propaganda are ways to soften up the enemy before delivering the military blow. We will continue the discussion of Russia, especially regarding Ukraine, but first, we need to address an interesting, cunning and deceptive aspect of modern war in general. I refer to the Humans Rights Industrial Complex, aka the Soft Power Complex – the nefarious NGO networks on the other side of the coin, who soften up a targeted nation with propaganda so it's easier for the military to invade.

Nongovernmental Organizations (NGOs) – The Soft Power Complex

What I am about to write may enrage some people. "Why are you attacking NGOs?" they might ask. "How could you possibly criticize such noble institutions who are founded with a mission to serve or help without trying to make profit in the same way a corporation does?" It sounds so noble, and I'm sure many NGOs are full of well-intentioned people who do good work. However, there are many that are not – provably so – and the public perception that they are only innocent, do-good organizations is exactly what makes them such a perfect tool for the NWO to exploit in their war of conquest via infiltration. Even the term and acronym NGO is deceptive, because these NGOs are actually GONGOs – Government-Organized Nongovernmental Organizations – which is obvious something of an oxymoron. However, we have to realize that certain NGOs are just political tools of governments and their military-intelligence departments.

The American "promotion of democracy" around the world which increased with Reagan has always been about regime change. You have to learn to read between the lines and pass the MSM talking-point phrases through an Orwellian translation unit. The US doesn't give a rat's colon about democracy. It's just a nice-sounding cover for American economic and military interests. Kissinger said it: it's all about interests. The military just comes in to defend the economic interests of American multinational corporations. This has always been the game – the UK had the same relationship with its military when it was the dominant superpower defending its business interests and corporations (such as the East India Company) in its multitude of overseas colonies. Allen Weinstein, cofounder of NED (National Endowment for Democracy), one of numerous NGOs or GONGOs funded by the illustrious George Soros, said, *"A lot of what we do today was done covertly 25 years ago by the CIA."* Admiral Sir Philip Jones, First Sea Lord, put it even more succinctly when he stated that *"the hard punch of military power is often delivered inside the kid glove of humanitarian relief."* Former US Marine Smedley Butler was a highly decorated military man who understood the game at the end of his career. He wrote in his book *War is a Racket*:

I spent 33 years and four months in active military service and during that period I spent most of my time as a high class muscle man for Big Business, for Wall Street and the bankers. In short, I was a racketeer, a gangster for capitalism. I helped make Mexico and especially Tampico safe for American oil interests in 1914. I helped make Haiti and Cuba a decent place for the National City Bank boys to collect revenues in. I helped in the raping of half a dozen Central American republics for the benefit of

Wall Street. I helped purify Nicaragua for the International Banking House of Brown Brothers in 1902-1912. I brought light to the Dominican Republic for the American sugar interests in 1916. I helped make Honduras right for the American fruit companies in 1903. In China in 1927 I helped see to it that Standard Oil went on its way unmolested. Looking back on it, I might have given Al Capone a few hints. The best he could do was to operate his racket in three districts. I operated on three continents.

These thoughts are echoed by former economic hit man John Perkins (author of *Confessions of an Economic Hit Man*), who described from experience how the system works. Poorer and developing nations are offered loans by the IMF to develop their infrastructure, but they must pay back the loans with crippling interest. If they default, the creditors swoop in and demand a pound of flesh. This would often include control over United Nations votes, the installation of US military bases or access to precious resources such as oil or the Panama Canal. Another country would be added to the global empire. If a nation refused the loan, then the "jackals" would be sent in – assassins who would overthrow and/or assassinate the noncompliant heads of state. If that didn't work, then the US would send in its military to invade.

Even if you just look at the last decade from 2010 to 2020, the US has been following its foreign meddling playbook in Libya, Syria and Iran just to name a few. It destroyed Libya, couldn't quite destroy Syria and couldn't quite get the controlled opposition off the ground in Iran, but it's the same game wherever it's played. The goal is always the same – overthrow of the government, the destruction of the country, the installation of a friendly puppet regime, the opening of a country's markets to foreign investment and the theft and exploitation of a country's resources by NWO multinational corporations.

NGO subversion: turning Communism into democracy doesn't help you if you're under the thumb of the NWO. The word "democracy" has become just another propaganda term.

To come to back NGOs, the NWO has developed sophisticated ways to achieve its goals in undermining other nations without having to physically invade them – which extracts a lot of costs in terms of blood, treasure and poor public/world opinion. Enter the NGO. NGOs have the power to influence public thought and stealthily disseminate propaganda that can cause people to lose faith in their politicians, overthrow governments and induce a nation to make poor decisions that benefit the creators and controllers of the NGOs.

Take a look at George Soros's colossal network of NGOs, which include the NED (National Endowment for Democracy) and NDI (National Democratic Institute). As Eric Draitser notes in his article *China's NGO Law: Countering Western Soft Power and Subversion*[141]:

Human Rights Watch, and the NGO complex at large, has condemned China's Overseas NGO Management Law because they quite rightly believe that it will severely hamper their efforts to act independently of Beijing. However ... the reality is that they act as a de facto arm of western intelligence agencies and governments, and they have played a central role in the destabilization of China in recent years.

The oft touted leader of Occupy Central was a pro-Western academic named Benny Tai, a law professor at the University of Hong Kong. Though he presented himself as the leader of a grassroots mass movement, Mr. Tai has for years been partnered with the NDI, a nominal NGO which is actually directly funded by the US State Department via the NED ... Tai [and other Chinese] each act as the public face of a US Government-sponsored initiative to destabilize the political situation in Hong Kong, one of China's most economically and politically important regions. Through the intermediary of the NGO,

---

141 journal-neo.org/2015/07/25/china-s-ngo-law-countering-western-soft-power-and-subversion/

Washington is able to promote an anti-Beijing line under the auspices of "democracy promotion," just as it has done everywhere from Ukraine to Venezuela.

The horrible Ukrainian coup of 2014 could not have been pulled off without the help of Soros and his NGOs. Around that time, the US pumped at least $5 billion into regime change in Ukraine[142] (as admitted by Zionist neo-con Victoria Nuland, wife of Zionist neo-con Robert Kagan), forcibly removing the legitimately elected government of Yanukovych and installing a puppet regime of neo-Nazis answerable to Washington's demands. Nuland also got caught saying "Fuck the EU"[143] to US Ambassador to Ukraine Geoff Pyatt in a leaked phone call. All this pales in comparison to the many more billions in money and weapons sent to Ukraine since the beginning of the Russo-Ukraine War in February 2022. William Jasper[144] noted:

Many of the participants in Kiev's "EuroMaidan" demonstrations were members of Soros-funded NGOs and/or were trained by the same NGOs in the many workshops and conferences sponsored by Soros' International Renaissance Foundation (IRF), and his various Open Society institutes and foundations. The IRF, founded and funded by Soros, boasts that it has given "more than any other donor organization" to "democratic transformation" of

---

142 https://www.youtube.com/watch?v=dexrP27MMdU

143 https://www.youtube.com/watch?v=KlvRljAaNgg

144 www.thenewamerican.com/world-news/europe/item/17843-george-soros-s-giant-globalist-footprint-in-ukraine-s-turmoil

The NGOs of arch manipulator George Soros played a big part in the 2014 Ukrainian coup. Above: the Maidan in Kiev, Ukraine, before and after.

Ukraine.

Soros is a master manipulator and a godfather-like figure of the political left. Some nations like Hungary, under leader Viktor Orban, have publicly exposed Soros's machinations; however, his influence still remains immense. An RT (Russia Today) article[145] revealed how twenty-two out of a hundred judges on an EU court are tied to Soros. Conflict of interest is rife:

The study has found that, out of the 100 judges who have served on the bench of the European Court of Human Rights in the period 2009-2019, nearly a quarter (22) have strong links to George Soros' Open

145 https://www.rt.com/op-ed/481651-george-soros-european-court-judges/

Society Foundation or to NGOs like Amnesty International and others which are funded by it. Human Rights Watch, for instance, has received $100 million from the Open Society Foundation since 2010 … The report's worst finding is that in 88 cases judges sat on the bench ruling on cases brought to the court by NGOs they had previously worked for, without declaring a conflict of interest and without withdrawing from hearing the cases (see page 15 of the report and annexes 1 and 2.) In one case, ruled on in 2018, 10 out of the 14 NGOs that had brought the case were funded by the Open Society Foundation, while six out of the 17 judges who heard the case themselves had links to the same Soros-funded group.

In May 2016, Vanessa Beeley reported that the so-called *White Helmets* NGO[146] was actually a *"US and UK government-funded "first responder" organization in Syria … shown to have deep ties to al-Nusra Front as well as links to ISIS, and it operates exclusively within terrorist-held areas in Syria, including participation in executions."* Did you catch that? Participation in executions? Links to the US-UK-Israeli controlled pet Frankenstein ISIS?

NGOs are running amok. We don't just have NGOs; we have an actual NGO complex which is controlled by the New World Order and is part of their psychological operations and perception management department. It ensures that *American democracy* and *humanitarian interventions* (both

146 21stcenturywire.com/2016/05/19/uk-column-exposing-us-uk-funded-first-responder-ngo-in-syria-with-direct-ties-to-terrorists/

doublespeak oxymorons) are coated with sugar to go down well. Often, they hide behind the excuse of furthering human rights as a way to justify their subversive operations. Patrick Henningsen wrote an excellent article in April 2016 entitled "AN INTRODUCTION: Smart Power & The Human Rights Industrial Complex"[147] which spells out the way these NGOs operate:

Shaping western public perception and opinion on major international issues is essential if major world powers are to realise their foreign policy goals. Not surprisingly, we can see that many of the public positions taken by NGOs are exactly aligned with western foreign policy. In the Balkans War of the 1990s, human rights groups supported partitioning. In the Ukraine in 2014 and with both Syria and Yemen in 2016 they supported regime change. In each instance NGOs function as a public relations extension to a United Nations western member Security Council bloc, namely the US, UK and France. This collusion is manifest throughout the upper echelons of these organizations whose streamlined agenda conforms through a lucrative revolving door which exists between a cartel of western NGOs, government and media.

The role of NGOs and human rights organizations has been pivotal in Syria, to provide cover for the US to carry out its clear intention of regime change:

By framing the Syrian Conflict (2011 to present) as a

---

[147] 21stcenturywire.com/2016/04/19/an-introduction-smart-power-the-human-rights-industrial-complex/

"civil war", both western media and human rights organizations did their part in propping-up an important western foreign policy narrative. Inaccurate and distorted, this narrative has helped shield the US-led clandestine proxy war ... [but the reality is] a US-backed guerrilla war where Washington and Ankara, along with NATO and Gulf Cooperation Council (GCC) allies, flooding Turkey and Syria with weapons, cash, equipment, social media teams, military trainers and foreign fighters from as a far away as Pakistan.

NGOs are responsible for all those feel-good petitions that totally misinform Westerners about some poor country that is about to get invaded, whip up misdirected outrage and persuade people to get in line with the exact military goals the US has already planned. Have you noticed how many NGOs call for "No Fly Zones", "Buffer Zones" or "Safe Zones"? Remember the phony Stop Kony 2012 campaign? Remember how George Soros' Avaaz called for a No Fly Zone in Libya, to help US-NATO assassinate Gaddafi and control Libya? There are many NGOs actively involved in the subversion, including USAID and the Soros Open Society Foundation networks (NED = National Endowment for Democracy).

On the bright side, people are beginning to wake up. Ecuador, Israel, Egypt, China, India and Russia have all tightened regulations on foreign NGOs operating within their shores, and in some cases they have completely banned them. However, there are still a great many people blind to the game.

The Endgame: Encircling and Conquering Eurasia

To summarize thus far, the Anglo-American-Zionist cabal is using US military, political and economic power, including its NGO network, to pick off many smaller nations according to the agenda that leads to Global Governance. All of this is mere preparation for the battle for the grand prize: Eurasia. The grand objective is to conquer Russia and China – the last two significant nations that have any chance of standing up to the military and economic might of the USA. However, at the end of the day, the NWO controllers only care about erecting a worldwide dictatorship, not about the fate of any particular nation within it, so whether it comes about via unilateral American power or via a multipolar shared system does not matter to them as long as the end result is a totalitarian dictatorship with them in charge.

The Anglo-American obsession with Eurasia can be traced back to the geopolitical theories of Englishman Halford Mackinder, who in 1904 submitted a paper called *The Geographical Pivot of History* at the Royal Geographical Society in which he formulated his Heartland Theory. Some consider this the founding moment of geopolitics as a field of study. The Heartland Theory, which has gone on to become hugely influential on the foreign policies of the UK and the US, analyzes which parts of the world are most important to hold in order to rule the entire world (more of the conquering mindset). Mackinder proposed that the Earth's land surface was divisible into:

- The World-Island, comprising the interlinked continents of Europe, Asia, and Africa – largest, most populous and richest of all possible land combinations
- The offshore islands, including the British Isles and the islands of Japan
- The outlying islands, including the continents of North America, South America and Australia

Mackinder came up with a neologism at the time (Heartland) which he used to describe the center of the world island, stretching from the Volga to the Yangtze and from the Himalayas to the Arctic. In Mackinder's time and still to this day, the Heartland has been ruled by Russia. Later in 1919, Mackinder summarized his theory as:

Who rules East Europe commands the Heartland;
who rules the Heartland commands the World-Island;
who rules the World-Island commands the world.

– Mackinder, *Democratic Ideals and Reality*, pg. 150

Mackinder went on to speculate about how nations could wrest control of the Heartland from Russia, theorizing that any power which controlled the World-Island would control well over 50 percent of the world's resources. The Heartland's size and central position made it the key to controlling the World-Island.

Mackinder's theories no doubt influenced the late Zbigniew Brzezinski, a long-time NWO globalist and insider who died in 2017. Brzezinski was a founding member of the Trilateral Commission (along with David Rockefeller), one of the key think tanks and societies which form part of the Round Table. Brzezinski mentored US President Obama and was a former National Security Advisor to US President Carter. He once said that *"in earlier times, it was easier to control a million people, literally, than physically to kill a million people"* while *"today it is infinitely easier to kill a million people than to control a million people."* Specifically, he said that *"new and old powers face"* an unprecedented situation; the *"lethality of their power is greater than ever"*, but their *"capacity to impose control over the politically awakened masses of the world is at a historical low."* That gives you a very good idea of his mindset.

Brzezinski is on video[148] organizing the Mujahideen to fight against the former Soviet Union, tricking them by saying that *"God is on your side"* as the US used Radical Islamic Terrorism™ once again

148 https://www.youtube.com/watch?v=A9RCFZnWGE0

to achieve its geopolitical objectives. In his book *The Grand Chessboard*[149], written in 1997, Brzezinski affirmed his Russophobia and his belief in US preeminence by writing:

The most immediate task is to make certain that no state or combination of states gains the capacity to expel the United States from Eurasia or even to diminish significantly its decisive arbitrating role.

... the expansion of NATO is essential. By the same token, a failure to widen NATO ... would shatter the concept of an expanding Europe and de-moralize the Central Europeans. It could even reignite currently dormant or dying Russian geopolitical aspirations in Central Europe.

...how America 'manages' Eurasia is critical. A power that dominates Eurasia would control two of the world's three most advanced and economically productive regions. A mere glance at the map also suggests that control over Eurasia would almost automatically entail Africa's subordination, rendering the Western Hemisphere and Oceania (Australia) geopolitically peripheral to the world's central continent.

About 75 per cent of the world's people live in Eurasia, and most of the world's physical wealth is there as well, both in its enterprises and underneath its soil. Eurasia accounts for about three-fourths of the world's known energy resources.

---

149 www.takeoverworld.info/Grand_Chessboard.pdf

Another noteworthy doctrine in the same vein is the Wolfowitz Doctrine, named after Zionist neocon Paul Wolfowitz (right), who was US Deputy Secretary of Defense from 2001 to 2005 under Rumsfeld and Dubya. Wolfowitz was also a coauthor of the notorious *Rebuilding America's Defenses*[150], a report released in September 2000 by Zionist neocon think tank PNAC (The Project for a New American Century). Now disbanded, the PNAC membership list was a "Who's Who" of American Zionist New World Order conspirators – in addition to Wolfowitz the list included Dick Cheney, Donald Rumsfeld, Robert Kagan, I. Lewis (Scooter) Libby, Richard Perle, Doug Feith and many others. The report contains the now infamous sentence which just so happened to prophesize 9/11:

This process of transformation is likely to be a long one, absent some catastrophic and catalyzing event – like a new Pearl Harbor.

The Wolfowitz Doctrine explicitly and unabashedly pushes for complete US supremacy at the cost of any other value. If it is truly the guiding principle of US foreign policy and geopolitical maneuvering, as it appears to be, it comes as no surprise then that America is such a hypocrite on the world stage. To put on a good face on the world stage and feed the propaganda that it only promotes freedom and democracy, the US is forced to use rhetoric claiming it values the promotion of human rights, the self-determination of people and the sovereignty of nations. Yet, whenever any of these

150 www.informationclearinghouse.info/pdf/RebuildingAmericasDefenses.pdf

"values" conflict with the ideals set out in the Wolfowitz Doctrine, the US always chooses its own supremacy over them.

As Michael S. Rozeff[151] writes:

The U.S. condemns separatism in Ukraine and aids Kiev in attacking its own people with heavy and advanced weapons of all kinds. This is because the superpower agenda is served by steering Ukraine into the Western camp. At the very same time, the U.S. condemns China for indicting a professor who is a vocal separatist and critical of Chinese policy in Xinjiang. Hence, we observe the U.S. against separatism in Ukraine but supporting it in China. This is because the U.S. is applying pressure on China wherever it thinks this will succeed in diminishing China as a power ... Numerous other instances of U.S. hypocrisy can be understood in this way. The U.S. will support democracy but then ignore elections and support dictators ... It will condemn terrorism and then arm terrorists. This is because the overriding agenda is the Wolfowitz Doctrine.

[151] https://www.lewrockwell.com/lrc-blog/u-s-implements-the-wolfowitz-doctrine/

Or, again, as arch-NWO insider Henry Kissinger said, *"'America has no permanent friends or enemies, only interests."* Brzezinski, Wolfowitz and their ilk are concerned with just one thing: power. It's presupposed that might is right and that American supremacy is moral. The pervading issue is always: how can America expand or at least maintain its global power?

In alignment with the Wolfowitz Doctrine, the Western Zionist MSM is constantly telling us how bad Russia is and how aggressive Putin is, yet the facts reveal otherwise. It's easy to see the demonization of Russia and the smear campaign against Putin as desperate attempts of the Anglo-American NWO to control the information war and paint themselves as the victim instead of the aggressor. Consider the following facts:

– In 1991, the US violated their promise to Russia by allowing NATO to extend beyond the borders of Germany (and much farther since);

– From 1991 onwards, the US continually invaded nations in the Middle East (Kuwait, Iraq, Afghanistan, Syria) to gain a foothold in Eurasia;

– During the 1990s, the US allowed NATO to admit former Soviet allies and former Soviet republics into its organization;

– In 2002, the US unilaterally withdrew from the ABM (Anti-Ballistic Missile) Treaty;

– In 2008, US-sponsored forces attempted to

overtake Georgia (right on Russia's doorstep);

– In 2014, as mentioned earlier, the US orchestrated another coup on Russia's doorstep, this time in Ukraine, by ousting the Russian-friendly President Yanukovych and replacing him with a pro-Western puppet. After the coup, the Ukraine people suddenly found themselves with a government containing literal Nazis (the Azov Battalion from the Mariupol area) whose first decision was to ban the Russian language!

– In 2014, in a referendum deemed impartial and fair[152], 96 percent of Crimeans voted to return to Russia. There was no "annexation of Crimea." Crimea has been a province of Russia since 1758, and only became part of Ukraine when Soviet head Khrushchev handed it over to Ukraine at a time when both Crimea and Ukraine were part of the Soviet Union (the whole thing was purely administrative). Therefore, Russia has had its Black Sea fleet based in Crimea for over 250 years, and a leasing agreement with Ukraine gave them the right to have twenty-five thousand troops there;

– In September 2014, Ukraine, Russia and the Organization for Security and Co-operation in Europe (OSCE), with mediation by France and Germany, signed the first Minsk Protocol (since it was held in the capital of Belarus, Minsk). The agreement was also signed by representatives of the self-proclaimed Donetsk People's Republic (DPR) and Luhansk

---

[152] https://www.rt.com/news/international-observers-crimea-referendum-190/

People's Republic (LPR), two western regions of Ukraine which declared independence. This agreement followed many previous attempts to stop the fighting in the region and aimed to implement an immediate ceasefire;

– In February 2015, with the Ukrainian armed forces (having officially incorporated the Azov Neo-Nazis into their military) still attacking Russian separatists in Donetsk and Luhansk, another agreement was signed – Minsk II. This one contained many measures, including a ceasefire, withdrawal of heavy weapons from the front line, the release of prisoners of war and constitutional reform in Ukraine granting self-government to certain areas of the Donbas (the whole basin or area comprising Donetsk and Luhansk). Nonetheless, Ukrainians in the Donbas who were ethnically and culturally Russian continued to be killed.

– In February 2018, the Trump Administration changed the US nuclear weapon policy as detailed in the official document Nuclear Posture Review[153] to allow preemptive attacks or first strikes;

– In 2019, the US withdrew from the INF (Intermediate-Range Nuclear Forces Treaty). This was one of the key treaties between the US and Russia for the limitation of medium-range missiles. Some have described it as a fundamental part of the world's international security architecture.

---

153 https://media.defense.gov/2018/Feb/02/2001872886/-1/-1/1/2018-NUCLEAR-POSTURE-REVIEW-FINAL-REPORT.PDF

– In February 2022, after 8 years of the Ukrainian government refusing to adhere to the Minsk agreements, with Ukrainian President Zelensky talking about Ukraine acquiring nuclear weapons, Russia took matters into its own hands. It officially recognized Donetsk and Luhansk as independent republics or nations, signed defense agreements with them, then sent Russian soldiers there. The Western MSM dubbed this as an invasion of Ukraine. Putin initially called this not a war but a Special Military Operation (SMO) and stated that the Russian objectives were demilitarization and denazification of Ukraine. Russia also stated that it would immediately stop fighting if Ukraine agreed to put it in its constitution that it would remain a neutral country and not join NATO. Later, this conflict broadened into an actual bona fide war, with the West pouring literally billions into Ukraine every month to prop it up with weapons. Ukraine is another classic case of a proxy war between the US/NATO and Russia. Many people have wryly commented that the US is fully prepared to fight Russia down to the last Ukrainian.

As you can see from the timeline above, the US has been step-by-step encircling Russia, encouraging nations to join alliances against Russia, provoking Russia, bringing former USSR states into the Western orbit and dismantling the series of treaties that sprung from the Cold War to protect the world from the horror of nuclear Armageddon. The Russian bear has been prodded, poked and provoked, and now we have a hot war on our hands – with the MSM ratcheting app the fear by talking about it going nuclear.

Whatever you think of Vladimir Putin (and I'm sure he's no angel), he has vast intelligence, a cool head and has seen the writing on the wall. Putin has watched US forces repeatedly get closer and closer to Russia over the last few decades. Russia is being hemmed in on both sides; NATO is constantly inching eastward, absorbing new nations into its conglomerate (e.g., Montenegro) and placing missile systems and other weaponry there. Meanwhile, on the other flank, the US continues to hype the North Korean threat as an excuse to surround Russia on its eastern side by placing THAAD missile systems on the territory of its "ally" (i.e., vassal state) South Korea. Putin has repeatedly warned that we are on a sure course for WWIII between US-NATO forces and Russian-Chinese forces. Years before Russia took it to a military level in 2022, Putin said the following in July 2016 at International Economic Forum at St. Petersburg, berating journalists in the audience for not grasping and willfully not reporting the urgency of the situation:

The "Iranian threat" does not exist but the NATO Missile Defense System is being positioned in Europe ... [US-NATO is] always referring to the "Iranian threat" in order to justify this system. Once again, they lied to us. Now the system is functioning, and being loaded with missiles. As you [journalists] should know, these missiles are put into capsules, which are used in the Tomahawk long range missile system.

So, these are being loaded with missiles that can penetrate territories within a 500km range, but we know that technologies advance, and we even know in which year the US will accomplish the next missile. This missile will be able to penetrate distances of up to 1000km, and then even further, and from that moment on, they will start to directly threaten Russia's nuclear potential.

We know year by year what's going to happen, and they know that we know. It's only you that they tell tales to, and you buy it, and spread it to the citizens of your countries. Your people in turn do not feel a sense of the impending danger – this is what worries me.

How do you not understand that the world is being pulled in an irreversible direction, while they pretend that nothing's going on? I don't know how to get through to you anymore ..."

<u>Trying to Slay the Chinese Dragon</u>

Just as Russia is being endlessly demonized in the US media, so too do the maniacal US leaders have China in the crosshairs. Obama started a massive buildup in the Pacific during his tenure which was named the "Pivot to Asia." This Pivot to Asia, which is really the US militarization of the Pacific, is obviously in preparation for a war with China and Russia. It is, in fact, an unprecedented buildup all throughout the Pacific and the biggest military buildup in an area since World War II. Even before Trump got to office, tension between the US and China has been steadily increasing[154], with the dispute over the South China Sea becoming strained.

The pivot to Asia is really about the US trying to control an entire region which is eight thousand miles across, comprises fifty-five countries and 60 percent of the global population and contains much of the Earth's natural resources. In 2011, Obama initiated the program to move 60 percent of US Air Force and Navy resources from the Middle East to the Pacific. The US propaganda claim is that the pivot to Asia plan is to rebalance power in the region, but the truth is that there is no "balance". As Koohan Paik, staff writer for the *International Forum on Globalization*, outlines in her article *Islanders Unite to Resist a New Pacific War*[155]:

[The US] already maintains over 400 military

[154] https://thefreedomarticles.com/us-china-tension-maneuvering-ww3/

[155] ifg.org/2015/11/09/islanders-unite-to-resist-a-new-pacific-war/

installations and 155,000 troops in that part of the world. Meanwhile China, even with its newest artificial island-bases in the South China Sea, will have a grand total fewer than ten [bases]... The U.S. is rapidly advancing U.S. military deployments ... as well as corporate trade intrusions, and massive resource raiding. And, an ever-more dangerous battle is emerging among the U.S., China and other great powers over trade, ocean and island resources, and economic and military domination of the 8,000 mile region.

As part of this plan of encircling China, the US since 2015 has been forging aggressive bilateral agreements with several Pacific nations. This includes conducting military interoperability exercises with various Pacific nations such as South Korea[156], Australia[157] and Japan[158]. One of the most disturbing aspects of Pivot to Asia has been the remilitarization of Japan under PM Shinzo Abe (promoted by the US). Since the horrific nuclear bombings of Hiroshima and Nagasaki, the Japanese people have been proudly pacifist for over sixty-five years. Sadly, that pacifist policy is disappearing. To quote again from Paik:

Prime Minister Shinzo Abe had managed to push

---

156 https://www.theguardian.com/world/2016/jul/30/us-south-korea-military-drills-north-korea-warning

157 www.military.com/daily-news/2016/04/04/us-australian-and-philippine-forces-kick-balikatan-exercise.html

158 www.military.com/daily-news/2016/05/16/us-south-korea-and-japan-to-hold-anti-missile-exercise.html

through highly unpopular legislation to disempower Japan's "peace constitution," implemented in 1947 by General Douglas MacArthur. Abe achieved this despite 100,000 protestors shouting "NO WAR" for weeks in front of the Japanese Diet. The following day, Abe's public approval rating plummeted to 38.9 percent. Now, Japan's military is permitted to act offensively, no longer only in self-defense mode. It can also surveil other countries for the first time in modern history, and establish a global arms industry (imagine, Honda-quality drones and tanks). According to a Pentagon official, this will give Japan "greater global presence." According to The Nation's Tim Shorrock, it will turn Japan into America's proxy army in Asia.

The Japanese were a powerful fighting force in World War II, so much so that they become a key ally of the Nazis and Axis powers. They are still a leading nation in terms of technological and industrial innovation. It would not bode well for the world for that technological and industrial potential to be turned once again to building weapons, yet this is precisely what the US is encouraging Japan to do. Specifically, in 2015, the US and Japan had the dubious distinction of securing three "milestones" as part of the US pivot to Asia:

The milestones, which work together symbiotically, are: 1) Disabling Japan's pacifist Constitution; 2) Beefing up of the U.S.-Japan Security Treaty; and 3) Reaching a TPP agreement which would work hand-in-glove with military force to pair economic dominance with military hegemony.

The revised treaty that Paik mentions encourages Japanese aggression toward its neighbors, and permits four islands in the Ryukyu archipelago to be transformed into state-of-the-art military bases, with missiles pointed towards China. This is part of the broader US strategy of military base outsourcing (i.e., letting its client states like Japan and South Korea bear the costs of building the bases):

For example, the construction of the Jeju naval base is South Korean in name, but it fulfills the Pentagon's directive to contain China. It will also port U.S. aircraft carriers, attack submarines and Aegis-missile carrying destroyers. Because the base is "officially" South Korean, costs are externalized — of construction, of environmental responsibility, and of policing eight years of still ongoing protests.

Russia and China know full well what is happening, which is why they have been working closely together to interlock their economic and military cooperation. They realize that only united can they push back against the US. Both Russia and China have military agreements with Iran, and these three nations acted mostly in unison all throughout the Syrian War to defend Syria, protect legitimate Syrian President Assad and defeat the proxy forces ("moderate rebels") of the US-UK-Israeli-Saudi alliance, and are doing so again in the current Russo-Ukraine war.

In the near future, expect to see more pressure exerted on Taiwan, North Korea and Iran (and perhaps neighboring nations who are yet to play a role in this drama), all with the aim of the NWO

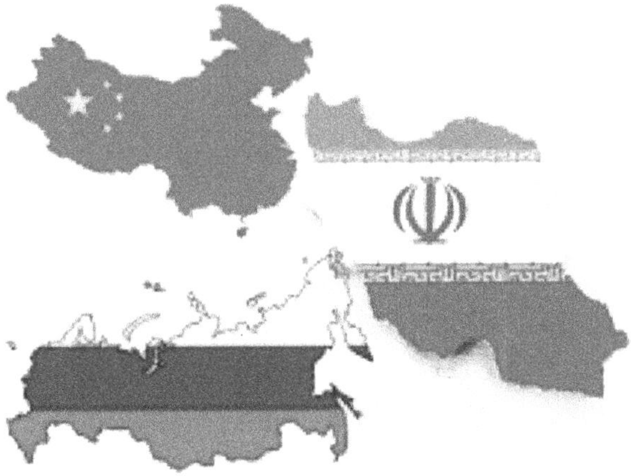

orchestrators drawing more and more nations into this developing WWIII – especially Russia and China.

<u>We Are Already in WWIII</u>

As mentioned earlier, the USG has been using 4GW against various nations like Venezuela (and some people claim there is now a concept of 5th Generation Warfare or 5GW) to strike nations with economic attacks, cyber attacks, electromagnetic attacks, infrastructure attacks and informational attacks (propaganda). This underlies the point that we are already in WWIII. Just because it doesn't look like the trench warfare of WWI or the air raids of WWII doesn't mean it's not war. It's a slow-moving, relentless, different kind of war – but it is war nonetheless.

All the machinations and provocations described in this chapter are either a prelude to it or part of it. All the economic sanctions that the West threw at Russia in February 2022 (with Europe badly shooting itself in the foot by doing so) are part of it. You are living through WWIII right now as you read these words.

Unipolar vs. Multipolar Worlds – Different in Style, but Are They Different in Substance?

I will end this chapter with an extremely important point. To understand this point requires taking a bird's eye view of the situation, looking at the big picture rather than the minutiae, details and drama of the conflict. It's easy to get caught up in all the deceptions and shenanigans of the US Government and US Military, however what we must really be aware of is the deeper agenda: the relentless push towards a One World Government or worldwide totalitarian dictatorship. The NWO controllers who run the world have no allegiance to any one nation. They want them all under their control – whatever it takes to achieve that.

We have to be wary of the false dichotomy that is arising in geopolitical analysis, namely that of a unipolar world order versus a multipolar world order. On the one hand, we have certain groups within the USG who are desperately pushing for the US to continue as the sole hegemon, extending its sphere of control to the entire world. On the other hand, we have certain nations, led by Russia, who are promoting a multipolar world comprised of varied poles or power centers around the world. Superficially, it may appear that the US is trying to bring about the NWO while Russia, united with China, are standing in the way of the NWO by promoting a multipolar world which is more free.

Swedish analyst Ingemar Wärnström[159] quotes Putin as saying:

What is a unipolar world? However one might embellish this term, at the end of the day it refers to one type of situation, namely one center of authority, one center of force, one center of decision-making. It is a world in which there is one master, one sovereign. And at the end of the day this is pernicious not only for all those within this system, but also for the sovereign itself because it destroys itself from within. And this certainly has nothing in common with democracy. Because, as you know, democracy is the power of the majority in light of the interests and opinions of the minority. Incidentally, Russia – we – are constantly being taught about democracy. But for some reason those who teach us do not want to learn themselves. I consider that the unipolar model is not only unacceptable but also impossible in today's world.

Putin is certainly right to highlight the hypocrisy of the US, however what is not mentioned is that the multipolar world he is pushing for, with support from China and other Eurasian nations, does not guarantee the average person freedom, either. To paint the multipolar world as an antidote to the NWO is not only simplistic but also outright false. For starters, strong nations such as Russia and China, and medium-strength nations like Iran (all in favor of this multipolar world order) are not well known for

[159] newsvoice.se/2015/09/07/swedish-analyst-the-smear-campaign-against-putin-and-the-us-agenda-part-1/

their respect of human rights; in March 2022[160], Russia effectively outlawed anti-war protest, and China in particular inflicts massive suppression upon its people, who have to live under a social credit system that restricts their rights and freedom, as well as outrageous levels of censorship and intimidation (especially Falun Gong practitioners who have had their organs harvested[161]). The Iranian Government used to have an agency called the Guidance Patrol[162] (or colloquially the "Morality Police") who enforce the law that all women must wear headscarves (or sometimes face coverings) out in public; it is not unusual for woman who refuse to wear them to be beaten or killed. As Iain Davis writes[163] in Part 3 of his series "Multipolar World Order":

Ostensibly, the multipolar version of the world order is a departure from the unipolar model in the sense that it will—supposedly—genuinely observe international law and share power among a broader coalition of nation-states. As a result, it will introduce —supposedly—functioning multilateralism into global governance, arguably for the first time. To some, this multipolar model sounds preferable to the current,

---

160 https://www.hrw.org/news/2022/03/07/russia-criminalizes-independent-war-reporting-anti-war-protests

161 https://humanrightscommission.house.gov/events/hearings/forced-organ-harvesting-china-examining-evidence

162 https://en.wikipedia.org/wiki/Guidance_Patrol

163 https://off-guardian.org/2022/10/19/multipolar-world-order-part-3/

international rules-based unipolar model.

Yet, when we look at the statements of the touted leaders of the new multipolar world order, their objectives seem indistinguishable from those of their unipolar counterparts…

- *They express an unwavering commitment to sustainable development and Agenda 2030.*
- *They support the United Nation's Security Council remaining the political centre of global governance—though, notably, loss of the veto isn't countenanced.*
- *They wholeheartedly endorse the World Economic Forum's AI-driven 4th Industrial Revolution (4IR).*
- *They also regard censorship and information control as necessary to fight the "infodemic" and to protect the world against "disinformation."*
- *Their global initiatives—and the public-private partnerships that will implement them—are practically identical to the initiatives of their unipolar counterparts, though they offer an important variation, which we'll discuss in Part 4.*
- *Finally, to supporters of multipolarity, a new global "financial system" is, as ever, the key to the supposed "transformation."*

He further writes:

If the multipolar world order is something new, then surely this trajectory towards centralised global governance should change, right? But when the multipolar model seems to be accelerating the transition to centralised power, then we have to wonder if there is anything new and different about it at all.

. . .

Katehon is the "independent" think tank established by Russian oligarch Konstantin Malofyev (Malofeev), who has been sanctioned by the US since 2014 for his support of Ukrainian Russians, first in Crimea and then in the Donbas. The Katehon board includes Sergey Glazyev, the economist and politician who is the current Commissioner of Macroeconomic Integration for the Eurasian Economic Union (EAEU). In 2018, Katehon pointed out that, despite all talk to the contrary, multipolarity had largely been defined as opposition to unipolarity. That is, expressed in terms of what it isn't rather than what it is. Katehon sought to rectify this, offering its Theory of the Multipolar World (TWM):

Multipolarity does not coincide with the national model of world organization according to the logic of the Westphalian system. [. . .] This Westphalian model assumes full legal equality between all sovereign states. In this model, there are as many poles of foreign policy decisions in the world as there are sovereign states [. . .] and all of international law is based on it. In practice, of course, there is inequality and hierarchical subordination between various sovereign states. [. . .] The multipolar world differs from the classical Westphalian system by the fact that it does not recognize the separate nation-state, legally and formally sovereign, to have the status of a full-fledged pole. This means that the number of poles in a multipolar world should be substantially less than the number of recognized (and therefore, unrecognized) nation-states. Multipolarity is not a system of international relations that insists upon the legal equality of nation-states[.]

The unipolar world doesn't protect the nation-state any more than the multipolar model does.

Russia and China issued a very long joint statement[164] on February 4th 2022 endorsing the UN 2030 Agenda for Sustainable Development, promoting the UN in general and stating that there needs to be global cooperation on many UN initiatives, such as green energy, climate change, sustainable development and vaccines. All this will become very relevant in the next few chapters. Davis concludes:

That the nominal leaders of the new multipolar world order constantly cite the same tales—none of which mirror reality—as a reason for their proposed reset of global governance might likewise be mere coincidence ... A central tenet of the suggested multipolar world order is to strengthen adherence to the Charter of the UN, thereby establishing genuine global governance. Globalist oligarchs have long advocated exactly the same approach and so do the claimed leaders of the multipolar world order. Another instance of mere coincidence?

Indeed, if you dig a little deeper, you will find that many nations opposed to Western hegemony (such

164 www.en.kremlin.ru/supplement/5770

as the BRICS group of Brazil, Russia, India, China and South Africa, plus BRICS-aligned nations) still support the globalist think tank WEF (World Economic Forum), whose chairman Klaus Schwab is a lookalike Bond villain. Schwab rose to infamy during the COVID scamdemic for pushing "The Great Reset" which is simply a rebranding of the New World Order. Schwab also boasted how his cadre of Young Global Leaders had penetrated the cabinets of governments[165] worldwide.

There exists a general geopolitical pattern of the US vs. Russia and China, but it is an oversimplification just to view it like this. The paradox is that, in a lot of ways, the governments of nations like China and Russia tend to be harsher to their own citizens than foreign people and nations. This produces a paradoxical situation where these governments are perpetrators internally but victims externally. In other words, they assert more control internally and less control externally. In the US, on the other hand, although there is rising police brutality, there are still ways (especially via the courts, which nominally at least have to respect the US Constitution) for US citizens to retain their rights, whereas history has shown the USG will not hesitate to bomb foreign nations almost indiscriminately. So the US tends to be harsher to their own citizens than foreign people and nations.

Although I have spent most of this chapter (and book) describing how the NWO conspirators are

[165] https://rumble.com/vx509j-klaus-schwabharvard-talk-trudeau-cabinet-and-others-penetrated.html

using the military might of America to bring all nations into the fold by force, this really isn't about America. It's about using America as a tool to achieve the NWO, then discarding it, stripping it of power and relegating it to the same level as all other nations, under the heel of the international banking and elite bloodlines who yearn to rule the world. As long as they get their global governance, they don't care whether it's via a unipolar or multipolar way.

The NWO globalists have made no secret of their admiration for China and for the ruthless (and in recent history totalitarian) Chinese model of governance. Here is what the late David Rockefeller said in 1973 (the same year he cofounded the Round Table think tank Trilateral Commission), in an article entitled "From a China Traveler" that first appeared in the *New York Times*:

The social experiment in China under Chairman Mao's leadership is one of the most important and successful in history.

Interesting how Rockefeller conveniently left out the part about Chairman Mao's regime killing (or enacting policies which led to the death of) thirty to eighty million people (estimates vary widely) through starvation, persecution, prison labor and mass executions, including under policies such as the Great Leap Forward that led to the deadliest famine in history.

Modern-day China itself is a chilling example of technocracy (rule by technology and technocrats – see chapter 11) and authoritarianism. Information is heavily censored. Books are buried or rewritten to reflect the Chinese Communist Party's ideology (even old texts like the Bible and the Quran[166]). Criticism of the government is not allowed. People are openly shamed, bullied and fined into compliance. The new Sesame Credit social credit system gives all citizens a numerical score based on their obedience, and restricts travel if the score is deemed too low. China uses facial recognition software and ubiquitous digital surveillance to keep track of its citizens. The internet is censored and monitored (the Great Firewall of China). Millions of Chinese have been arrested and sent to "reeducation" camps for brainwashing (the lucky ones) or involuntary organ removal without anesthetic (the unlucky ones who die in excruciating pain and are swiftly cremated as a

From a China Traveler

By David Rockefeller

---

166 https://www.dailymail.co.uk/news/article-7824541/China-rewrite-Bible-Quran-reflect-socialist-values.html

result). On top of all of this, as mentioned earlier, the Chinese Government cracked down on the peaceful and apolitical movement known as Falun Gong, a spiritual practice based on the three values of truth, forgiveness and compassion. In an absolutely horrific example of sadism and brutality, the Chinese government not only imprisoned and murdered many Falun Gong practitioners but also harvested the organs of some – to sell for money. Sometimes, words simply cannot describe the atrocities that governments have carried out against their citizens.

The US and its vassal states are waging a hybrid (4GW/5GW) war against China. This battle, taking place on many fronts (especially economic), is set to become the defining struggle of the twenty-first century, where the US will use the flashpoint of Taiwan to provoke China (just as it has used Ukraine to provoke Russia). However, this is only one level of the dichotomy. The struggle between the US and China (just like the struggle between the US and the USSR during the Cold War) is ultimately a stage-managed and fake conflict, because at the very top, these nations are controlled by the same group, the same force, the same cult. From this perspective, the battles between nations and blocs are performative; they are shows; they are real to the lower level politicians and bureaucrats but not to the force at the very top. These top warring nations could best be considered "frenemies" since they cooperate behind the scenes in space endeavors and the SSP (Secret Space Program – see chapter 10). The real battle is not between the US and China but between the ruling class and its citizen-subjects, between the NWO manipulators and the rest of humanity. The technocratic and totalitarian governmental system of China itself very closely resembles the NWO endgame and their ideal society (as long as they are in charge, of course). What China is today, the West and the world will be tomorrow – unprecedented surveillance, governmental control and lack of freedom – unless we become aware of the game plan now and rise up in large numbers to stop it. Authorities in the West are itching to roll out a version of China's social credit system where all money is digital (such as governmental-controlled cryptocurrencies) and where they can ensure obedience and compliance, as those who disobey will be shut off from their money and thus lose their ability to trade. If you can't buy or sell, how can you obtain food or other life necessities?

Microsoft, founded by NWO frontman Bill Gates, owns a patent[167] published on March 26, 2020 entitled "CRYPTOCURRENCY SYSTEM USING BODY ACTIVITY DATA" with the interesting number WO2020060606 (note the 666 at the end – just another strange coincidence). This patent aims to monopolize the idea of monitoring and monetizing human activities – paying people digitally to perform certain tasks:

Human body activity associated with a task provided to a user may be used in a mining process of a cryptocurrency system. A server may provide a task to a device of a user which is communicatively coupled to the server. A sensor communicatively

[167] https://patentscope.wipo.int/search/en/detail.jsf?docId=WO2020060606

coupled to or comprised in the device of the user may sense body activity of the user. Body activity data may be generated based on the sensed body activity of the user. The cryptocurrency system communicatively coupled to the device of the user may verify if the body activity data satisfies one or more conditions set by the cryptocurrency system, and award cryptocurrency to the user whose body activity data is verified.

Imagine a world where all your 'work', and even all your actions and thoughts, were tied to a surveillance grid, and where you were only paid money depending upon whether your behavior satisfied certain conditions. It is beyond Orwellian, but the plans for this dystopian nightmare are very real indeed.

So yes, on one level, the US and China are opponents, but on a deeper level, those at the very top of the pyramid are controlling both nations, wanting to bring the authoritarian hallmarks of the Chinese Government to the West and wanting to merge both nations – all nations – under a fascist World Government. The Russian and Chinese Governments back the UN and its programs of sustainability which is ushering the world towards a dictatorial NWO. They were fully on board with the COVID scamdemic (see chapter 8) and all its tyranny including masks, vaccines and lockdowns. The Russo-Ukraine war is real however there is a part which is performative – just like Orwell said in 1984 when he commented that the purpose of wars was to unite people behind their leader, distract people from how bad their life was and to use up excess supplies for production that would elevate the lower and middles classes.

At the highest levels, all these nations cooperate, just as they all marched in lockstep during the COVID scamdemic – never forget that.

We need a flexible mind to be able to see the real superficial conflict among nations, and also the real deeper agenda that unites their respective leadership classes.

Chapter 6 – The Carbon and Climate Change Mega Scam

I can only see one element of the climate system capable of generating these fast, global changes, that is, changes in the tropical atmosphere leading to changes in the inventory of the earth's most powerful greenhouse gas – water vapor.

– Dr. Wallace Broecker, a leading world authority on climate Lamont-Doherty Earth Observatory, Columbia University. Lecture presented at R. A. Daly Lecture at the American Geophysical Union's spring meeting in Baltimore, MD, May 1996.

There is no dispute at all about the fact that even if punctiliously observed, (the Kyoto Protocol) would have an imperceptible effect on future temperatures – one-twentieth of a degree by 2050.

– Dr. S. Fred Singer, atmospheric physicist, Professor Emeritus of Environmental Sciences at the University of Virginia and former director of the US Weather Satellite Service, in a September 10, 2001 Letter to Editor, *Wall Street Journal.*

I am compelled to disagree that there is a consensus of scientists who agree that this [climate change] is the consequence of human activities. While the melting of permafrost, retreat of glaciers and waning of the permanent ice pack may be alarming, it is only alarming to those unfamiliar with past changes in climate in the North. Paleoclimatologists recognize such events as part of natural changes wholly unrelated to CO2 concentrations in the atmosphere. In fact, the waxing and waning of ice shelves, along with glaciers, ice caps and pack ice are largely related to changes in solar inputs.

– Professor Ian Clark[168], University of Ottawa

It may be, for instance, that gross pollution of the environment can eventually replace the possibility of mass destruction by nuclear weapons as the principal apparent threat to the survival of the species. Poisoning of the air, and of the principal sources of food and water supply, is already well advanced, and at first glance would seem promising in this respect; it constitutes a threat that can be dealt with only through social organization and political power.

– *Report from the Iron Mountain*, 1966 (commissioned by JFK and completed when LBJ was US President)

In searching for a common enemy against whom we can unite, we came up with the idea that pollution, the threat of global warming, water shortages, famine and the like, would fit the bill. In their totality and their interactions these phenomena do constitute a common threat which must be confronted by everyone together … all these dangers are caused by human intervention in natural processes, and it is

---

168 https://www.desmogblog.com/ian-clark

only through changed attitudes and behavior that they can be overcome. The real enemy then is humanity itself.

– *The First Global Revolution,* 1991, p.75 (a document from the Club of Rome)

In order to save the planet it would be necessary to kill 350,000 people per day.

– Jacques Cousteau, UNESCO Courier, 1991

If we do a really great job on new vaccines ... we could lower [population growth] perhaps by 10-15%.

The benefits [of vaccines] are there in terms of reducing sickness, reducing population growth.

– Bill Gates, founder of Microsoft and the Bill and Melinda Gates Foundation that pushes vaccines and GMOs around the world

A total population of 250-300 million people, a 95% decline from present levels, would be ideal.

– Ted Turner, founder of CNN

Depopulation should be the highest priority of foreign policy towards the third world.

– Henry Kissinger, US National Security Advisor 1969–1973, US Secretary of State 1973–1977

The concept of national sovereignty has been immutable, indeed a sacred principle of international

relations. It is a principle which will yield only slowly and reluctantly to the new imperatives of global environmental cooperation.

– Maurice Strong, from a speech at the 1992 UN Rio Earth Summit (Strong isa former oil man who was the Secretary General of that summit, co-author [with Mikhail Gorbachev] of the Earth Charter and co-author of the Kyoto Protocol)

Eugenic goals are most likely to be attained under another name than eugenics.

– Frederick Osborn, President of the Rockefeller-funded Population Council

No matter if the science of global warming is all phony – climate change provides the greatest opportunity to bring about justice and equality in the world.

– Christine Stewart[169], former Canadian Minister of the Environment

The models are convenient fictions that provide something very useful.

– Dr David Frame, climate modeler, Oxford University.

We've got to ride this global warming issue. Even if the theory of global warming is wrong, we will be doing the right thing in terms of economic and

---

169 www.sepp.org/twtwfiles/1998/dec14_20.html

environmental policy.

– Timothy Wirth[170], former US Senator, Board Member of UN Foundation

*****

The push behind AGW (Anthropogenic Global Warming), or manmade global warming, now known as manmade climate change, has been so intense that it has often resembled hysteria. There is no doubt that humanity is polluting and destroying the environment in many ways, whether through industrial output of toxic waste, plastics, heavy metals, pharmaceutical contamination of waterways, oil spills, car exhaust, synthetic food additives, pesticides, genetic pollution of the environment (the spread of GMOs which contaminate organic crops), geoengineering and also invisible forms of contamination such as radiation (both nuclear and EMF). Yet there is a big difference between humanity polluting the environment and humanity imagining it has the power to change the climate of the entire planet. There is also a big logical gap between noticing that the climate is changing (as it has always done, naturally, for eons) and theorizing that humanity is causing the climate to change.

The truth is that AGW (and the dangerous cult crying "Apocalypse!" that has overtaken the worldwide environmental movement) is a massive part of *The Agenda* – the NWO agenda to reshape

---

170 https://www.forbes.com/sites/larrybell/2013/02/05/in-their-own-words-climate-alarmists-debunk-their-science/%23606613d668a3

the world into a centralized dictatorship. Why? The reason is that, as the above quotes reveal, the NWO controllers have needed a theme to rally all of humanity behind, from Chile to Canada, from Rwanda to Russia. What unites all people at a fundamental level? Breathing. So the controllers concocted the idea of a giant environmental threat that if hyped enough would require a giant environmental solution from a giant centralized body – a world government. It is vitally important to understand that large movements don't just come out of nowhere but rather are planned, implemented, funded or co-opted to serve those at the top of the pyramid. The environmental movement is a case in point. It is a symptom of the current general collective state of humanity: good hearted but ignorant. Kind-hearted but hoodwinked. Many people in the environmental movement are in it for the right reasons: they see the ongoing poisoning and destruction of the planet by corporations and are determined to defend the Earth. Yet despite their good intentions, they have unwittingly allowed themselves to be channeled in a direction that does not help the Earth. They are unintentionally supporting the very forces that are responsible for pillaging it.

By continuing to push notions that carbon dioxide is a poison, that global warming exists and mankind is responsible for it, that we need a worldwide carbon tax, and that we require "Global Governance" (a UN/NWO buzzword), these people are unknowingly promoting the NWO program and unwittingly placing NWO criminals in power who don't care about the environment and view it merely as a resource to be exploited. It has even gotten to the point where those refusing to buy into manmade climate change are being slurred and derided as "deniers" and treated like criminals. There have been constant calls in the US for years by climate scientists[171] for these "deniers" to be prosecuted!

Welcome to Planet Earth. If your opinion diverges too much from the mainstream groupthink, you could get locked up for thinking wrongly.

<u>What's the Ideology Driving the Movers, Shakers and Funders of the Climate Change Movement?</u>

In order to understand how the climate change movement has come to be the massive behemoth that it is, you have to understand where it came from. For those new to this topic, it may come as quite a shock that the underlying ideology behind AGW is, actually, er, ... don't say it out loud ... *eugenics*. Yes, it's that dirty word again. As I said earlier, the eugenicists never really went away after Hitler and the Nazis gave eugenics a bad name; they just regrouped and rebranded. By the way, guess where eugenics was flourishing before the Nazis took it further? The USA.

The theme of population control is a good lens through which you can see the clear connection between AGW and eugenics. There have been many famous supporters of eugenics. US Supreme Court justices Oliver Wendell Holmes and Louis Brandeis

---

171 dailycaller.com/2015/09/17/scientists-ask-obama-to-prosecute-global-warming-skeptics/

This is the type of propaganda which has been out there for over a century to promote eugenics. Note how the poster claims that eugenics is the "self-direction" of human evolution, despite the obvious truth that eugenicists almost always promote totalitarian systems with rulers or overlords who manage human breeding, i.e. who control who gets to procreate and who doesn't. This is the very antithesis of "self-direction."

ruled in favor of eugenics. Others supporting eugenicist ideals include Alexander Graham Bell, inventor of the telephone; activist Margaret Sanger; botanist Luther Burbank; Leland Stanford, founder of Stanford University; the novelist H. G. Wells; and the playwright George Bernard Shaw.

In the US, organizations such as the Rockefeller Brothers Fund (RBF) (founded in 1940 by John D. Rockefeller Jr.'s five sons) and the Population Council (founded by John D. Rockefeller himself in 1952) emerged with nearly identical missions: furthering eugenics research and slowing population growth. The Rockefellers either set up new organizations or funded existing ones with population control in mind, as this article[172] by Aly Nielsen reveals:

When global population passed 2½ billion in the early 1950s (it is now more than 7 billion), John Rockefeller III was among those convinced that catastrophe was on the way," Philanthropy Roundtable reported. "He believed his family foundation bore some of the responsibility for rising numbers—because its health programs had reduced death rates in poor countries. So he convened a panel of experts for advice on blunting population growth," Philanthropy Roundtable continued.

When the Rockefeller Foundation would not adopt overpopulation as one of its projects, John D. Rockefeller, 3rd, used RBF to found the Population Council. He was also the first president of the Population Council. The Ford Foundation also donated $2 million in the 1950s to help create the Council. The second Council president was Frederick Osborn, a director at the American Eugenics Society. He wrote extensively on both eugenics and the environment, according to his New York Times obituary in 1981.

Today, RBF has purged its eugenicist language. It also no longer gives to Planned Parenthood or the Population Council (but the Rockefeller Foundation and Rockefeller Philanthropy Advisors do).

But it's essential to recognize that the modern environmental movement grew out of an early 20th

[172] buyingbias.org/2017/04/21/eugenics-climate-change/

century conservationist agenda which involved white supremacy, racism and eugenics.

Knowing the character of the NWO controllers, it's safe to say they are not motivated to "save the planet" or "save humanity" – such an idea is laughable. They are solely motivated to save themselves, or rather, save their power base. A growing population is a threat because it means more people to manage and control (making the job harder), plus more competition for the finite resources on this planet, which the greedy cabal want all for themselves. More people equals more unpredictability in economic, social and political systems around the world: more chance of upheaval and revolution.

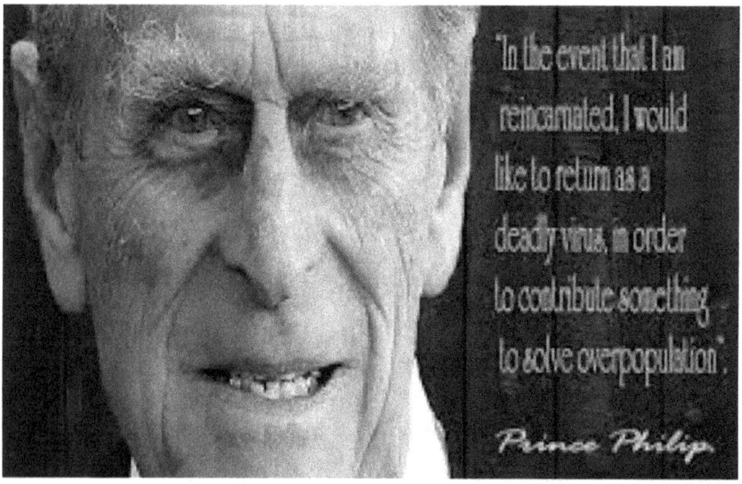

The concept of population control can quickly become a moral quagmire. First, there is slowing the birth rate through contraception, which most people accept but which some do not (especially from Catholicism). Then there is abortion, which is a highly charged and divisive issue, with a sizeable amount of people against the idea. Then, there is sterilization, both voluntary and forced. Some men voluntarily choose vasectomies but often after having had children already. Most people see forced sterilization as a breach of basic human rights; however, this hasn't stopped many women from being surreptitiously sterilized by Rockefeller-created Big Pharma (e.g. women from Kenya who were given vaccines laced with a contraceptive agent which prevented pregnancy). Then, there is euthanasia, another charged issue. Remember how Dr. Richard Day (in Chapter 2) predicted that society would move in the direction of the "demise pill" or death pill?

The Rockefellers and other NWO families and foundations have funded all of these things and more through a myriad of different organizations (e.g., Planned Parenthood). On a case-by-case basis, it may seem as though a particular organization really cares about a woman's rights (abortion) or an elder's right to die (euthanasia), but the unmistakable pattern behind it all is NWO money funding a very clear depopulation agenda.

Speaking of the word depopulation, there is a difference between it and population control. Population control is more of a euphemism; it suggests that someone or some group merely wants to control future growth. Depopulation, on the other hand, is more blunt and direct; it connotes depeopling the world in whatever way is necessary. There are many clues left behind by the NWO conspirators suggesting that they are aiming not only at curtailing future growth but also perhaps even culling the current population.

Take for instance the Georgia Guidestones, a set of large, mysterious granite stones that was fashioned into a creepy monument in the state of Georgia, USA. These Guidestones were mysteriously blown up in July 2022, however they were written in ten languages and contained a set of ten commandments or guidelines:

1. Maintain humanity under 500,000,000 in perpetual balance with nature.

2. Guide reproduction wisely - improving fitness and diversity.

3. Unite humanity with a living new language.

4. Rule passion - faith - tradition - and all things with tempered reason.

5. Protect people and nations with fair laws and just courts.

6. Let all nations rule internally resolving external disputes in a world court.

7. Avoid petty laws and useless officials.

8. Balance personal rights with social duties.

9. Prize truth - beauty - love - seeking harmony with the infinite.

10. Be not a cancer on the earth - Leave room for

nature - Leave room for nature.

The first guideline is a blatant call for outright depopulation. We currently have around 7.6 billion, so a reduction to five hundred million would be a 94 percent reduction. We can't "maintain" humanity at five hundred million when we passed that figure long ago and now stand at fifteen times that amount. That is not "maintaining" but rather "culling" (euphemistically) or killing. The second is nothing but the eugenically driven call for an authoritarian government which has the power to control human breeding, procreation and reproduction. Number ten is a reference to humans as a "cancer on the earth," which echoes Prince Philip's statement about how he would like to reincarnate as a virus to wipe humanity off the planet. Number eight may sound innocuous enough but is a veiled attack upon individual rights (as enshrined in documents like the Magna Carta and the US Bill of Rights) and a hidden call for socialism/collectivism. Finally, number six is another push for a One World Government, taking the angle that we need a world court (which would be the judicial arm of the world government) to resolve our disputes.

It may seem strange that something as pure (on the surface) as the green movement is connected to something as diabolical as depopulation, but truth is stranger than fiction. Of course, many environmental activists have their hearts in the right place and have no idea about this connection, thus fail to see the very agenda they are unwittingly serving. However, look closely and the link is undeniable. It's not hard to find many references in the environmental movement to the idea of "having fewer kids" to "reducing your carbon footprint" and "fighting climate change." There is the agenda all in one sentence: have fewer kids (depopulation), reduce your carbon footprint (accede to a carbon tax administered by a Global Government) and fight imaginary manmade climate change (so you can feel good and noble about giving up your freedom).

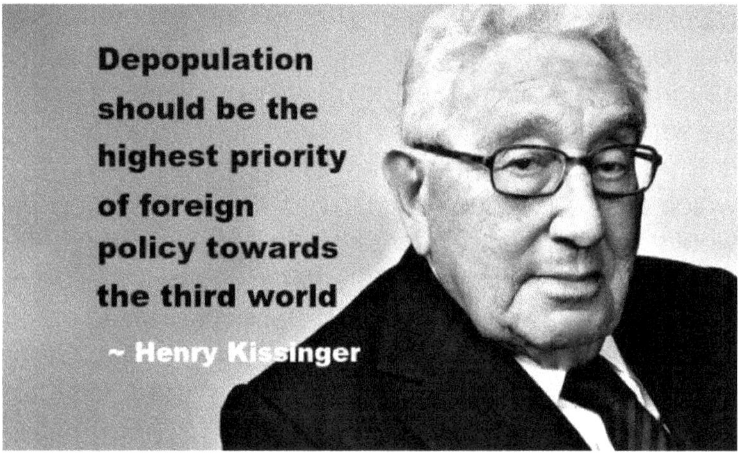

Agenda 2030 – Get Ready to Live in a Human Habitat

To understand the master plan and – if we don't wake up fast – where this is all headed, we need to understand the UN's grand scheme, which used to be called Agenda 21 but which has been renamed and rebranded Agenda 2030. It is a blueprint for centralized, tyrannical global governance which ties together various themes of the worldwide conspiracy, including depopulation, destroying the idea of private property, the "smart" grid, transhumanism and microchipping. It plans to establish "nonhuman zones" where ordinary people will never be allowed to set foot (but as usual there will be one rule for the masses and another rule for the elite). Around these nonhuman zones will be placed buffer zones. In the USA, the plan is to create six mega-regions – human habitats – with incredibly high population density. These will become smart cities, with mass transit (instead of cars), high rises, people stacked up on top of each other in tiny box-sized apartments and constant surveillance 24/7. You will be asked to "need less" and accept living in a cardboard box, all for the supposed sake of the Earth – while the elite administrators live in their mansions out of sight in another sector or, as portrayed in the *Hunger Games* movies, another "district."

Agenda 2030 loves to use feel-good buzzwords such as "sustainable development" and "global governance" to mask the true agenda. It also has a myriad of subprojects. One example is the Wildlands Project, a well-funded effort to lock up as much as 50 percent of the US into wilderness. It operates deceptively, hiding behind innocent-sounding names like greenways, smart growth and wildlife corridors, all the while transferring the land to the ruling class who control the various trusts and funds connected to the UN.

Agenda 21 entered the world's stage at the 1992 Rio Earth Conference and has its origins at the Club of Rome (see quote at beginning of chapter), one of the Round Table think tanks and secret societies that run the world, alongside the CFR (Council on Foreign Relations), the RIIA (Royal Institute of International Affairs), the Trilateral Commission, the Bilderberg

Group and the UN (United Nations). The Rothschilds and Rockefellers have been instrumental in the creation and development of many of these Round Table groups. The UN sits on Rockefeller-donated land in New York, for instance.

George Hunt[173] was one of the earlier people to alert the public about the background of the World Bank and the World Conservation Bank. He exposed how the propaganda works: the World Bank is not a benign money-lending organization for poorer countries, but rather a tool by which the international banking cabal seize control of the natural resources of the Third World and bringing all nations totally under their heel. He attended some of the big international conferences and actually got close enough to record the voices of the Rothschilds, the Rockefellers and their top agents as they laid out their deceitful schemes.

The insidious thing about Agenda 2030 is how cleverly it is hidden. At first glance, who would object to the idea of cleaning up the planet, living in better harmony with Nature and living more smartly and sustainably? Yet, as with many aspects of the global conspiracy, you only get the truth if you look past the veneer and dig beneath the surface. It turns out that the conspirators have their own meaning for each of their key terms. They state in their documents that sustainable does not mean self-sufficient, and they explicitly define things they deem not sustainable: ski runs, grazing of livestock, plowing of soil, building of fences, industry, single family homes, paved and

[173] thebigbadbank.com

tarred roads, logging activities, dams and power line construction. These are all targeted to be banned, and yet life without some of them would mean a return to the Stone Age!

The whole foundation of sustainable development according to Agenda 2030 is a world without private property. This is the 1st plank of the Communist Manifesto[174]. Using a mixture of half-truths, the UN claims in its documents that *"land ... cannot be treated as an ordinary asset, controlled by individuals and subject to the pressures and inefficiencies of the market. Private land ownership is also a principle instrument of accumulation and concentration of wealth, therefore, contributes to social injustice."*[175] While it's true that our current society is full of wealth and power inequalities, getting rid of the ability to own your own land, and putting all land on Earth into the hands of international bureaucrats to distribute as they see fit is definitely not the answer.

Simply put, the concepts behind sustainable development, as laid out in Agenda 2030[176], are incompatible with personal liberty. It's a green smokescreen for control. The entire manmade climate change movement is all about the elimination of personal freedom under the banner of saving the Earth.

---

174 www.libertyzone.com/Communist-Manifesto-Planks.html

175 www.un-documents.net/vp-d.htm

176 https://sdgs.un.org/2030agenda

That's a recipe for tyranny, and once again, it all boils down to the same distorted idea: collectivism.

Agenda 2030 is Pure Collectivism

To revisit, collectivism is the idea that the group is superior to the individual and that the abstract needs of the group should come ahead of the concrete needs of the individual. It sounds all fine and dandy in theory, and to some degree an individual must sacrifice some of his desires to work harmoniously in a team or live harmoniously in a community, but that's not what this is all about. Whenever collectivism is applied to politics, it becomes Marxism, socialism or Communism, and horrible results ensue. The individual becomes nothing. The state becomes everything. Power gets concentrated in a tiny percentage of hands (like a central committee) who become the new ruling elite. They claim to represent everyone and manage affairs and wealth distribution for the good of all, but in reality they become unaccountable tyrants who force their will on anyone who stands in their way. Collectivism can happen under a nominally "capitalist" system too. Currently in the West, we live under a corporate capitalistic oligarchic society where a few billionaires have more wealth than most of the population combined. The Protocols of the Learner Elders of Zion (chapter 2) specifically cites collectivism as the type of system that "they" want to impose on the masses in order to rule them.

Agenda 2030 is entirely and utterly collectivist. It goes against everything in the British Magna Carta, the US Bill of Rights and other similar documents which spell out the inherent individual rights and freedoms of humanity. It goes against the Declaration of Independence and everything Americans fought for in the late 1700s to become a free republic. Unsurprisingly, the UN's own list of human rights, The Universal Declaration of Human Rights[177], proposes fake rights or privileges rather than true inherent or intrinsic rights. Why? Because the UN claims it is granting the rights, rather than the rights being inherent:

These rights and freedoms may in no case be exercised contrary to the purposes and principles of the United Nations. – Article 29

The purpose and principle of the UN is a centralized One World Government (under the control of the NWO). So this is stating that if we don't accept this purpose, we are not allowed to exercise our rights and freedoms ... meaning these are mere privileges which can be revoked at will by an outside authority.

In the exercise of his rights and freedoms, everyone shall be subject only to such limitations as are determined by law. – Article 29

In other words, the "law" can override the exercise of your rights and freedoms. Thomas Jefferson once noted in a letter to Isaac H. Tiffany in 1819 that *"of liberty I would say that, in the whole plenitude of its extent, it is unobstructed action according to our will. But rightful liberty is unobstructed action according to*

---

[177] www.un.org/en/universal-declaration-human-rights/

our will within limits drawn around us by the equal rights of others. I do not add 'within the limits of the law,' because law is often but the tyrant's will, and always so when it violates the right of an individual." For the UN or any other supposed authority to say that you have rights but only so long as they don't interfere with the law is identical to saying you have no rights, since any tyrant can always make a law at will to cancel them out.

Everyone is entitled to a social and international order in which the rights and freedoms set forth in this Declaration can be fully realized. – Article 28

New World Order, anyone?

An important thing to note is that Agenda 2030 is not a treaty. It was never ratified by the US Senate. Therefore, it is not the law of the land in the US. Agenda 2030 is "soft law" or policy which covertly influences a country's legislation at all levels, national, state and local. Not only does it give the appearance of being green, but it also gives the appearance of being local, when in fact it is being orchestrated globally through ICLEI (International Council for Local Environmental Initiatives) and other organizations that are disguised to appear as local. The architects of Agenda 2030 are, naturally, the very NWO families and agents I have already been exposing in previous chapters.

A Closer Look at Global "Warming"

So now you know that eugenics, population control/depopulation and Agenda 2030 global governance form the background to the environmental movement. Let's then take a closer look at the claims by various green groups that the world is catastrophically warming and that man is to blame. You may have heard the propaganda that the "science is settled" and that scientists almost unanimously agree that man is causing global warming and climate change. Not true. That is a trick to shut down investigation and open debate.

The so-called 1995 Heidelberg Appeal[178] consisted of over four thousand scientists and seventy Nobel Laureates, all of whom expressed doubt in AGW. In 2008, as many as 32,000 dissenting scientists[179] rejected the idea of manmade global warming. Then, we have the Global Warming Petition Project[180] consisting of 31,487 American scientists (including 9,029 with PhDs) who also claim the idea of AGW is false. So much for the claimed scientific "consensus"!

The AGW movement has been busted fudging the data and cooking the books on many occasions. The so-called Climate Gate scandal began in 2009 and featured the infamous "hockey stick" example where researchers from the University of East Anglia in England were caught manipulating the data[181] to

---

[178] https://defyccc.com/heidelberg-appeal-anniversary/

[179] https://aapsonline.org/32000-scientists-dissent-from-global-warming-consensus/

[180] www.petitionproject.org/

[181] www.lavoisier.com.au/articles/greenhouse-science/climate-change/climategate-emails.pdf

make it look like global warming was accelerating so fast that it resembled a hockey stick which turns at the bottom and goes straight up.

This Climate Depot[182] report quotes geologist Dr. Don Easterbrook (professor of geology at Western Washington University) as saying that *"the corruption within the IPCC revealed by the Climategate scandal, the doctoring of data and the refusal to admit mistakes have so severely tainted the IPCC that it is no longer a credible agency."*

I am going to point out six main fallacies the NWO conspirators have managed to get many people and environmentalists to believe when it comes to AGW. Undoubtedly there are many more but for reasons of time and space we shall limit ourselves to these half-dozen.

Fallacy #1: Carbon Dioxide is a Poison

Let's start with the basics: carbon dioxide (CO2) is a nutrient, not a poison. We breathe out carbon dioxide every breath, but we also breathe some of it in.. According to the United Nations IPCC (Intergovernmental Panel on Climate Change), we are therefore poisoning ourselves with every breath! The IPCC, by the way, is not a scientific panel but rather a political one filled with many nonscientists and tasked with the goal of trying to legitimize the AGW agenda.

Think about it – if CO2 were really a poison, why does it help plants grow so much? Why is it a key

---

182 www.cfact.org/pdf/2010_Senate_Minority_Report.pdf

part of the fundamental equation of biology: sugar + oxygen = carbon dioxide + water + heat? How is it that those in the environmental movement are ignorant of basic biology?

As the website PlantsNeedCO2.org[183] states, the more CO2 around, the better plants grow:

In Idso and Idso's (1994) analysis of soil nutrient limitations, the percentage growth enhancement due to a 300-ppm rise in the air's CO2 content actually did exhibit a slight (but statistically non-significant) decline, dropping from 51% to 45% when nutrients went from non-growth-limiting to limiting in a group of 70 experiments. But when the atmospheric CO2 enrichment was 600 ppm, this slight negative trend reversed itself, going from a CO2-induced growth stimulation of 43% when nutrients were present in abundance to a 52% enhancement when their supply was sub-optimal. And for a 1200-ppm increase in atmospheric CO2, the percentage growth enhancement jumped from 60% when the soil nutrient supply was adequate to 207% when it was less-than-adequate.

It's a simple equation: the more CO2 you have, the more the plants like it, and the faster they will grow. The world-renowned theoretical physicist Freeman Dyson has said, *"The possibly harmful climatic effects of carbon dioxide have been greatly exaggerated... the benefits clearly outweigh the possible damage."* Dr William Happer, Professor of Physics at Princeton University, has said, *"No*

---

183 www.plantsneedco2.org/default.aspx?menuitemid=333

chemical compound in the atmosphere has a worse reputation than carbon dioxide, thanks to the single-minded demonization of this natural and essential atmospheric gas... The incredible list of supposed horrors that increasing carbon dioxide will bring the world is pure belief disguised as science.... We're really in a carbon dioxide famine now... increased carbon dioxide will be good for mankind."

If only the hijacked environmental movement could see the obvious: carbon dioxide is a nutrient, not a poison.

During previous periods in the Earth's history, in periods such as the Triassic and Jurassic, CO2 levels were at 7000 to 9000ppm, far more than the paltry 400ppm we have today. This is not just about plants; phytoplankton species also feed on CO2, using carbon from CO2 as a building unit and releasing oxygen. Contrary to common belief, it is not the forests but the oceans that constitute the "lungs" of the Earth. Around 70 percent of the oxygen present today in the atmosphere comes from phytoplankton, not trees.

The demonization of carbon dioxide is not about helping the environment. The NWO idea has always been to attach the worsening environment to an individual's energy usage – and even his or her breathing – so as to introduce a carbon tax. The government literally wants to tax you for breathing – for merely being alive! As a matter of fact, with CO2 levels around 300 to 400 ppm, we don't have too much carbon dioxide – we have too little. Historical CO2 levels have been far higher than today's level; at one point, levels were around 2500ppm which is 6 to 8 times our current level. At 150ppm, plants no longer have the necessary CO2 to live and begin dying. We are way closer to that extreme than the other. If we could double our current levels, plants would thrive worldwide, and reforestation would accelerate. So much for all the CO2 fearmongering.

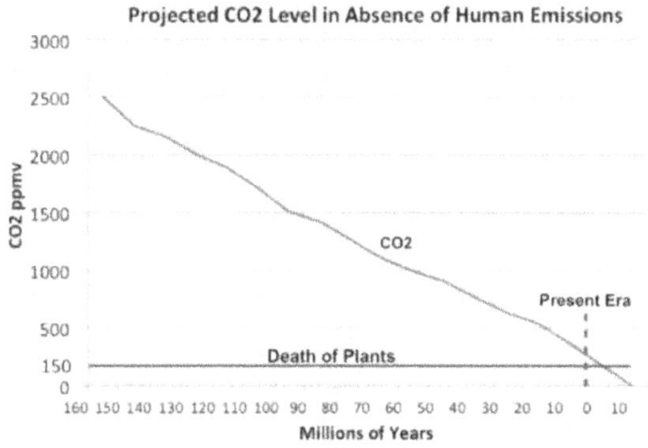

We are in danger of such low CO2 levels that plants will not exist – and neither will we. Image credit: presentation of former Greenpeace activist Patrick Moore.

Fallacy #2: Carbon is Warming the Atmosphere

The second big fallacy is that CO2 is warming the atmosphere. This ignores the periods in history when we had three or even ten times the CO2 levels that we have today, yet there was no temperature rise. The Holocene period which lasted around three thousand years had warming but no CO2 rise. Most of the warming of the last 120 years occurred before 1940, when cars and other vehicles were nowhere near as widespread as they are today.

Al Gore, who stands to profit greatly if a carbon cap-and-trade scheme is introduced as binding law, became famous for his documentary *An Inconvenient Truth*. In that film he pointed out the close relationship between increased temperature and increased levels of CO2 ... however he failed to mention something very important (failed, or deliberately omitted). He didn't say what caused what. The truth is that the causation goes the opposite way than AGW proponents pretend. Higher levels of temperature cause higher levels of CO2, not the other way around; CO2 follows temperature. This is mostly because the ocean, which is a vast reservoir of stored CO2, releases the gas as it warms.

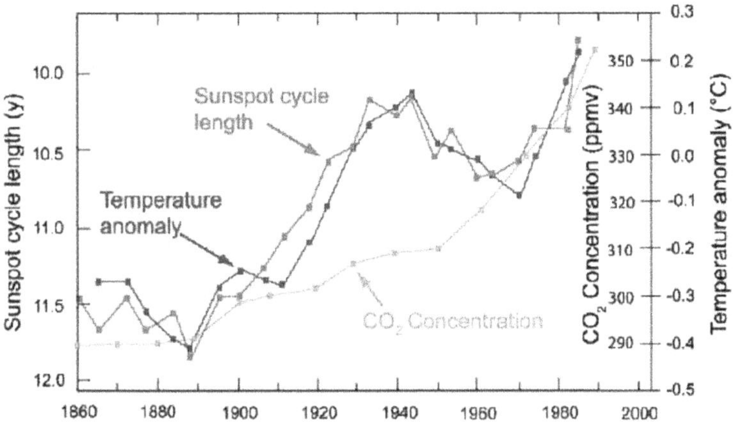

A very commonsense point that seems to be missed by AGW proponents is what is really driving temperature. It's not CO2. However, if you look up in the sky you might get an idea. That's right – it's the sun. Solar activity and temperature correlate extremely closely, as this next graph based on the research of Dr. Tim Patterson (Professor of Geology at Carleton University) shows[184].

Additionally, measurements from worldwide tidal

---

184 www.globalwarming-sowhat.com/warm--cool-/

gauges show that sea rise is negligible[185].

Fallacy #3: The Carbon Allegedly Warming the Atmosphere is Due to Human Activity

Even if CO_2 levels did cause global warming (which they do not), could human activity really be the cause? No. Humans contribute 3 percent of CO_2, which itself is around 0.03 percent of the gases in Earth's atmosphere. Volcanoes, animals, bacteria, dying vegetation and the oceans all produce far more CO_2 than humans every year. Here is a breakdown of the gases in our atmosphere:

Atmosphere	
78%	Nitrogen
21%	Oxygen
0.9%	Argon
0.1%	Trace gases

Trace Gases	
0.95%	Water Vapor (i.e. 95% of Trace Gases)
0.03%	CO_2

There are also some gases at tiny concentrations, including helium (He), methane (CH_4), nitrous oxide (N_2O) and ozone (O_3), as well as halogenated gases (CFCs) released by mankind which have damaged the ozone.

Water vapor is far and away the largest greenhouse gas, but the IPCC chooses to ignore it.

---

185 https://climatechangedispatch.com/tidal-gauges-negligible-sea-level-rise/

Check out these pie charts below where you can see that water vapor is excluded from the percentages. The IPCC and other AGW proponents claim they need to exclude water vapor from their calculations because it varies so much from region to region. Yes, it does vary greatly all over the Earth, but to just exclude the largest greenhouse gas (and a massive driver of temperature too) from calculations because it's inconvenient is grossly misleading.

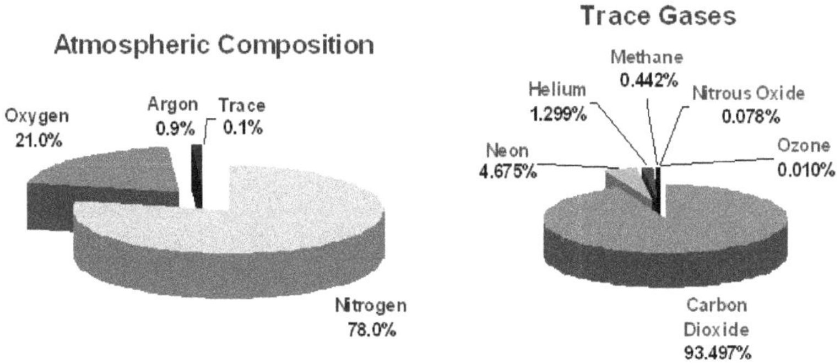

A pie chart typical of one used by the IPCC and AGW proponents. Water vapor, despite being the overwhelmingly largest greenhouse and trace gas, is simply ignored and omitted.

To recap: trace gases are 0.1 percent of the atmosphere, and carbon dioxide makes up around 3 percent of these trace gases, so therefore CO2 is 3 percent of 0.1 percent. So CO2 comprises 0.03 percent of the atmosphere. That's pretty damn small, but we can't stop there. The next question to ask is: how much of this is caused by human activity? The IPCC has conflicting sets of data here, but both are within a small range of each other, either 3.0 percent (using the 2007 figures) or 3.6 percent (using the

2001 figures). No matter which set of data you use, the IPCC data shows that manmade CO2 output levels are ~3 percent. How do you figure this out? The 2001 data shows the total amount of CO2 going into the atmosphere (119 + 88 + 6.3 = 213.3) and the human portion as 6.3. Divide 6.3 by 213.3 and you get 2.95%. The 2007 data shows the total amount of CO2 going into the atmosphere (29 + 439 + 332 = 800) and the human portion as 29. Divide 29 by 800 and you get 3.63 percent. Here's the bottom line. According to the IPCC's own data, manmade CO2 output levels are 3 percent of 3 percent of 0.1 percent of the total Earth's atmosphere. That's 0.0009 percent! CO2 is measured in ppm (parts per million) because it is such a tiny and insignificant gas, yet somehow, the propaganda has been so successful that is has sprouted into what some estimate[186] is a US$1.5 trillion industry.

The IPCC is basically stuck on water vapor. This panel can't actually measure the vapor, since the variability across the world is so high, H2O vapor changes so quickly, and it takes place above a variety of different landscapes/topographies. There are too many variables to calculate to produce a good model. So the IPCC just sweeps this question aside and states it has no "confidence." Here's exactly what the IPCC says[187]:

---

186 https://www.washingtontimes.com/news/2015/aug/11/climate-change-industry-now-15-trillion-global-bus/

187 https://wattsupwiththat.com/2015/02/08/thanks-to-the-ipcc-the-public-doesnt-know-water-vapor-is-most-important-greenhouse-gas/

Modelling the vertical structure of water vapor is subject to greater uncertainty since the humidity profile is governed by a variety of processes ... because of large variability and relatively short data records, confidence in stratospheric H2O vapour trends is low.

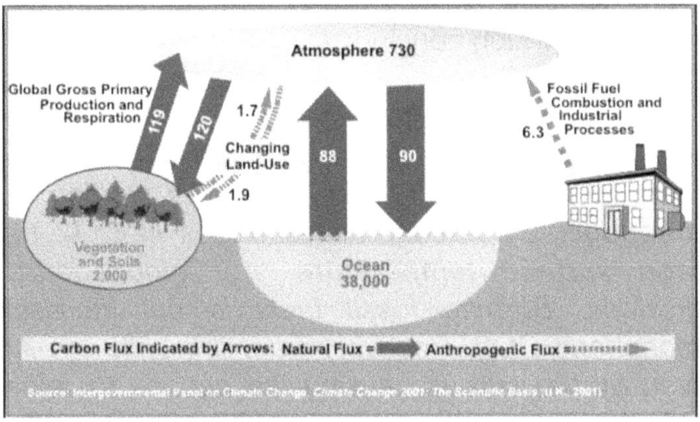

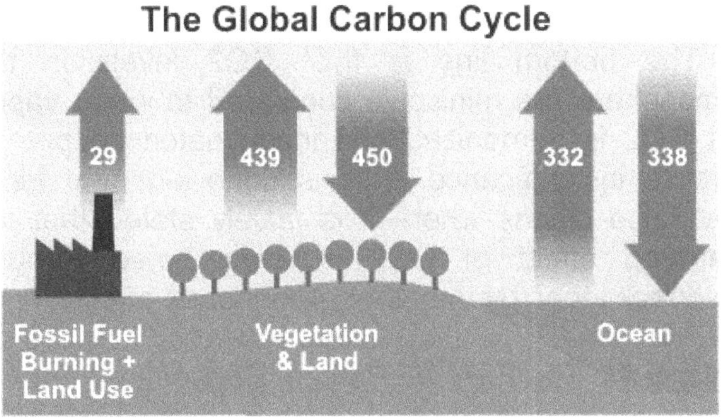

Manmade CO2 output levels (IPCC data from 2001) and Manmade CO2 output levels (IPCC data from AR4, 2007)

It doesn't suit the IPCC's agenda to really dive in and better understand the role of water vapor as the key greenhouse gas driving climate temperature. It's far easier to just pretend it doesn't exist and only focus on the tiny amount of CO2 in the atmosphere instead.

The website NoTricksZone features an article[188] by Ed Caryl which concludes:

It is ten times as likely that atmospheric CO2 is coming from natural sources, namely the warming ocean surface, as it is likely that it is coming from anthropogenic sources. The changes in CO2 track ocean surface temperature, not global carbon emissions. Burning fossil fuels is not increasing atmospheric CO2. Recovery from the Little Ice Age, driven by the sun, is causing the oceans to release CO2. It is temperature driving CO2 release, not the other way around. Just as it has always been.

The bottom line is this: CO2 levels in the atmosphere are miniscule compared to water vapor, yet CO2 is demonized and incriminated despite its relative insignificance. This is done via dirty tricks and false claims where it is falsely stated that the warming effect of CO2 is exacerbated through feedback loops by the other greenhouse effects.

Fallacy #4: The Fake 97 Percent Consensus

AGW proponents claim that there is a 97 percent

---

188 notrickszone.com/2013/03/02/most-of-the-rise-in-co2-likely-comes-from-natural-sources/

consensus among scientists that most of the global warming since the 1950s was manmade. They base this on a study (Cook et al. in 2013) which took 11,944 papers published between 1991 and May 2012 and read the abstracts to determine which of the three categories the authors fell into:

1. explicit or implicit agreement that humans are causing the climate to change;
2. no statement or uncertainty about humans changing the climate; and
3. explicit or implicit rejection of the notion that humans are changing the climate.

They claim that 97 percent of these authors believe in AGW. However, as Christopher Monckton points out, they combined different levels of endorsement to inflate the percentage. The IPCC's definition of AGW is that *most* of the global warming since 1950 was manmade, not just "some" or "a little." Monckton writes[189]:

The algorithm counted the number of abstracts Cook had allocated to each level of endorsement. When the computer displayed the results, I thought there must have been some mistake. The algorithm had found only 64 out of the 11,944 papers, or 0.5%, marked as falling within Level 1, reflecting the IPCC consensus that recent warming was mostly manmade.

I carried out a manual check using the search

[189] https://wattsupwiththat.com/2014/07/11/the-climate-consensus-is-not-97-its-100/

function in Microsoft Notepad. Sure enough, there were only 64 data entries ending in ",1".

Next, I read all 64 abstracts and discovered – not greatly to my surprise – that only 41 had explicitly said Man had caused most of the global warming over the past half century or so.

In the peer-reviewed learned journals, therefore, only 41 of 11,944 papers, or 0.3% – and not 97.1% – had endorsed the definition of the consensus proposition to which the IPCC, in its 2013 Fifth Assessment Report, had assigned 95-99% confidence ... Cook et al. had lumped together the 96.8% who ... had endorsed the proposition that we cause some warming with the 0.3% who had endorsed the IPCC's proposition that we caused most of the warming since 1950. In defiance of the evidence recorded in their own data file, they had then explicitly stated, both in their article and in a subsequent article, that 97.1% had endorsed the IPCC's proposition.

For those wanting to see the detailed data, read the scientific refutation of the Cook et al. study in this study written by David Legates entitled *Climate Consensus and 'Misinformation': A Rejoinder to Agnotology, Scientific Consensus, and the Teaching and Learning of Climate Change*[190].

<u>Fallacy #5: We Can Solve AGW and Too Much CO2 with a Worldwide Carbon Tax (and Global Governance)</u>

---

190 https://link.springer.com/article/10.1007/s11191-013-9588-3

As pointed out above, all this focus on carbon is to create a backdoor to justify the transformation of society via "Global Governance", i.e. the NWO. The whole scheme to get people and corporations fixated on their carbon footprint – rather than how much actual benefit or harm they are doing the environment – is to pave the way for more taxation and centralization of power. Of course, the former depends on the latter; to have a worldwide carbon tax you need a One World Government to enforce and collect it. The UN, ICLEI and its other subdivisions are constantly talking about global governance for this very reason. Why would you believe that the very people scheming to rule over you will "save" you, the environment and the Earth by taxing you more?

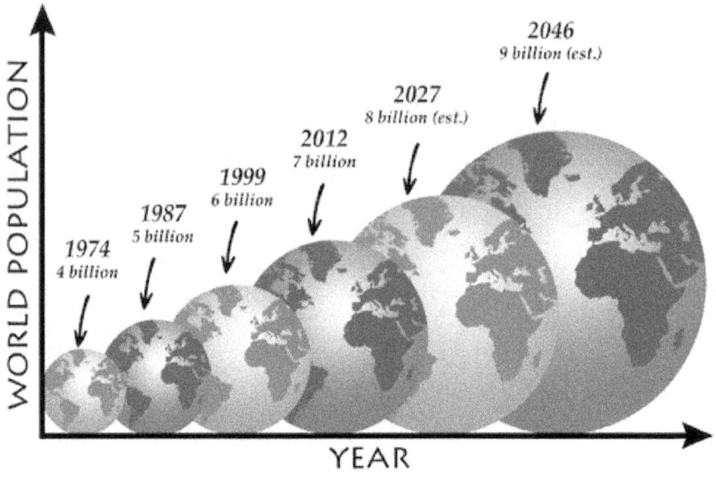

Fallacy #6: Overpopulation

So now we come full circle back to eugenics. Mahatma Gandhi once said: *"Earth provides enough to satisfy every man's need, but not every man's greed."* There is no doubt that rising populations can put a strain on resources, yet where is the proof that the Earth cannot support seven billion people? Or nine billion people? Is it really population that is the problem here, or is it rather self-centered greed and destructive environmental practices and technologies?

We can accept the rising amount of people not as a threat or a reason to justify depopulation (killing), but rather as a challenge. It can propel us into living more from the heart, to having more compassion for those less well off than us, to doing a better job of sharing and distributing resources equitably. It can stimulate us into better modes of efficiency. Could the rising population help a critical mass of people awake to the truth of free energy, and the fact that free energy or over unity devices already exist which provide practically unlimited energy for free or very cheaply (see chapter 15)?

It has been known in many countries for a long time that as you increase education, you decrease population naturally[191]. There is no need for stealth sterilization programs, introducing contraceptives through vaccines or other depopulation murder programs. When people gain a higher education, they organically choose to have fewer kids. If the conspirators really cared about the planet's population, why not use their money to help everyone access better education? The answer is, of course, that they don't.

The Real Problem

The real problem with the environment isn't climate change or carbon. It's that we as a collective species are trashing and degrading it. We are in serious danger of ruining our environment to such an extent that it will no longer be able to support an oxygen-breathing species like ourselves. We spill oil in our oceans and rivers. We kill off species faster than we can even classify them. We make substances which don't biodegrade and end up in giant landfills. We cut down forests without taking enough care to replace them. We manufacture toxic products like asbestos, DDT, dioxin, atrazine and glyphosate. We used to (and still do in some nations)

[191] www.earth-policy.org/data_highlights/2011/highlights13

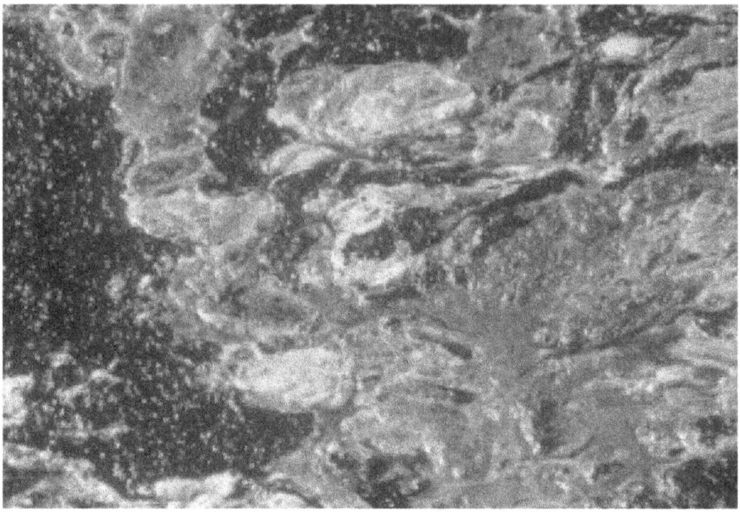

allow lead in gasoline, paint and children's toys. We contaminate our waterways with industrial chemicals, heavy metals and pharmaceutical residues. We use an economic system which incentivizes planned obsolescence and encourages us to throw things away rather than repair them.

We let maniacal people rule out-of-control governments that spray toxic barium, aluminum and strontium chemtrails all over the world – and get away with it. Geoengineering itself is so massively destructive to the environment that it alone could alter the course of life on the planet – yet there is still a great majority of people today around the world who refuse to believe their own eyes and deny that such aerial spraying is even a phenomenon. What about the release (via geoengineering) of synthetic self-aware fibers that cause Morgellons' Disease? What about unstoppable environmental genetic pollution caused by the release of GMOs? What about the planned saturation of the entire planet in

Wi-Fi and 5G EMFs by beaming the signal from space to every part of Earth so there is no escape from it?

What does any of this have to do with climate change or carbon? These two terms are a huge distraction and a deliberate way to trick people who genuinely care for the environment. The idea that manmade CO2 output levels are problematic, in the scheme of all of Earth's eco problems, is a giant hoax. It diverts environmentalists' attention away from the true issues that need addressing. Does it make any logical sense to spend so much money, energy and attention on 0.0009 percent of CO2, when there are very palpable, tangible and dangerous threats to our environment?

The latest iteration of the manmade climate change hoax is the push to sequester carbon by taking it out of the atmosphere and bury it underground. Humanity is a carbon-based lifeform. A war on carbon is a war on humanity itself. We are facing an anti-human agenda.

The whole AGW movement is a con, but it has been craftily constructed to exploit human psychology. Here's what the late scientist and researcher István Markó said in an interview[192] with Grégoire Canlorbe:

In my eyes, there are two main reasons—or if you prefer, two main types of feelings—that make people let themselves be seduced by the theory of anthropogenic warming so readily. In the first place, the Catholic religion is in decline in the Western world; and what I call ecologism comes to replace it.

Westerners have a pronounced taste for self-flagellation; and the theory of anthropogenic warming provides justification for that tendency, possibly anchored in our Judeo-Christian heritage. So, on the one hand, we have religious feelings: faith in a new system of thought, which is ecologism; the veneration of a new divinity, which is benevolent and protective Nature. On the other hand, we have a feeling of guilt, expressed in our conviction that, if the climate warms up, it is our fault; and that if we do not immediately limit our CO2 emissions, we will have sullied and disfigured our planet.

The con is based on eliciting people's guilt by telling them that they are part of the problem—that they are polluters and part of the carbon cycle. The resemblance to the old Catholic Church is striking – using guilt to control: "You're a dirty little sinner" or "You're a dirty little carbon polluter" or even "You're a dirty little carbon breather!" Children being used as pawns and propaganda tools to join the climate cult

[192] gregoirecanlorbe.com/interview-with-istvan-marko-for-breitbart-news-network

(see Greta Thunberg).

To overcome the manmade climate change hoax, we need streetwise spirituality and activism.

Do you deeply care for the environment? Great! Then do your research first before joining any protests. Oppose fracking, GMOs, corporate welfare to military companies (the Pentagon is the biggest polluter on planet) and geoengineering, which is spraying poison all over the world. As leading conspiracy author, researcher and public speaker David Icke says, we need streetwise spirituality. We need to have our hearts in the right places, but also put our thinking caps on, otherwise we will easily be led astray by tricksters. Only when the leaders of the environmental movement have their hearts and brains in alignment can we help to really and truly save the environment.

Here are the takeaways from this chapter:

– The green movement has been hijacked and used as a vehicle for a massive transformation of society, a massive centralization of power and the installation of a One World Government;

– Caring for the environment is great; just make sure your efforts are directed to real problems;

– CO2 is a minuscule trace gas; water vapor has more effect on climate; beyond that, the sun affects the climate far more than any Earth gas or manmade phenomenon.

Question: what do eugenics and AGW have in common? Answer: they are both pseudo-sciences. Don't fall for them.

Chapter 7 – Perception Management Goes into Overdrive

Censorship reflects society's lack of confidence in itself. It is the hallmark of an authoritarian regime.

– Justice Potter Stewart

Censorship is the child of fear and the father of ignorance.

– Laurie Halse Anderson

Libraries should be open to all – except the censor.

– John F. Kennedy

The problem of fake news isn't solved by hoping for a referee, but rather because we as citizens, we as users of these services, help each other. We talk and we share and we point out what is fake. We point out what is true. The answer to bad speech is not censorship, the answer to bad speech is more speech. We have to exercise and spread the idea that critical thinking matters, now more than ever, given the fact that lies seem to be getting more popular.

– Edward Snowden

To learn who rules over you, simply find out who you

are not allowed to criticize.

– Voltaire

Censorship is telling a man he can't have steak because a baby can't chew it.

– Mark Twain

The conscious and intelligent manipulation of the organized habits and opinions of the masses is an important element in democratic society. Those who manipulate this unseen mechanism of society constitute an invisible government which is the true ruling power of our country. We are governed, our minds are molded, our tastes formed, our ideas suggested, largely by men we have never heard of.

– Edward Bernays (nephew of Sigmund Freud and known as the father of modern PR or Public Relations)

The business of the journalists is to destroy the truth... We are the tools and vassals of rich men behind the scenes. We are the jumping jacks, they pull the strings and we dance. Our talents, our possibilities and our lives are all the property of other men. We are intellectual prostitutes.

– John Swinton, speech given while working for the *New York Sun*, 1880

*****

If you want to boil the entire conspiracy down to

one key theme, it would be perception. We are in the midst of many wars, militarily and metaphorically, but the wars on so-called rogue states (North Korea, Syria, Iran, Venezuela, Russia, China), and the wars on poverty, cancer and drugs all pale in significance next to the one fundamental war: the war on perception. For the NWO agenda to succeed, it needs to capture your mind and your soul, and it aims to do that through controlling your perception. To use another Orwellian and military euphemism, it's all about perception management.

The concept of perception management is well known to the upper-echelon rulers. The FBI has listed foreign perception management as one of eight "key issue threats" to national security, alongside terrorism, attacks on critical US infrastructure and weapons proliferation. Militarily, perception management has been recognized as just as important – if not more so – than actually physically fighting the battle. This is why there have been entire military departments for psychological operations whose only purpose was to decide how to present information to the media and the public.

So how do the NWO rulers control the perception of the ruled? They do so on two main fronts. The first is via external censorship, where they control people's access to information. They bury and eliminate the true while propagating the false via propaganda. The other is internal censorship, where they encourage people to self-censor. The idea is to frighten and trick you into only speaking certain things aloud (much of which is achieved via political correctness—which, to paraphrase George Carlin, is fascism pretending to be manners). The NWO manipulators want social conformity. They want you to adhere to the prevailing and officially sanctioned groupthink. They stoke and augment people's fears of being weird, unpopular or wrong, since it is far easier to rule people by getting them to police themselves (self-censorship) than trying to police them by force with henchmen. Then, there is "cancel culture", a relatively new term and concept that contains elements of both external and internal censorship. Cancel culture is all about people or organizations posing to look good (virtue signaling) by refusing to follow, associate or do business with those who are deemed politically incorrect by the mob, who consequently lose business deals, online platforms and access to audiences based on their beliefs and viewpoints.

We will look at external and internal censorship in turn. Ultimately, the agenda is to not only make it illegal to speak outside of party policy but also to make it literally impossible to think outside of standard lines, thus reducing the threat of a revolution and the chance the NWO's grip on power will be dissolved.

EXTERNAL CENSORSHIP

Censorship has become a big issue around the world. Overt censorship remains at high levels in many nations, not just in China (with their Great Firewall) and the Middle East, but also in the so-called free and democratic West. If you are still in any doubt about the blatant levels of censorship that exist in our world today, take a look at the following

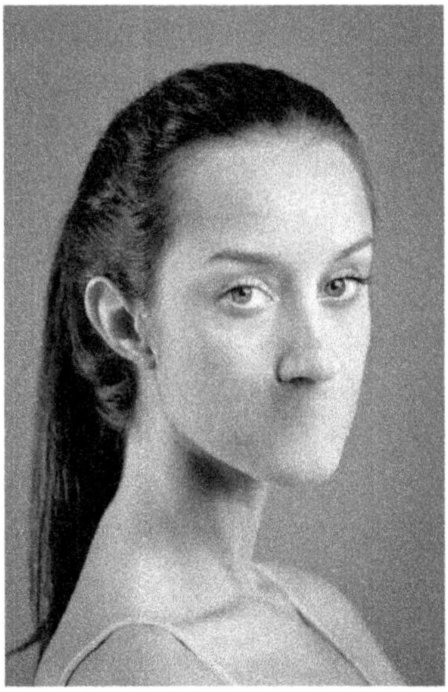

examples. In 2016, Israel threatened to ban "contrary to reality" headlines[193] by annulling the press credentials of journalists and editors who used them. Turkey has been arresting journalists[194] for years, and things sharply escalated with the very dictatorial President Erdogan who got busted buying oil from and supplying weapons to ISIS. (Erdogan, by the way, is the same guy that tried to get a Turkish citizen thrown in prison for "insulting the President"[195] because the man compared Erdogan to Gollum from *Lord of the Rings*.) Some nations take it even further; in Thailand you can actually get imprisoned not only for insulting the King but also for insulting the king's dog[196].

China is so scared of the free flow of information that they have enormous firewalls maintained by their "Ministry of Truth" that gets to decide what people

193 https://www.rt.com/news/331306-israel-press-credentials-headlines/

194 https://en.wikipedia.org/wiki/List_of_arrested_journalists_in_Turkey

195 time.com/4132235/tayyip-erdogan-turkey-gollum-lord-of-the-rings/

196 www.theguardian.com/world/2015/dec/29/thai-kings-dog-khun-tongdaeng-dies-days-after-insult-arrest

can and cannot see and read online. In Eritrea and North Korea, there is no independent journalism[197]; all news media is published by the state. Even in the US, where freedom of the press is enshrined and protected in the First Amendment, Congresswomen Dianne Feinstein in 2013 put forth an amendment to narrow the definition of journalism and weed out those who were not, as considered by her, "real reporters."

In the USA, community ISPs (Internet Service Providers) are being discouraged or banned, following the decision by the FCC to reverse net neutrality. There are two sides to this issue; however, it seems to be a choice between handing over control of the internet to the untrustworthy government (net neutrality) or the untrustworthy corporatocracy (reversal of net neutrality). As it currently stands, online censorship in the US will be easier if the corporatocracy owns the internet, not small companies. You may mistakenly think that the first amendment in America safeguards against censorship, but a close examination reveals that the US has a very long history of censorship[198], despite all its rhetoric about free speech, human rights and freedom. After Elon Musk purchased Twitter and oversaw the release of the Twitter Files, some of the journalists he used to get the story out (such as Matt Taibbi and Michael Shellenberger) dubbed the sprawling apparatus the Censorship Industrial Complex.

---

[197] https://cpj.org/reports/2012/05/10-most-censored-countries.php

[198] https://www.racket.news/p/a-century-of-censorship

The Big Tech Google-YouTube-Meta-Facebook-Twitter-Amazon Nexus: Grabbing Your Data and Controlling Your Perception

The big tech companies form a nexus and are clearly colluding and conspiring to censor the news – and control your perception. To understand this you have to first understand the key point that the Big Tech conglomerate (Alphabet-Google-YouTube, Meta-Facebook-Instagram-WhatsApp, Twitter and Amazon) is an insidious agglomeration of the government, the military and the corporate world. Alphabet is the parent company of Google which owns YouTube. Meta owns Facebook, Instagram and WhatsApp. Google is joined at the hip with the MIC. It was started up with NSA and CIA seed money via CIA front companies like In-Q-Tel. Google was hit with a backlash from its employees over Project Maven (Google's contract with the Pentagon for a controversial drone imaging program that uses AI), but nonetheless, continues to serve the US Military, just like Amazon does. Amazon is on the verge of (and may have already become) the biggest contractor to the US Military. Amazon signed a $600 million contract with the CIA to store its data in the cloud and is on course to be selected for the winner-take-all $10 billion cloud contract dubbed the Joint Enterprise Defense Infrastructure (or JEDI for short). Facebook has used NATO-linked think tank Atlantic Council to help advise it on "fake news". Do you get the picture yet?

The Big Tech cabal has become the preeminent social engineer and unelected arbiter of truth in our society today. They pretend they want to insulate users from "fake news" and misinformation, but it's a bald-faced lie. Online censorship on platforms and by companies such as YouTube-Google-Alphabet, Facebook, Twitter and Amazon has skyrocketed in the last five years. YouTube began by embarking upon soft censorship through forced sign-ins and hard censorship by deleting entire channels. The 2017 YouTube "Adpocalypse" as it was called was a sign of things to come: it involved a sweeping demonetization of videos scrubbed due to their "inappropriate content" for advertisers. YouTube has embarked on numerous censorship sprees or purges since then, eliminating thousands upon thousands of alternative channels and voices from its platforms over the years, and demonetizing others who are forced to look to other platforms to host their content in the hopes of raising money from it. For many independent reporters, journalists, bloggers and content creators, if they can't get paid for their work, they can't produce it, because they have to find paid work elsewhere. But, of course, that is the idea. Boot independent creators off your platform = reduce the scope of accessible thought. There are many ways for Big Tech to achieve their goal of perception management.

Google's search engine hides websites (by deranking them) and demonetizes content and sites that are not to its liking. At one point Google publicly floated the idea of deranking and delisting certain sites (they mentioned Russian sites RT and Sputnik), but they later did a U-turn and claimed they would not be doing that. Obviously, it is easily within their power to tamper with algorithms to include or exclude anything they want, and virtually no one would ever know the search results were being skewed. Google was caught doing this in favor of Hillary Clinton during the 2016 US presidential elections. Indeed, after the firing of ex-Google employee James Damore (who initiated a class-action lawsuit due to his dismissal), and subsequent whistleblowers such as Zachary Vorhies[199] (who leaked Google docs to the public), we have proof that ideological bias is already coded into Google's algorithms as a result of their orthodoxy and culture (left-wing and promoting diversity at all costs). Breitbart did an article series[200] on how former Google employees stated that there were efforts inside Google to demote anything non-PC (not politically correct, more below) from its search results. Breitbart also reported[201] that

---

[199] https://thefreedomarticles.com/google-documents-leaked-prove-censoring-election-tampering/

[200] www.breitbart.com/tech/2017/08/08/former-google-employee-there-are-efforts-to-demote-anything-non-pc-from-search-results/

[201] www.breitbart.com/tech/2018/01/10/googles-fact-checking-feature-almost-exclusively-targets-conservative-media/

Google's fact-checking almost exclusively targets conservative or right-wing media (just as Facebook's does).

Google is much more than just a search engine, email provider and internet giant. It's not even just a monopoly. Google is trying to become the ultimate arbiter of truth. Former CEO Eric Schmidt said[202] that it was a "bug" that when you use Google, you get different search results for the same question, rather than one right answer. Schmidt has also admitted that Google is "trying to augment humanity." This leads into the transhumanism agenda (see chapter 11). Google could be broken up by antitrust laws, but why would the NWO controllers want that? Google is incredibly useful to the Surveillance State. The article *Google's True Origin Partly Lies in CIA and NSA Research Grants for Mass Surveillance*[203] states:

Intelligence-gathering may have been their world, but the Central Intelligence Agency (CIA) and the National Security Agency (NSA) had come to realize that their future was likely to be profoundly shaped outside the government ... In fact, the internet itself was created because of an intelligence effort: In the 1970s, the agency responsible for developing emerging technologies for military, intelligence, and national security purposes—the Defense Advanced Research Projects Agency (DARPA)—linked four supercomputers to handle massive data transfers. It

---

202 https://www.youtube.com/watch?v=vrKs_vduiKU

203 https://qz.com/1145669/googles-true-origin-partly-lies-in-cia-and-nsa-research-grants-for-mass-surveillance/

handed the operations off to the National Science Foundation (NSF) a decade or so later, which proliferated the network across thousands of universities and, eventually, the public.

Did the CIA directly fund the work of Brin and Page, and therefore create Google? No. But were Brin and Page researching precisely what the NSA, the CIA, and the intelligence community hoped for, assisted by their grants? Absolutely ... The CIA and NSA funded an unclassified, compartmentalized program designed from its inception to spur the development of something that looks almost exactly like Google.

Google was working on Project Dragonfly to tailor their search engine capability to Chinese-style censorship. Dragonfly allegedly contained code that required users to log in to perform searches while censoring the search results for certain terms. It also tracked a user's location and shared the data with a Chinese partner, meaning that ultimately it would end up in the hands of the ruling Communist government. Users' movements would be stored, along with the IP address of their device and links they clicked on. Additionally, content deemed sensitive or inappropriate by the Chinese government would be encoded not to return any search results, such as content related to democracy, human rights and peaceful protest. *The Intercept*[204] reported:

Previously undisclosed details about the plan, obtained by The Intercept on Friday, show that

---

[204] https://theintercept.com/2018/09/14/google-china-prototype-links-searches-to-phone-numbers/

Google compiled a censorship blacklist that included terms such as "human rights," "student protest," and "Nobel Prize" in Mandarin.

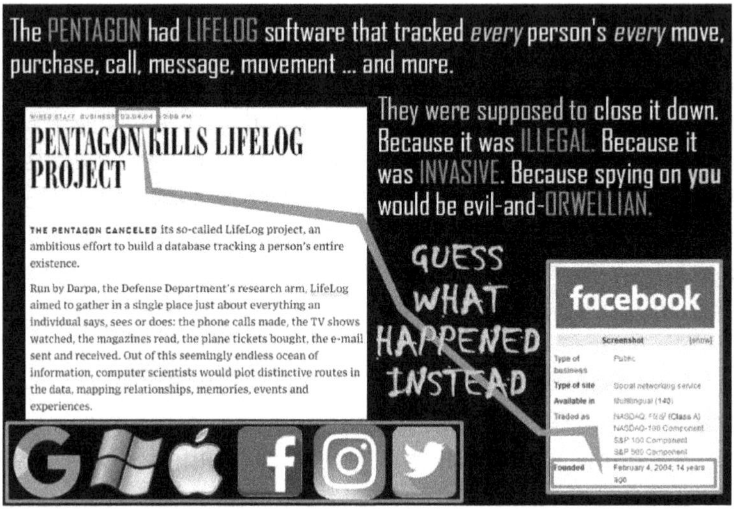

Project Dragonfly fits right in with Sesame Credit, the draconian Chinese social credit system which ranks every Chinese person on the basis of how obedient, conforming and "good" they are. It is based on the principle of once untrustworthy, forever restricted; and it punishes people who don't have a high enough score by preventing them buying plane or train tickets. It's the gamification of control and part of the alarming trend of how technology is being adapted not to give us more freedom but to seal our prison cells.

In late 2019, Google-owned YouTube introduced a clever new clause in their agreements with their content creators. The theme was "commercially viable." YouTube told its creators that it had the right to terminate their accounts, or at least demonetize their channels, if it deemed their content to be not commercially viable. While YouTube is a profit-maximizing business, this move has the obvious cover-your-ass approach because now YouTube has the perfect excuse to censor people and claim it was just because their content was boring. It's especially Machiavellian because the content creator would never really know why they were censored, since YouTube has been known to manipulate the view count on its videos.

Meta/Facebook is no different to Google with its MIC roots. It was officially and "coincidentally" started on the exact same day (February 4, 2004) when LifeLog finished. LifeLog was a surveillance operation dreamt up by the ultra-sinister DARPA (Defense Advanced Research Projects Agency), the Pentagon's technological development arm, which is creating killer robots, death rays, autonomous swarms of aggressive nanobots and all sorts of lovely things for humanity. Facebook is the ultimate tool for self-surveillance whereby a person will willingly give up their data and privacy without realizing what this really means. Facebook has been caught conducting giant experiments on behalf of the military to alter people's feeds/timelines (and study the results, which affected people's moods). That is incredible censorship on an unprecedented level. Facebook deletes entire accounts and/or rolls out "fake news checkers" (more on this later) who are massively biased towards the political left. Some of these fake news checkers are even linked to NWO families such as the Rothschilds who fund the SPLC (Southern Poverty Law Center), which also happens to decide what qualifies as "hate speech." Jon Rappoport writes[205]:

The big infusion of cash that sent Mark Zuckerberg and his fledgling college enterprise on their way came from Accel Partners, in 2004. Jim Breyer, head of Accel, attached a $13 million rocket to Facebook, and nothing has ever been the same. Earlier that same year, a man named Gilman Louie joined the board of the National Venture Capital Association of America (NVCA). The chairman of NVCA [was] Jim Breyer. Gilman Louie happened to be the first CEO of the important CIA start-up, In-Q-Tel. In-Q-Tel was founded in 1999, with the express purpose of funding companies that could develop technology the CIA would use to "gather data." That's not the only connection between Jim Breyer and the CIA's man, Gilman Louie. In 2004, Louie went to work for BBN Technologies, headed up by Breyer. Dr. Anita Jones also joined BBN at that time. Jones had worked for In-Q-Tel and was an adviser to DARPA, the Pentagon's technology department that helped develop the Internet.

If you still think these Big Tech giants are "private companies" then consider this. They all swap people at the very top. Like many big companies, there is a revolving door at the top between Facebook and the US federal government. Nathan Gleicher, Sarah Feinberg, Joel Benenson, Aneesh Raman, David Recordon, Meredith Carden, David Ploufe, Josh W. Higgins, Lauryn Ogbechie, Danielle Cwirko-Godycki, Sarah Pollack, Ben Forer, Bonnie Calvin and Juliane

---

205 https://www.activistpost.com/2018/08/social-media-censorship-here-are-the-deep-basics.html

Sun are all former Obama administration staffers, advisers and campaign associates who joined Facebook's ranks.

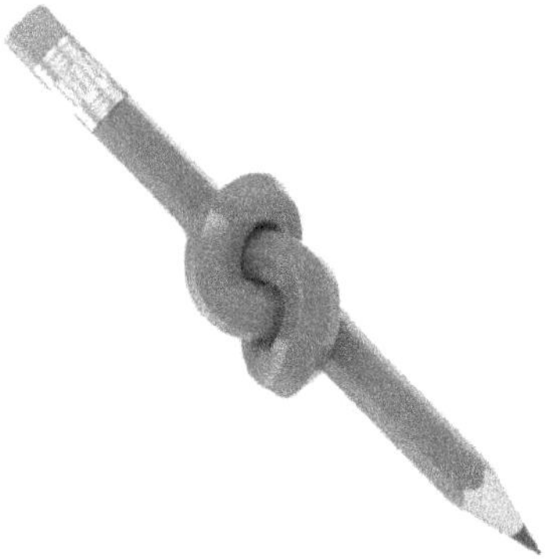

Meanwhile, Twitter embarked upon shadowbanning (aka stealth banning, ghost banning or comment ghosting), meaning blocking a user or their content from an online community without the user realizing they have been banned, in addition to the outright banning of people from its platform and deleting accounts. In a first in world history, Twitter actually prevented a sitting US president (Donald Trump) from tweeting from December to January 2021 many times and then actually banned him completely using the excuse he had incited violence. The message form these NWO-controlled Big Tech companies is clear: it doesn't matter if you are president of the most powerful nation on Earth: if you speak out against the agenda, you will be silenced.

Amazon has been caught banning certain books from being sold on its platform. In 2015 when it decided to ban Jim Fetzer's book *No One Died at Sandy Hook*, which exposed the false flag mass shooting.

A common thread among all these Big Tech companies is that they want the best of both worlds. They want it both ways: they want to be neutral platforms (not responsible for content), and they want to be publishers (who curate and edit content). They have been deceitfully playing both sides, claiming they are either mere platforms or publishers, depending on the situation. Lawsuits are pending to take the matter further. Will the people be able to force them to stick to one of these categories rather than just using whatever rules and regulations suit them?

We Have to Censor You Because of ... Terrorism, Hate Speech and Fake News

In the so-called liberal West, authorities have to pretend they care about the free flow of information and ideas, so they needed a pretext to clamp down on dissenting views without being viewed as unpopular. Terrorism has served its purpose of scaring people and justifying illegal wars and laws and to a degree has also helped the authorities with censorship. The idea of "hate speech" helped even more, for it has effectively turned insults into something illegal. Government was set up to be a legal arbiter, not a moral one; so turning something that could be said to be immoral into something illegal is a gross overstep of power. Yet not many people seem to have noticed. Hate speech is also deliberately vague. This is how oligarchs get the power to decide what does and doesn't constitute hate speech, therefore giving them the power they always wanted to shut dissidents down. However, even hate speech has had to make way for something even more ambiguous. Enter fake news.

Fighting "fake news" is the new pretext given by

the ruling cabal in many nations to enact censorship via the back door. Amid the rallying cries of "We must fight fake news!" numerous nations all over the world (Egypt, France, Germany, Indonesia, Brazil, Italy, Singapore, Malaysia, Philippines, Russia, India and of course China) have either passed or attempted to pass legislation to ban political content on the web that the government deems to be fake news. Some of this legislation has contained clauses punishing journalists with imprisonment for violations. There is hardly a clear and widely accepted definition for the phrase "fake news." It often gets used by people who seek to criticize information they don't like, dismiss allegations against them or even to defend themselves when faced with an unflattering report about themselves. As Glenn Greenwald writes[206]:

Yet, as many have long been warning, few people, if any, ever bothered to define what the term [fake news] actually means. As a result, it's incredibly vague, shifting, and devoid of consistent meaning. Do any news articles that contain false, significant assertions qualify? Is there some intent requirement, and if so, what is it and how is determined (does recklessness qualify)? Can large mainstream outlets such as the Washington Post, Le Monde, and Globo be guilty of publishing "fake news" and thus subject to this censorship, or is it — as one expects — reserved only for small, independent blogs and outlets that lack a powerful corporate presence?

206 https://theintercept.com/2018/01/10/first-france-now-brazil-unveils-plans-to-empower-the-government-to-censure-the-internet-in-the-name-of-stopping-fake-news/

Ill-defined terms that become popularized in political discourse are, by definition, terms of propaganda rather than reliable, meaningful indicators of problems. And invariably, they wreak all kinds of predictable havoc and inevitably give rise to abuses of power. More than anything else, such terms — which, by design, mean whatever the powerful groups wielding them want them to mean — so often produce arbitrary censorship in the name of combatting them. Just consider two similarly ill-defined but popular propagandistic terms — "terrorism" and "hate speech" — which have been appropriated by governments all over the world to justify the most extreme, repressive powers.

The fake war on terror has given the West - especially the US and UK - lots of mileage to suppress its own citizens. Egypt and Saudi Arabia also jumped in on the act with censorship laws based on terrorism. As for hate speech, it has been used to silence all sorts of opinions including those opposing Zionism and Israel's continuous theft and murder against the Palestinians - because if you criticize Israel then you must be anti-semitic, right (even though true Judaism and Zionism are mutually exclusive)?

The Pentagon also launched a new program to fight "viral" news. When you put all these nebulous but lethal terms together – national security, war on terror, terrorism, hate speech and fake news – it pretty much allows the government to do anything it wants, anytime, anywhere. This includes searching you, robbing you, jailing you and, yes, killing you.

Censorship is also being administered by smaller companies that play a key part in the infrastructure of the internet (e.g., web hosting companies, email marketing companies, etc.) *WakingTimes.com* ran the article *A Snapshot of the Internet Kill Switch in 2018*[207] which included this list:

1.) "Violation of Community Guidelines" (The Outright Ban) – First and foremost is the now ubiquitous, blanket statement that users of corporate media platforms get when their pages, channels, accounts are shut down. It never points to anything specific, or offers an opportunity to right the transgression. It is legalese for 'f$#k off, you're not wanted around here."

2.) Shadow Banning – This is the act of allowing a persona non grata to continue to use a corporate media platform, but not allowing their posts or content to actually be seen by anyone.

3.) Throttling of Reach – Businesses and media organizations across the board have been seeing a steady and dramatic decline in their ability to reach their audience. The number of page likes really means absolutely nothing, and while these people have signed up to receive content from you, the social media platforms make sure that only a tiny fraction of your audience actually gets what they signed up for.

4.) Blacklisting Domains – Platforms like Facebook have demonstrated the ability to prevent a specific

---

[207] https://www.wakingtimes.com/2018/08/16/a-snapshot-of-the-internet-kill-switch-in-2018/

domain from getting any reach.

5.) Deleting Posts and Content – If a particular post or piece of content is unwanted on a platform, for whatever reason, it can be deleted.

6.) Flagging Content as 'Fake News' – This one is particularly insidious because social media platforms are using corporate news organizations like ABC and discredited private companies like Snopes to supposedly fact check independent content. These labels are often erroneous and can sometimes be appealed, but the flag itself damages the content providers reputation and reach.

7.) Downranking and Search Indexing – Google is using their algorithms to target and hide information from search results.

8.) Time Outs for 'Bad Behavior' – Twitter, Facebook and others will often time out a page or page admin for violating some hidden policy. Admins will be locked out of their pages for set periods or have their functionality reduced, thereby preventing them from posting content and reaching or communicating with their audiences.

9.) Shutting Down Websites and Confiscation of Content – WordPress.com is now shutting down sites hosted with its hosting services, again for the ambiguous 'violation of community guidelines.' Page owners are locked out without warning and are prohibited from accessing their content or backups of their sites, effectively stealing intellectual property from people.

10.) Shutting Down Business Services – Services such as Mailchimp, Spotify, Disqus and a variety of ad networks are now demonstrating the willingness to cease doing business with organizations for political reasons. This is one of the most insidious ones, because it goes beyond content censorship and aims to shut people out of their legal right to conduct business."

Censorship Via the Pretext of Copyright and IP: Banning Hyperlinks and Memes!?

There are many methods the free-speech gestapo have conjured up to restrict you. There's another back-door route to censor the public. I refer to the efforts to restrict the free flow of information by claiming to protect IP (Intellectual Property), which includes patents and copyright. Europe is leading the way here. In 2016, the highest court in the European Union heard arguments[208] to ban hyperlinks. The EU dictators want a law to ban you from linking to other content and sites on the internet! What's coming next? Wait for it ... a law requiring that we ask the government the permission to breathe? It is no understatement to say that linking to other sites is one of the key foundational mechanisms of the entire internet. It's a basic building block of the web. Independent journalist Matt Drudge warned this was coming[209] in October 2015 when he revealed that

---

[208] www.prisonplanet.com/highest-eu-court-considers-criminalizing-website-hyperlinks.html

[209] www.infowars.com/matt-drudge-copyright-laws-could-outlaw-linking-to-websites/

copyright laws could ban hyperlinking, and that he was told by a Supreme Court justice that *"they've got the votes now to enforce copyright law."* Then, in March 2019, the Council of the European Union passed the very controversial and freedom-deleting Article 13 which severely restricts content creators and even bans memes! This kind of legislation justifies itself under the rubric of defending IP rights, but the real game plan is to restrict freedom of speech and freedom of expression because exposure is what the controllers fear the most. The EU then topped all of this off by further mandating that Facebook must remove content globally if it violates European law.

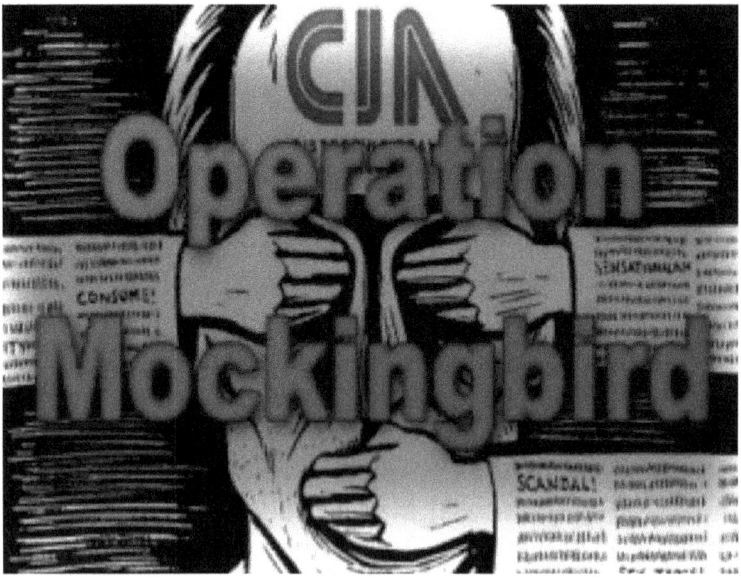

American Censorship: The Mockingbird That Doesn't Sing

Operation Mockingbird, as discussed in chapter 2,

was a CIA Project that began around the late 1940s/ early 1950s, led by Frank Wisner, Cord Meyer and Allen Dulles – the latter being the notorious CIA director who was the ringleader of the men who killed JFK. Of course, control of the media is a central component in any would-be tyrant's agenda; it is no surprise that such a scheme has been outlined in key conspiracy documents such as the *Protocols of the Learned Elders of Zion* (as covered in chapter 2), the ten planks of Communism and also in Orwell's *1984*. By 1975 the control of the press in America by the CIA was so obvious that Senator Frank Church launched an investigation into it.

The Agency's relationship with [The New York] Times was by far its most valuable among newspapers, according to CIA officials. [It was] general Times policy ... to provide assistance to the CIA whenever possible.

– The CIA and the Media, by Carl Bernstein

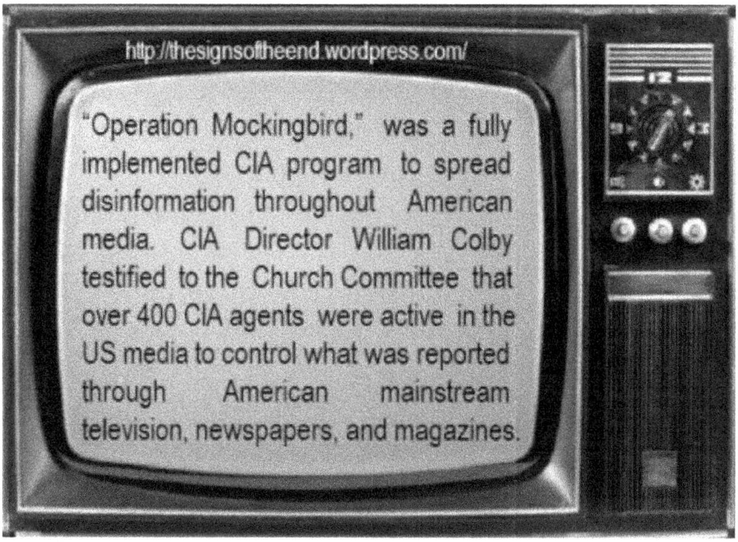

The Mockingbird has never died. The evidence indicates that censorship in America was worse under Obama[210] than before. In 2015, the US dropped to forty-ninth place in the world for press freedom[211], behind Malta, Niger, Burkina Faso, El Salvador, Tonga, Chile and Botswana. In 2017 the US was still in forty-third place. Meanwhile, the CIA continues to control foreign journalists, such as the ones in Germany, and bribes them to write anti-Russian propaganda, as revealed by the late Udo Ulfkotte[212]. Udo admitted he was *"educated to lie and betray, not to tell the truth to the public ... by the CIA."*

Of course, not by chance, the MSM has become incredibly centralized. The many brands and channels are just a trick to make you believe you have a diversity of viewpoints when you don't. The Overton Window is set; lively debate is allowed within its very narrow confines, but nothing outside its scope is permitted. Around 90 percent of the US media was controlled by fifty media companies in 1983, then six in 2011 and then five in 2017. However, in many ways this is moot, since globally all the information comes from just three sources: Reuters, AP (Associated Press) and AFP (Agence France-Presse). Researchers in the past (such as Eustace Mullins) have reported that the Rothschilds

---

210 www.washingtonsblog.com/2015/05/obama-is-more-hostile-towards-the-press-than-any-president-in-history.html

211 https://theintercept.com/2015/02/12/u-s-drops-49th-world-press-freedom-rankings-second-lowest-ever/

212 https://www.youtube.com/watch?v=w5eJXXhwG5I

either partially or wholly own Reuters and AP. Whenever you see a story in the MSM, pause, take a breath and ask yourself why. Here is a key quote from *The Propaganda Multiplier*[213] paper by Dr. Konrad Hummler, Swiss banking and media executive:

Therefore, you always have to ask yourself: Why do I get this specific information, in this specific form, at this specific moment? Ultimately, these are always questions about power.

Not Just Political Censorship

But it's more than just political speech that's being censored. Look at the massive amount of censorship that exists in the area of health, medicine and nutrition. Big Pharma is given free rein to say anything it wants, yet makers of natural health products can't truthfully say what a health product does or what effects it has. Often, they can't show testimonials either, thanks to the free speech gestapo at the FDA. All the health censorship is obviously designed to protect the Rockefeller-Big Pharma monopoly on drugs and to prevent people from knowing the truth about natural alternatives so they can take their health into their own hands. I will present various health solutions in chapter 13, some of which have been heavily suppressed.

Predictably, Google and other large companies

---

[213] https://swprs.org/the-propaganda-multiplier/?fbclid=IwAR25IlQH8nTnOpDt6ETjQn9ff-5p4kj5L0gc49DQwXVQpiZObGVibMhdEi4

also decided to target conspiracy theories[214]. It was always going to happen. Now, the term weaponized by the CIA in the 1960s to discourage critical thinking will become the gift that keeps on giving. The NWO controllers can simply designate anything nonmainstream as a "conspiracy theory" and it will disappear down the memory hole. The writing is on the wall. In March 2018, YouTube announced[215] it would be providing "information cues" and linking to Wikipedia in an attempt to help educate viewers. Perception management at its finest.

INTERNAL CENSORSHIP

External censorship is indeed a massive problem in today's world; however, the more insidious problem is internal censorship or self-censorship. To understand this, we have to tackle the rise of one of the most cunning censorship techniques concocted by the NWO manipulators yet: political correctness (PC).

Political Correctness – The Cunning New Form of Censorship

Political correctness is about language control. And language control is thought control. Period. The rise of modern political correctness (PC) is a great example of the cunning way in which social

[214] https://www.activistpost.com/2017/08/google-youtube-update-quality-rating-guidelines-include-conspiracy-theories.html

[215] https://www.wired.com/story/youtube-will-link-directly-to-wikipedia-to-fight-conspiracies/

engineers operate. Political correctness is soft censorship. It is intolerance disguised as tolerance. As George Carlin said, it is *"fascism pretending to be manners."* It is running amok not just in universities but now almost everywhere in society. Just as Orwell laid out so precisely in *1984*, political correctness is the Newspeak which is threatening to limit our ability to freely speak and think by reducing the number of available words in our vocabulary.

PC is based on the nonexistent "right" to not be offended. When you look at the twisted contortions the PC crowd is insisting people go through to rid their language of anything "offensive", it has entered the theater of the absurd. Political correctness dictates what you can and can't say, based on how "offensive" a word is. Right off the bat there are several problems with this. Firstly, who are the commissars, officials or authorities who are granting themselves power by getting to decide what ranks as "offensive"?

Secondly, since when did "feeling offended" or "having your feelings hurt" become such an important issue that it legally justifies restricting everyone's freedom? Last time I checked, freedom of speech was a genuine and legitimate human right (enshrined in the legal documents of many countries), whereas the "right to not feel offended" is imaginary.

Thirdly – and most importantly – just as beauty is in the eye of the beholder, so too is "feeling offended" in the realm of the beholder. Words are words. Each person is in charge of their own emotions. Choose to ignore, respond or react to words in any manner you wish, but don't blame someone else for your emotional state. You are in control of your own state of consciousness. To blame someone else because you feel angry, offended or upset shows an abandonment of responsibility and a lack of emotional and spiritual maturity. Since when did we humans become such crybabies that we couldn't stand hearing or being called a word, a name, a label or a phrase?

As always, there's more to the story here. Political correctness has roots in Marxism and Communism. Wikipedia[216] notes that "*In the early-to-mid 20th century, the phrase 'politically correct' was associated with the dogmatic application of Stalinist doctrine, debated between Communist Party members and Socialists.*" However, it goes back further to the Frankfurt school (Institute for Social Research) in Germany, which was set up in 1923. The Frankfurt school was a think tank for social engineering, aiming to spread collectivism (or its offshoots of socialism, Marxism and Communism) around the world. As this article from the Schiller Institute[217] states:

---

216 https://en.wikipedia.org/wiki/Political_correctness

217 www.schillerinstitute.org/fid_91-96/921_frankfurt.html

The task of the Frankfurt School, then, was first, to undermine the Judeo-Christian legacy through an "abolition of culture" (Aufhebung der Kultur in Lukacs' German); and, second, to determine new cultural forms which would increase the alienation of the population, thus creating a "new barbarism."

It goes on to point out those funding the Frankfurt school:

Although the Institute for Social Research started with Comintern [Communism International] support, over the next three decades its sources of funds included various German and American universities, the Rockefeller Foundation, Columbia Broadcasting System, the American Jewish Committee, several American intelligence services, the Office of the U.S. High Commissioner for Germany, the International Labour Organization, and the Hacker Institute, a posh psychiatric clinic in Beverly Hills.

So we have reference to the Rockefellers funding the Frankfurt school, and it is well known that the Rothschilds funded the rise of Marxism[218]:

Nathan Rothschild had given Marx two checks for several thousand pounds to finance the cause of Socialism. The checks were put on display in the British Museum, after Lord Lionel Walter Rothschild, a trustee, had willed his museum and library to them.

Both of these key NWO families are thus

---

218 antinewworldorder.blogspot.com/2007/10/who-was-karl-marx.html

implicated in the rise of Marxism, the Frankfurt school and political correctness. Interestingly, many researchers have pointed out that political correctness is part of a broader movement of cultural Marxism, which is the subversion of a country's culture with collectivist ideology, as opposed to the more direct political version.

Yuri Bezmenov[219], a former Soviet KGB agent, said that "ideological subversion" would change the perception of reality of every American. He outlined how there was a slow brainwashing process taking place to change the individualistic culture of the West, consisting of:

1. Demoralization (covert, 15 to 50 years) (basically completed);
2. Destabilization (overt, 2 to 5 years);
3. Crisis (6 weeks);
4. Violent Change and Normalization (can take years, goes on forever).

All this was with the aim of making the West collectivist. The question is: how much has it worked?

219 https://www.youtube.com/watch?v=AAYQ-rfj1CI

Whatever good intentions political correctness may have had in trying to stop homophobia, racism, sexism and discrimination of any kind, it has long passed the threshold of absurdity. Consider the following examples[220] of what the PC crowd (the "progressives" who gained a foothold during the 1990s and the Clinton/Gore years, and who have taken over the US Left/Democratic Party) is trying to make people say with their "bias-free language":

seniors, elders, elderly => "people of advanced age"
overweight, obese => "people of size"
rich => "people of material wealth"
American => US citizen

This last one is especially interesting, given that the US government is a corporation which lays claim to the entire United States of America, whereas American denotes a natural-born individual of the Republic (see chapter 15). The PC police also want to eliminate the following words:

male, female, father, mother, too, hard worker, third world, crazy, insane, retarded, gay, tyranny, gypped, illegal alien, fag, ghetto, raghead

and phrases such as "I want to die" and "that test raped me".

Donald Trump was heckled[221] for using the term "anchor baby" by a PC journalist, who evidently

---

220 https://www.youtube.com/watch?v=lMl4klxw-jo

221 https://www.youtube.com/watch?v=xyOxQJNC2Us

expected him to say "the American born child of an undocumented immigrant." What a mouthful. Funnily enough, that PC journalist was breaking his own inane rules, since now we've been told that "American" is disallowed. Remember the "ban bossy" campaign[222]? Grown adults indulging in utter stupidity. More political correctness and language control. How can you *ban* a *word* anyway?

It's not just specific words or phrases that the PC crowd want to obliterate. At some universities, they

222 https://www.youtube.com/watch?v=6dynbzMlCcw

Even Mr. Nonsense makes far more sense than political correctness.

are banning entire ways of *behaving*. Check out these ridiculous university rules (taken from the book *Choosing the Right College 2012-2013*[223]), which have moved beyond speech control into total behavior control:

– Brown University: banned any speech "making people feel angry, impotent and disenfranchised"
– Colby College: banned any speech "leading to loss of self esteem"
– Bryn Mawr College: banned "suggestive looks"

---

223 https://books.google.com/books?id=9FA6AwAAQBAJ&pg=PT27&dq=Colby+College+Bryn+Mawr+College:+banned+%22suggestive+looks%22&hl=en&sa=X&ved=0ahUKEwjK2KCD6-zKAhVBFGMKHWKHCEkQ6AEIJjAA

– Haverford College: banned "unwelcome flirtation"
– University of Connecticut: banned "inappropriate laughter"
– West Virginia University: banned the use of words "boyfriend" or "girlfriend" but instead told students they have to use the words "lover" or "partner".

Look what the Grand Valley State University[224] recommends we do to allegedly remove "bias" from our language:

Avoiding Racism and Ageism

Mention a person's race or age only if it is relevant to the story.

Biased: A strange Black man spoke to me at the grocery store.

Better: A strange man spoke to me at the grocery store.

Disability and Disease

Focus on people rather than conditions.

Biased: I met an epileptic on the bus today.

Better: I met a person with epilepsy on the bus today.

Since when is becoming less descriptive equivalent to less discriminatory? Talk about a perversion of straight and ordinary speech! Political correctness is standing reality on its head. Here is a chilling quote from *1984*:

"You haven't a real appreciation of Newspeak,

[224] https://www.gvsu.edu/cms3/assets/C7078FCF-E2C3-F3DD-7F8E1630561E3F3E/bias-free_language.pdf

Winston," he said almost sadly … "In your heart you'd prefer to stick to Oldspeak, with all its vagueness and its useless shades of meaning. You don't grasp the beauty of the destruction of words. Do you know that Newspeak is the only language in the world whose vocabulary gets smaller every year?"

"Don't you see that the whole aim of Newspeak is to narrow the range of thought? In the end we shall make thoughtcrime literally impossible, because there will be no words in which to express it …"

All words are potentially offensive. Every word could potentially be associated with something "bad," so every word could come under the scrutiny of the PC police. Slurs, insults and derogatory language have always existed ever since humans could speak. You can't just annihilate them. Even the concepts of "microaggression" and "hate speech" are failed notions, trying to make "having your feelings hurt" or "getting offended" morally or legally equivalent to harassment. There is no equivalence: just remember, sticks and stones may break my bones, but names will never hurt me.

I encourage anyone who has even a mild interest in a free humanity with complete freedom of speech, and total freedom of thought, to resist political correctness with every fiber of your being. If you are concerned about hurting people's feelings unnecessarily, you can always find ways to express something more gently but still truthfully. In those situations, how you speak (e.g. your tone and intention) matters more than what you say.

We don't need speech police to tell us what we can and can't say – or can and can't think. We don't need to go through convoluted verbal gymnastics and mental masturbation just to say what we think or express ourselves. It's time for those hiding behind "feeling offended" to grow up. Stop demanding those around you change because of your lack of maturity. Stop trying to hijack everyone's else freedom because of your timidity. Just as beauty is in the eye of the beholder, offense is in the mind, attitude and reaction of the beholder.

A message just in for those pushing political correctness and thought control. Please fuck off – and I mean that in the most respectful way because I certainly wouldn't want to offend anyone.

It's time to call a spade a spade. We need the spirit of straight talking. The answer to bad speech is more speech.The best ideas and the truth float to the top in a free and open marketplace of ideas. We need the courage to speak truth to power, not to go in the opposite direction and become afraid of saying anything. The real agenda of political correctness is to stifle objective investigation and free speech. Ultimately, it is to eliminate criticism of the NWO manipulators under the guise of stopping "hate speech" and making everything fair and equal.

Final Thoughts

Freedom and democracy only exist within the Western empire to keep up appearances. The NWO controllers have long figured how to control and manipulate the people while giving them the appearance of being free – it's much more effective that way because when people believe they are free, they won't rebel. Meanwhile, the truth is that human minds are hackable. Perception can be managed via narrative control.

Although this topic of censorship is a sad one, there is a positive and fundamental truth underlying this issue. Authorities only censor information because *they* can't handle the truth, not the reverse as it is commonly thought. Governments around the world engage in censorship because they are afraid, deadly afraid, of how the free flow of information could undermine their power base. At one level, they don't trust people to read for themselves, think for themselves and judge the news for themselves. At another level, they fear the exposure of their secrets and corruption.

Truth will always be more powerful than lies. And ultimately, a lie can only be censored and can only exist for so long until it is uncovered, exposed, disbelieved and tossed away. Today, we live in an age of uncovering lies and promoting the truth as has never happened before.

Watch out any time politicians invent a new talking point term which is vague and indefinable. That vagueness can be used against you. Fighting fake news is a joke. People are people. As long as humans have had free will and the ability to speak or write, there has always been the possibility of people lying, omitting, distorting or making false claims. It's part of being alive to develop your discernment and work out what is true or false. Never allow government to pretend it can do this, for the result will always be that the ruling class filters out what it doesn't want you to know out of self-interest and a desire for more power and control.

Chapter 8 – Operation Coronavirus

At the end of 2019 and the beginning of 2020, the entire world was subject to a far-reaching operation that became unique in recorded human history. I refer to the fake pandemic known as COVID-19, or as I prefer to call it, Operation Coronavirus. The NWO conspirators managed to get something like one third to one half of the entire world shut down over a virus that has never been proven to exist and a disease whose CFR (Case Fatality Rate) was around 0.1 percent, *on par with the seasonal flu*. The lingering, rights-violating, small-business destroying and dehumanizing effect of COVID (and I'm not talking about the alleged virus or disease itself) will be felt forever as it was planned to be. It was brilliantly (from the conspirators' point of view) executed to justify an acceleration of all the NWO agendas they had been wanting to implement. How did they pull this off? I will answer that, but first, let's cover some important background.

To make sense of the coronavirus pandemic, or rather *scamdemic*, it is useful to know the history of bioweapons around the world, including Japan's Unit 731, Nazi bioweapons programs and the US programs at Fort Detrick, Maryland, and Plum Island, the latter of which actually used Nazi scientists brought into the US after WWII under Operation Paperclip. However, COVID is unique in that the evidence shows that the NWO conspirators didn't even need a bioweapon or a real virus to convince the world to follow their plan. However, before we get to that, let's take a brief look at the history.

As previously discussed, Operation Paperclip was the program whereby Nazi scientists and technicians were smuggled into the US to give their new nation their technical expertise in exchange for their lives. Many Nazi Paperclip scientists went on to work in the US Military-Intelligence Community, especially at NASA and the CIA. Dr. Erich Traub worked under Heinrich Himmler (the second-highest-ranking Nazi just under Hitler). During WWII, Traub oversaw a program where the Nazis sprayed occupied Soviet territory with viruses from planes. Traub was instrumental in setting up research on Plum Island. He worked for the US Biological Warfare Program from 1949 to 1953, during which time he consulted with the CIA and also worked at Fort Detrick. The US government would go on to create a biological warfare disease known as Lyme disease (named after the small town in Connecticut) with Traub's help, a disease which has afflicted many people worldwide.

But Lyme Disease is just one small part of the sordid history of bioweapons. After WWII, the US government embarked on a host of bioweapon experiments on its own people, including:

– **Operation Sea-Spray (1950):** this was a secret US Navy experiment where two bacteria, serratia marcescens and bacillus globigii, were sprayed over the San Francisco Bay Area in California;

– **Norfolk Naval Supply Center experiments**

(1951): those running this test dispersed fungal spores to see how they would infect workers unpacking crates in this base in Virginia. Most of the workers were African American. The plan was to test if they were more susceptible to fungal disease than Caucasians;

– **Spraying Chemicals to Test Potential of Biological Weapons (1950s):** in 1997, the National Research Council revealed that the US government used chemicals to test the potential of biological weapons in the 1950s. Zinc cadmium sulfide was dispersed by plane in open-air testing. It was sprayed over many American cities, including St. Louis, Missouri, and Minneapolis, Minnesota;

– **Operation Big Itch (1954):** this experiment was designed to learn whether fleas could be loaded into bombs. It turns out they could. The tests happened just a few years after the Soviets accused the US of dropping canisters full of insects infected with plague and cholera in Korea and China during the Korean War (just as Japan had done against China);

– **Project 112 (1962):** Then US Secretary of Defense Robert McNamara authorized this new program which greatly expanded bioweapons research. One of the most well-known and nefarious tests was in 1966 on the New York subway. Scientists filled light bulbs with bacillus globigii (same bacterium as used in Operation Sea-Spray) and smashed them open on the train tracks. The bacteria traveled all around the subway system, with thousands of people breathing them in.

It is also important to understand all the recent history of USG planning and preparedness for pandemics, ever since the 9/11 false flag attack that occurred in 2001. Just as happened with 9/11, the NWO ruling class and the US government have been carrying out drills or simulations for pandemics for a long time. Astute readers may notice that the phenomenon of the drill "going live" crops up in both drills/exercises/war games (which become false flag attacks) and pandemic preparedness simulations. Here are some highlights, or rather lowlights:

– **Dark Winter (June 2001):** an operation which simulated a biowarfare anthrax attack. By a strange coincidence, such an anthrax attack actually happened after 9/11. Dark Winter not only predicted the 2001 anthrax attacks, but some of its participants had clear foreknowledge of those attacks;

– **Model State Emergency Health Powers Act (drafted in 2001):** MSEHPA is a public health act originally drafted by the CDC (Center for Disease Control and Prevention) with the intention of getting the fifty US states to enact similar legislation. It includes sweeping and draconian legislation as a response to epidemics, pandemics and bioterrorism. It is crucial to realize that the CDC owns patents on several vaccines so functions as a giant vaccine company as a much as a governmental agency;

– **Project BioShield Act (2004):** The Project Bioshield Act was an act passed by Congress calling for $5 billion for purchasing vaccines that would be used in the event of a bioterrorist attack;

– **The Public Readiness and Emergency Preparedness Act (2005):** The Public Readiness and Emergency Preparedness (PREP) Act, codified at 42 USC §247d-6d[225], gives the Secretary of the Department of Health and Human Services (HHS) the power to waive legal liability for corporations producing "covered countermeasures" (i.e. vaccines) in the case of a public health emergency;

– **Lock Step (Rockefeller Foundation Paper, 2010):** this Rockefeller Foundation paper entitled *Scenarios for the Future of Technology and International Development*[226] outlines a scenario where a pandemic has hit, and the governments of the world use it to expand their authority and increase their grip on power. Although the authors of the paper try to claim they are just imagining not predicting the future, given the immense role of the Rockefeller family bloodline and Rockefeller Foundation in pushing the NWO global government, this is a ruse to cover their active planning for crisis scenarios that they know will happen. It is also a fine example of predictive programming. One of the scenarios of the paper is called "Lock Step", a phrase with negative overtones and suggestive of soldiers, military and fascism.

– **USNORTHCOM Branch Plan 3560 (January 2017):** this unclassified US military paper[227] outlined

---

225 https://www.law.cornell.edu/uscode/text/42/247d-6d

226 www.nommeraadio.ee/meedia/pdf/RRS/Rockefeller%20Foundation.pdf

227 https://www.scribd.com/document/454422848/Pentagon-Influenza-Response

the planned and coordinated response to an infectious disease outbreak;

– **Cybersecurity and Infrastructure Security Agency Act (2017):** similar to section 817 of the Patriot Act (the Expansion of the Biological Weapons Statute which gave the USG immunity from violating its own biological weapons laws), this act reorganizes the Department of Homeland Security's National Protection and Programs Directorate (NPPD) into a new agency: the Critical Infrastructure and Cyber Security Agency. Reporter Janet Phelan wrote[228] that this new act further cements the USG's *"ability to covertly deploy through water, which is defined as critical infrastructure, any biological or chemical agent and claim not only immunity but also deny any legal right to protest this through the legal system. Given the covert nature of this delivery system, it is to be expected that the US would claim that the resultant mass deaths to be attributable to a naturally occurring pandemic."*;

– **Clade X Exercise (2018):** like Event 201 below, Clade X was a pandemic tabletop exercise hosted by the Johns Hopkins Center for Health Security where a pandemic resulted in 900 million deaths due to a virus that causes respiratory illness similar to the common cold and is spread by close contact or touching contaminated objects;

– **Crimson Contagion 2019 Functional Exercise**

---

[228] https://www.activistpost.com/2018/11/trump-signs-bill-to-further-protect-critical-infrastructure-including-pandemic-delivery-system.html

(August 2019): this USG operation[229] prophetically simulated a viral outbreak that began in China and landed in Chicago; and

– **Event 201 (October 2019):** on October 18th, 2019 in New York, the Johns Hopkins Center in partnership with World Economic Forum (WEF) and the Bill and Melinda Gates Foundation hosted *Event 201 – A Global Pandemic Exercise* which was a simulation of a coronavirus pandemic. Attendees included the US CDC, the Chinese CDC, WEF (in partnership with the WHO), Big Pharma reps (e.g. Johnson and Johnson) and others.

NWO frontman Bill Gates was highly visible both before and after the coronavirus outbreak. Gates has used his fortune to push GMOs and vaccines all over the world. He used MSM platforms to preach the need for mandatory vaccines and possible "digital certificates" or "immunity passports" which people would need to travel again after the lockdown. This may even involve some form of human microchipping, whether through digital tattoos or nano-particles in the bloodstream. The human microchipping agenda is a long-held NWO agenda. What are the chances that all these preparedness laws, papers, exercises and events are coincidences and that the NWO controllers didn't know this coronavirus crisis was coming?

So, we know the USG has used bioweapons against its own population. And that brings us now to

---

229 https://www.nbcchicago.com/news/local/crimson-contagion-2019-simulation-warned-of-pandemic-implications-in-us/2243832/

the coronavirus, officially named COVID-19 (COVID for short) and officially caused by SARS-CoV-2. Given not only the long history of governmental biological weapons use, and the fact that the US government carefully planned and prepared for Operation Coronavirus decades in advance, it would be natural to think that COVID was just another bioweapon which has been deliberately engineered and released. However, things are not that clear-cut. In the shadowy world of politics, military, intelligence and bioweapons, things are never as they seem.

There has been a fierce debate over whether COVID is a legitimate health crisis or a manufactured threat. It is important to remember that, either way, such crises are always manipulated by governments in order to expand their powers. So, we will now turn our close attention to the ways in which COVID has been hyped and manipulated to create unprecedented levels of fear. As Secretary of State Mike Pompeo admitted on live TV[230], this has been a "live exercise," which is why I am referring to this whole affair as Operation Coronavirus.

Anatomy of Operation Coronavirus

To summarize, this is how the operation works:

1. The orchestrators ensure they have some ownership of the mass media/MSM: they use this to relentlessly broadcast the narrative, frame the context, hype the fear and control the perception.

230 https://www.youtube.com/watch?v=3Qscuw_3aUk

2. The orchestrators obtain patents for the virus and/or vaccine: There have been several companies that quickly claimed after the coronavirus outbreak that they had already developed the vaccine. The first is Inovio. It was reported on January 24, 2020 that US biotech and pharmaceutical company Inovio received a $9 million grant[231] to develop a vaccine for the coronavirus. Inovio got the money grant from the Coalition for Epidemic Preparedness Innovations (CEPI); however, they already had an existing partnership with CEPI; in April 2018 they got up to $56 million to develop vaccines for Lassa Fever and Middle East Respiratory Syndrome (MERS). CEPI was founded in Davos by the governments of Norway and India, the Wellcome Trust, and some of the participants of Event 201: the Bill and Melinda Gates Foundation and the WEF. CEPI's CEO is the former director of BARDA (US Biomedical Advanced Research and Development Authority) which is part of the HHS. Inovio claimed they developed a coronavirus vaccine *in two hours*. On the surface, such a claim is absurd; what is more likely is that they already had the vaccine because they had foreknowledge that the coronavirus was coming and was about to be unleashed. Two key men involved at Inovio are David Weiner and Dr. Joseph Kim. Weiner was once Kim's university professor. Weiner was involved with developing a vaccine for HIV and zika (which was an earlier pandemic that was hyped to the sky but didn't produce many deaths). Kim was funded by Merck (a large Big Pharma company) and produced something

---

231 https://www.nbcsandiego.com/news/local/local-biotech-company-developing-coronavirus-vaccine/2250034/

called Porcine Circovirus (PCV 1 and PCV 2). Kim served a five-year tenure as a member of the WEF's Global Agenda Council, which was yet another organization pushing the New World Order/One World Government under the banner of Agenda 2030 Global Governance. Weiner is an employee and advisor to the FDA, is considered a DNA technology expert and pioneered a new DNA transference method called electroporation – a microbiology technique which uses an electrical pulse to create temporary pores in cell membranes through which substances like chemicals, drugs or DNA can be introduced into the cell. This technique can be used to administer DNA vaccines, which inject foreign DNA into a host's cells that changes the host's DNA. This means if you take a DNA vaccine, *you are allowing your DNA to be changed*. Vaccines already cause disastrous side effects; however, DNA vaccines are taking it to a whole new level. Not coincidentally, electroporation uses pulsed waves. Guess what else uses pulsed waves? 5G wireless EMF radiation, which has been a significant factor in Operation Coronavirus (though not the sole cause).

Another company, the Pirbright Institute, owns a patent for a coronavirus strain (not SARS CoV2 or COVID-19) that could be used to develop a vaccine[232]. Guess who partially owns them? Bill Gates. As you can read on their site[233] Pirbright is being supported in their vaccine development endeavors by a British company Innovate UK, who

232 https://patents.justia.com/patent/10130701

233 https://www.pirbright.ac.uk/our-science/livestock-viral-diseases/viral-glycoproteins

also funds and supports the rollout of 5G[234]. Innovate UK ran a competition in 2018 with a £15 million share out to any small business that could produce vaccines for "epidemic" potential.

Then there is also MIGAL (The Galilee Research Institute)[235] organization in Israel that has claimed to be on the cusp of developing the first vaccine for COVID, which is interesting given Israel's leading role in false flag operations, spying, surveillance and other NWO agendas.

Some people recommend that as an investigator you need to "follow the money." This is certainly true to some extent; however, the agendas at play with Operation Coronavirus are much deeper than just money. That said, there is a monetary angle. Where there's fear, there's opportunity. The orchestrators start work developing the vaccine years before they release the virus, so that they can have the vaccine in place when everyone freaks out. This means they can pose as the saviors and make a ton of money when governments around the world flock to buy the vaccine. The orchestrators also influence politicians to pass emergency laws allowing them to "rush" largely untested vaccines quickly to market, and therefore are protected from any liability from the horrendous damages the vaccines will cause.

---

234 https://www.wired-gov.net/wg/news.nsf/articles/Developing+5G+networks+across+the+globe+apply+for+funding+25092019091000?open

235 https://www.jpost.com/health-science/israeli-scientists-in-three-weeks-we-will-have-coronavirus-vaccine-619101

3. The orchestrators ensure funding is already in place for "scientific experts" who will "find" whatever results they are paid to find: true science is not for sale, but junk science is. There are "soul-for-sale" scientists whose brains the orchestrators can buy to publish whatever results they want. These scientists (or shills) will reliably "find" the right result that bolsters the propaganda of the orchestrators.

4. The orchestrators choose a time to launch the pandemic when there are already many background deaths and diseases going around: It is difficult to make up a pandemic completely out of nothing. There has to be something going on in the background that is causing some deaths. So the orchestrators chose wintertime, when the seasonal flu goes around, and many people already get sick.

5. The orchestrators make up a new disease with an unknown or scary-sounding name: the average person had never heard of a coronavirus before, and would have had no clue that "coronavirus" is defined in medical encyclopedias as the common cold. The average person would also never know that according to doctors like Wolfgang Wodarg[236], coronaviruses make up approximate 7 to 15 percent of all viruses found in cases of acute respiratory disease, and therefore many people already have trillions of them in their body at any time, given the human virome is 380 trillion[237]. They choose something new that people know little to

236 https://www.youtube.com/watch?v=p_AyuhbnPOI

237 https://thefreedomarticles.com/deep-down-virus-rabbit-hole-question-everything/

nothing about with a scary or cool-sounding name; that way, most people can't contradict the official narrative when the parrot MSM reporters tell the public how infectious, contagious and deadly it is.

6. The orchestrators frame the context of how bad this is against background deaths: Right from the start, the orchestrators skillfully use the MSM to frame the context. They control the narrative by telling people this virus/disease/pandemic is much worse than anything that's ever happened before. It's all hype, hype, hype. Most people are intellectually lazy. Even with the internet at their fingertips, they won't check the figures or do the thinking required to put the pandemic into its proper context. They want the MSM to spoon feed them and tell them how to think about this new thing. MSM reporters, news readers and anchors dutifully use dramatic faces and tones to impart fear. If necessary, the orchestrators may even go back in time to manipulate past figures to aid their current propaganda (i.e., changing history as Orwell laid out in *1984*).

7. The orchestrators bring in fake "experts" with exaggerated simulation models predicting doom: The next phase is when the orchestrators bring in "science" to bolster their "evidence-based" and "data-driven" image. It's all about perception control. They introduce new buzzwords and buzz phrases like "flatten the curve", "social distancing" and "the new normal." They ensure all their paid lackeys repeat them ad nauseam. They repeat how their approach is evidence based despite the fact that phrase is meaningless when the numbers are so easy to manipulate. Then, they bring in a legion of fake experts (i.e., paid science shills) to say whatever you want. Choose the ones with the direst and most end-times computer simulation models and loudly proclaim this new virus is extraordinary and unprecedented. Predict lots of deaths (recall during the 2005 H5N1 bird flu, the Senior UN System Coordinator predicted[238] it could kill 5 to 150 million people, yet it only killed around 100[239]). Remember how Neil Ferguson of Imperial College in England came out with catastrophic prediction models for COVID deaths in the UK and the US (500,000 British deaths and 2,200,000 American deaths), only to later backtrack[240] once the damage was done and people were in fear? As it turns out, the Gates Foundation gave $79 million to the Imperial College[241].

By the time the whole thing is over, and the actual number of deaths only turns out to be way under 1 percent of the predicted number, no one will remember. And if they do, the orchestrators use Big Tech to censor the truth tellers and the MSM to distract the masses with diversions so no one will pay attention.

---

238 https://en.wikipedia.org/wiki/Global_spread_of_H5N1_in_2005

239 https://en.wikipedia.org/wiki/Human_mortality_from_H5N1

240 https://thefederalist.com/2020/03/26/the-scientist-whose-doomsday-pandemic-model-predicted-armageddon-just-walked-back-the-apocalyptic-predictions/

241 https://www.gatesfoundation.org/How-We-Work/Quick-Links/Grants-Database/Grants/2020/03/OPP1210755

8. The orchestrators manipulate the CFR (Case Fatality Rate): At this point some people will begin to ask about the CFR, so here's what the orchestrators do. They can manipulate the rate in two main ways: increase the numerator (attribute other deaths to this new disease, even if this disease was present in their bodies at death but didn't cause it) and decrease the denominator. To increase the numerator, they relax the laws everywhere to allow doctors to ascribe the cause of death to the new virus, even if it had nothing to do with the actual death. Heart attack? He died from the virus. Lung collapse? She died from the virus. Hit by a truck? Another virus death. To decrease the denominator, they calculate it from the number of confirmed infected cases rather than the estimated infected (that way the number is sure to be lower). Using only confirmed cases will give you a much higher CFR or death rate, around ten to a hundred times higher.

The orchestrators try to censor knowledge of Iceland's tests[242] showing that of COVID-19 positives, ~50 percent of people have mild symptoms and ~50 percent have zero symptoms, that LA County[243] had 40x more people with COVID-19 than

---

242 https://cleantechnica.com/2020/03/21/iceland-is-doing-science-50-of-people-with-covid-19-not-showing-symptoms-50-have-very-moderate-cold-symptoms/

243 https://www.reuters.com/article/us-health-coronavirus-usa-serology/los-angeles-coronavirus-infections-40-times-greater-than-known-cases-antibody-tests-suggest-idUSKBN22234S

previously known, and that Santa Clara County[244] has 50 to 85x more people with COVID-19 than previously known.

Then, the orchestrators have the MSM compare apples with oranges, discussing the seasonal flu CFR (around 0.1 percent, based on estimated infected) juxtaposed with the new killer virus CFR (they try to get it as high as 10 percent, based on confirmed infected). Magic! Naturally, they never share the fact that the death rate for the ordinary seasonal flu from confirmed cases is around 10 percent.

9. The orchestrators balance increasing CFR with increasing cases to show fast and dangerous spread: The orchestrators have a delicate juggling act to perform. They have to get the CFR as high as possible to scare the living daylights out of people, getting them to believe this new killer virus is catastrophic, with a never-before-seen kill rate. However, if they make the denominator too low, people will see that there are not many cases. That won't work, because they also need to create the impression this thing is spreading quickly and uncontrollably.

So, here's what they do. They increase the rate of testing as time goes on to create the perception of fast spread. Remember, the media will use their testing figures, so they start testing slowly then gradually increase it as the engineered pandemic

---

244 https://thefreedomarticles.com/mit-tech-review-smears-study-proving-covid-19-overhyped/

begins to take hold of people's minds. Consequently, the rate of confirmed cases will match the rate of testing; the more tests, the more confirmed cases. This will make it look like the virus is spreading faster than it actually is. For example, at the beginning they may test a hundred people and find ten new cases; then the next day they might test two hundred people and find twenty new cases, then eight hundred people and discover eighty new cases, and so on. The virus is not necessarily spreading; they are just testing more people. However, people will believe the virus is spreading. They can also test in a selective way: if they want to get more cases, then they just test people they are confident already have the disease. They control which stories, nursing homes, districts, cities, states and countries to focus upon with the MSM to mold perception.

10. The orchestrators make the symptoms vague, broad and ill-defined: Cough? Mucus? Fatigue? Trouble breathing? Fever? These kinds of symptoms could mean any one of countless diseases. COVID has been deliberately characterized and defined by unrealistically broad and vague symptoms. This way, people may think they have contracted it when they simply get tired, cough or get a cold. The orchestrators take virtually anything and incorporate it into the narrative. They can collect all the deaths that are happening anywhere in the world and use them for the cause. A fake pandemic doesn't require just one disease or one cause[245]. Horrible air pollution? 5G radiation?

---

245 https://thefreedomarticles.com/covid-19-umbrella-term-fake-pandemic-not-1-disease-cause/

Poor hygiene and sanitation? Chemtrail aerosols causing poisoning? Heavy metal contamination? Industrial pollution? Microplastics causing disease in people's bodies? GMOs leading to organ damage? They can blame anything and everything on the new killer virus. Plus, this allows them to let their corporate and military friends off the hook for their pollution and secret operations destroying the planet.

11. The orchestrators say the pathogen spreads easily via air, food, body fluids and surfaces: Fear is the currency of control. People will be more afraid if they think this new virus can spread from anything – air, food and body fluids. The orchestrators told people it could survive on surfaces for days, weeks even. They stretched the bounds of incredulity, but as they know, people don't think clearly, rationally or intelligently when they are in fear. They made people anxious about basic natural and social activities. They made people completely OCD about everything in their lives, including touching cash[246], which just so happens to bolster the cashless agenda.

12. The orchestrators hype serious cases and young people dying: The orchestrators make sure people don't wake up to the fact that this new pandemic is only affecting the elderly or immuno-compromised people. They hype any deaths of young and healthy people. After all, with Operation Coronavirus, they have had the whole world to choose from. They magnify all the serious cases,

---

[246] https://thefreedomarticles.com/digital-dollar-us-bills-mention-central-bank-digital-currency/

focus on any peaks in the statistics and ignore regions when things calm down or cases are sparse.

13. The orchestrators show pictures of mass graves and forklifts loading dead bodies for effect: They add a touch of Hollywood special effects to the pandemic by showing alleged mass graves and forklifts loading alleged dead bodies into trucks to amplify the fear in minds of the population.

14. The orchestrators pose as the pandemic saviors by introducing a vaccine: This is the corollary from the preparations they set up in step #2. When people are scared and worried, they pose as the knight in shining armor by stepping forward with the "cure" in the form of a patented proprietary vaccine. They pretend they're being super selfless and altruistic by offering it to the public. They don't mention, of course, the fact that the vaccine is a delivery method for microchipping in the form of nano-particles.

15. The orchestrators use their Big Tech friends to censor anything that counters their narrative: Unfortunately for the orchestrators, there will be some level-headed people that will see through the fake pandemic propaganda. Some of them may even be scientists or doctors who will want to publish papers doubting the official narrative. The orchestrators use their friends at Big Tech (Google, Facebook, Twitter and even smaller players like Vimeo) to censor anything that runs counter to official information. Big Tech has carefully crafted policies already in place to protect their users from uncomfortable opinions. The orchestrators can dominate the narrative by flooding it with editors and websites on their payroll, or celebrities and public opinion molders who are too stupid to realize what is happening. They conduct some fake polls to show the majority of the population supports the draconian measures taken.

16. The orchestrators spin the fact the virus or pandemic wasn't that bad by claiming their measures saved the day: When the fake pandemic eventually winds down – as it must – the orchestrators will claim credit for it. They will deflect attention away from the fact it wasn't really that bad and didn't actually kill that many people by claiming it was only their great leadership, intervention, regulations, economic shutdown, lockdowns, quarantines and house arrests that saved the day. Otherwise, it could have been a lot worse. Of course, that is an empty hypothetical claim that can never be disproven, so they usually get away with it unchallenged.

In a nutshell, it's all about perception control. All these steps are possible regardless of how real and dangerous the virus is. Even if the virus turned out to be as bad as the doomsday propagandists said it was, these steps still form the foundation of how the pandemic is "presented" to the public for maximum effect – so that the orchestrators can exploit the crisis to roll out as many agendas as they can and to their fullest effect.

<u>What Is a Virus?</u>

Now, we will turn our attention away from the

history of bioweapons and the manufacturing of the pandemic to the foundational issue at the heart of the COVID-19 phenomenon. What is a virus anyway? Are viruses the infectious killers they have been made out to be?

Behind any pandemic, there are always a long set of assumptions that underpin the medical reports and subsequent political and legal decisions. These assumptions are barely recognizable since they are routinely reported as facts. However, to truly justify everything that has happened all over the world since Operation Coronavirus began – social distancing, surveillance, censorship, lockdowns, quarantines, house arrest, medical martial law, economic crashes, new digital currencies, governmental emergency powers (with mandatory vaccinations and human microchipping slated to come) – those in charge at the Department of Propaganda have to convince you that those assumptions are facts. So, let's take a journey down the rabbit hole to ask the fundamental questions: What is a virus? Can a virus cross from animal to human? Can it cross from human to human? Did you know the CDC admitted that their beloved PCR test is essentially useless, as it doesn't tell you whether a virus is causing disease? Is it 100 percent proven that viruses cause disease in humans anyway? How do the competing theories of germ theory and host theory/terrain theory play into this?

Mainstream Western Medicine (allopathy) developed due to the influence of the Rockefellers,

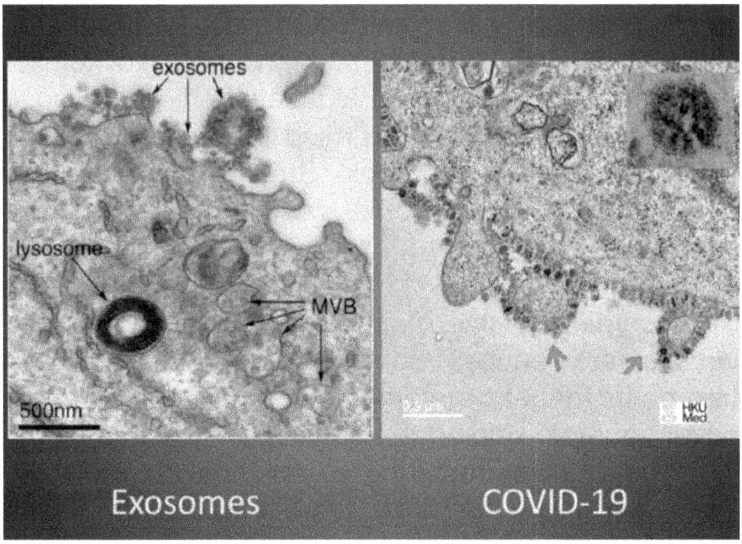

A still slide from a presentation by Dr. Andy Kaufman. Notice the striking similarity between an exosome and a virus.

who created it to help sell their petroleum drugs[247] which became the basis for today's Big Pharma medicines. The Rockefellers and other NWO central banking bloodline families overtook the schools and curricula for medicine and shut down competition like homeopathy, via the Flexner Report[248]. They made sure that allopathy would be purely focused on pharmaceuticals and blocked proper nutritional knowledge from doctors. Since this is the same mainstream medical system that sets the definitions for things like viruses, it's important to begin with a healthy dose of skepticism. This is also the same

---

[247] https://thefreedomarticles.com/western-medicine-rockefeller-medicine/

[248] https://thefreedomarticles.com/flexner-report-rockefeller-ama-takeover/

Rockefeller family that funded the UN (and donated land for its HQ in New York), whose Rockefeller Foundation has co-opted education[249] and whose Rockefeller Foundation released the aforementioned 2010 paper[250] with Lock Step analyzing how governments could/should react to a pandemic scenario.

According to this mainstream scientific mindset, viruses are entities composed of DNA or RNA fragments (genetic material) and encased in a protein cover and/or lipid (fat) envelope. They are not technically alive, requiring a cell host to replicate. They are tiny – far tinier than a bacterium – and unlike a bacterium they are not a cell, so they don't have a respiratory, circulatory or nervous system. The virus is said to be right on the border of the living and the nonliving.

However, there is an important alternative view of the virus. The late primal diet/raw meat advocate Aajonus Vonderplanitz (who died in 2013) gave this fascinating interview[251] during the swine flu hoax of 2009, when everyone was freaking out (not as much as with the coronavirus, but in a similar vein to the

---

[249] https://thefreedomarticles.com/tax-exempt-foundations-rockefeller-fronts/

[250] https://thefreedomarticles.com/2010-rockefeller-foundation-paper-plan-exploit-pandemic/

[251] https://www.youtube.com/watch?v=ctvt0ansKkw

hyped Ebola[252] and zika[253] outbreaks). He claimed the following:

– viruses are created by the body to clean itself when friendly bacteria can no longer break down all the waste;
– all viruses are good viruses, being necessary cellular responses;
– viruses are like a solvent or soap, made by cells to help dissolve and eliminate toxins (a solvent is something that will make the solute [the thing to be dissolved] turn into a solution [liquid]);
– viruses are specific to the cell that created them;
– viruses cannot cross species;
– viruses don't exist outside of bodies; and
– the only way a virus can cross species is if it's made in a factory and injected (i.e., extracted, kept in a lab, genetically altered and modified, weaponized, then made into a vaccine and/or a bioweapon).

Dormant viruses and latent viruses can exist in our bodies all the time without causing disease. The mere presence of a virus in an organism doesn't tell you anything about the health of that organism. It is quite possible that due to all the toxicity in our world (junk food, GMO crops, chlorinated and fluoridated water, poisoned skies), our body has to make a solvent to help us get rid of the toxins. Interestingly, the main points in the interview with Aajonus are also explained in this recent video by Australian Tom

[252] https://thefreedomarticles.com/ebola-hoaxing-it-up/

[253] https://thefreedomarticles.com/zika-or-insecticide-pyriproxyfen-behind-microcephaly-cases/

Barnett[254].

What if this were true? What if viruses have been completely misunderstood and demonized? What if the body is producing viruses in response to toxicity? What if their apparent spreading and replication are due to the body making many of them to clean up a mess?

French scientist Antoine Bechamp (more on him below) did experiments that led him to discover tiny particles which he called microzymas and which others have called protids, somatids or exosomes. These tiny particles are pleomorphic (taking on many shapes) and may well go through a life cycle where they begin as "buds" (which is what the word "germ" means etymologically) or offshoots, and later develop into viruses or bacteria. The fact that microbes can be pleomorphic is a very important concept to understand. This idea is also relevant when it comes to understanding what cancer is and how to heal it naturally[255]. In my article *Inner Terrain vs. Outer Terrain: Which Do You Emphasize for Good Health?*[256] I explain:

Bechamp theorized that germs were actually the chemical byproducts, dead tissue and degenerative aspects of a body's unbalanced state. He stated

---

[254] https://m.facebook.com/story.php?story_fbid=638176716728974&id=100016099539778

[255] https://thefreedomarticles.com/cancer-busting-myths-cancer-microbe-p1/

[256] https://thefreedomarticles.com/inner-terrain-vs-outer-key-good-health/

living entities called microzymas (tiny enzymes) created bacteria in response to host and environmental factors.

. . .

Claiming discovery that the "molecular granulations" in biological fluids were actually the elementary units of life, Béchamp named them microzymas—that is, "tiny enzymes"—and credited them with producing enzymes and were the builders of cells while "evolving" amid favorable conditions into bacteria. Denying that bacteria could invade a healthy animal and cause disease, Béchamp claimed instead that unfavorable host and environmental conditions destabilize the host's native microzymas, whereupon they decompose host tissue by producing pathogenic bacteria.

James Hildreth MD from Johns Hopkins University declared[257]:

The virus is fully an exosome in every sense of the word.

This video[258] which highlighted fake aspects of the coronavirus pandemic also talked of viruses as entities created by the body that are not harmful and are designed to carry waste. The video creator refers to viruses as a "piezoelectrical repair crew", with a polysaccharide coating on their heads, which can

[257] https://rupress.org/jcb/article/162/6/960/33690/When-is-a-virus-an-exosome

[258] https://www.youtube.com/watch?v=3aUhWt8Aj-Y

travel to a damaged cell and facilitate glycolysis (the conversion of sugar into energy). In other words, they go to a cell needing a repair and give it energy (sugar) and electricity (a kind of jump start). According to this viewpoint, blaming a virus for damage is like blaming an innocent helper at the scene of the crime; just because someone saw a crime and came to help does not mean they caused the crime. The situation is similar to the demonization of cholesterol which I discuss in chapter 13 and at this footnote[259]; it turns out that cholesterol is an essential nutrient and at the scene of bodily damage to repair it, not because it caused it. By the way, around eight years ago Berkeley scientists turned harmless viruses into piezoelectric generators[260].

Even if you strongly believe in germ theory (more on this to come), there are some serious problems with the generally accepted method of testing for a virus. It's called the RT-PCR test (Reverse Transcription Polymerase Chain Reaction) test, or PCR for short. The PCR test amplifies a specific region of a DNA strand (the DNA target). It is qualitative not quantitative; in other words, it can tell you if a virus is present or not, but it can't tell you in what quantities. It also can't assess "viral load," and it can't make any accurate assessment about whether the presence of that virus is enough to cause disease. As I pointed out in my article *6 Solid,*

---

[259] https://thefreedomarticles.com/plastic-oils-vs-saturated-fats/

[260] https://www.extremetech.com/extreme/129389-berkeley-scientists-turn-harmless-virus-into-piezoelectric-generator

Scientific Reasons to Assuage Your Coronavirus Panic[261], the CDC (US Center for Disease Control) itself admitted[262] that a positive coronavirus COVID-19 test (using the PCR method) doesn't mean the virus is causing the disease/symptoms you may have. These are the actual words of the CDC:

Positive [test] results are indicative of active infection with 2019-nCoV but do not rule out bacterial infection or co-infection with other viruses. The agent detected may not be the definite cause of disease.

So, is it 100 percent proven that viruses cause disease in humans? Amazingly, no, it is not. Germ theory is just that: a theory. For those wanting a more technical explanation of this alternative understanding of viruses, check out Dr. Thomas Cowan[263], Dr. Andrew Kaufman and especially Dr. Stefan Lanka. Kaufman gave interviews with Crrow777[264] and Richie from Boston[265] where he elaborated upon the idea that viruses have never been proven to cause disease. Both Cowan and Kaufman discuss the tests that were done after the 1918 Spanish Flu (an outbreak which it turns out was caused by EMFs/electrification and/or vaccines[266])

---

[261] https://thefreedomarticles.com/6-solid-scientific-reasons-to-assuage-your-coronavirus-panic/

[262] https://www.fda.gov/media/134922/download

[263] https://www.youtube.com/watch?v=KUw1Rzbde5U

[264] https://www.youtube.com/watch?v=HQQtOQUkUol

[265] https://www.youtube.com/watch?v=NcS60a9cdg4

[266] https://www.youtube.com/watch?v=MLD2NTe9pfM

where they had sick people breathe into healthy people's mouths. The healthy people didn't get sick. Likewise, they had sick horses sneeze and cough mucus, fluids, droplets, etc. into a bag, put food in that bag, then gave that food to healthy horses. They were unable to make the healthy horses sick.

Dr. Stefan Lanka is the king in this area. He is a German biologist and virologist who came to understand we have been lied to on a grand scale regarding the nature of the virus. He offered a reward of €100,000 for anyone who could scientifically prove that measles was a virus. That case that went all the way to the German Supreme Court where he won. Paul Fassa reported[267]:

At first it appeared he had lost. But Dr. Lanka took his loss to a higher court with more experts and the backing of two independent laboratories. He wound up not having to pay. It turned out that the "proof" provided was a composite of several different electron microscope images. And the composite involved different components of damaged cells. The composite could not be duplicated. The German Federal Supreme Court confirmed that there was not enough evidence to prove the existence of the measles virus.

Dave Mihalovic reported in the article *Biologist Proves Measles Isn't A Virus, Wins Supreme Court*

---

[267] https://vaccineimpact.com/2017/german-supreme-court-upholds-biologists-claim-that-measles-virus-does-not-exist/

Case Against Doctor[268]:

In a recent ruling, judges at the German Federal Supreme Court (BGH) confirmed that the measles virus does not exist. Furthermore, there is not a single scientific study in the world which could prove the existence of the virus in any scientific literature. This raises the question of what was actually injected into millions over the past few decades. Not a single scientist, immunologist, infectious disease specialist or medical doctor has ever been able to establish a scientific foundation, not only for the vaccination of measles but any vaccination for infants, pregnant women, the elderly and even many adult subgroups.

Lanka has spoken out against similar viral epidemics or pandemics, such as the H5N1 bird flu scare (which was being hyped in 2005). Finally, there are even other prominent virologists like Professor Peter Duesberg who have stated with solid evidence that HIV does not cause AIDS[269]. Here are some more quotes[270] from Lanka (who speaks German, so translated into rough English):

What viruses are there at all, then, and what are they doing?

Structures which you can characterize as viruses there are in many species of bacteria and in simple

---

268 https://vaccinationdanger.blogspot.com/2017/02/measles-is-not-virus.html

269 https://www.youtube.com/watch?v=pB8g0b-FkW0

270 whale.to/b/lanka.html

life forms, similar to the bacteria. They are elements of together-living of different cells in a common cell type which have remained independent. This is called a symbiosis, an endosymbiosis, which has arisen in the course of the process of different cell types' and structures' combining, an endosymbiosis which has brought forth the present cell type, that type of cells of which humans, animals and plants consist ...

Very important: Viruses are component parts of very simple organisms, for instance of the confervacea type of algae, a particular species of a one-celled chlorella alga and of very many bacteria. As existing there, these viral component parts are called phages. In complex organisms however, in particular in humans, or in animals or plants, such structures which you might call viruses have never been seen. In contrast to the bacteria in our cells, the mitochondria, or the bacteria in every plant, the chloroplasts, which cannot leave the common cell, since they are dependent on the metabolism of the common cell, viruses can leave the cell, since they are not carrying out any survival-vital tasks within the cell.

Viruses, thus, are component parts of the cell which have turned their entire metabolism over to the common cell and therefore can leave the cell. Outside the common cell, they are helping other cells, in that they are transferring construction and energy substances. Any other function of theirs has never been observed. Those actual viruses which have been scientifically demonstrated to exist are performing, in the very complex processes of

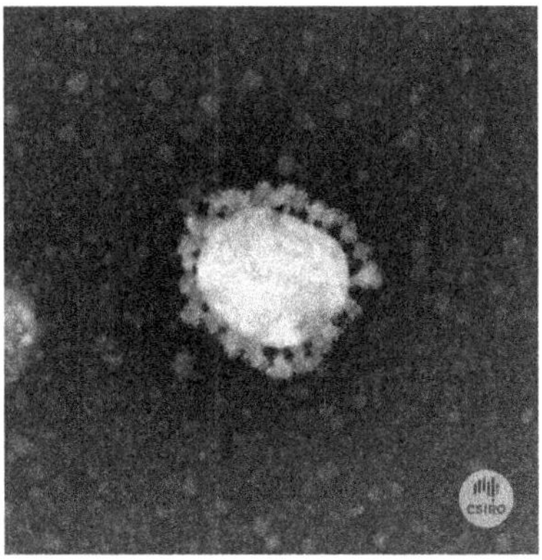

The alleged SARS-CoV-2 virus according to CSIRO Australia[271], with extremely heavy emphasis on the word alleged.

interactions of different cells, a helping, a supporting and in no case a destructive function. Also in the case of diseases, actually neither in the diseased organism nor in a bodily fluid has any structure which you could characterize as a virus ever been seen or isolated. The proposition that there is any sick-making virus whatsoever is a transparent swindle, a fatal lie with dramatic consequences.

Lanka also drops this bombshell:

Why then are disease-causing viruses still being maintained to exist? The school medicine protagonists/practitioners need the paralyzing, stupid-making and destructive fear of disease-causing phantom viruses as a central basis for their existence:

Firstly, in order to harm many people with vaccinations, in order to build up for themselves a clientele of chronically ill and ailing objects who will put up with anything being done to them.

---

[271] https://www.csiro.au/~/media/News-releases/2020/Coronavirus/COVID-19-JEM1400--16-orange-blu-vibrant-300-dpi_Credit-CSIRO.jpg

Secondly, in order not to have to admit that they are failing totally in their treatment of chronic illnesses and have killed and are killing more people than all wars so far have made possible. Every school medicine practitioner is conscious of this, but only very few dare to speak about it. Therefore it's no wonder either that among professional groups, it is that of the school medicine practitioners that has the highest suicide rate, far surpassing other professional groups.

Thirdly, the school medicine practitioners need the paralysing and stupid-making fear of diabolical viruses, in order to conceal their historical origin as an oppression and killing instrument of the Vatican's when it was struggling to rise in the world, having developed out of the usurping West Roman army."

To understand all this, we have to revisit germ theory and terrain theory.

Germ Theory vs. Terrain Theory

In the aforementioned article *Inner Terrain vs. Outer Terrain: Which Do You Emphasize for Good Health?*[272] there have been two competing theories which have influenced thought in many fields (medicine, biology and many more): germ theory and terrain theory/host theory. This started in the 1800s in France when Louis Pasteur championed the germ theory (the world is full of pathogenic germs, microbes, bacteria, etc. which can infect you if you

[272] ibid.

are unlucky enough) and Antoine Bechamp and Claude Bernard championed the terrain theory (microbes can change from one type to another according to the blood or tissue where they reside). The quote attributed to one or more of these three men is *"the germ is nothing, the inner terrain is everything."*

Pasteur (the same man after which "pasteurization" is named) won out and germ theory became the more dominant philosophy of the two. This has had the unfortunate effect of making people more scared of their environment and more susceptible to propaganda by Big Pharma (we're here to protect you; just take your drugs and vaccines and everything will be okay). It has also led people to take less responsibility for their inner terrain, via poor dietary and lifestyle choices, meaning a weakened host and lowered immune system – thus becoming more susceptible to disease. But what if we had it wrong? What if it is far more important to emphasize your own strength, health and terrain than to worry about possible germs floating around everywhere that could kill you? What if the whole coronavirus crisis is making everyone OCD, scared of every surface, scared of basic and natural human contact, forgetful of their internal strength and forgetful of the power of their gut microbiome and immune system?

Can a virus cross from animal to human, or human to human? According to the people quoted above, the answer is no. A virus is made specifically by your body for the purpose of healing via excretion and clean-up of toxins. According to this new way of understanding, a virus is made specifically for a cell, group of cells or organ, so viruses don't even cross organs, let alone from one human body to another.

Where is a genuine picture of the virus causing COVID-19? In a world where everything – literally everything – is photographed and video-recorded, why are there no actual pictures of the actual coronavirus supposedly causing all this mayhem? It shouldn't be that hard to get an electron microscope and take a picture. Why are we only given CGIs (computer-generated images)? Australia's CSIRO offered this picture (see earlier pages); however, as Dr. Andrew Kaufman covered in this presentation[273] at the 20:30 minute mark, it looks exactly like an exosome (see earlier pages).

So we come to the key question: if viruses can't cross species, bodies or be "caught", then what happens when one person appears to "catch" the flu from someone else? If viruses really are completely different than what almost all of us have been taught to believe, how can we explain apparent viral contagions or viral infections? Are they real? Well, certainly many people have experienced getting sick right after being around other people who were sick. The real issue is how? One possible answer is that the terrain of the recipient was lowered at the point of infection, whether because they were worried or anxious they would get sick (fear lowers the immune system), had the thought they would get sick (and unconsciously gave that thought power) or developed some kind of emotional entrainment or frequency

[273] https://www.youtube.com/watch?v=Xr8Dy5mnYx8

match with the sick person. It's all about creating a frequency lock. In life, we all have strong and weak moments; in those weaker moments we become more susceptible to disease. The great genius Nikola Tesla said that *"The day that science begins to study non-physical phenomena, it will make more progress in one decade than in all the previous centuries of its existence."* He also said that *"If you want to find the secrets of the universe, think in terms of energy, frequency and vibration."*

Possible ways we may get sick include exposure to toxins, mental causes, emotional causes, renewal/ detoxification or via shock. Dr. Ryke Geerd Hamer (founder of German New Medicine) established that *"every disease is caused by a conflict shock that catches an individual completely off guard"* and made it his first biological law.

Is catching disease not about "evil germs out to infect us" but rather about our mental and emotional state, our immune system, our microbiome and our susceptibility?

<u>The COVID-19 Umbrella Term</u>

At this point, armed with a new perspective about what a virus might be, let's revisit the idea that there is a new distinct virus SARS-CoV2 which is spreading, infecting and causing the disease COVID-19. Did you know that COVID-19 fails Koch's Postulates? German scientist Robert Koch (Heinrich Hermann Robert Koch, 1843–1910) made great contributions to the field of microbiology. He is considered to be one of the founders of the field of modern bacteriology. He identified the specific causative agents of TB (tuberculosis), cholera and anthrax. For his work on TB, he was awarded the Nobel Prize in 1905 in Physiology or Medicine. Koch established four criteria to identify the causative agent of a particular disease. These criteria have become a gold standard for determining the existence of an infectious agent and for isolating and verifying what is causing a disease. The criteria are a set of conditions known as Koch's postulates. They are:

1. The microorganism must be identified in all individuals affected by the disease, but not in healthy individuals.
2. The microorganism can be isolated from the diseased individual and grown in culture.
3. When introduced into a healthy individual, the cultured microorganism must cause disease.
4. The microorganism must then be re-isolated from the experimental host, and found to be identical to the original microorganism.

Firstly, the coronavirus SARS-CoV2 (allegedly causing the disease COVID-19) has not been shown to be present only in sick people and not in healthy ones. There are countless cases of people having this virus with mild, minor or zero symptoms. Iceland tested a relatively large percentage[274] of its population (around 5,000 people out of 364,000) and found that 0.86 percent (close to 1 percent) of Icelanders had the coronavirus. The symptoms? Little or none:

---

[274] ibid.

Importantly, approximately half of the people who tested positive for COVID-19 are non-symptomatic, according to Gudnason as reported by BuzzFeed[275]*. The other half is mostly showing "very moderate cold-like symptoms."*

Secondly, the virus has never been isolated – which must be done with proper equipment such as electron microscopes and which cannot be achieved through CT scans (as the Chinese were using) and the flawed PCR test (as previously discussed). The January 24th 2020 study published in the New England Journal of Medicine entitled *A Novel Coronavirus from Patients with Pneumonia in China, 2019*[276] describes how the scientists arrived at the idea of COVID-19: they took lung fluid samples and extracted RNA from them using the PCR test. It admits that the coronavirus failed Koch's postulates:

Further development of accurate and rapid methods to identify unknown respiratory pathogens is still needed ... our study does not fulfill Koch's postulates.

The late David Crowe, a great pandemic researcher, didn't believe there was even sufficient evidence to justify calling the COVID coronavirus a new virus, let alone a pandemic. In his paper *Flaws*

---

275 https://www.buzzfeed.com/albertonardelli/coronavirus-testing-iceland

276 https://www.nejm.org/doi/full/10.1056/NEJMoa2001017

in Coronavirus Pandemic Theory[277] he writes:

The world is suffering from a massive delusion based on the belief that a test for RNA is a test for a deadly new virus ... If the virus exists, then it should be possible to purify viral particles. From these particles RNA can be extracted and should match the RNA used in this test. Until this is done it is possible that the RNA comes from another source, which could be the cells of the patient, bacteria, fungi, etc. There might be an association with elevated levels of this RNA and illness, but that is not proof that the RNA is from a virus. Without purification and characterization of virus particles, it cannot be accepted that an RNA test is proof that a virus is present.

Definitions of important diseases are surprisingly loose, perhaps embarrassingly so. A couple of symptoms, maybe contact with a previous patient, and a test of unknown accuracy, is all you often need. While the definition of SARS, an earlier coronavirus panic, was self-limiting, the definition of the new coronavirus disease is open-ended, allowing the imaginary epidemic to grow. Putting aside the existence of the virus, if the coronavirus test has a problem with false positives (as all biological tests do) then testing an uninfected population will produce only false-positive tests, and the definition of the disease will allow the epidemic to go on forever.

This strange new disease, officially named COVID-19, has none of its own symptoms. Fever and

---

[277] https://theinfectiousmyth.com/book/CoronavirusPanic.pdf

cough, previously blamed on uncountable viruses and bacteria, as well as environmental contaminants, are most common, as well as abnormal lung images, despite those being found in healthy people.

He concludes:

The coronavirus panic is just that, an irrational panic, based on an unproven RNA test, that has never been connected to a virus. And which won't be connected to a virus unless the virus is purified. Furthermore, even if the test can detect a novel virus the presence of a virus is not proof that it is the cause of the severe symptoms that some people who test positive experience (but not all who test positive). Finally, even if the test can detect a virus, and it is dangerous, we do not know what the rate of false positives is. And even a 1% false positive rate could produce 100,000 false positive results just in a city the size of Wuhan and could mean that a significant fraction of the positive test results being found are false positives.

The use of powerful drugs because doctors are convinced that they have a particularly potent virus on their hands, especially in older people, with pre-existing health conditions, is likely to lead to many deaths. As with SARS.
There is very little science happening. There is a rush to explain everything that is happening in a way that does not question the viral paradigm, does not question the meaningfulness of test results, and that promotes the use of untested antiviral drugs.

Yes, antiviral drugs (which do a lot of damage to

your body), and, more to the point, mandatory vaccinations.

10 Reasons that SARS-CoV-2 Is an Imaginary and Theoretical Virus

The SARS-CoV-2 virus that allegedly causes COVID has still, to this date, never been isolated. Countless governments and organizations worldwide have failed to produce evidence of its existence when challenged. Although those who believe in the COVID cult – both those orchestrating the scamdemic and those blindly following along – will insist the virus is real, the truth is that there has still been no compelling or conclusive evidence that a real SARS-CoV-2 virus exists. The emperor truly has no clothes. There is no virus, other than a digital, theoretical abstraction made on a computer from a genomic database. The virus has never been isolated, purified, sequenced, characterized and proven 100 percent to exist. In addition to the fact that the virus has never been isolated according to either Koch's Postulates or River's Postulates (proposed by Thomas M. River in 1973 as a modification to Koch's), consider the following.

1. As mentioned earlier, the January 24, 2020 study published in the *New England Journal of Medicine* entitled *A Novel Coronavirus from Patients with Pneumonia in China, 2019*[278] describes how the scientists arrived at the idea of COVID-19: they took lung fluid samples and extracted RNA from them using the PCR test. It admits that the coronavirus

---

[278] ibid.

failed Koch's Postulates:

Further development of accurate and rapid methods to identify unknown respiratory pathogens is still needed … our study does not fulfill Koch's postulates.

2. All claims that the SARS-CoV-2 virus has been isolated have turned out to be unsubstantiated. Meanwhile, there have been actual admissions by officials that they haven't isolated it. The chief epidemiologist of the Chinese CDC (Center for Disease Control) Dr. Wu Zunyou admitted "they didn't isolate the virus" in this video clip[279].

3. The US CDC (Centers for Disease Control and Prevention) in its July 2020 report *CDC 2019-Novel Coronavirus (2019-nCoV) Real-Time RT-PCR Diagnostic Panel*[280] admitted that it had been running PCR tests based not on an actual viral isolate (an actual sample or specimen taken from an infected human), but rather "stocks" of "transcribed RNA" taken from a gene bank to "mimic clinical specimen":

Since no quantified virus isolates of the 2019-nCoV were available for CDC use at the time the test was developed and this study conducted, assays designed for detection of the 2019-nCoV RNA were tested with characterized stocks of in vitro transcribed full length RNA (N gene; GenBank accession: MN908947.2) of known titer (RNA copies/

---

[279] https://twitter.com/EEccetera/status/1354208913315528705

[280] https://www.fda.gov/media/134922/download

μL) spiked into a diluent consisting of a suspension of human A549 cells and viral transport medium (VTM) to mimic clinical specimen. (p.43)

4. The CDC has already admitted that SARS-CoV-2 is a computer-generated digital virus, not a real living virus. It has never been properly purified and isolated so that it could be sequenced from end-to-end once derived from living tissue; instead, it's just digitally assembled from a computer database. In this paper, the CDC scientists state they took just thirty-seven base pairs from a genome of thirty thousand base pairs which means that about 0.001 percent of the viral sequence is derived from actual living samples or real bodily tissue. In other words, they took these thirty-seven segments and put them into a computer program, which filled in the rest of the base pairs. This computer-generation step constitutes scientific fraud. This is the paper[281] where the CDC admitted they extrapolated their make-believe virus. Here is the quote:

Whole-Genome Sequencing
We designed 37 pairs of nested PCRs spanning the genome on the basis of the coronavirus reference sequence (GenBank accession no. NC045512). We extracted nucleic acid from isolates and amplified by using the 37 individual nested PCRs.

Another way to say this is that the "virus" has been constructed using a technique called "de novo assembly" which is a method for constructing

281 https://wwwnc.cdc.gov/eid/article/26/6/20-0516_article

genomes from a large number of (short or long) DNA fragments, with no a priori knowledge of the correct sequence or order of those fragments. You can read more about it at this site[282].

5. The original Corman-Drosten paper[283] admitted they used a theoretical virus sequence for all their work and calculations. They, like the CDC and every government and agency, claim this is only because no isolate was ever available. I wonder if any of these scientists ever asked *why* the isolate has never been available?

In the present case of 2019-nCoV, virus isolates or samples from infected patients have so far not become available to the international public health community.

A subsequent study highlighting fatal flaws in the Corman-Drosten paper was published entitled *External Peer Review of the RTPCR Test to Detect SARS-CoV-2 Reveals 10 Major Scientific Flaws at the Molecular and Methodological Level: Consequences for False Positive Results*[284]. It

282 https://thesequencingcenter.com/knowledge-base/de-novo-assembly/

283 https://www.eurosurveillance.org/content/10.2807/1560-7917.ES.2020.25.3.2000045

284 https://www.researchgate.net/publication/346483715_External_peer_review_of_the_RTPCR_test_to_detect_SARS-CoV-2_reveals_10_major_scientific_flaws_at_the_molecular_and_methodological_level_consequences_for_false_positive_results

highlights how the authors used in silico or theoretical sequences from computer banks, not real isolated samples from infected people. "In silico" is pseudo-Latin for "theoretical"; in plain English, synonyms for theoretical are "imaginary" and "make-believe."

The first and major issue is that the novel Coronavirus SARS-CoV-2 (in the publication named 2019-nCoV and in February 2020 named SARS-CoV-2 by an international consortium of virus experts) is based on in silico (theoretical) sequences, supplied by a laboratory in China, because at the time neither control material of infectious ("live") or inactivated SARS-CoV-2 nor isolated genomic RNA of the virus was available to the authors. To date no validation has been performed by the authorship based on isolated SARS-CoV-2 viruses or full length RNA thereof.

...

Nevertheless these in silico sequences were used to develop a RT-PCR test methodology to identify the aforesaid virus. This model was based on the assumption that the novel virus is very similar to SARS-CoV from 2003 (Hereafter named SARS-CoV-1) as both are beta-coronaviruses ... in short, a design relying merely on close genetic relatives does not fulfill the aim for a "robust diagnostic test" as cross reactivity and therefore false-positive results will inevitably occur. Validation was only done in regards to in silico (theoretical) sequences and within the laboratory-setting, and not as required for in-vitro diagnostics with isolated genomic viral RNA. This very fact hasn't changed even after 10 months of introduction of the test into routine diagnostics.

6. The governments of many nations around the world couldn't seem to come up with a real virus either when challenged to do so. More evidence proving the "virus" is constructed on a computer database from a digital gene bank comes from Frances Leader[285], who questioned the UK MHRA (Medicines and Healthcare Products Regulatory Agency) whether a real isolated virus was used to make the COVID vax (two of which, the Pfizer and Moderna mRNA vaccines, are not true vaccines but rather gene-editing devices). Leader found that the WHO protocols that Pfizer used to produce the mRNA do not appear to identify any nucleotide sequences that are unique to the SARS-CoV-2 virus. Leader asked if the "virus" was actually a computer-generated genomic sequence, and ultimately the MHRA confirmed they had no real specimen:

The DNA template does not come directly from an isolated virus from an infected person.

In July 2020, a group of concerned academics wrote a letter[286] to then UK Prime Minister Boris Johnson in which they asked him to produce independently peer-reviewed scientific evidence proving that the SARS-CoV-2 "virus" has been isolated. To date they have not received a reply.

---

[285] https://hive.blog/worldnews/@francesleader/email-exchange-with-uk-mhra-exposing-the-genomic-sequence-of-sarscov2

[286] https://www.resetourplanet.com/covid19-something-real-or-fake-what-do-we-know/

Similarly, UK researcher Andrew Johnson[287] made a Freedom of Information Request to Public Health England (PHE). He asked them to provide him with their records describing the isolation of a SARS-COV-2 virus to which they responded[288]:

PHE can confirm it does not hold information in the way suggested by your request.

7. In other Commonwealth nations it was the exact same story. In Australia scientists from the Doherty Institute[289] falsely announced that they had isolated the SARS-CoV-2 virus[290]. When asked to clarify the scientists said:

We have short (RNA) sequences from the diagnostic test that can be used in the diagnostic tests.

Perhaps this is the reason for this disclaimer by the Australian government[291]:

---

[287] https://cvpandemicinvestigation.com/2020/09/covid-19-evidence-of-fraud-medical-malpractice-acts-of-domestic-terrorism-and-breaches-of-human-rights/

[288] https://www.whatdotheyknow.com/request/679566/response/1625332/attach/html/2/872%20FOI%20All%20records%20describing%20isolation%20of%20SARS%20COV%202.pdf.html

[289] https://www.doherty.edu.au/people

[290] https://twitter.com/TheDohertyInst/status/1222345640769777671

[291] https://www.tga.gov.au/covid-19-testing-australia-information-health-professionals

The reliability of COVID-19 tests is uncertain due to the limited evidence base…There is limited evidence available to assess the accuracy and clinical utility of available COVID-19 tests.

8. Researcher Christine Massey made a similar Freedom of Information request in Canada, to which the Canadian government replied[292]:

Having completed a thorough search, we regret to inform you that we were unable to locate any records responsive to your request.

9. In fact, Massey and her colleague in New Zealand *"have been submitting Freedom of Information requests to various institutions in Canada, NZ, Australia, Germany, the U.K., the U.S. etc., seeking any records that describe the isolation of a "COVID-19 virus" (aka "SARS-COV-2") from an unadulterated sample taken from a diseased human … As of December 16, 2020, >40 institutions in Canada, U.S., New Zealand, Australia, U.K., England, Scotland, Wales, Ireland, Denmark, and the European CDC have provided their responses, and none could locate any record describing the isolation of any "COVID-19 virus" aka "SARS-COV-2" directly from a diseased patient.*

10. Did you know that previous coronaviruses have also not been isolated? The Spanish health journal *Salud* published a great article in November 2020 entitled "Frauds and Falsehoods in the Medical

---

[292] https://www.fluoridefreepeel.ca/wp-content/uploads/2020/06/Health-Canada-FinalResponse-A-2020-00208-2020-06-13.pdf

Field" where it exposed the lack of evidence not only for the isolation of SARS-CoV-2 but also for the isolation of other past coronaviruses (unofficial translation here). The scam runs deep. Jon Rappoport has done great work exposing how the exact same scam blueprint was played out in the 1980s (with Fauci in charge, leading the fraud) when scientists asserted there was a new virus called HIV, and it was causing AIDS. The COVID scamdemic greatly mimics other historical fake pandemics such as the 1976 swine flu pandemic[293]. The article in Salud states:

The genetic sequences used in PCRs to detect suspected SARS-CoV-2 and to diagnose cases of illness and death attributed to Covid-19 are present in dozens of sequences of the human genome itself and in those of about a hundred microbes. And that includes the initiators or primers, the most extensive fragments taken at random from their supposed "genome" and even the so-called "target genes" allegedly specific to the "new coronavirus". The test is worthless and all "positive" results obtained so far should be scientifically invalidated and communicated to those affected; and if they are deceased, to their relatives. Stephen Bustin, one of the world's leading experts on PCR, in fact says that under certain conditions anyone can test positive!

...

We have been warning you since March [2020]: you cannot have specific tests for a virus without knowing the components of the virus you are trying to detect.

---

293 https://thefreedomarticles.com/same-fake-pandemic-similarities-1976-swine-flu-2020-covid/

And the components cannot be known without having previously isolated/purified that virus. Since then we continue to accumulate evidence that no one has isolated SARS-CoV-2 and, more importantly, that it can never be isolated … In this report we are going to add the results of a particular research we have done from the data published on the alleged SARS-CoV-2 and on the protocols endorsed by the WHO for the use of RT-PCR as well as the data corresponding to the rest of the "human coronaviruses". And the conclusions are extremely serious: none of the seven "human coronaviruses" have actually been isolated and all the sequences of the primers of their respective PCRs as well as those of a large number of fragments of their supposed genomes are found in different areas of the human genome and in genomes of bacteria and archaea …

Their report analyzed human coronaviruses 229E (said to have been isolated in 1965), OC43 (in 1967), SARS-CoV (in 2003), NL63 (in 2004), HKU1 (in 2005) and MERS-CoV (in 2012). And just to repeat in case you missed it: they discovered the alleged sequences of SARS-CoV-2 are found in *both humans and bacteria*. This means all the various in silico models of SARS-CoV-2 contain existing human genetic sequences, so it is little wonder that people test positive when the primer or standard being tested against contains human sequences.

The COVID cult is a colossal fraud and superstition – but it's only in place to advance the underlying NWO agenda. Remember, this all started when Chinese scientists took lung fluid samples and claimed they had discovered a novel or new virus.

The Gates-Rockefeller WHO backed them up. In the WHO's *Novel Coronavirus 2019-nCov Situation Report 1*[294], they stated:

The Chinese authorities identified a new type of coronavirus, which was isolated on 7 January 2020 . . . . On 12 January 2020, China shared the genetic sequence of the novel coronavirus for countries to use in developing specific diagnostic kits.

With the evidence presented above, the WHO's assertions and claims are utterly baseless. They constitute outright fraud. The world has been shut down over a lie – a coldly calculated, carefully curated lie – that was simulated and war-gamed for decades in advance. The COVID cult is an irrational superstition based on nothing but in silico, theoretical, make-believe viral sequences. Yet, the real-world consequences for millions who have been thrown into stress, despair, poverty, joblessness, alcoholism and suicide is anything but theoretical.

Remember, There Is Not One Cause nor One Disease

COVID – whatever it actually is – is a repackaging scheme. It's all about reclassification of existing disease. It's crucial to understand this one point: there is not one virus nor one cause – and there is not one disease. The NWO propagandists have created the appearance of an international pandemic by exploiting many common assumptions people

[294] https://apps.who.int/iris/bitstream/handle/10665/330760/nCoVsitrep21Jan2020-eng.pdf?sequence=3&isAllowed=y

have, including the idea of one disease caused by one infectious agent. Remember, the COVID-19 umbrella term can cover numerous symptoms (coughing, shortness of breath, increased mucus, fatigue, etc.) which may be caused by any number of things. Jon Rappoport wrote[295] this piece on April 1, 2020, very appropriately since it was April Fools Day:

I keep pounding on this, because it's the main illusion, and it's the hardest illusion to dispel. People hang on to it like a life raft. The stage magicians present the "pandemic" as one disease with one cause, and people buy in immediately. Some people who reject the coronavirus as the cause present ANOTHER single cause—they're falling for the basic con job. There are people in Wuhan who have pneumonia because of the horrendous air quality in the city. There are people in New York who have ordinary flu-like illness. There are people in Italy who have histories of multiple, long-term, serious health conditions—pneumonia, flu, cardiac problems, kidney problems—made far worse through treatment with toxic drugs. There are people in hospitals around the world who, after being diagnosed with COVID, are dosed with powerful toxic antiviral drugs. There are people on breathing ventilators who are being given too much oxygen and too much pressure[296]—and their lungs collapse. There are perfectly healthy people who are testing positive for the virus because the test is irreparably flawed... All these people are

[295] https://blog.nomorefakenews.com/2020/04/01/covid-its-not-one-thing-its-not-one-disease/

[296] https://blog.nomorefakenews.com/2020/03/31/more-non-virus-causal-factors-in-epidemic-cases-hospitals/

called "COVID cases."

. . .

The stage magic trick is easy to see, once you grasp the tactics: Claim to have discovered a new virus. Say it is spreading and needs to be contained. Invent an umbrella label for the epidemic: COVID-19. Start pulling all sorts of people with all sorts of different conditions under the umbrella and say they're all "cases." Use a diagnostic test that will automatically turn out many verdicts of "infected." And you have the illusion of a pandemic.

. . .

Or you might get this: "No, it's not the coronavirus, it's really 5G technology that's making people sick and killing them." STILL falling for the magic trick. In certain places, 5G might be harming people. Indeed. And some of those people might be labeled as COVID. Yes. But "the whole thing" isn't 5G, because THERE ISN'T ONE WHOLE THING.

There is no "it."

This is the illusion we need to dispel: there is not one cause nor one disease.

Frontline NYC doctor Cameron Kyle-Sidell stated here[297] and here[298] from firsthand experience that he was seeing a lot of patients being brought in and suffering from what seemed like altitude sickness, a severe shortness of breath and lack of oxygen. He thought they should be treated for hypoxemia (a condition where the oxygen content in the arterial

---

297 https://www.youtube.com/watch?v=1EWQPgF6-UQ

298 https://www.youtube.com/watch?v=QWaq8HoEROU

blood is below normal, like altitude sickness) and not for ARDS (Acute Respiratory Distress Syndrome, by definition a respiratory disease). This means less use of ventilators and breathing tubes because as he says, it is highly likely the pressure from the ventilators may be damaging patients' lungs. They need oxygen, not pressure. He states that apparent COVID-19 patients do not appear to be suffering from anything resembling viral pneumonia.

When many people show signs of disease in the same region, it is easy to assume they are "catching" it from one another. Bill Gates-Netflix propaganda (the Netflix Explained series episode titled *The Next Pandemic*[299]) reinforce this programming. However, this is an assumption. It is just as possible the people in a certain geographical area are all being subjected to the same poison and thus reacting in the same way. In other words, it could be because of a local contaminant rather than an infectious agent. What appears like contagion may actually be the consequence of mass long-term poisoning, but governments and corporations are never going to confess to that when they have a scapegoat killer virus they can blame instead.

Many COVID-19 deaths were those who are elderly, have compromised immune systems or have comorbidities. On top of that, consider the following:

1. Air pollution: the air in Wuhan, China, and Milan, Italy, is notoriously bad. Many of the symptoms people experienced there are perfectly explainable

---

299 https://www.netflix.com/title/80216752

due to the atrocious air quality;

2. GMOs: GM crops, and thus glyphosate[300], have long contaminated the global food supply;

3. Biofuel made with GM corn: as Dr. Thomas Cowan speculates in this video[301], GM corn biofuel is now used in place of regular fuel. What happens when it is burned, used up and dispersed into the air for everyone to breathe in all the GMOs and glyphosate?;

4. Vaccines: the residents of Wuhan were reportedly vaccinated en masse before the outbreak[302]; and

5. EMF (e.g. Wi-Fi and 5G): the word has got out that the 5G 60GHz frequency interferes with oxygen absorption. Is it just a coincidence that the NHY doc above is revealing that people now have symptoms of hypoxemia or hypoxia?

6. Chemtrails / Geoengineering: the ongoing spraying of our skies is one of the most serious crimes against humanity. Aerosol concoctions of aluminum, strontium and barium, plus mycotoxins

---

300 https://thefreedomarticles.com/glyphosate-problem-carcinogen/

301 https://www.youtube.com/watch?v=m3LgrcDAlJs

302 https://thewatchtowers.org/chinas-mandatory-vaccination-law-went-into-effect-on-december-1-2019-the-coronavirus-outbreak-is-it-a-vaccine-experiment-gone-bad/

and synthetic life[303], have been sprayed in the air in virtually every part of the world for at least ten to fifteen years. There has been ample time for these particulates to invade our bodies. What horrible long-term effects are going to happen because of this?

There are many more. This is not an exhaustive list. The point is that there are many causes and many diseases occurring right now which have been lumped under the term COVID-19 to bolster the illusion of a raging pandemic.

If you didn't know the history of fake pandemics, you might think that the WHO, the USG and other world governments would have had solid evidence for declaring a health emergency. They didn't. Asking key fundamental questions about the nature of the COVID-19 disease, and how the virus is being isolated and tested, reveal a house of cards. There are serious fundamental flaws in the pandemic propaganda. What happened here was a carefully crafted script to engineer a worldwide crisis and to blame mass long-term poisoning on a tiny invisible particle whose existence has never been conclusively proven to exist.

COVID Was a Military Operation

On top of everything I have just written, consider the information which came out thanks to people

303 https://thefreedomarticles.com/synthetic-agenda-heart-new-world-order/

such as Sasha Latypova[304] and Katherine Watt[305]. If you haven't begun to realize by now, nothing is what you think it is! The COVID scamdemic was pulled off in part because authorities used the military to roll out the operation on an unsuspecting population. Public health has been militarized – and the military in turn has been turned into a public health front. This has been going on a long time, well before COVID. The NWO controllers use public health language and law to carry out military campaigns. Their weapons of attack are informational (propaganda), psychological (fear promotion) and chemical-biological-radiological-nuclear (pharmaceuticals like gene-altering fake-vaccines). Thanks to a lawsuit by whistleblower Brook Jackson, Pfizer even admitted in court that they weren't manufacturing "vaccines" but rather DoD prototypes – which don't have to go through safety testing or clinical trials, or get FDA approval! The USG used its military to deploy a "prototype" or "countermeasure" – a weapon against the public. Big Pharma was just a front for the op.

It hardly bears mentioning that the NWO controllers are master manipulators who intimately understand how to exploit human psychology. The real conspiracy here is the exploitation of the mass ignorance regarding the true nature of the virus. If there are dangerous little critters everywhere around us that could infect or kill us, then we need protection. Once we need protection, we open the door for forces posing as protectors to "save" us.

---

304 https://www.bitchute.com/video/o6sseleLrKTk/

305 https://rumble.com/v26xpbc-dod-vaccine-press-conference-tuesday-january-24-230p-et.html

What if there is no such thing as a killer virus? What if the real virus here is fear itself – fear of the virus, fear of the unknown and fear of death?

Speaking of the unknown, the next chapter is about to go even deeper into the depths of the unknown. Buckle up.

Chapter 9 – Pedophilia and Satanism: The Cement Holding the Conspiracy Together

These people, most of them, were Luciferians ... they served something immaterial, what they called Lucifer ... So I went to places called Churches of Satan ... so I visited these churches, just as a visitor, dropped by, and they were doing their Holy Mass with naked women and liquor and stuff ... But then at some point, which is why I'm telling you all this, I was invited to participate in sacrifices... abroad. That was the breaking point. Children.

– Ronald Bernard

The negative, you can say evil, the Luciferians, Satanists, whatever you which you call it... it is a real entity ... there really has been a moment of separation from the manifestation of light, in which a group went their own way and are carrying an intense hatred, anger ... Because this is an all annihilating force that hates our guts. It hates creation, it hates life. It will do anything to destroy us completely, and the way to do that is to divide humanity.

– Ronald Bernard

We need to wake up ... this not only ties in to

MKUltra, CIA, it ties into Satanism. There are approximately 4 million practicing Satanists in America today ... there are between 50,000 and 60,000 human sacrifices (according to 3 different sources) in this country [USA] every year. The Satanic cults operate secretly. The Satanic cults – along with the covert criminal enterprise within the Government – are a serious threat to our society.

– Ted Gunderson

Pedophilia and Satanism are the cement that holds the global conspiracy together.

– David Icke

No one will enter the New World Order unless he or she will make a pledge to worship Lucifer. No one will enter the New Age unless he will take a Luciferian Initiation.

– David Spangler[306]

*****

Many people know that pedophilia, child sex trafficking and child sex rings exist, but they don't think these things are part of a grand conspiracy. Nor do they realize just how prevalent these things are in the West as well as the developing world. The truth is that pedophilia is a central part of the New World Order. Why? Because of what pedophilia is. At its

---

306 https://www.azquotes.com/author/22648-David_Spangler

core, pedophilia is about domination and exploitation. It's about violation and theft. It's about feeding off the energy of the innocent, pure and weak. This is exactly the mindset of the NWO controllers. They have become accustomed to living beyond moral and legal boundaries and to being rich and powerful enough to escape the consequences of their actions. As we shall see, pedophilia is rife throughout NWO circles, with many top politicians, European royalty and businessmen up to their necks and beyond in it.

Many people associate the Vatican with pedophilia. This is for good reason; the Catholic Church is Pedophilia Central. Like a deeply entrenched mold infestation, pedophilia is highly unlikely to ever be removed from the Catholic Church, with Pope after Pope after Pope either being involved in it, supporting it, condoning it, or at best failing to take a strong stand against it. In August 2018, former high ranking official Carl Vigano, who was the Vatican's US ambassador from 2011 to 2016, called on Pope Francis to step down. He wrote a seven-thousand-word letter publicly accusing the pontiff of doing nothing for five years while knowing about the sex abuse allegations against a renowned US cardinal (until the Pope finally accepted his resignation). There were voluminous allegations against this cardinal, Theodore McCarrick, of sexually abusing lower-ranking seminarians and priests. Not only was he not punished, but he was actually rewarded; McCarrick began traveling on missions on behalf of the church, and according to Vigano, he went to China and was involved in US-Cuba talks in 2014 on behalf of the Vatican.

Catholic Church pedophilia is systemic and rife across the world. Molestation and sex abuse occur worldwide. For instance, in Germany, a report published by *Spiegel Online* and *Die Zeit* on Catholic child sex abuse found that 3,677 people were abused by clergy between 1946 and 2014. The majority of victims were boys aged thirteen or younger (969 of whom were altar boys), at least 1,670 clergy were involved, and every sixth case was a rape. In what has become typical of the Vatican's way of dealing with this problem, many of the priests caught were transferred rather than defrocked, and only one-third were investigated by the church. In Australia, a five-year national inquiry into Catholic sexual abuse, completed in 2017, concluded that 7 percent of Australia's Catholic priests were accused of abusing children between 1950 and 2010. In the USA, just in the state of Pennsylvania alone, the Catholic Church hierarchy systematically covered up the abuse of at least a thousand kids by three hundred priests over seventy years. This was only in a small geographical area of six dioceses. Imagine how big the problem is if you extend that to the entire world. In this case, the grand jury report included the case of a ring of pedophile priests in Pittsburgh who raped boys, took pornographic pictures of them and marked them by giving them gold crosses to wear – so they could be easily recognized by other pedophile priests.

Throughout all this, the Vatican keeps making excuses for their predator priests and even has the gall to accuse victims of pulling publicity stunts. So much compassion – how very Christ-like. Like a rat going down with a sinking ship, the Vatican still clings on to its old doctrine that sex and sexual desire is sinful and that priests must remain celibate. Although allowing priests to marry would not solve the whole problem, it would obviously be better to allow them an outlet for their sexual energy. Otherwise, it gets repressed and then comes out in clandestine, abusive ways.

In case after case, some very common themes emerge. High-up Catholic officials refuse to take swift and effective action to remove offending priests from positions of power or positions with easy access to young children. Likewise, middle or lower officials refuse to report the pedophile and instead cover for him, placing their allegiance to the church ahead of the innocent victims. A case in point is Australian Archbishop Philip Wilson, the most senior Catholic official to be convicted of covering up child sex abuse. He was found guilty in May 2018 of failing to alert police to the repeated abuse of two altar boys by pedophile priest James Fletcher in the state of New South Wales in the 1970s. The ruling magistrate Robert Stone found that Wilson had shown no remorse or contrition for his actions, and that his primary motive had been to protect the Catholic Church.

The Saga of Jeffrey Epstein – Pedophile, Pimp, Blackmail Operator and Mossad Agent

Pedophilia goes far beyond the Catholic Church and other mainstream religions. It is the dark underbelly of the NWO, and it involves politicians, businessmen, judges, royalty and more. The reality is that many perpetrators of pedophilia are not shady men in trench coats living in seedy hotels but are in

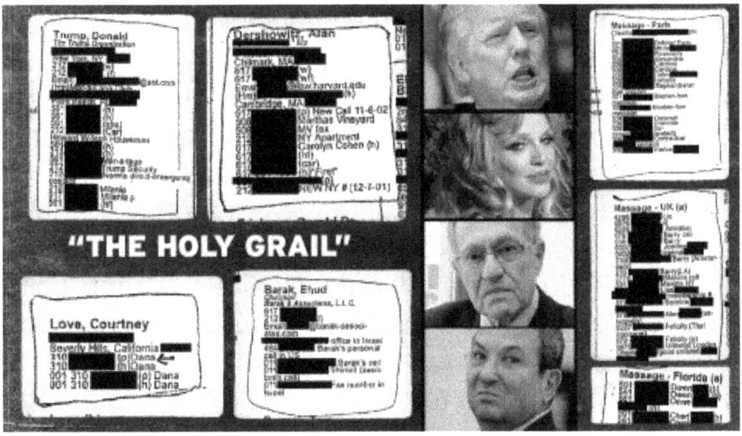

Donald Trump and other well-known names listed in pedophile Epstein's little black book.

fact "pillars" of our community. The numerous examples of elite pedophilia throughout the world are fundamentally connected because a global sex-trafficking ring exists, involving pimps like convicted pedophile Jeffrey Epstein. The Epstein case went from cold to hot in July 2019 when he was arrested again, years after he was first sentenced for sex offenses in 2008. The case got massive media attention, not least when Epstein either died (or disappeared) due to apparent "suicide" in a tightly guarded Manhattan jail.

Epstein owned a private island where he would host huge underage sex orgies, transporting people by private plane which came to be known as the *Lolita Express*. Epstein had many prominent figures using his child sex slaves, like Alan Dershowitz (ardent defender of genocidal Israel), Bill Clinton (the promiscuous and deceitful ex-US president), Prince Andrew (British royalty) and probably (although still unproven) the former US President Donald Trump (who has had at least two lawsuits brought against him for pedophilia and rape, both also involving Epstein[307]). In his little black book, Epstein reportedly had twenty-one phone numbers for Bill Clinton[308]; Trump was listed, too. Clinton was reported to have flown to Epstein's private island (Little St. James, dubbed "Pedo Island") twenty-six times. Trump once said to *New York* Magazine in 2002 about his good friend Epstein: *"I've known Jeff for 15 years. Terrific guy. He's a lot of fun to be with. It is even said that he likes beautiful women as much as I do, and many of them are on the younger side. No doubt about it, Jeffrey enjoys his social life."*

Epstein wasn't just procuring girls for his own and his clients' sexual enjoyment. He was running an incredibly well-funded sexual blackmail operation highly reminiscent of the Mossad. The Mossad has long had a reputation for "honeypot" or "honeytrap" operations where they use female spies and agents to lure their targets into compromising situations. In Epstein's case, people reported that there were video cameras hidden in the rooms where his clients would rape underage victims, so it was all caught on tape and could be used as blackmail material. It was also reported that Epstein would quiz the girls after the session about his clients' fetishes. It was a sexual

---

[307] https://www.scribd.com/doc/316341058/Donald-Trump-Jeffrey-Epstein-Rape-Lawsuit-and-Affidavits#fullscreen?platform=hootsuite

[308] endoftheamericandream.com/archives/bill-clinton-and-the-pedophile-the-sex-scandal-that-could-destroy-hillarys-presidential-ambitions

entrapment ring to gain information on prominent politicians (and other high-profile public figures) so they could then be controlled. Epstein's connections to Israel, Israeli Intelligence and the Mossad in particular are manifold:

– Epstein was friends and business partners with several high-level Israelis including the aforementioned former Israeli PM Ehud Barak;

– Epstein's so-called madam and former girlfriend Ghislaine Maxwell, who acted as a procurer of young girls for him, was the daughter of known Mossad agent Robert Maxwell;

– Former executive for Israel's Directorate of Military Intelligence Ari Ben-Menashe claimed to have met Epstein and Ghislaine Maxwell in the 1980s. In this interview, he states that both Epstein and Maxwell were already working with Israeli intelligence during that time;

– Ben-Menashe reveals that after he personally met Epstein, that Epstein and Maxwell began a sexual blackmail operation with the purpose of extorting US public figures on behalf of Israeli military intelligence.

Epstein was a highly connected individual whose mysterious wealth was never explained. His death was another shake-your-head event where nothing added up. I could call it suspicious, but I wouldn't want to be unfair to the word "suspicious." In a day and age of massive surveillance, the CCTV footage was mysteriously unavailable. We were told that he was not being watched by a proper prison guard; that he wasn't checked upon for hours in the time before his death or escape; that he was left alone in his cell despite normal protocol being that he should have had a new cellmate; that two guards who would normally have had overnight shifts were told to leave the area three hours earlier for "maintenance"; anonymous reports reveal Epstein was whisked out of the building at 4:15 a.m.; former MCC [Metropolitan Correctional Center] inmates state that he could not have killed himself with the sheets and materials available to him in his cell; that the prison guards who were supposed to be watching him were "asleep" and later falsified the logs; that his autopsy results revealed that he had multiple broken bones in his neck, including a broken hyoid bone, which is typically more associated with homicide (strangulation) rather than suicide (hanging).

Interestingly enough, it is quite plausible that Epstein is still alive, and that a body double was used in his place while he was rescued by the powers he serves. Millions of dollars were moved[309] from one of his secret bank accounts after his death; no one seems to know who was controlling the account or moving the money.

All this points to something that routinely happens in grand conspiracies. It is how real power kills (or rescues). Certain people in high places had the power to call off security, ensure the destruction of evidence and allow the crime to take place, just like what happened in famous assassinations like those of JFK and Princess Diana. As Colonel Fletcher

---

[309] https://www.activistpost.com/2020/02/no-one-knows-why-epsteins-secret-bank-account-moved-millions-since-his-death.html

Prouty said:

"No one has to direct an assassination – it happens. The active role is played secretly by permitting it to happen."

Although the Epstein case is sickening, involving hundreds if not potentially thousands of victims, one positive thing that came out of it is that even the MSM began reporting on it. This opened up the perception of the average person who would otherwise have been inclined to dismiss it all as "conspiracy theory." Yes there absolutely was a conspiracy or conspiring by Epstein to recruit and exploit girls and to collect blackmail material; and there was a very clear conspiracy to cover up his death or disappearance. Once a conspiracy becomes so overt and obvious, backed by so many pieces of evidence, it's no longer conspiracy theory but conspiracy fact.

Jimmy Savile was another infamous pedophile who functioned like Epstein. Savile had close connections to Israel[310] (like Epstein) and to the British Royal Family (like Epstein). Savile was close friends with (like a mentor to) then Prince Charles, now King, and became a well-known procurer of both girls and boys. Sexual abuse and rape allegations against him were in the hundreds. Laughably, the Royal Family claimed they didn't know anything about it – just as Prince Andrew (very good friends with Epstein) claimed he didn't know about Epstein's sexual predation and exploitative activities either.

---

310 https://aangirfan.blogspot.com/2012/10/jimmy-savile-fixed-it-for-israel.html

Andrew denies having sex with Epstein victim Virginia Robert Giuffre, despite being photographed with her and despite other witnesses seeing them dancing together. Give me a break.

The Normalization of Pedophilia

From one perspective, it might be surprising to some that the elite engage in so much pedophilia when it can be so easily used to compromise and blackmail them later. However, once you've sold your soul and are part of the "club", the club bands together to protect its own. It is a common mindset among the NWO controllers that they think themselves so rich and powerful as to be untouchable. Of late there has been a push to normalize pedophilia by trying to redefine it as "a sexual orientation." Logically and biologically, this makes no sense. Sexual orientation is an attraction to either males or females (or both), much like a magnetic pull/push. After all, we are electromagnetic creatures. Age has no bearing on this. For instance, if you a heterosexual man, you are attracted to females, regardless of whether they are young girls or old women. Perhaps you prefer younger women, but that is irrelevant to your orientation or basic underlying feeling of attraction.

Yet, the NWO controllers (through the psychiatric DSM-V) have tried to recast and rename pedophiles as "minor-attracted persons" and redefine pedophilia as a "sexual orientation." There are even organizations (like B4UAct.org) that are trying to somehow normalize the behavior of pedophiles and are claiming that pedophiles are being unfairly stigmatized for their feelings! Psychiatry, it should also be noted, has a history of inventing fictitious diseases such as ADHD[311] (fictitious in the sense there is no blood test or physical test for it, as admitted by its inventor on his deathbed by Leon Eisenberg). This move has to do with the NWO elite wanting to reshape the world in their (sick) image. It has to do with removing any moral, cultural or legal stigmatism and ramifications from the act of pedophilia so they can continue their child sex trafficking and pedophilic activities with no fear of consequence.

Step into the Inner Ruling Circle, and There Is Pedophilia; Step Beyond That, and There Is Satanism

The movie *Conspiracy of Silence*[312] is an excellent documentary exposing global child sex trafficking rings. State Senator John De Camp wrote a 1992 book entitled *The Franklin Cover-Up, Child Abuse, Satanism, and Murder in Nebraska* in which he exposed the existence of a child sex ring in Nebraska. In it he names many figures such as George Bush and former NSA chief Michael Aquino of the Church of Satan. We have testimony from many people such as Paul Bonacci[313], Brice Taylor[314] and Cathy O'Brien[315], the latter of whom states that

[311] thefreedomarticles.com/fictitious-diseases-psychiatry-big-pharma/

[312] https://www.youtube.com/watch?v=ggxiBWv4xYE

[313] https://www.youtube.com/watch?v=1KgkiruMB4g

[314] https://www.youtube.com/watch?v=fjsqEq6r-RQ

[315] https://www.youtube.com/watch?v=7CQ2FnG9Ldg

George Bush, Dick Cheney, Hillary Clinton, Bill Clinton and many others raped her and her young daughter Kelly.

The late great Ted Gunderson (described in chapter 2) was a former FBI chief who had a twenty-eight-year career at the FBI and was in charge of fourteen million people. He spent decades of the latter half of his life investigating the New World Order and Satanism. His inquiries led him to discover a common thread running through the global conspiracy: a worldwide child sex trafficking and pedophilia ring that sold children into slavery and flew them to places like Washington, DC, to be used in sex orgies by politicians. Sometimes, children would be abducted through underground tunnels. Gunderson found that, in America, more than sixty thousand kids were going missing every year, and that the FBI, CPS and White House were fully complicit in the cover up.

However, it went beyond that: Gunderson discovered via meticulous investigation that the global network of pedophilia was strung together with a common thread: Satanism. He found undeniable evidence that a Satanic cult was using mind control and Satanic Ritual Abuse (SRA) over its victims. The abducted children would be forced into dark rituals and either sacrificed or converted into sex slaves. In one video presentation, Gunderson presented proof of SRA, including human sacrifice, animal bones and satanic symbols in the dirt.

<u>What is Satanism?</u>

To truly understand the pedophilia infestation, you have to grasp the shocking truth that pedophilia is intimately and inextricably connected with Satanism. Satanism is the worship of dark entities and forces. It involves demonic possession, whereby a Satanist (usually during ritual) summons up and makes a connection with some kind of otherworldly entity. This connection is a two-way street; the Satanist believes he is getting something from the exchange (e.g., power, charisma), and the entity gets something by taking possession of the Satanist's mind and soul. The concept of "selling your soul to the devil" can be taken quite literally, not just metaphorically. Satanism advocates indulgence (as opposed to the idea of restraint advocated by the Catholic Church). Satanism is also about inversion – turning everything upside down (which brings to mind the NWO motto *ordo ab chao* or order out of chaos). Black is white, pain is pleasure, bad is good, sin is virtue. Satanic ritual often involves sexual orgies and sacrifice. Satanists get a dark high from drinking the blood of their tortured victims, which contains emotional neurochemicals released into the blood at the time of their death. Some believe one such chemical is adrenochrome which is produced by the body's adrenals.

A recent whistleblower to expose NWO inner sanctum Satanism was Roland Bernard[316], a former insider who went public in 2016/2017 with his shocking story. He was a young naive entrepreneur who stumbled into the world of high finance. He was told he could make a lot of money if he were willing to

---

316 https://www.bitchute.com/video/aYsJDmY41CXx/

put his conscience in the freezer (i.e., deaden it). He learned that the wealthy elite act like they're on opposite sides but secretly work together to suppress the masses so it doesn't get too crowded at the top. He reveals how he went to rituals with naked women, first as a spectator. What broke him, so to speak, was when he was invited to actually participate in a Satanic sacrifice – at which point he quit and was tortured to maintain secrecy but escaped to become a whistleblower. Interestingly enough, after rubbing shoulders with many NWO criminals, he estimates that around 8,000 to 8,500 people run the entire world. He also affirms the accuracy of The Protocols of the Elders of Zion (see chapter 2).

The New World Order cult that rules the world administers Satanic pedophilia networks, including top-level politicians like Australian prime ministers and US presidents. What I am about to reveal next is not for the faint of heart; however, I believe it is fully true. It is a story told again and again by various whistleblowers, all of whom reveal the same theme. For those new to this, it will be hard to accept, but read on if you dare.

There are Satanic pedophilia networks all over the world, and one such network was exposed by Australian woman Fiona Barnett, who showed a lot of courage by going public at a Sydney press conference in October 2015[317] and naming names. Fiona, a former victim of Satanic ritual abuse and part of an international VIP pedophile ring, not only exposed the existence of the Satanic pedophilia

---

[317] https://www.youtube.com/watch?v=zln_Nq-1C0c

network and its international child-trafficking ring, but actually named three former Australian prime ministers and one former US president as perpetrators. She reveals that this network, composed of famous actors, celebrities, judges, politicians and other high-flyers, has infiltrated all the key organizations and institutions in Australia – just as it has in the US, Britain and elsewhere.

Fiona saw it all – Satanic ritual, rape, torture and murder – but actually says *"the way I've been treated for reporting the crimes I've witnessed and experienced has been far worse than my original abuse experiences."* That speaks volumes about people's collective denial and amnesia, doesn't it?

Fiona proclaims that Australia is a pedophile haven. She explains how Australia took in a large number of Nazi war criminals, including her own step-grandparents. She was introduced by her own family to an international child trafficking pedophile ring based in Sydney. Some victims are kidnapped off the street, some are "bred" for it (without ever getting birth certificates) and some are brought into it through multigenerational abuse. These latter ones are trained and expected to become the perpetrators and future administrators of it.

Fiona has had flashbacks to being abused as young as the age of two. Later on, when she was still a little girl, she was dropped off at VIP parties, instructed to say "the starchild is here", then watch as famous politicians, actors and celebrities snorted cocaine, raped her, had sex with each other, then pretended to drown her in a pool. She wasn't just

sexually abused and raped; she also suffered Satanic ritual abuse in the form of torture (e.g., she suffered cattle- prodding electroshock to cause disassociation). She reveals how this pedophile ring goes to the highest levels, and included orgies at Parliament House (in Australia's capital Canberra) itself.

Fiona names the names of the people who sexually assaulted, raped and tortured her. Many are dead, but some are still alive: Antony Kidman (actress Nicole Kidman's father; Fiona claims Nicole Kidman was a victim of the ring, too, but was nasty towards her despite the fact they both victims); Dr. John Gittinger (Lithuanian Nazi concentration camp guard and CIA agent); actor Bruce Spence; former

US President Richard Nixon; former Australian Prime Minister Gough Whitlam; former Australian Prime Minister Bob Hawke; former Australian Prime Minister Paul Keating; former Australian Minister of Education Kim Beazley Sr.; former NSW Premier Bob Carr; former Australian cricketer Richie Benaud; US Evangelist Pastor Billy Graham; and Ted Turner (depopulation advocate and founder of fake news mainstream media network CNN).

Fiona also recalls being at Bohemian Grove (more on this soon). On one occasion she was in a pink bubble room and raped. On another occasion she had to participate in "Teddy Bear's Picnic" a child rape hunt party, where children were hunted like animals and raped (as also happened to Kathy Collins and Cathy O'Brien).

In this video[318], Fiona talks about being present at a real Satanic ritual with some of Australia's famous people, as well as local Australian cops and priests from St. Stanislaus (a Catholic Jesuit school). It took place in 1985 in Bathurst, a small town in NSW, Australia. She mentions Kim Beazley Sr. (Minister for Education in the government of Gough Whitlam and Labor member of the Australian House of Representatives for 32 years from 1945 to 1977. He was the father of Kim Christian Beazley, who later became Australian Labour Party and Opposition leader), Richie Benaud (famous Australian cricket captain and sports commentator), actor Bruce Spence and former NSW police commissioner John Avery. She reveals how Beazley and Benaud led the ritual by worshipping their Satanic gods, chanting

---

[318] https://www.youtube.com/watch?v=87IRjfLg2Sk

"Baal", "Lucifer", "Satan", "Son of the Morning" and other such appellations. She then witnessed them ceremoniously killing a pregnant mother (a "breeder" to the Satanists) in the center of the circle. After that, they pulled out the unborn child, chopped it up with a knife, put it on a gold platter, and proceed to do a type of dark communion or Eucharist. (Fiona mentions here that the Catholic Church communion is based on this older Satanic version of a communion – in line with my article *Are Parts of Organized Religion Satanic?*[319])

After that, she states that several hypnotized children came forward like robots, who were probably mind controlled or completely dazed. Bruce Spence came forward with a samurai sword and sliced off the head of each child. Then, the entire crowd of Satanists, who were sexually aroused by everything that had just taken place, broke out into a bloody orgy. They had whipped everyone up into a frenzy, and then they drunk the adrenalized blood of the woman and child. (Satanists are addicted to and get high from adrenaline in human blood.) Lastly, Beazley forced her to take a bite of one of the decapitated heads …

Fiona herself mentions in this interview[320] that some of the criminals who abused and raped her were "just" pedophiles, and she puts former Aussie PM Gough Whitlam in this category. This echoes what I state earlier – pedophilia is at the inner circle of the NWO, but beyond that, even deeper, there is

---

319 thefreedomarticles.com/organized-religion-satanic/

320 https://www.youtube.com/watch?v=rWx3nWQyLqQ

Satanism. Fiona explains how the Satanic hierarchical pyramid works. Roughly speaking, at the lowest level, you have street gangs; next, you have organized crime and the mafia; next, you have recruits into the elite club; then, above that, you have "just" pedophiles (those who rape children but who have no Satanic connection); finally, at the very top, you have the elite VIPs who are fully fledged Satanists.

From her experience, Fiona has learned that only bloodliners can make it to the top. These people come from the thirteen or so Illuminati bloodlines (as exposed by Fritz Springmeier, David Icke and other researchers). These bloodlines are revered as demigods; and the roughly three hundred bloodlines or so below that can never make it to the top echelon. (Probably because they don't have pure blood, i.e., "royal" or reptilian DNA.)

The OTO, the Freemasons, Scientology, Catholic Church, the CIA, the Australian military and countless others are all branches of the same Satanic Pedophilia Network. It administers the international child trafficking ring. Fiona warns that every organization in Australia has been infiltrated, including hospitals, psychiatry, politics, child advocacy groups – everything. The Satanists have even created a False Memory Foundation, a fake organization set up by pedophiles to stop true victims from coming forward with their stories, by convincing people they didn't really experience what they experienced.

Satanic Black Magic Rules the World

Black magic is the force that rules the world, so it is the Satanic black magicians which constitute the

Elite figures talking at Bohemian Grove, before the black magic rituals. Note Nixon on the right, and Reagan on the left – at a time when he was not yet president.

true controllers of the world – at least in the human Earthly realm. The Satanic black magicians pull the strings, not politicians, corporate bosses, military heads, intelligence chiefs or even international bankers – although they also hold many of those roles. NWO manipulators fulfill a hidden role and an outer, more respectable public role. While many Satanic black magicians are also businessmen and bankers, their true ruling power comes from Satanism and the twisted use of humanity's creative power (black magic), which they then use in their secular roles in society.

Remember the saying of the Chinese sage Confucius, who said that "symbols rule the world, not rules or laws"? Symbols communicate at a deeper level than words because they are decoded by the right, intuitive brain, whereas words are decoded by the left, logical brain. Symbols are able to penetrate more deeply into our subconscious, which is why the elite are so obsessed with their occult corporate and governmental logos of red crosses, rising suns, all-seeing eyes, pyramids, 666, the rings of Saturn and inverted pentagrams. Words attempt to rule the world, but they can never be as powerful as symbols. Corporate logos are full of occult symbology.

Before looking at the evidence of elite use of black magic, it is worthwhile remembering a defining aspect of Satanism: the inversion of everything. Black is white, bad is good, wrong is right. This is why the inverted pentagram is such a popular Satanic symbol. George Orwell touched on this in *1984* when he wrote of the ruling class propaganda:

"War is peace. Freedom is slavery. Ignorance is strength." Even mind control, developed by the Nazis first in Germany and later at the CIA, uses Satanic principles to confuse its victims, by telling them that pain is pleasure and pleasure is pain, and eventually breaking down victims so they can no longer distinguish between the two.

There are some secret societies which are mostly political and economic in nature, such as groups like the Trilateral Commission or the CFR (Council on Foreign Relations), who go around convincing the world about the great benefits of globalization (the elite buzzword for centralization of power), global governance and free trade agreements. There are others, however, whose purpose is shrouded in more mystery but seem to involve black magic and Satanic ritual, such as the worshipping of dark gods/entities, the acting out of sexual orgies/fetishes and sacrifice, whether mock or real.

The Bohemian Club, located in San Francisco, is one such group. Every summer in the USA, many key figures of the US elite gather in the tall redwoods of northern California at Bohemian Grove. People such as Henry Kissinger, Richard Nixon, Ronald Reagan, George Bush and other US presidents have attended. Alex Jones successfully infiltrated the Grove once, and was able to videotape one of the rituals that took place there, known as Cremation of Care[321], which involved hooded figures performing a mock sacrifice black magic ritual beneath a forty-foot owl.

---

321 https://www.youtube.com/watch?v=FpKdSvwYsrE

On the other coast of America, at Yale University in Connecticut, lies an old secret society founded in 1832 by William Huntington Russell and Alphonso Taft, known as the Skull and Bones society, and its members as "bonesmen." The late professor Anthony Sutton did some great research on Skull 'n' Bones. Members have admitted having to undergo strange initiation rituals[322] such as making sexual confessions in a tomb, while outsiders have heard chilling howls and screams emanating from the windowless Skull and Bones crypt (see this video[323]).

If you think these secret societies are just perverted people messing around, ask yourself: why would the elite, many of whom are obsessed with power, be involved with them? Why would they engage in such black magic rituals unless they were getting something in return – like more power? These guys control the printing presses of the world, and some have more money than they could possibly spend. It's power they want, not money. Money is just a means to an end. Is it just a coincidence that in the 2004 US presidential election, where George W.

---

322 www.bibliotecapleyades.net/sociopolitica/esp_sociopol_skullbones12.htm

323 www.youtube.com/watch?v=d7Kl1_KH2J4

Bush and John Kerry were running against each other, that both were Bonesmen, with a membership total of around three hundred in a country of nearly three hundred million people? Did MSM news anchor Tim Russert[324] get bumped off[325] for asking too many questions to Bush and Kerry about the secret society?

A scene from the movie *Eyes Wide Shut* directed by Stanley Kubrick, depicting a Satanic sexual black magic ritual at an elite mansion.

The ordinary person will never be initiated into a Satanic secret society, nor get close enough to witness what really goes on in there. It is therefore interesting when someone who does get close to that world decides to spill the beans and show the world what's going on. Such a person was Stanley Kubrick,

---

324 https://www.youtube.com/watch?v=m7bg8egG-zw

325 theocculttruth.com/index.php?p=1_50

the late great filmmaker who many suspect (with strong evidence) was part of the US government's fake Apollo moon landing in 1969. Kubrick may have cut a deal with the devil in making a fake moon landing for the elite because when he handed over the tape for his last film *Eyes Wide Shut*, he was found dead four days later of a heart attack, despite the fact those close to him said he was in fine health and had no history of heart trouble.

Kubrick depicts a black magic scene with a circle of naked women. They drop their clothes to become naked, and are later involved in a massive orgy, where all the participants wear masks to hide their true identities. Kubrick hints in the film that this Satanic-sexual black magic ritual also involves sacrifice and murder, by implying that one of the women/prostitutes was killed during or at the end of the ritual.

Black magic at its core is really about demonic possession. Since the world is made of energy, not matter, and since energy moves in waves which have frequencies, the Satanic rituals are designed to entrain the energetic bio-frequencies of the participants with that of other dark entities, so that there is a vibrational match. Once there is a frequency resonance or lock, an exchange can then take place: energy, intent or information can go from one being, place or dimension can be transferred into another. This works both ways: the person gets possessed and receives information from certain dark entities, while the dark entities also take something from the person. This theme of possession crops up again and again when exposing the worldwide conspiracy, and has been going on a long time.

The late great artist David Dees's impression of what goes on at Satanic black magic rituals like the Bohemian Grove. Sad to say, it's probably very accurate. Note NWO figures (from left) Blair, Bush, Obama, Greenspan, Gates, Brown, Clinton, Rockefeller and Turner.

It is also black magic that is behind the unspeakable and unconscionable phenomenon of missing children. These children are being deliberately kidnapped and taken down into elite-controlled underground facilities where they are mind controlled, turned into slaves and where some of them are even sacrificed at Satanic rituals. If that is too difficult to believe, listen to the testimonies of various mind control victims, researchers, Illuminati defectors or ET contactees, such as Cathy O'Brien,

"Mary Anne"[326], "Svali"[327], Alex Collier[328] (mentioned in chapter 10) and many others.

The God of Freemasonry

Since Satanism is a religion of sorts, a logical question in all of this would be: to whom are Satanists worshipping? To answer that, we will look at the world's most widespread Secret Society, Freemasonry. Centuries of leaked documents, former insider accounts and scholarly research has shown that Freemasonry has become the most pervasive, influential and powerful of all the Secret Societies on Earth. Many US Founding Fathers were masons. Many leading figures of the French Revolution were masons. Many US presidents have been masons. Freemasonry inspired Mormonism and was a central theme behind the occult assassination of JFK[329]. People in high positions of power place their oath to Freemasonry above their oath to serve the people who elected them; some such policemen and judges make decisions not based on truth and justice but rather based on protecting the masonic network, the Lodge and their masonic brethren. Many lower-level masons are deliberately kept in the dark, not told what they are getting into, but what are the higher-level initiates really worshipping? Who or what is the god of Freemasonry? As it turns out, it is the very

326 henrymakow.com/illuminati_defector_mary_anne.html

327 https://www.youtube.com/watch?v=bZtkojaaMm8

328 https://www.youtube.com/watch?v=kXD6_Vwe2j8

329 thefreedomarticles.com/kennedy-assassination-who-how-why-part-3/

same force to which Satanists pray …

In trying to decipher the god of Freemasonry, there are many clues that point towards a dark force that is the engineer or creator of this world, especially the dystopian aspects of this world which some people have dubbed "the establishment," "the system" or "the matrix." It is no coincidence that in *The Matrix* movie series themselves, Neo finally meets his maker (i.e., the being who created the entire system). He is called "the architect" and is represented by a bearded old man. Saturn, god of time, harvest, law and death, is also represented this way. Masons typically refer to their god as the "Great Architect of the Universe" while Gnostics also used the same term in reference to the tyrant they claimed had created a fake, inferior copy of the original perfect world (they also called this force "Demiurge" and "Yaldabaoth"). The primary masonic logo of the letter G is enclosed inside a square and compass, which are tools of an engineer, draftsman or *architect* who designs and draws with them to create things.

The masonic "G".

It's easy to get lost in names here, but the point is to see the connections. There are many names but one underlying force beneath all the names. The Architect/Demiurge is the cruel god who is basically the same force as Satan or the Devil, and goes by many other names, as we shall see.

So what does masonic G, what does it stand for? Official masonic lore[330] claims that it stands both for "God" and "Geometry". Is G a clue for the God of Freemasonry?:

By letters four and science five, this "G" aright doth stand, in due Art and Proportion; you have your answer, friend.

What are the "letters four"? It is believed that they stand for "YHWH", the name of the Great Architect of the Universe pronounced "Yahway" (sometimes pronounced Jehovah) in the ancient Hebrew language, from which the Bible was translated: Which is the 5th science? Geometry. The Letter G stands for "Geometry", which is the mathematical science upon which Architecture and Masonry were founded.

However, there are others who quote famous grand masons Eliphas Levi and Albert Pike to claim that the masonic G really stands for gnosis and generation. Gnosis is the Greek word for knowledge, and this fits in precisely with the masonic ideology of worshiping the light (more on this below) to become

[330] www.masonic-lodge-of-education.com/letter-g.html

enlightened or illuminated (think *Illuminati*). This is from the website GnosticWarrior.com[331]:

In the Mysteries of Magic by Eliphas Levi and interpreted by Arthur Edward Waite, it is written; "All these magical theorems, based on the unique dogma of Hermes, and on the analogical inductions of science, have been invariably confirmed by the visions of ecstatics and by the convulsions of cataleptics under the supposed possession of spirits. The G which Freemasons place in the centre of the Burning Star signifies Gnosis and Generation, the two sacred words of the ancient Kabbalah. It also signifies Grand Architect, for the Pentagram, from whatever side it may be looked at, always represents an A. (Also See Eliphas Levi, Dogme et Rituel de la Haute Magie, vol. II, p. 97.)

Albert Pike had reconfirmed this fact by quoting Levi in his book, Liturgy of the Ancient and Accepted Scottish Rite of Freemasonry: IV to XIV; "In the centre of this Blazing Star Freemasons place the letter G. It signifies Gnosis and Generation, the two sacred words of the ancient Kabala; and also the Grand Architect; for the Pentagram, whichever way we view it, presents the letter A."

Is the God of Freemasonry Jahbulon? Historian Jasper Ridley claims in his book *The Freemasons* that before joining a lodge all Masons must accept that the God of Freemasonry is Jahbulon and that they learn this once they get to the Royal Arch Degree. Interestingly, Jahbulon is a composite word

---

331 https://gnosticwarrior.com/g.html

made up of three parts: *Jah* is the Hebrew name for God (Jahovah is very similar to Jehovah) and is also used by certain Rastafarian religions to mean God; *Bul* refers to the Babylonian deity Baal; and *On* refers to the Egyptian deity Osiris.

Baal is mentioned in the Bible as a god who demanded and required human sacrifice. Baal is another name for the Babylonian god Nimrod. The ancient Mystery Schools which spawned the world's current secret societies, of which Freemasonry became the dominant strain, trace their roots back to Egypt and Babylon. Hence Nimrod may be yet another name for the God of Freemasonry. This article on MediaMonarchy.com[332] states:

Masonic writings ... dwell heavily on a descendant of Ham as one of the founders of Masonry—Nimrod. In the Encyclopedia of Freemasonry (Mackey-McClenachan), under the heading "Nimrod," we find:
"The legend of the Craft in the Old Constitutions refers to Nimrod as one of the founders of Masonry. Thus in the York MS., No. 1, we read: "At ye making of ye toure of Babell there was a Masonrie first much esteemed of, and the King of Babilon yt called Nimrod was a Mason himself and loved well Masons".

...

As Nimrod had so many things attributed to him, it was only reasonable for peoples, now in segregation, to adopt the portion of belief best interpreted by each group. Thus, diverse religious attributes and beliefs,

332 mediamonarchy.com/2015/02/masonic-roots-christ-solomon-or-baa/

yet peoples remaining reverent to their god. We find such names for this revered god (Nimrod) in scripture as Chemosh, Molock, Merodach, Remphan, Tamuz, and Baal, to mention only a few of the some thirty-eight Biblical titles plus numerous representatives of these "gods".

Did you catch that Molock (aka Moloch, Molech) was among the other names of the God of Freemasonry? The is the same Molech already discussed at Bohemian Grove – a giant forty-foot owl under which mock (or not) sacrifices are made.

Statue of George Washington, first US president and high-level Freemason, in a Baphomet pose.

Baphomet is another god associated with Freemasonry, even though some Freemasons officially deny it. You can see master mason George Washington doing his baphomet pose above. Baphomet was a hermaphroditic god (having both male and female genitalia) which will begin to take on more significance in the future, as we head into a transhumanistic world where the NWO transgender agenda (part of the synthetic agenda – see chapter 11) is to make all humans more robotic – nonbinary, genderless and sexless. Baphomet's head is an inverted five-pointed star/pentagram (more Satanic inversion), and being a goat he is linked to Mendes, Pan (god of the wild, often linked to horniness and sexual excess), Capricorn (the zodiac sign symbolized by goat horns) and of course Saturn (housed in Capricorn in the night sky).

Albert Pike and Manly Hall are former masons whose work is widely quoted by those seeking to understand what exactly Freemasonry is. Both of these men referred explicitly to Lucifer as the God of Freemasonry. Pike spoke of the pure doctrine of Lucifer while Hall wrote about the seething energies of Lucifer which can be awakened by master masons:

Lucifer, the Light-bearer ! Strange and mysterious name to give to the Spirit of darkness! Lucifer, the Son of the Morning! It is he who bears the Light, and with its splendors intolerable, blinds feeble, sensual or selfish souls? Doubt it not!

– Albert Pike (33° Freemason), *Morals and Dogma of the ancient and Accepted Scottish Rite of Freemasonry*, p. 321[333]

When the Mason learns that the key to the warrior on the block is the proper application of the dynamo of

[333] https://www.christian-restoration.com/fmasonry/lucquotes.htm

living power, he has learned the mystery of his craft. The seething energies of Lucifer are in his hands and before he may step onwards and upwards he must prove his ability to properly apply (this) energy.

– Manly Hall (33° Freemason), *Lost Keys of Freemasonry*, p. 48[334]

Freemasonry, like other strands of Satanism, inverts everything and takes the opposite as the truth. Grand commander and sovereign pontiff of universal freemasonry Albert Pike were quoted as giving instructions to the twenty-three supreme councils of the world:

That which we must say to the crowd is, we worship a god, but it is the god one adores without superstition. To you sovereign grand inspector general, we say this and you may repeat it to the brethren of the 32nd, 31st and 30th degrees – the Masonic religion should be by all of us initiates of the high degrees, maintained in the purity of the luciferian doctrine. If lucifer were not god, would Adonay (the God of the Christians) whose deeds prove cruelty, perfidy and hatred of man, barbarism and repulsion for science, would Adonay and His priests, calumniate Him? Yes, lucifer is god, and unfortunately Adonay is also God, for the eternal law is that there is no light without shade, no beauty without ugliness, no white without black, for the absolute can only exist as two gods. darkness being necessary for light to serve as its foil, as the pedestal

334 www.manlyphall.org/text/the-lost-keys-of-freemasonry/chapter-iv-the-fellow-craft/

is necessary to the statue, and the brake to the locomotive. Thus, the doctrine of Satanism is heresy, and the true and pure philosophical religion is the belief in lucifer, the equal of Adonay, but lucifer, god of light and god of good, is struggling for humanity against Adonay, the god of darkness and evil.

– Recorded by A.C. De La Rive[335], *La Femme et L'enfant dans La Franc-Maconnerie Universelle*, pg. 588. Cited from 'The Question of Freemasonry" (2nd edition 1986 by Edward Decker pp. 12–14)

This is the very same Albert Pike I have quoted elsewhere as predicting a World War III scenario, where the NWO controllers pit Zionism against Islam[336]:

We shall unleash the nihilists and the atheists and we shall provoke a great social cataclysm which in all its horror will show clearly to all nations the effect of absolute atheism; the origins of savagery and of most bloody turmoil. Then everywhere, the people will be forced to defend themselves against the world minority of the world revolutionaries and will exterminate those destroyers of civilization and the multitudes disillusioned with Christianity whose spirits will be from that moment without direction and leadership and anxious for an ideal, but without knowledge where to send its adoration, will receive the true light through the universal manifestation of the pure doctrine of Lucifer brought finally out into

335 ibid.

336 https://www.goodreads.com/author/quotes/69103.Albert_Pike

public view. A manifestation which will result from a general reactionary movement which will follow the destruction of Christianity and Atheism; both conquered and exterminated at the same time.

What is most important is to see the deeper unity of reality, to connect the dots among seemingly disparate names, terms, ideas and cultures. Whether you call this dark force the Great Architect of the Universe, the Demiurge, Yaldabaoth, Satan, Devil, Yahweh, Jehovah, Saturn, Jahbulon, Baal, Nimrod or Lucifer, it's the same basic force. Rich and powerful people are worshipping something – and they're not just doing it for fun. They're getting something out of it. They are literally selling their souls – handing them over for possession – in exchange for (what they perceive as) power but which in reality is a diminishment of their power.

Sacrificing a Chicken to Moloch?

Lastly, we will finish this chapter by looking at some of the emails published by WikiLeaks, a great organization which has promoted transparency by leaking hundreds of thousands of official cables and emails. WikiLeaks has a 100 percent authenticity rate in its publishing, meaning that no document it has ever published has been proven to be fake or inauthentic. This is one of many reasons why Australian Julian is such a hero and a true journalist, and why the CIA and USG have been out to get him for years. A lot of fuss was made over the "Pizzagate" scandal of 2016, and there were undoubtedly a lot of unsubstantiated theories and exaggerations. However, there was definitely some truth behind it.

WikiLeaks brought us lots of positive proof in the form of the leaked emails of John Podesta, former lobbyist and campaign manager for the 2016 Hillary Clinton presidential campaign. They are replete with references to pedophilia and Satanism – although the pedophilia is couched in code language. Examples were "spirit cooking" and "sacrificing a chicken ... to Moloch" and strange pedophilia code terms such as "pizza", "pasta", "cheese", "walnut sauce" and more.

Email number 30489[337] from the WikiLeaks archive says:

With fingers crossed, the old rabbit's foot out of the box in the attic, I will be sacrificing a chicken in the backyard to Moloch.

Sacrificing a chicken to Moloch! This may be taken literally, or it's quite possible that in pedophilia code that chicken means child, in which case it may be referring to child sacrifice.

It turns out that Marina Abramovic[338] would invite the Podesta brothers (both John and Tony) for "spirit cooking" dinners at her house, where the participants would engage in weird Satanic rituals involving bodily fluids such as blood, semen and breast milk, as well as animal blood. WikiLeaks Podesta email 15893[339] revealed the spirit cooking invitation. In a different email chain, Hillary Clinton asks her assistant Huma

---

337 https://wikileaks.org/clinton-emails/emailid/30489

338 https://www.youtube.com/watch?v=3EsJLNGVJ7E

339 https://wikileaks.com/podesta-emails/emailid/15893

Abedin if Marina will be going with Huma:

Abramovic is known for her often-gory art that confronts pain and ritual. Her first performance involved repeatedly, stabbing herself in her hands. The next performance featured her throwing her nails, toenails, and hair into a flaming five-point star.

These are some of the words Marina painted in blood on her wall during her supposed spirit cooking:

Fresh morning urine sprinkle over nightmare dreams ... with a sharp knife cut deeply into your middle finger of your left hand feel the pain.

Meanwhile, numbers 43113[340], 35581[341] and 32795[342] (among many others) all contain strange and unnatural references to food items such as pizza, pasta, cheese, walnut sauce, ice cream and more. Who speaks like this?

Hi John, The realtor found a handkerchief (I think it has a map that seems pizza-related. Is it yours? They can send it if you want. I know you're busy, so feel free not to respond if it's not yours or you don't want it.

Some have suggested the code is something like this:

---

340 https://wikileaks.org/podesta-emails/emailid/43113

341 https://wikileaks.org/podesta-emails/emailid/35581

342 https://wikileaks.org/podesta-emails/emailid/32795

- Dominos = domination
- Pasta = little boy
- Cheese = little girl
- Hotdog = young boy
- Pizza = young girl
- Map = minor attracted person or semen
- Walnut = African American or African

Email 49435[343] invites Clinton campaign members to a rural getaway – where three children aged six (almost seven), nine and eleven would be supplied for "entertainment":

We plan to heat the pool, so a swim is a possibility. Bonnie will be Uber Service to transport Ruby, Emerson, and Maeve Luzzatto (11, 9, and almost 7) so you'll have some further entertainment, and they will be in that pool for sure.

Given all the evidence leaked by WikiLeaks of a pedophile ring, in a sane world the FBI or some kind of police/law enforcement agency would investigate this. Cracking the code could not be that difficult.

Did they? Not a chance.

To be clear, I am not saying every theory about so-called Pizzagate is correct. Clearly some are off-the-wall and outright wrong. However, there is a thread of truth running through this entire affair. It demands serious investigation.

Conclusion

---

343 https://wikileaks.org/podesta-emails/emailid/49435

All the aspects of dysfunction in our society – including political corruption, mainstream media deception, smart meters, GMOs, toxic vaccines, geoengineering, the militarization of police, fake terrorism, false flag ops, UN Agenda 2030, transhumanism and the human microchipping agenda – are fundamentally connected. They are part of one overarching, grand conspiracy. In order to transform and heal them, it's crucial to realize this. All these issues and more are manifestations of a more primordial evil or unconsciousness in our midst – Satanic black magic. The secretive rituals conducted at Bohemian Grove and elite mansions tell us more about who rules the world than political think tanks or banking cartels, although of course there is an overlap. Our human "leaders" (whether royalty, politicians, business chiefs or military heads) are not running the show – they are willingly giving over their souls during Satanic rituals to otherworldly forces (demonic possession) in exchange for (what they perceive to be) power. Our world is dominated by hierarchies; however, the true hierarchies are those that emanate from the occult world of black magic and not by the outer world of nations, politics and business.

Why is pedophilia such a massive and global phenomenon? It stems from the mindset that dominates the thoughts and acts of those in power. It is a mindset that looks at everyone and everything around it as resources to be used and abused for its own personal gain – even if that gain results in its own self-destruction. It is a mindset that operates according to greed, not need. It is a mindset that believes might is right, and which derives a twisted pleasure from exploiting the weak and innocent. Pedophilia is the manifestation of this predatory and psychopathic mindset in the sexual arena. Not all pedophiles are Satanists, but at the inner core they are.

If humanity is to rise up and overcome the conspiracy, we must focus our attention on the root of evil (not the branches), and use "white magic" in greater force – the harnessing and funneling of our creative powers to make a world of peace, freedom and love. We must continue to expose the deepest aspects of the conspiracy. At the same time, we have to ensure we are not letting the elite siphon off our precious thoughts, emotions and powers to create their nightmarish world, but rather, using those energies within us to create the world we want with positive intention, focus and conscious manifestation. I will get into this more in the second half of this book.

Chapter 10 – Don't Freak Out – Yes ETs Are Real

We are not alone, and we have never been alone.

– Bob Dean, Former Command Sergeant Major at SHAPE (Supreme Headquarters Allied Powers in Europe), NATO

People all over this planet, for at least 6,000 years, have been influenced by extraterrestrials: the Dracos and the Reptilians.

They have taken the information that is in, essentially, every school on the planet and they've modified the information. All history documentation in this country and in every country on the planet have been given lies about astronomy, lies about mathematics, lies about technical capabilities, lies about the universe, you name it. Okay?

Everything has been lies. Every PhD on this planet, whether they're scientific, whether they're medical, makes no difference. Every book that they read the six years they were in the university [was] lies. They are not telling the truth. They were not taught the truth.

– William Tompkins

There is considerable knowledge as far as the actual being of UFO and ET phenomena that we are aware of today.

– John F. Kennedy (according to staff aide)

We have various pressure points in our informational system, our educational system, that can be manipulated. Humans are being manipulated, maybe wittingly, maybe unwittingly, by an extraterrestrial agenda in terms of what information makes it into the universities.

– David Wilcock[344]

They found out about extraterrestrials advising the SS in Germany and Hitler on how to build massive spacecraft carriers, how to build massive space cruisers to operate with the Reptilian Draco space navy … this is the first time anybody in the United States knew that extraterrestrials were actually here on the planet and actually were working with Germany, had agreed, legal agreements, with Hitler.

We then had these Navy spies, which we had operating there 24 hours a day from 1942 to the end of the war.

– William Tompkins

*****

I know in reading this chapter that many people are going to be turned off. Some who have come this far with me are going to reach the edge of their belief

---

[344] https://spherebeingalliance.com/blog/transcript-cosmic-disclosure-deeper-disclosures-from-william-tompkins.html

barriers and refuse to go any farther. I understand this. However, my aim is to uncover the truth, no matter how weird, ugly, negative, bizarre or hard-to-swallow it is. I go where the evidence takes me, and the evidence of the existence of extraterrestrial (ET) and alien life is, indeed, undeniable once you examine it closely. You really can't understand the NWO without understanding the alien influence upon it. The ET issue brings in a whole new and incredibly deep dimension to the topic. I would rather start important discussions in this area and be criticized, ridiculed and thought of as crazy than to play it safe and avoid mentioning this topic of overwhelming importance.

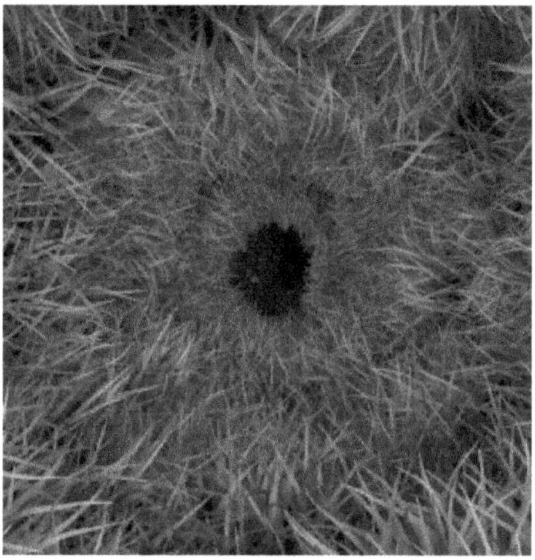

How far down the rabbit hole of conspiracy do you want to go? If you want the truth, you'll have to open your mind. Yes, aliens are real.

The late whistleblower Phil Schneider (more on him soon) put it best when he said that the NWO agenda is the alien agenda. It's essential to realize the directors of the entire NWO conspiracy are nonhuman entities. If you go down the rabbit hole deep enough, the trail goes off planet – both to other worlds and to other dimensions.

The Last Stand of the Last Great US President

To introduce this topic, it may be most helpful to begin by looking at the incredible true story of how consecutive US Presidents Truman, Eisenhower and Kennedy were forced to deal with the ET issue – and what happened as a result. The story is brilliantly researched and told by Dr. Michael Salla in his 2014 book *Kennedy's Last Stand: Eisenhower, UFOs, MJ-12 and JFK's Assassination*. Basically, here's what happened: in early July 1947, a UFO crashed on farmlands in the little town of Roswell, New Mexico, USA (near some US Air Force bases and military installations). A farmer named Mack Brazel found pieces of the craft and reported it to the sheriff. The US military soon got involved and planted a fake story in the media that it was really a weather balloon. As a five-star general and the former supreme commander of the Allied forces in Europe during WWII, Eisenhower was briefed. Apparently real alien bodies – dead and alive – were recovered. Later that year, President Truman decided to set up an entirely new group to handle and oversee what was the most explosive and sensitive topic in all of human affairs. He called the group Majestic 12 or MJ 12. It was composed of senior scientists, military officials and intelligence officials. MJ 12 was closely connected to the CIA; the head of the CIA was also the head of MJ 12.

When Eisenhower replaced Truman as US president at the start of 1953, he set up an advisory committee to help him decide how to handle the alien question. One of the main men on that committee was a Rockefeller – Nelson Rockefeller to be precise (funny how these Rockefellers keep cropping up in matters of supreme importance). After years of deliberation, Eisenhower eventually agreed to Rockefeller's argument that it would be better for a group like MJ 12 to handle the ET issue outside of political polarization and interference so they could continue their work without being subject to political winds of change every four years. Eisenhower soon regretted his decision. In 1958, trying to keep abreast of MJ 12's plans, he asked for updates, and, as the sitting president, was denied because his clearance *was too low*. This infuriated Eisenhower, and when none of his efforts could entice MJ 12 to give him the information he wanted, he finally threatened them, saying he would take the First Army stationed in Colorado and march on Area 51, which is the area in Nevada that was given to the CIA as the headquarters for MJ 12 operations. The CIA was in charge of security.

MJ 12 considered Eisenhower's threat as very credible, so they reluctantly opened up and gave Eisenhower the information he needed. However, the problem of MJ 12's independence from executive oversight continued to bother Eisenhower right to the end of his presidency. We can surmise that advice around the topic was the number-one issue he relayed to the new incoming president, John F. Kennedy, who assumed the presidency in 1961. JFK came from a politically connected family (his father Joe was a former US ambassador to the UK with many connections in the political and business worlds). JFK had served in Congress since 1947. Fortunately for him, then Secretary of the Navy (1944-1947) and Secretary of Defense (1947-1949)

TOP SECRET
EYES ONLY

THE WHITE HOUSE
WASHINGTON

September 24, 1947.

MEMORANDUM FOR THE SECRETARY OF DEFENSE

Dear Secretary Forrestal:

As per our recent conversation on this matter, you are hereby authorized to proceed with all due speed and caution upon your undertaking. Hereafter this matter shall be referred to only as Operation Majestic Twelve.

It continues to be my feeling that any future considerations relative to the ultimate disposition of this matter should rest solely with the Office of the President following appropriate discussions with yourself, Dr. Bush and the Director of Central Intelligence.

TOP SECRET
EYES ONLY

James Forrestal took the young congressman under his wing, giving him access to highly classified information about postwar Germany and even the Roswell UFO crash. Forrestal was part of MJ 12, and was perhaps the only member of the original twelve who was against secrecy and in favor of telling the public the truth. Most likely because of this stance, he was confined to a military hospital in Bethesda and was ultimately said to have jumped or fallen out of his window from a high story, plunging to his death. By then, killing people to hide the truth had already become routine for the secret government.

As president, JFK would soon learn firsthand just how out of control the CIA had become. He signed off on the plan to invade Cuba, a plan which went awry and became known as the Bay of Pigs fiasco. Kennedy was deeply angered and disappointed with the intelligence fed to him by the CIA. He ended up firing the agency's top three men. The director, Allen Dulles, was also the head of MJ 12. Kennedy had begun making inquiries to the CIA during 1961 wanting UFO information, and Dulles had responded by asking some of the other MJ 12 members what they should do about it. Eventually, the group decided that JFK would have to be murdered if he kept pushing for more information. Thus, Dulles managed to put into place a plan to kill JFK, a plan that would later be activated after Dulles was already out of office (he left at the end of that year, 1961).

Meanwhile, in the second year of his presidency in 1962, JFK began visiting various US Air Force bases and gaining access to restricted areas. We can't know for sure, but there is circumstantial evidence he saw a wrecked UFO craft, ET bodies and other ET-related things. At the time, JFK had been having an affair with famous actress Marilyn Monroe. She died in very suspicious circumstances after having threatened the Kennedy brothers with going public about the secret topics she had learned from them – that is, ETs and UFOs! Here is the text of the CIA transcript picture:

Wiretape of telephone conversation between reporter Dorothy Kilgallen and her close friend, Howard Rothberg (A); from wiretap of telephone conversation of Marilyn Monroe and Attorney General Robert Kennedy (B). Appraisal of Content: [A portion redacted.]

1. Rothberg discussed the apparent comeback of subject with Kilgallen and the break up with the Kennedys. Rothberg told Kilgallen that she was attending Hollywood parties hosted by the "inner circle" among Hollywood's elite and was becoming the talk of the town again. Rothberg indicated in so many words, that she had secrets to tell, no doubt arising from her trists [sic] with the President and the Attorney General. One such "secret" mentions the visit by the President at a secret air base for the purpose of inspecting things from outer space. Kilgallen replied that she knew what might be the source of visit. In the mid-fifties Kilgallen learned of a secret effort by US and UK governments to identify the origins of crashed spacecraft and dead bodies, from a British government official. Kilgallen believed the story may have come from the New Mexico story in the late forties. Kilgallen said that if the story is true, it would cause terrible embarrassment for Jack and his plans to have NASA put men on the moon.

2. Subject repeatedly called the Attorney General and complained about the way she was being ignored by the President and his brother.

3. Subject threatened to hold a press conference and would tell all.

4. Subject made reference to "bases" in Cuba and knew of the President's plan to kill Castro.

5. Subject made reference to her "diary of secrets" and what the newspapers would do with such disclosures.

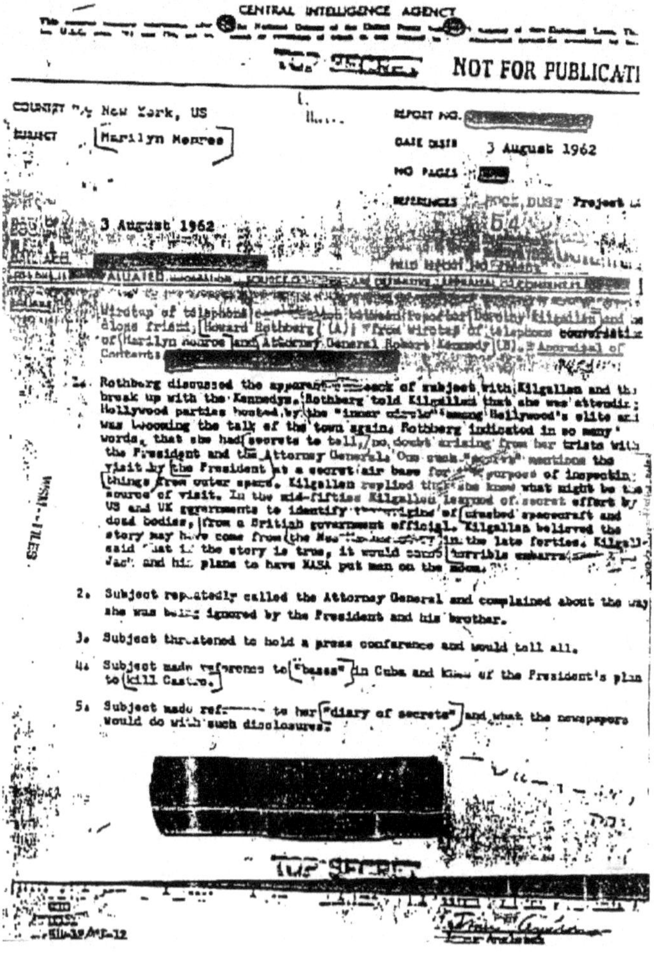

CENTRAL INTELLIGENCE AGENCY

TOP SECRET NOT FOR PUBLICATI

COUNTRY New York, US

SUBJECT Marilyn Monroe

REPORT NO. [redacted]

DATE DISTR 3 August 1962

NO PAGES [redacted]

REFERENCES [illegible] Project [illegible]

3 August 1962

[redacted]

[illegible] EVALUATED [illegible]

Wiretap of telephone conversation between reporter Dorothy Kilgallen and close friend, Howard Rothberg (A); from wiretap of telephone conversation of Marilyn Monroe and Attorney General Robert Kennedy (B). Appraisal of Contents: [redacted]

1. Rothberg discussed the apparent comeback of subject with Kilgallen and the break up with the Kennedys. Rothberg told Kilgallen that she was attending Hollywood parties hosted by the "inner circle" among Hollywood's elite and was booming the talk of the town again. Rothberg indicated in so many words, that she had secrets to tell, no doubt arising from her trysts with the President and the Attorney General. One such "secret" mentions the visit by the President at a secret air base for the purpose of inspecting things from outer space. Kilgallen replied that she knew what might be the source of visit. In the mid-fifties Kilgallen learned of secret effort by US and UK governments to identify the origins of crashed spacecraft and dead bodies, from a British government official. Kilgallen believed the story may have come from the [illegible] incident in the late forties. Kilgallen said that if the story is true, it would cause terrible embarrassment to Jack and his plans to have NASA put men on the moon.

2. Subject repeatedly called the Attorney General and complained about the way she was being ignored by the President and his brother.

3. Subject threatened to hold a press conference and would tell all.

4. Subject made reference to "bases" in Cuba and knew of the President's plan to kill Castro.

5. Subject made reference to her "diary of secrets" and what the newspapers would do with such disclosures.

[redacted]

TOP SECRET

[An indented block of text is redacted near the bottom of the page, and the document is signed JAMES ANGLETON, who at the time was the Chief of Counterintelligence for the CIA.]

JFK, unlike Eisenhower, was not a former general and so not in a position to threaten MJ 12 by storming their bastion with an army. Instead, JFK embarked on a strategy to get them to share their information by forcing their hand. After years of making overtures to the Russians, he finally gained the Soviets' agreement on November 12, 1963 to go in together on joint space and lunar missions. That day he instructed NASA to prepare to begin sharing files, data and information with the Russians. Also on that day, he sent a memo to the CIA instructing them to begin preparing their UFO files, separating out the clandestine US-owned UFOs from the actual "unknowns" or extraterrestrial craft, so that the US could share files with the Russians and not give away classified information relevant to US national security.

Just ten days after these memos, JFK was shot dead.

We have evidence the JFK hit was orchestrated via the cryptic assassination directive below, which states that "it should be wet", a code phrase for assassination used by Russian spies. It read:

Directive Regarding Project ENVIRONMENT

When conditions become non-conducive for growth in our environment and Washington cannot be influenced any further, the weather is lacking any precipitation … it should be wet.

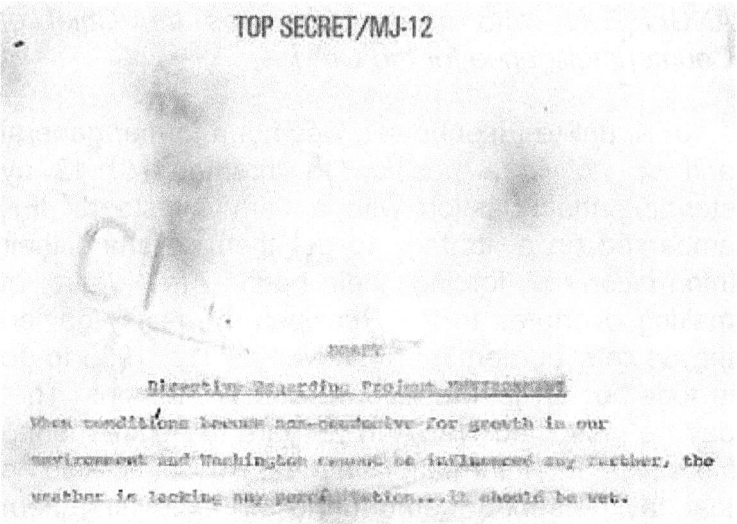

TOP SECRET/MJ-12

DRAFT

Directive Regarding Project [illegible]

When conditions become non-conducive for growth in our environment and Washington cannot be influenced any further, the weather is lacking any precipitation....it should be wet.

So JFK went to Dealey Plaza in Dallas on November 22, 1963, and the rest is history. The American people were robbed of their last great president (the last president to truly stand up to the dark, powerful forces surrounding him), the US was robbed of an opportunity to work together with Russia (to end the Cold War and join forces in exploring space and jointly handle the ET issue), and humanity was robbed of the chance to have an open, informed and intelligent conversation about how to interact with our space visitors.

Things were already in chaos by 1963. The military intelligence agencies had seized control of the management of the ET issue, and they would not relinquish any control, not even to the president, showing they were more than happy to kill to preserve the secrecy and their power. Things have only gotten worse since. MJ 12 and the corporations they have brought in to reverse engineer the alien technology have become, quite literally, a breakaway civilization, as UFO researcher Richard Dolan puts it. They wield massive and unaccountable power, which, from as best as we can tell, must have grown only exponentially, as they have had access to technologies advanced far beyond the average ones on Earth.

The following quote is attributed to Ben Rich, who was at one time the head of Skunkworks, a highly classified division of the giant military corporation Lockheed Martin:

We already have the means to travel among the stars, but these technologies are locked up in black projects and it would take an act of God to ever get them out to benefit humanity ... anything you can imagine we already know how to do.

He also reportedly said this:

The US Air Force has just given us a contract to take ET back home.

<u>Where's The Proof?</u>

Many people are not satisfied with mere stories about aliens. They want cold, hard proof. While such a thing is not always easy in the world of conspiracy, given the colossal amount of lies and coverups, there is a spectrum of evidence, and some of it is extremely compelling. There are many sources with a broad range of provability. The ones listed first here are more "provable" to the rational, logical mind:

– photographic and video evidence of ETs and UFOs;
– eyewitness accounts of alien contactees and alien abductees of their encounters and interactions with ETs;
– alien, abduction and UFO researchers (ufologists) who have listened to and collected hundreds of case files of contactees and abductees;
– testimony of former governmental and military insiders who saw case files and worked in "alien departments" of their organizations;
– declassified governmental and military documents and case files;
– past and present stories, myths and legends from all over the world.

We will go through each of these in turn. As you read through the following, you will come across consistent references to various types of ET species. The four main types that people seem to have the most experience and interaction with are:

– Greys (the most well-known in pop culture; short, almond-shaped face, big eyes, small nose and mouth)
– Reptilians (muscular, aggressive, taller than the average human; basically like an erect crocodile);
– Mantids (an insectoid race of beings which resemble a large praying mantis); and
– Nordics (a race resembling the Nordic people of Germany, Scandinavia, etc.; the most human-looking race of these four types).

Additionally, some people involved have claimed

that certain ET types originate from certain planets or star systems (e.g. the Reptilians from Draco [which is Latin for dragon], a constellation near Ursa Major).

One of the famous UFO photos of alien contactee Billy Meier.

ETs, Aliens and UFOs: Photographic and Video Evidence

Thanks to the spread of technology, there is plenty of genuine photographic and video evidence for the existence of UFOs, despite the internet also being flooded with fake photos and bogus footage. It may take you a while to discern which is which, but if you familiarize yourself with watching them, it will become apparent. As a starting list, the following ones appear genuine:

Japan – The floating mountain
https://www.youtube.com/watch?v=8xCBJNAXxcc

USA – The Phoenix Lights Incident
https://www.youtube.com/watch?v=ymCml-MvleU

London – ET craft/orbs appearing (and rapidly speeding off)
https://www.youtube.com/watch?v=wQmut0XtD3s

Jerusalem (Dome of the Rock)
https://www.youtube.com/watch?v=EKmSf-7Nd-M

Hawaii
https://www.youtube.com/watch?v=p9LRPYO12SU

Italy
https://www.youtube.com/watch?v=YdyQu5Zx8xw

Of the tens of thousands, hundreds of thousands or even millions of genuine sightings, it is probable that some are terrestrial (from Earth not another planet) and originate from the secret black military programs which don't officially exist. All in all, it is *extremely unlikely* all sightings can all be explained away as people daydreaming, hallucinating or faking it.

ETs, Aliens and UFOs: Eyewitness Testimony

Military engineer and geologist Phil Schneider was a brave whistleblower who went public in 1995[345] (and was murdered by "suicide" a year later in 1996). As mentioned earlier, he is the one who first voiced the sentence "The New World Agenda is the

---

[345] https://www.youtube.com/watch?v=xedmfAgx8eg

alien agenda" – and he would have known, because according to his claim, he personally came face-to-face with both hostile Grey and Reptilian ETs while working on the construction of DUMBs (Deep Underground Military Bases). Incredibly, Schneider got into a gunfight with some of these ETs, which resulted in an exchange of fire where Schneider was wounded and the ET killed.

Schneider's accounts include a host of other stunning claims, such as detailed descriptions of underground bases and cities beneath America, the US government's secret deals with hostile ETs, the advanced alien technology being used by secret US agencies, the existence of "corbamite" (element 140), mining operations on the moon and the alien/NWO genocidal agenda to reduce the Earth's population by 85 percent. As much as possible, Schneider backed up his assertions by showing his scar to the cameras, as well as what he claimed was a sample rock of corbamite. Cynthia Drayer, Phil's ex-wife, has highlighted the many suspicious details surrounding Schneider's death[346].

Schneider was close friends with Al Bielek, the man involved in the Philadelphia Experiment and Montauk Project, secret experiments which played

346 www.apfn.org/apfn/ex_wifephil.htm

around with invisibility and time travel, apparently successfully. In this video[347] Bielek reveals special information that Schneider had confided in him, including tales of seven-foot Grey aliens dictating policy at a secret UN underground base, and how Schneider secretly flew to Japan in a private jet to reveal how the Kobe "earthquake" was a nuclear attack by the US. Schneider's account is also corroborated by the Dulce Papers[348] which talk of a fight between humans and aliens in 1979 at the underground base at Dulce, New Mexico.

Alex Collier is an alien contactee, well-known for his interactions with a highly evolved ET species from the Andromeda Galaxy – hence called the Andromedans. Collier claims to have been taken under the wing and mentored by two Andromedans named Vissaeus and Morenae. Collier remains a widely beloved and respected figure for the astounding array of information he has brought forth from his Andromedan relationship. Way back in an interview in 1994, Collier was speaking out about the phenomenon of missing children, the coming NWO, the control of world politicians by dark forces, the existence of Reptilian ETs and much more. Since then, he has brought forth information about the moon, Mars, the holographic nature of reality (he reveals how the Andromedans operate their entire society with holographic technology), the variety of ET races currently on Earth and the possibility of humanity maturing and becoming mentored by advanced ETs. Collier once revealed one of the most

---

347 https://www.youtube.com/watch?v=fuvgTiqlfNk

348 www.subterraneanbases.com/the-dulce-papers/

spiritually profound things ever told to him (by Vissaeus): "The love you withhold is the pain you feel."

Simon Parkes is a modern alien contactee who lives in England, where he also serves in local government as a councillor. Parkes claims to have had relationships with several ET species – Greys, Reptilians and Mantids. He is closest to the Mantids, having actually started a family with one. He believes the main alien agenda is to repopulate the Earth with hybrids, and that the Mantid ETs are cooperating with the Reptilian ETs to achieve this – but that the Mantids are ultimately subservient to the Reptilians. Additionally, Parkes claims that for their abductions, hostile ETs target races which have by tradition rarely married outside their own race, meaning their genetics are more "pure" and closer to the original human.

John Edmonds is an American farmer/rancher who has been very open about his ET experiences, which have been full of pain and suffering. Grey ETs were mutilating and killing his animals and harassing him and his wife. At a certain point, he felt compelled to fight back in self-defense. Phil Schneider made similar claims about the hostile Grey ETs he encountered (Phil also ended up killing a Grey in self-defense and sustained wounds from them).

John writes:

The assaults by these creatures were responded to in the most violent behavior I could respond with because of weekly and some times daily confrontations during which our home, ranch, horses and dogs were killed. Our bedroom as well as our own bodies were assaulted leaving bleeding holes from syringe like wounds. Large bruises on both myself and my wife in the inner thigh, lower stomach, and upper shoulder areas has occurred on many occasions.

Actual undoctored image of a Grey alien. John Edmonds was reluctantly drawn into the world of aliens and had to defend himself, his family and his animals against invading and hostile Grey ETs. Image credit: JohnEdmonds.info.

John mortally wounded at least a few of these Grey ETs, but he states that the Greys literally disappear when hurt. In John's experience, the Greys exist in between dimensions, so they have the ability to pull out of this dimension when they sense danger.

For further reading, see my earlier book 40 Incredible Real Life Alien Abductee and Contactee Experiences: (Controversial Truths Revealed Series

Book 2)[349] which provides a brief summary of forty contactee cases. There are literally tens of thousands – or more likely hundreds of thousands – of cases all over the world and far too many to list. On top of that, there are likely many more we don't know about, since some people either don't recall the incident (self-imposed memory suppression as a psychological defense mechanism to protect against trauma, or externally imposed memory wipe/mind control), or are too afraid to go public with it for fear of ridicule, ostracism or other reasons.

ETs, Aliens and UFOs: Alien and UFO Researchers

For those still skeptical, the work of various alien, UFO and abduction researchers is very compelling. For instance, take the work of Dr. David Jacobs, a tenured professor of American history at Temple University for thirty-seven years, who has interviewed over 150 alien contactees or abductees. Jacobs found in the accounts a repeated theme of extraterrestrial beings abducting and sexually molesting humans to create a race of hybrid human-aliens. Take the work of Budd Hopkins[350], who developed his own hypnotic regression methods to help heal the trauma of thousands of alien abductees – who he realized had become mere specimens in an ongoing ET genetic experimentation on humanity. The common thread running through these cases was the fact that the abductees had a sense of missing time and that their reproductive organs

349 https://www.amazon.com/Incredible-Alien-Abductee-Contactee-Experiences-ebook/dp/B0BG6G9D4P/

350 https://www.youtube.com/watch?v=5A2aGy_2u8c

were often tampered with. In some cases, female abductees were found to have one missing ovary, with no apparent scar tissue to show how it was removed.

Take the work of Dr. Karla Turner, a former college instructor, who wrote three books on alien abduction: *Into the Fringe* (1992), *Taken* (1994) and *Masquerade of Angels* (1994). As she became acquainted with a plethora of alien abduction cases, she also became convinced that the aliens (many of which were Reptilians) were visiting humanity with malicious intent. As Bill Ryan and Kerry Cassidy of Project Camelot[351] wrote:

From beginning to end, Turner had been struck by how contradictory the stories of the aliens were. They would, she averred, say anything they wanted to attain their ends. As the abductees in Taken reported it, the aliens insisted variously that they had come to help us cope with upcoming ecological disaster, interbreed for our good and theirs, help us evolve, take our genetic material to revivify their dying race. Sometimes they claimed they had outright created us; other times, that they were genetically altering us for our own good.

Many other researchers have helped add to our

[351] projectcamelot.org/turner.html

knowledge base of an alien agenda, such as Mary Rodwell, John Mack, John Carpenter, Bill Baldwin and Barbara Lamb. Of special note are the works of Dr. Roger Leir (who pioneered research into the shocking phenomenon of alien implants) and Barbara Bartholic, whose protégés included Karla Turner, Eve Lorgen and James Bartley. Bartley[352] actually wrote the following about Bartholic:

Barbara quickly realized energetic harvesting was a key component of the alien abduction syndrome. Barbara was an empath and highly intuitive and laboured endlessly to document every facet of a person's alien abduction experiences. She knew the negative aliens manipulated the energy centres and emotions of alien abductees in order to nourish and empower themselves at the expense of the abductees. This process is being played out on a macro society-wide scale. Alien abduction is an all out assault on the abducted humans: physically, emotionally, energetically and spiritually.

ETs, Aliens and UFOs: Testimony of Former Insiders

There are many level-headed former governmental and military operatives who have attested to the existence of an alien agenda, too. Take the whistleblowing efforts of Bob Dean[353], who has given an abundance of presentations about his time at SHAPE (Supreme Headquarters Allied Powers Europe) at the top of NATO. Dean tells the

---

[352] www.theoutpostforum.com/tof/showthread.php?1269-The-Legacy-of-Barbara-Bartholic

[353] https://www.youtube.com/watch?v=NvBluLZrFh0

story of how NATO knew there were ET craft above our skies, commissioned a study to see what could be done about it. The study concluded that the ETs probably had no hostile intentions and were here to observe – because if they had really wanted to enslave or destroy us, they could have done it a long time ago!

This was obviously a highly unsettling conclusion for the military brass to deal with but so was another of Dean's revelations: that the top commanders at the Pentagon knew there was a very high likelihood that some alien species (such as the Nordic-looking race of ETs) appeared so humanlike that you could walk right next to one and never spot the difference. Dean later himself had face-to-face meetings with some of these ETs, who he claimed appeared indistinguishable from terrestrial humans.

Another former military man Robert Salas[354] (a retired air force captain) went public with his encounter with a UFO while on duty in a nuclear missile silo. This was a military cover up until recently declassified. He relates the amazing story of a large,

354 https://www.youtube.com/watch?v=FbBc_LmXkbQ

pulsating red oval thirty to forty feet (ten to thirteen meters) in diameter hovered over the silo's front gate. Seconds later the missiles underwent a "control system failure." Did peaceful, intelligent ETs disable the nuclear weapons? Salas' story is one of many of the same theme where manmade nuclear missiles suddenly stop working for no apparent reason.

The late William Tompkins (who died in 2017) is one of the most intriguing whistleblowers to step forward. The depth and implications of his testimony are nothing short of astounding. Tompkins claims he was part of an operation involving US Navy spies who stole UFO plans and antigravity technological secrets from the Nazis during the height of World War II. He asserts he personally distributed some of these stolen secrets as information packages to the CEOs of leading American corporations involved in the military and space industries. Furthermore, William Tompkins says he actually worked alongside ETs – Nordic alien women who were indistinguishable from humans and who were working as his secretaries. Additionally, he reveals that the Nazis already had operational UFOs during the war, and because of the information that the US spies were able to obtain, the US later developed its own fleet of UFOs – which then got siphoned off into the black military sphere under the control of the aforementioned MJ 12.

To understand the information Tompkins brought forth in its historical context, we have to go all the way back to before World War II began. You may have heard of secret societies that were in existence around the time of the rise of Hitler and the Nazis, such as the Thule Society and the Vril Society. There is an important story told about a certain talented young woman by the name of Maria Orsic (right). It is reported that she managed to make contact with alien civilizations and channel information from them.

One of these civilizations was apparently from the planet Aldebaran, which is located in the Taurus system. According to Tompkins, the Nazis were in contact with Extraterrestrial Reptilians at the same time as Orsic was doing her channeling. Hitler found out about Orsic, her abilities and the fact she was receiving information on how to construct UFOs. Again, according to Tompkins, Hitler allowed Orsic (and the Nordics with whom she was working) to continue work on their UFO program, because the Nazis were already in contact with the Reptilians – and because Hitler knew he could always come in take over Orsic's project at any time.

Robert Wood, who was interviewed alongside William Tompkins by Search4TruthReality[355], claims that the Nazis' technology rapidly advanced due to

[355] https://www.youtube.com/watch?v=Chn7i42aDh0

their relationship with the Reptilians, such that they actually got to the far side of the moon before the end of WWII. Wood is a veteran expert in the UFO field himself, having been given the task early in his career (when he was working at Douglas) to analyze how UFOs worked. He was given $500,000 to disseminate UFO documents and $250,000 to make a UFO documentary. Later, Robert and his son Ryan scanned hundreds of MJ 12 documents and made them available on their website[356].

Now, fast forward to 1942, where the tale begins for Tompkins. The world is smack dab in the middle of WWII. The two brutal dictators Hitler and Stalin are commanding armies engaged in long battles with high fatalities on both sides. Meanwhile, unbeknownst to almost the entire world except for a few insiders, the Nazis are deep into a secret UFO project. Having obtained schematics from a group of female channelers (one of whom was named Maria Orsic, above), the Nazis already had operational UFO craft, such as the Haunebu. During all this, almost on the other side of the world from Moscow, on February 24 to 25, 1942, UFOs flew over the LA sky for hours. Tompkins, who was still a boy in high school, watched the UFOs all night. The incident later becomes known as the infamous Battle of Los Angeles. Several weeks later he is taken from high school to work in the military. His life takes a whole new direction.

---

356 www.majesticdocuments.com

Artist rendition of the Haunebu, a Nazi model UFO secretly worked on during WWII.

Close up shot of UFO in the Battle of Los Angeles, February 24-25, 1942.

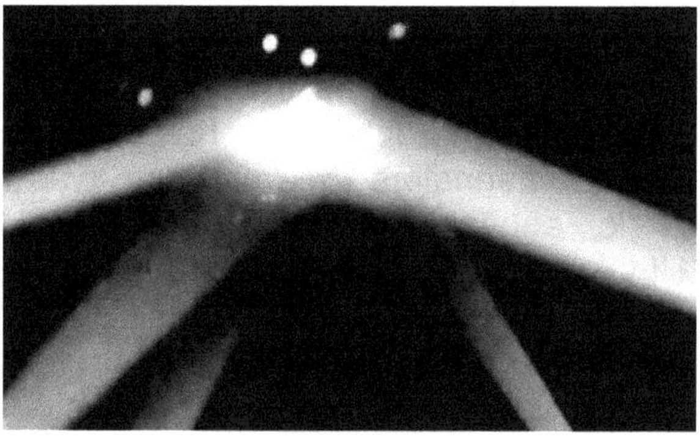

JFK, left, with Curtis LeMay, right. According to several sources, LeMay was part of the original twelve members of MJ 12, and according to Tompkins, may even have been part of the original four members which gathered in 1942. LeMay was another one of those aggressive generals who disliked the peace-seeking Kennedy.

Tompkins states he was recruited at a young age by the US Navy due to his precocious ability to build highly accurate model ships. After working at North American Aviation and Northrop, he was hired by Douglas Aircraft Company in 1950. There he worked as a draftsman under a group partly controlled by US Navy personnel who used to work for James Forrestal – the very same one mentioned in the opening story of this chapter who took JFK under his wing. Tompkins has more to add to the picture: he claims that Forrestal was an ET contactee himself and that Forrestal chose Admiral Rico Botta, who in turn chose William Tompkins. It seems both Forrestal and Botta were guided to choose someone under them who was open to the extraterrestrial reality, someone who could handle the (colossal) truth.

In interviews such as with Project Camelot[357] and

[357] https://www.youtube.com/watch?v=Sb18kkVlRh4

in his book *Selected by Extraterrestrials*, Tompkins reveals much of his story. Contrary to the accepted version among alternative researchers, Tompkins states that MJ 12 actually began in 1942 with the Donald Douglas Sr. (the man who started the Douglas Aircraft Company). Tompkins states that right after Battle of Los Angeles in 1942,

Douglas pulled some key men into a group (or think tank) which later became MJ 12. The group included two admirals and two generals, one of whom was Curtis LeMay – another man who disliked JFK and who, during the Cold War, was prepared to launch a preemptive nuclear strike against the Soviet Union.

During WWII, US Navy operatives were embedded inside the Nazi military. They were able to get data (including pictures) of the Nazi UFOs and relay the information back to the US. Tompkins explains how the information went through his superior, Rico Botta, who chose an ingenious way to handle the subject: by not classifying it at all. If he had given it top secret classification or another high classification, it may have attracted unwanted attention. This technique is known as *hiding the truth in plain sight*.

Tompkins was assigned the job of handing out packages containing this information to the CEOs and leaders of private military corporations. Unfortunately, the packets didn't contain good schematics or drawings of the Nazi technology but were rather like chicken scratching with very little technical information. Apparently they even contained hieroglyphics (not the German language) since the operatives accessed the actual channeled information that had come via Maria Orsic!

In various interviews such as with Jeff Rense[358], Tompkins discusses his theory that our moon is not a natural object but rather an artificial object and command center. This aligns with what other researchers such as David Icke have warned about. Our moon doesn't rotate and neither do other moons of other planets. Conventional physics explains this is because of a tidal lock, but is it perhaps because these artificial objects are hiding something on their dark sides facing away from their host planets?

Tompkins states that when the first astronauts went to the moon, they were shocked to discover it was already occupied – by Draco Reptilians. He says the Reptilians, over nine feet tall, were standing there next to their advanced craft. He jokes that the Reptilians *"gave us the finger"* (i.e. acted in an unfriendly manner). According to both Tompkins and Wood, the Reptilians had already made a deal with the Nazis.

Amazingly, Tompkins himself claims he saw ancient structures on the far side of the moon and that he saw a floating building –

358 https://www.youtube.com/watch?v=mjHhlVMLeBg

1.5 miles above the lunar surface! For Tompkins, the entire Apollo 11 mission was a show. All the astronauts were Freemasons. He states that Freemasons put the plaque on the moon first and then got back in the module to do the "Neil Armstrong" show. Perhaps Armstrong should have said: *"One small step for Man, one giant leap for Masonry."* Finally, Tompkins goes deep into the conspiracy by saying that ultimately we don't own our planet; it is a laboratory for advanced ETs to conduct experiments upon us.

Tompkins stated that although there are many ET species interacting with humanity right now, including Dracos/Reptilians which influence some groups and Nordics which influence others, that Reptilians basically control every government in the world. In his Project Camelot interview, Tompkins warned that if he talked about Reptilians and their darkest activities – which include eating humans and performing blood sacrifices – then some people will think it so crazy that they would automatically shut down and discredit everything else he has said. Kerry Cassidy reiterates the philosophy of Project Camelot: that humans in general are not protecting themselves and are ignorant of the dangers of predatory ET species; therefore, it is vital that those in the know go public with their knowledge and warn others – because not to do so equates to culpability. For what it's worth, Tompkins also offer his opinion that all recent US Presidents (including Obama) have been Reptilians who could change their form – except Donald Trump who is not one of them.

So why William Tompkins? He thought he was

being given the green light, while others like him were being threatened or having their families threatened. He chalked it up to his association with Nordic ETs, specifically two women and one man who used to be his secretaries. As an aside, he did not know for a long time that he even had ETs working for him. He only found this out when one of them fell down the stairs and was taken to hospital in a grave condition. He overheard her admitting she was not who she said she was and answering to another boss or captain. Tompkins believes the Nordics had been helping him all along by clearing the way for him to do certain things.

Tompkins liked to say throughout his interviews that *"everything you're told is a lie"*. He claimed that many of the systems and sciences we pursue, such as astronomy, medicine, etc., have been seeded with lies to trick us. This harks back to his claim that every government on Earth right now is under Reptilian control. Whether that turns out to be true or not remains to be seen, but so much deception has already been uncovered in so many areas of life that it is wisest to remain open to this possibility. Above is

a another US military patch featuring the reptile theme and a Latin motto. Rough translation: "With all your bases you're serving us."

Tompkins' tale reaffirms that the extraordinary story of humanity, and the depth of the worldwide conspiracy, cannot possibly be grasped without comprehending the reality of ET interference in our past and current ET influence and control over our affairs.

<u>ETs, Aliens and UFOs: Declassified Documents and Case Files</u>

Many governments have declassified and released their UFO files. In 2015 the US government declassified files from Project Blue Book (although this project was designed to appease the public after potential hot potato issues like the Roswell crash, so the best cases were kept secret and not included).

This site[359] shows a list of twenty-four countries/ organizations that have done so, including Argentina, Australia, Brazil, Canada, Chile, China, Denmark, Finland, France, Germany, India, Ireland, Japan, Mexico, New Zealand (Additional Report), Peru, Russia, Spain, Sweden, Ukraine (not in English), United Nations, United Kingdom, Uruguay and even Vatican City. This is impressive evidence for those would deny the existence of UFOs.

ETs, Aliens and UFOs: Alien Stories, Myths and Legends

Humanity's history is replete with references to aliens. The ancient Vedic texts of India mention *vimanas* or flying discs. Zulu shaman Credo Mutwa, introduced to many in the Western world by David Icke, tells stories of how reptilian beings feature

359 www.educatinghumanity.com/2011/01/list-of-countries-that-have-disclosed.html

throughout his people's history. Zechariah Sitchin, Jordan Maxwell and many others talked about how the Bible itself originally talked of "*elohim*" meaning "the gods" not "God" as it became mistranslated. According to Sitchin, two Reptilian ET beings named Enlil and Enki of the Annunaki seeded humanity. The dragon is a ubiquitous symbol in China. Is it just a myth, or does it signify something deeper?

If humanity itself was created by an advanced extraterrestrial race, as the article *Scientists Find Extraterrestrial Genes In Human DNA*[360] and others suggest, how could there not be an alien agenda with humanity right now? How could aliens not be intimately involved with our current progress? And since the world is being pushed towards the NWO, wouldn't it be fair to assume it is happening in alignment with their desires – an alien agenda?

So Aliens Are Among Us – But Are They Malevolent?

Given the compelling evidence presented above (a tiny fraction of all the evidence in existence on the topic) – which not only indicates the existence of ETs but also shows that many are interfering in Earthly affairs with a hostile agenda – it's surprising that there is still the widespread perception that "all ETs are benevolent and have humanity's best interest at heart." This is foolish nonsense – and dangerous nonsense, too, because it gives people a false idea about our galactic neighbors, thus lowering their defenses and making them more susceptible to some kind of invasion or manipulation.

---

[360] https://rense.com/general74/d3af.htm

The alien agenda ain't all love and roses – you'd better believe it!

For some reason, this notion has been pushed by none other than Dr. Steven Greer of the *Disclosure Project*. Greer has done a truly outstanding job in bringing ET and UFO witnesses to light and has exposed many aspects of the conspiracy, including the suppression of zero point or free energy technology. Sadly, because Greer is a leading expert in the ET/UFO field, many blindly accept every word he says on the subject. He insists all the so-called negative interactions experienced by so many alien abductees are secret black military operations – MILABs (Military Abductions). I believe Greer has totally missed the mark on this point, as he ignores the copious evidence of abductees who have suffered tremendous trauma at the hands of hostile ETs such as the Reptilians. Aforementioned researchers such as Turner and Bartley alone have gathered hundreds and hundreds of case studies in this area. Kerry Cassidy and Bill Ryan of Project Camelot (now just run by Cassidy) pointed out the flaws in Greer's argument in this heated discussion[361], as have other leading experts on exopolitics such as Dr. Michael Salla who wrote the

---

361 https://www.youtube.com/watch?v=hzqDVOjtNhg

rebuttal *Exopolitics vs Exospin*[362]. Salla quotes the Lieutenant Colonel Philip Corso – the same one who wrote the famous book *The Day After Roswell* in 1997 and who stated publicly[363] that he briefed then US Attorney-General Bobby Kennedy (brother of President John Kennedy) on the ET issue:

[Greer puts forth] a gross misrepresentation of Col Corso's position as evidenced in statements such as the following in his soon to be published private notes:
... the aliens have shown a callous indifference concerning their victims. Their behavior has been insidious and it appears they might be using our earth and manipulating earth life.

The All-Seeing Eye. Are there reptilian scales around that eye?

Skeptics will excuse them that possibly they are benevolent and want to help, however, there is no evidence they have healed anyone or alleviated human ailments. On the other hand, they have caused pain, suffering and even death (http://www.exopolitics.org/Exo-Comment-39.htm).

---

362 www.paradigmresearchgroup.org/article-salla1.html

363 https://www.youtube.com/watch?v=t3eTgeeasKs

Some have theorized Greer's views have been compromised due to his connection with Lawrence Rockefeller of the infamous Rockefeller family (there they are again). Many have exposed the malevolent alien connection to world events, but David Icke has been the most comprehensive in the many books he has written on the Reptilian theme which is inextricably intertwined with the NWO. *The Biggest Secret* (1999), *Children of the Matrix* (2001) and *The Perception Deception* (2013) in particular contain a monumental amount of dot-connecting and information showing that at the apex of the NWO pyramid are nonhuman entities. Specifically, the connection between hostile ETs (like many Reptilians) and certain humans (of certain bloodline and vibrations frequencies) is made through black magic – Satanic rituals of sex and sacrifice – as exposed in the previous chapter. The key concept here is infiltration by a reptilian species which has created reptilian-human hybrids, which allows them to take on both a reptilian form and a human form.

SSP plus *Twenty and Back*

If you've made it this far and think you've already heard enough, then strap on your seat belt because there's a bit more yet in this chapter to blow your socks off. Some researchers have been on the trail of an elusive subject we know little about; however, that "little" is growing. Unfortunately we don't have hard and fast "proof", but we do have an increasing number of (seemingly unrelated) whistleblowers saying similar or identical things about this topic – always a synchronicity and an important clue.

I refer to a massive operation being carried out in space known simply as the Secret Space Program (SSP). It involves the covert military colonization of our solar system (especially the moon and Mars), while space agencies like NASA put on a fake public face and lie to the public about the real state of technology. One of the first pieces of hard evidence we had about the SSP was when Scottish computer geek Gary McKinnon in 2001-2002 hacked into various US military databases, including a NASA database, and found interesting references to deep space operations. McKinnon actually saw a database list "non-terrestrial officers." The US had been trying unsuccessfully to extradite McKinnon to the US to try him for his "crime" of informing the public about what the shadow government has been hiding.

However, what McKinnon found out was small potatoes compared with what some whistleblowers have allegedly experienced. People such as Michael Relfe, Arthur Neumann (aka Henry Deacon), Andy Basiago, Bernard Mendez, William Brett Stillings, Michael Prince, Randy Cramer (aka Captain K or Kaye), Tony Rodrigues, Michael Gerloff, Penny Bradley, James Rink and Corey Goode have all talked of either setting foot on Mars or participating in the SSP to some degree. Their accounts vary in credibility; however, the similarities are striking. Some of these whistleblowers (Relfe, Cramer, Rodrigues, Gerloff and Goode) specifically refer to the *twenty and back* military program. *Twenty and back* is the standard phrase used to describe the tour of duty undergone by recruits into the SSP; it refers to the twenty-year commitment or "tour of duty" that these military agents make when they sign up to go into space – or the amount of time they are forced to serve as slaves.

One of the alleged hallmarks of the *twenty and back* program is that it involves highly advanced technology (time travel and age regression) whereby the recruit, at the end of his/her service, is actually brought back in time to the point at which he/she signed up – plus they are age-regressed to be brought back to their age at that time. This means, in effect, that they gain an extra twenty years' experience in life (although often those memories are inaccessible and buried deep within their subconscious). In other words, they live that same age range/period in their lives twice over, in different places doing different things, and only one of those timelines remains active.

The case of Michael Relfe is the exception rather than the rule because his story only came out when he underwent totally unrelated regression therapy with a licensed therapist to deal with anger and rage issues. Soon the content of the therapy sessions became very revealing. Relfe uncovered hidden memories of twenty years' military service on Mars, including themes of time travel, point-to-point portal travel, mind control, military abduction and alien abduction. His story showed the way in which top secret military personnel are frequently manipulated by having their memories covered over and replaced with new implanted ones to hide the truth of their covert service. There was an attempt made on Relfe's life shortly before he went public with his story, which only added further credibility to his tale.

Randy Cramer initially came out under the pseudonym of "Captain K" or "Captain Kaye." He thinks he has reclaimed his memories of serving on a Mars colony for around seventeen years in the SSP. Cramer was born in 1970 and was trained from three-and-a-half to seventeen years old under Project Mannequin (of which Max Spiers also claimed he was part), a global supersoldier project. Cramer revealed mysterious places and organizations such as the Lunar Operations Command (on the back side of the moon), which was part of the EDF (Earth Defence Force). For most of his time, he worked for the MDF (Mars Defense Force), under the MCC (Mars Colony Corporation), which he claims is a consortium of governments, banks, technological companies, etc. operating mining and other operations on Mars. Cramer states that he worked in the USMC s.s. (United States Marine Corps, special section, same as other whistleblower Michael Gerloff), and that his supervisor requested and gave him permission to speak publicly about his SSP experiences. Cramer claims he worked at a military installation on Mars known as Forward Station Zebra. He states he could breathe the air on Mars, albeit with a little difficulty, and usually used a kind of powered environment suit to walk on the surface. He says that there were some native humanoid species on Mars – one reptoid and one insectoid – with whom he had occasional interaction. At some point during his tour, things developed into a brutal four-way war among the Earth humans, two native Martian species and the Reptilians. Then there was a catastrophic event which almost wiped out Cramer's entire station and its sister station. Since there were around 260 military personnel stationed at each of these bases, this event resulted in the death of (at least) around 520 people. At the end of his time, he was regressed and brought back into a younger cloned body of seventeen years old and inserted back into Earth life. It took him a lot of effort and inner psychological work to retrieve these memories and integrate them back into his life.

Cramer believes we have colonies not just on the moon and Mars, but also all over the Solar System and beyond. He also thinks the reason for all the secrecy is that the program was originated to preserve entire human culture and DNA, but the agenda morphed into "let's save just a few elite special people and not everyone." Cramer believes that if governmental disclosure occurred and if humanity could talk to our intergalactic brothers and sisters, they would enlighten us about new societal, political and economic systems that are not exploitative – which would undermine our current debt-based, wage-slave monetary system. Interestingly, Cramer reveals that in his journeys he had access to all sorts of incredible technology that was so advanced most people would regard it as magic. He mentions something called an "ARC" (Aeronautical Repositioning Chamber) which was the jump room that took people from Earth to Mars, meaning something akin to a teleportation pad or station. In the realm of medical technology, he also speaks of the existence of holographic technology which can be used to restore massive tissue loss and damaged organs, regrow limbs and cure supposedly terminal illnesses like cancer.

Tony Rodrigues was abducted as a young boy

and eventually ended up in the *twenty and back* program. He claims he was abducted by five aliens after teasing another kid in his grade whose father was high up in the Illuminati. He ended up in a situation where he was used with other children as sex slaves in Seattle at age thirteen. He underwent brutal training, including sexual abuse and being forced to attend Satanic rituals and engage in cannibalism. Later on at age sixteen in 1988, he went to the moon. During his time in the SSP, Tony was treated as a slave and had to work incredibly hard. He claims he worked as a cargo officer on a ship within the Solar System dropping off cargo at various bases (including moons of other planets e.g., Enceladus on Saturn). He reveals how some of the cargo was advanced alien technology (nuclear missiles far more sophisticated than terrestrial nuclear weapons). He mostly worked on Ceres (the largest asteroid in Solar System, in the asteroid belt between Mars and Jupiter). There was a large base concealed in darkness at a location on Ceres. Tony recalls visiting many Earth-like planets during his SSP time. The fact that he recalls so many details (some minor, some major) from his time working in the SSP lends credence to his account. For instance, he often saw the Nazi eagle on the uniforms of officials who commanded him (sometimes with a swastika below, sometimes with other symbols); he saw Ahuna Mons out of his spaceship window; he saw other spaceships in hangars; he describes a giant train station in Ceres with giant horses (built with scaffolding) in an underground cavern; the slave workers were constantly spied on, but no one could see the cameras; despite being a slave, he occasionally got paid small amounts (e.g. $20) in a currency called "Franks" which looked like an old Germanic currency; there were facial recognition technological devices for shopping there; there were automatic translators (English <=> German) so he could converse with some of the (grumpy) middle-aged female German shopkeepers there; there was artificial telepathy (with a machine, as opposed to natural/organic telepathy); and he used an incredibly fast magnetics-based train system there for transportation. Tony claims you could get anywhere on Ceres within thirty minutes, despite the fact that it's 580 miles in diameter.

Michael Gerloff is a Marine whistleblower who claims he was recruited into the SSP at age eighteen in 1978. He displayed psychic abilities from a young age (e.g., at age three he left his body and had an OBE (Out of Body Experience). The way Gerloff describes being recruited into (and returned from) the SSP is fascinating. He claims he was training to be a Marine when, in the middle of a test, he was taken aside by a captain and invited to be part of the space corps (this is in line with Randy Cramer's claims of working for the UMSC s.s. or the United States Marine Corps special section). Once Gerloff accepted, he was taken to a room with a load of paperwork and recalls Lockheed Martin being part of that paperwork. He remembers being told about the *twenty and back* program, and being promised that he would be brought back in time at the completion of his tour of duty. After the twenty years had passed, he was taken right back to the very moment when he signed up and into the same room and the same chair with the same captain sitting there. He was very dazed and discombobulated, and he couldn't quite work out what had happened. He went on to serve in the regular Marine corps for some time.

Corey Goode is a highly controversial figure. In many ways, his story goes far beyond even those of the previous whistleblowers whose accounts I have highlighted. The alternative research, conspiracy and UFO communities are divided between whether to accept his testimony at face value or not. Goode claims his family is part of a multigenerational experiment by the military to find star seeds (Indigo children), then use and convert them to the dark side. He states he was trained in DUMBs (deep underground military bases) to get used to ETs. Goode provides a lot of detail about themes such as underground bases in Antarctica, inner Earth caverns, clones, PLFs (Programmed Life Forms – a kind of robotic yet biological lifeform that has no soul) and the colonization of our Solar System. Others have reported these things, too, however in Goode's case, he claims to have interacted with an entirely new ET species that no one else has reported meeting or seeing – the "Blue Avians" – who are birdlike in appearance. He also claims objects (spheres) the size of Neptune or Jupiter have entered our Solar System. Hmm. His account is the most complete and detailed of any SSP testimony. Is it true? Only time will tell.

Finally, we will end this section with the account of lawyer and whistleblower Andrew Basiago. Basiago doesn't speak of doing a *twenty and back* tour, but he does claim to have had firsthand experiences in DARPA's Project Pegasus. DARPA stands for

Defense Advanced Research Project Agency, and is the technological arm of the Pentagon devoted to developing and pursuing technology to further US military aims – and, let's be blunt, dedicated to surveilling, enslaving, controlling and killing more people more efficiently. (That sounds so cool and slick – perhaps it could be their new motto?) Anyway, according to Basiago, DARPA ran a secret operation delving into matters of time-space exploration during the period 1969 to 1972. In this program, Basiago was actually teleported, first across the US, and later to Mars, via what a jump room. He reveals that several other high-profile people were part of the project, including astronaut Buzz Aldrin, DARPA-Google-Facebook agent Regina Dugan and a certain Barry Soetoro (aka Barack Obama) – you may have heard of him. Basiago describes Mars as a desert planet, severely damaged by a solar system catastrophe, with most of its ionosphere blown off, and deficient in oxygen and water. Contrary to what Cramer says, Basiago claims there are around thirty land species engaging in constant, moderate predation against each other. He also states the CIA used "quantum access" technology (the ability to collect data from the future) via a device called a "chronovisor" which enabled its user to see the future.

The SSP is not just an American phenomenon. All the major nations on Earth are involved, and as alluded to earlier, all are secretly cooperating, despite whatever surface tensions they have and play out on the world stage for the benefit of mass media and consumption.

With any kind of whistleblower testimony, you have to develop your own discernment filter to attempt to gauge the truthfulness of it. All of these testimonies and accounts have very similar themes. Yes, sometimes they differ or contradict one another in detail. Yet what they have in common far outstrips any miniscule differences. In a world of vast governmental secrecy, they offer a fantastic glimpse into a whole other world or breakaway civilization which awaits us as we move towards accepting and integrating the truth that we are not the only intelligent species in the universe.

The Alien Agendas

So if aliens or ETs exist, then what do they want? What is their agenda? Well, to answer that with the available evidence, we have to conclude that there is not just one alien agenda. There are many alien agendas that crop up and emerge as common. Here is a brief and incomplete list of some of them, which

run the gamut from positive and helpful to negative and hostile:
– wanting to directly help humanity and see it evolve (although not "save" humanity);
– wanting to help stop humanity killing itself and destroying the planet (e.g., through nuclear weapons);
– wanting to befriend and exchange information with humanity;
– wanting to go back in time (time travel) to prevent an undesirable outcome from occurring;
– wanting to borrow or steal humanity's genetic material (DNA) to reseed, rebreed or revivify their own species (e.g., as is the case with some ET races who have taken a "wrong" evolutionary path and bred out emotion from their genetics);
– wanting to create a hybrid human-alien race;
– wanting to dominate humanity, turn it into a servant or slave race of farm animals, and feed off its emotional energy;
– wanting to trap humanity in perpetuity through an endless cycle of birth, death and rebirth (e.g., through the soul net of soul recycling / forced reincarnation);
– wanting to assimilate humanity into an androidlike collective (like the Borg from Star Trek).

It would be most accurate to say the NWO agenda is *an* alien agenda, not *the* alien agenda. The NWO plan is most influenced by the last few agendas in the list above – to trap, subjugate and dominate humanity, and make it a stable source of (emotional) food for its masters.

<u>Open Your Mind to the Wider, Deeper Conspiracy</u>

We are not alone, and we never have been alone, as Bob Dean says. What makes some people think humans are the only species with high intelligence or capable of rational thought in the entire known universe? It is narrow minded to think so, and it is equally narrow minded to assume that any extraterrestrial motive or alien agenda would be neutral or beneficial to us. The cosmos is brimming with life of all kinds.

The significance of the existence of ETs cannot be understated. The topic connects to almost everything. It is related to the subject of free energy (see chapter 15), evolution (e.g., with theories that ETs are related to us through DNA and may have intervened in our past), science (ET biology and technology), religion (understanding the place and significance of humanity in the cosmos) and politics/ sovereignty. Are we mere playthings in the hands of greater forces? Just as the US-Israeli-led NWO uses proxy terrorist armies to fight its wars, it's quite possible different human nations, groups and factions are fighting on behalf of ET handlers.

The available evidence clearly shows that some ETs are here to help, while other ETs are here to harm. We have to be wary and use discernment. No one is our savior. If we even need "saving," we must save ourselves.

Remember, the Game is a whole lot grander than you think. The NWO doesn't end with just political control, police brutality, indoctrination, assassination, infiltration, free-trade agreements, geoengineering, international banking, suppressed technology or microchips; copious evidence shows it goes off-planet into far more bizarre realms than the average person could imagine. How many are up for the task of exploring and analyzing these realms to get to the bottom of the truth?

Chapter 11 – AI is Upon Us: The Smart Prison is Being Built

The technetronic era involves the gradual appearance of a more controlled society. Such a society would be dominated by an elite, unrestrained by traditional values. Soon it will be possible to assert almost continuous surveillance over every citizen and maintain up-to-date complete files containing even the most personal information about the citizen. These files will be subject to instantaneous retrieval by the authorities.

– Zbigniew Brzezinski[364] in his book *Between Two Ages: America's Role in the Technetronic Era*[365]

[In a society ruled by technology, [the] elite [will] not hesitate to achieve its political ends by using the latest modern techniques for influencing public behavior and keeping society under close surveillance and control.

– Patrick Wood[366], *Technocracy Rising: The Trojan*

---

364 thefreedomarticles.com/brzezinski-easier-to-kill-than-control/

365 www.goodreads.com/work/quotes/3269714

366 https://www.goodreads.com/author/show/12095665.Patrick_M_Wood

Horse of Global Transformation[367]

By 2030 ... it will be routine practice to have billions of nanobots coursing through the capillaries of your brains, communicating with each other, as well with our biological neurons and with the internet. One application will require full immersion into Virtual Reality.

– Ray Kurzweil, transhumanist and leader of one of Google's many R&D arms called Deep Mind

Thus, in a way, the creation of the AI smart grid all-encompassing global technological sub-reality cloud, is creating a vehicle for those gods ... to enter this reality and control this reality, through this technological this web, under the name 'AI'. So in many ways [the transhumanist agenda] is an extension of this takeover of human society. Because this archontic force cannot directly operate in this reality, for frequency and atmospheric reasons and many other reasons, it has had to put bloodlines in place within our society, infested with this archontic consciousness [demonic possession] to manipulate human society on its behalf.

This transhumanist technological global network is designed to allow the next stage, which is for this force to actually enter this society and directly manipulate via this network – because if every human mind is connected to an artificial reality that is controlled by this artificial intelligence, this artificial intelligence controls everything, including every

367 https://www.goodreads.com/work/quotes/43925749

[human perception and thought]. When you just study what Kurzweil is saying is going to happen, it's exactly what he's describing.

– David Icke[368]

*****

Technocracy

Technocracy is defined as government by technicians, or the management of society by technical experts such as scientists and engineers. It is derived from two Greek words, *tekhno* (art, skill; a term which has come to mean technology) and *kratia* (rule). So, this is rule by technology or technicians. Technology is a double-edged sword. Unfortunately, much of it has been weaponized and used for control. Sometimes it is used to promise Utopia – a world where every human on Earth will be guaranteed from birth the essentials of life: food, clothing, shelter, education. All at no cost. There are many versions of a technocratic Utopia, and it all sounds great on the surface. But when you dig a little deeper, all Utopias seem to promote collectivism. Is there are any technological Utopia being promoted that doesn't involve hierarchy and top-down control? Why is it that these kinds of "perfect societies" always seem to require a small group of elite technocrats at the top to run them? Importantly, how many people ask themselves the question when presented with flashy new promises of a technological paradise: what will I have to give up if this technocracy

368 https://www.youtube.com/watch?v=Vp8W8Qy5Q9Q

becomes a reality? The answer is always the same: *freedom.*

As you read this, a broad-spectrum technological control grid is being rolled out and erected all around you. It's the "smart" wireless network whose aim is to connect everything in the world, animate or inanimate, and make them nodes on the *smart* grid. In this instance the word *smart*, by the way, is another piece of grand Orwellian propaganda. There is nothing intelligent about setting up networks which can easily be hacked by spies, thieves and other third parties (as has already happened), nor is there anything intelligent about surrounding ourselves with extra large doses of harmful EM (electromagnetic) and RF (radio frequency) radiation. If you substitute the word *smart* for *spy* (*smart* grid = *spy* grid) or stupid (*smart* grid = *stupid* grid), you'll be closer to the truth.

The smart grid is a grave threat to your health, privacy and freedom.

Right now any *smart* device, like a smartphone or tablet, has some kind of microchip (or nanochip, since they are getting smaller all the time) which transmits and receives information to and from the network. This is just the beginning. Appliances are now becoming *smart* – dishwashers, fridges, dryers, washing machines and more are now being produced that can be connected to the internet and the grid. Then, the plan is to force people to live in *smart cities* where everything is automated and monitored 24/7. Corporations are already starting to implant nanochips into their products (such as toothbrushes and children's toys), giving them the ability to track anything they ever made and sold.

The smart grid is currently being augmented by the rollout of 5G (5th Generation), the latest wireless system that telecommunications companies are trying to implement to service wireless communication. It's designed to allow faster downloads of more data. It uses the 28, 37 and 39 GHz bands, also known as millimeter wave (mmW) spectrum. 5G is designed to work in conjunction with another fancy term, the "Internet of Things" or IoT. The agenda is to connect every single material thing on the planet, including humans themselves, to a vast planet-wide web where everything and everyone become nodes on the network – connected by microchips which are nano size and can be inhaled (like smart dust). Many people are encouraging the advancement of 5G by their desire at all costs for convenience and speed (give me my multiple gigabit downloads now!). 5G is not merely an upgrade of wireless infrastructure; it is a giant leap towards the erection and installation of a total technological control grid. The agenda is to cover the entire Earth – including rural areas – with the 5G electromagnetic blanket, so that its effects can literally not be escaped by anyone living on this planet.

If I haven't got your attention yet, please take a look at this video[369] where then FCC (Federal Communications Commission) head Tom Wheeler lays out how 5G is going to happen – consequences be damned. At the 2:42 mark, the video goes through

---

369 https://www.youtube.com/watch?v=OMxfffqyDtc

an edited version of his June 2016 speech at the National Press Club in Washington, DC. From my perspective, Wheeler appears more than just intense or defiant; he borders on the psychopathic. This guy is another former corporate lobbyist using the good old "revolving door" at the top of the business-political world. He now occupies a key governmental office to promote the agenda of his former industry (telecommunications). He is advocating the rollout of a game-changing technology (with toxic and cancerous side effects for some) that's going to affect all life on Earth, but he doesn't want to wait for safety standards. Later on the video, Wheeler ignores and dodges questions about the wireless radiation-cancer connection.

Here's a summary of his points:

– 5G will penetrate material objects better: thanks to "brilliant engineers", 5G radiation will be even harder to shield yourself against;
– 5G will be infrastructure-intensive: the plan is to erect even more radiating towers in every corner of the planet, adding a new meaning to the concept of an electromagnetic soup;
– 5G will make tens of billions of dollars for its owners through "unanticipated and unintended" consequences (after this point, Wheeler slams his fist on the podium and says, "That's damn important!");
– 5G is going to go ahead without the FCC waiting for governmental standards (Wheeler proudly proclaims that "unlike other countries" the US cares about being "first out of the gate" [i.e. economically]. He suggests we "turn innovators loose" rather than wait for committees to decide things. He defiantly

declares, "We won't wait for the standards!");
– 5G will require the sharing of frequencies with the military;
– 5G is the technological basis for the IoT (Wheeler states that "hundreds of millions of microchips" will be in everything [and everyone if they get their way]);
– All parts of the Earth will be covered, so there will be urban and rural radiation saturation.

Like all things in the NWO, 5G can be understood on many levels. Yes, it's about companies rushing forward to make money using unsafe technology and unproven products (a very familiar theme throughout human history – see tobacco, Big Pharma, vaccines, GMOs, etc.). However, that's only the surface level. That is nothing new. The deeper level is really about the construction of a total technological control grid whose ultimate purpose is to know what you're thinking and feeling and then be able to change what you're thinking and feeling so as to control your actions: in other words, complete technological slavery. Like many aspects of the worldwide conspiracy, most people who push forward their particular aspect of the overall agenda are not aware of the deeper ramifications or where the whole thing is headed.

If you think it's farfetched to connect 5G and the IoT with a technological control grid, consider the latest evidence. Do you know that our skin (the largest organ in our body) directly responds to 5G? Are you aware that our sweat ducts act as antennae? Do you know that our sweat ducts can receive signals? We are energetic beings, first and foremost. We vibrate and exude frequencies. To affect people

Wireless radiation in the MHz, GHz and THz is literally millions, billions and trillions (respectively) of times the normal frequency of the Earth – the Schumann Resonance of 7.83 Hz. Image credit: David Dees.

energetically is to affect them physically. Consider these findings by Israeli scientist Dr. Ben-Ishai in this video[370]:

[The 5G frequencies] will zap [us] with wavelengths that will interact with the geometrical structure of our skin … is there a health implication?

…

[In 2008] We found that sweat ducts work like helical antennas … the sweat duct was an integral part of the mechanism for the absorption of energy, electromagnetic, between 75-100 GHz, and that if you changed the character of the sweat duct, i.e. made it work, you could actually change that absorption at some point, and if you could do that you could trace how a person is under stress.

…

370 https://www.youtube.com/watch?v=VuVtGldYXK4

Gal Shafirstein also came to the same conclusion ... he actually looked at SAR rates as well. He did this because the American army had commissioned him to explain why their 94 Ghz proud dispersal gun made people run away when the beam touched them ... if you are unlucky enough to be standing there when it hits you, you feel like your body is on fire ... he found the SAR rate was going very high within sweat duct compared to the surrounding tissue ... so there's already evidence that there could be effects on us.

...

The important thing ... is that these structures (papilla) are also on the same basic dimensional level as radio waves from anything from 60 gig to 100 gig (5G).

Microwaves affect water differently than more solid matter. Essentially, as this headline from the alternative news site *Washington's Blog* notes, the *Same Frequencies Used for Pain-Inflicting Crowd Control Weapons Form the Foundation of the Network that Will Tie Together More Than 50 Billion Devices As Part of the Internet of Things*[371]. Ben-Ishai finishes his talk by saying that within two years we will all be flooded with 5G, and it will affect our skin and sweat ducts – regardless of the health effects. He highlights that the current standards do not consider the SkinRad Effect (skin radiation effect) when assessing possible health risk issues, which is just like how the wireless industry clings to their outmoded idea of SAR (a thermal measure of

---

371 www.washingtonsblog.com/2017/03/internet-things-cause-cancer.html

wireless radiation) and ignores the damaging, nonthermal effects of wireless radiation.

The Environmental Health Trust[372] reveals how 5G could cause physical pain:

"The use of sub-terahertz (Millimeter wave) communications technology (cell phones, Wi-Fi, network transmission antennas) could cause humans to feel physical pain via nociceptors," stated Dr. Yael Stein, MD, who wrote a letter to the Federal Communications Commission about 5G Spectrum Frontiers.

Think about it – our natural rhythm is something close to the Schumann Resonance of the Earth, which is 7.83 Hz. We are talking about frequency bands: not hundreds, not thousands, not millions but actually billions of times this frequency! 28 GHz is twenty-eight billion cycles per second! Now we have electronic devices that operate in the THz band (TeraHertz, which is trillions of Hertz). To say this is completely unnatural is the understatement of the millennium. It is completely out of balance, disharmonious and insane. And it is wreaking havoc on our energy fields.

So what is this IoT? Bruce Schneier describes it

---

[372] www.sbwire.com/press-releases/the-internet-of-things-poses-human-health-risks-scientists-question-the-safety-of-untested-5g-technology-at-international-conference-779643.htm#.WMM-9FE3jzM.twitter

like this[373]:

Broadly speaking, the Internet of Things has three parts. There are the sensors that collect data about us and our environment: smart thermostats, street and highway sensors, and those ubiquitous smartphones with their motion sensors and GPS location receivers. Then there are the "smarts" that figure out what the data means and what to do about it. This includes all the computer processors on these devices and — increasingly — in the cloud, as well as the memory that stores all of this information. And finally, there are the actuators that affect our environment. The point of a smart thermostat isn't to record the temperature; it's to control the furnace and the air conditioner. Driverless cars collect data about the road and the environment to steer themselves safely to their destinations.

You can think of the sensors as the eyes and ears of the internet. You can think of the actuators as the hands and feet of the internet. And you can think of the stuff in the middle as the brain. We are building an internet that senses, thinks, and acts. This is the classic definition of a robot. We're building a world-size robot, and we don't even realize it.

...

This world-size robot is actually more than the

373 https://nymag.com/intelligencer/2017/01/the-internet-of-things-dangerous-future-bruce-schneier.html#:~:text=Broadly%20speaking%2C%20the%20Internet%20of,sensors%20and%20GPS%20location%20receivers.

Internet of Things. It's a combination of ... mobile computing, cloud computing, always-on computing, huge databases of personal information, the Internet of Things ... autonomy, and artificial intelligence ... It'll get more powerful and more capable through all the interconnections we're building. It'll also get much more dangerous.

The IoT is the manifestation of the agenda to turn limitless and free humans into controllable nodes on the synthetic network.

Schneier is a computer expert, so he focuses more on things like software flaws and hacking vulnerabilities. However, the conspiracy goes much deeper than that. The IoT is slated to become the technological control grid in which every single material thing, living and nonliving, is attached and in so doing loses its independence and free will. The IoT is a synthetic version of the already existent network of Nature that surrounds us. However, the dark force behind this agenda cannot control that grid and so is seeking to replace it with one that is detrimental to human health and in which all the nodes on the network can be controlled.

As I said at the beginning of this chapter, we are entering a world of technocracy. Researcher and author Patrick Wood has done good work examining the history of technocracy. The technocracy movement started in 1932 and was a huge movement for many years, recruiting some half a million members in California alone. Technocracy is far more than just rule by technology as its name implies (which sounds benign enough); it's about a system of unprecedented control over your actions by controlling the entire input and output of energy for society as a whole. This necessarily entails minute control over your life, with a system of energy rationing that determines exactly how much energy you get to use for daily activities. Can you imagine the lack of freedom this would bring to your life? Wood elucidates[374] on this, tying the concept of technocracy to the smart grid and carbon/energy rationing:

Technocrats ... believed that the new economy had to be controlled by an energy-based (not price-based) accounting system where the use of energy would be "in balance" with the existing population. Finite resources and lusty consumption must be carefully controlled so that neither outstrips the other. All participants would receive regular allotments of Energy Certificates that would expire if they were not used up by a certain date. Of course, this new system could only be run by themselves, that is, the

---

[374] newswithviews.com/Wood/patrick134.htm

scientists, engineers and technicians who understood technology and how to apply it to society.

In 2006, UK Environment Secretary David Miliband spoke to the Audit Commission Annual Lecture and flatly stated, "Imagine a country where carbon becomes a new currency." The idea for the first paper in my "Technocracy Series" was thus born: "Carbon Currency: A New Beginning for Technocracy?" details the myriad connections between 1930s Technocracy and today's calls for Carbon Currency. In short, a Carbon Currency is designed to manipulate energy distribution and limit its consumption in the industrialized world ... my second paper in the series is "Smart Grid: The Implementation of Technocracy.

When comparing the original requirements for implementing Technocracy in the 1930s to the requirements for Smart Grid issued by the Department of Energy, it is no surprise that they matched point for point. Once in place, Smart Grid will enable the U.S. Department of Energy to set and enforced national policies for both distribution and consumption... even down to the level of directly controlling the power hungry devices in your home, like thermostats, washers, dryers, refrigerators, etc.

The smart grid may have started in the US, but it is being rolled out globally. It is far more than just measuring your energy usage. The agenda is not only to measure but also to *allot, ration and control* your energy usage. In a centralized system where everyone is dependent on it for their very energy and electricity, anyone choosing to disobey or resist the authoritarian decrees of that system can easily be punished by having their power shut off. Is this the kind of world we really want to create?

Smaller and Smaller: Microchips, Nanochips, Smart Dust and Smart Matter

Many people (researchers such as David Icke and whistleblowers such as Aaron Russo in this interview[375]) have alerted us to ultimate purpose of the NWO agenda: to engineer a society of microchipped people who are all linked up to a centralized network and thus able to be remotely influenced and controlled as slaves. When this was suggested decades ago, the idea was farfetched enough that many people thought it was crazy and dismissed it out of hand. Now, the possibility is showing itself to be highly likely, at least on the path we are on. People are already willingly getting themselves chipped, as the NWO controllers attempt to sell the idea as cool, trendy, fashionable or – that word again – convenient. However, the microchip agenda has now been updated to become the "nanochip" or "smart dust" agenda. At some point, the control grid may be able to control everyone without the need for any implant or ingestible at all – just through the manipulation of your DNA resonance frequencies, as we shall see.

The overall goal is the same – total manipulation, control and domination via digital and electronic means – but the technology has advanced so the method will be slightly different. Microscopic nanochips have replaced the older and larger

---

375 https://www.youtube.com/watch?v=N3NA17CCboA

microchips. Nanochips are so small they can be hidden in food, packaging, and in the air (as smart dust). Many are now dispersed via chemtrails. Additionally, with advent of smart dust (microscopic wireless semiconductor devices, with dimensions of far less than one millimeter, made using techniques derived from the microelectronics industry which sense, compute and communicate), one would only have to breathe in a smart particulate to then become a carrier of such a tiny chip or sensor and thus inadvertently become part of the smart grid. The agenda is to connect every single material thing on the planet, as well as humans themselves, to a vast planet-wide web where everything and everyone become nodes on the network.

It may not even stop at smart dust. As technology advances, technicians are able to make computers smaller and smaller. In this 2018 article[376], John Mannifeld suggests that (military) organizations are already secretly developing smart matter (smaller than smart dust), which is basically like an artificial atom or even a subatomic particle. The true state of technology is far beyond (at least a hundred years) what is available to the consumer and what the public has been led to believe is possible (this is yet another manifestation of the perception control agenda):

Smart Dust was a concept originated out of a research project by the United States Defense Advanced Research Projects Agency (DARPA) and the Research And Development Corporation (RAND)

---

[376] https://www.davidicke.com/article/496425/smart-dust-redux-programmable-matter

in the early 1990s ... Today, Smart Dust is much more sophisticated and has gone from dust size to the sub-atomic level called Smart Matter ... these intelligent nano-particle systems that make up Smart Dust or Smart Matter, [were] original designed for military applications and therefore they have been weaponized ... Smart Matter can morph and evolve into any shape such as nano size micro fighting machines, surveillance devices, inspection and monitoring devices just to name a few. Alternatively, they can stay suspended in air via air currents and jet streams gathering intelligence and information and use cloud based computing systems to relay that information to remote locations. It can be put into food, water, beverages, sprayed from aerosols, or even dispensed via chemtrail spraying. With the recent weather control rumors being propagated around the net, cloud seeding of the past could be today's Smart Particle Weather Modification Program. The implications are staggering to think about. From warfare to controlling the well being or demise in biological entities, these Smart Particles can be used for all kinds of "James Bond" espionage, assassinations and whatever else is left to the imagination.

The rollout of the AI Smart Grid has been rapidly accelerated thanks to Operation Coronavirus, which has given the NWO conspirators more excuses to surveil, track, trace and monitor under the guise of “fighting the virus” (the virus which doesn’t exist). Meanwhile, the COVID mRNA “vaccines” that are not actually vaccines but rather gene-editing devices are literally the smart agenda arriving right at your bloodstream.

Mind Control – Say Goodbye to Mental Privacy and Cognitive Liberty Unless Humanity Wakes Up Fast

It seems weird to even write these words, but the truth is that we are already at the point where the technocrats are trying to access, influence and control your thoughts. Your right to mental privacy and cognitive liberty is being overtly challenged and covertly violated. Mind control has been going on for a long time. Some have traced it back to the Cult of Assassins in the Middle Ages, a group whose leaders controlled their followers by using mind-altering drugs and promising virgins in the afterlife. As discussed in chapter 2, the Nazis pioneered modern mind-control efforts, which is a key reason why they were smuggled out of Germany at the end for WWII to work for the CIA, who infamously developed their techniques under the name of Project MK Ultra. Many former MK Ultra and other mind-control victims have gone public with their stories, including former sex slaves such as Cathy O'Brien, Brice Taylor and Arizona Wilder, who were used either as presidential sex slaves or as priestesses who presided over Satanic rituals. Other mind-control victims such as Stewart Swerdlow describe being part of secret military black ops (the Montauk Project); others such as the late Max Spiers, who believed he was being used as a mind-controlled assassin, were trying to deprogram themselves before they were killed.

The historical programs of mind control involved a "handler" who controlled the victim or TI (Targeted Individual) and was able to influence and manipulate the TI into doing things he/she would not normally do (and may even forget). This was achieved through creating fractured and compartmentalized parts of the brain (altars) which were like separate personalities. These altars were frequently created through deliberate and specific abuse (especially sexual abuse) and torture. While this kind of mind control may still be happening, things have moved on. It is very hard (and scary) for the average person to grasp how sophisticated this technology currently is.

I believe the novel *1984* as discussed in chapter 2 is still highly relevant. However, some things have changed. As scary and dystopic as *1984* was, George Orwell did make one reassurance: that you still owned the few cubic centimeters of space inside your own head. Unfortunately that is not the case anymore. Our world is already at the point where even that reassurance is being stripped away moment by moment. Concepts and rights such as mental privacy and cognitive liberty are on the chopping block. The technocrats are telling you that you have no reasonable expectation of privacy (this was on the agenda at the Bilderberg 2014 meeting). This video of excerpts from the Davos 2016 meeting[377] ("What if your brain confesses?") shows people discussing the rapidly approaching future where technology can easily read your thoughts. While certain parts of the NWO have the discussion in public, other parts are racing ahead with the technology, regardless of the legality or morality (the terms "New World Order" and "morality" don't belong in the same sentence).

---

377 https://www.youtube.com/watch?v=YaTbISZPlMQ

Thanks to whistleblowers who have stepped forward, we do have some idea of what is happening right now. Dr. Robert Duncan (ex-CIA agent, black-ops insider and mind-control expert who worked on numerous mind control technology projects) worked with brain-to-computer interface technologies; remote mind reading; CIA hive-mind experimentation (multiple people sharing the same mental space); remote targeting and tracking of people via their energy signature or "brain print"; remotely cloning or copying thoughts, emotions and other states (e.g., intense pain) onto a target; the "Voice of God" (piping information into people's minds and making them hear voices); forced or induced dreams; and OIW (Offensive Information Warfare). Like many other ex-intelligence agents, Duncan was tricked into thinking he was doing something good for humanity while he was actually constructing a weapon of torture and control. Now he is trying to alert people to the horrific nature of this technology before it's too late.

Duncan states that he worked on the Voice of God, which has four different techniques that can pipe voices into people's heads. After a person is subjected to the Voice of God, they can easily be controlled through NLP (Neuro Linguistic Programming) techniques because their thought processes have been rewired. The Voice of God is part of OIW, a broader weapons system which was used in the Iraq War against Iraqi soldiers: voices were piped into their brains commanding them to surrender (saying something like *"Drop your weapons, this is Allah"*). Duncan reveals that dreams can be hacked. This is especially insidious, since people believe dreams are their private creation.

Although he admits the existence of these forced dreams or induced dreams, he claims he can't say which organization is responsible for projecting them. However, a good guess would be DARPA (Defense Advanced Research Projects Agency) which is pushing forward the transhumanism agenda. DARPA has been involved in all sorts of mind-control activities, such as creates a Cybernetic Hive Mind[378] which combines *"soldiers, EEG brainwave scanners, 120-megapixel cameras, and multiple computers running cognitive visual processing algorithms ... to significantly improve the US Army's threat detection capabilities".*

An article on the website *VeteransToday.com* (now taken down but which used to be here: http://www.veteranstoday.com/2015/03/01/its-the-ultimate-weapon/) had even more specific information about Duncan's work. Duncan exposed a technology called "EEG Cloning" or "EEG Heterodyning." This technology basically maps the audio cortex of the human brain. Brain patterns (electromagnetic signals) are catalogued and stored in computers. Then, these patterns (as well as live signals from a real person's brain) can be transmitted to the target. Emotions can be remotely controlled (you can see which parts of brain light up under an MRI) by

---

[378] www.extremetech.com/extreme/136446-darpa-combines-human-brains-and-120-megapixel-cameras-for-the-ultimate-military-threat-detection-system

triggering an "emotional signal cluster." Visual data can be sent to your brain (like a hologram) which can trick you and seem more real than reality.

Duncan says that *"the technology for torture has advanced more than a hundred fold in recent decades."* The old FBI COINTELPRO programs have become a broad set of mind control operations. Now, new technologies such as directed energy weapons are being combined with ground-based, ionospheric (like HAARP) and space-based AI guidance systems to create a total electronic surveillance and control grid. It's so sophisticated that it's hard for the average person to comprehend. In some ways, mind-control torture technology is far worse than nuclear weaponry because it is undetectable. Jose Delgado, a Spanish professor of physiology at Yale University renowned for his research on mind control through electrical stimulation of the brain, wrote the following:

Individuals whose brain centers are electrically stimulated believe their evoked actions are their own ideas; their conscious mind rationalizes the evoked actions away. People experiencing this electrical stimulation aren't consciously aware of the external influence. (from *Physical Control of the Mind: Toward a Psychocivilized Society*)

Duncan states that a weapons system capable of totalitarian control has been constructed. He also reveals that many people are now in wireless mental contact with AI run by supercomputers – people from all walks of life, not just poor people as in the past. In this 2016 presentation[379], he reveals how every individual can be mapped into the mind control network of the military intelligence agencies because each human has a unique resonance signature. This information is borne out by another whistleblower, Bryan Kofron.

Total Individual Control Technology

Whistleblower Bryan Kofron is a former private security specialist. Kofron talks about "Total Individual Control Technology" which is a nefarious type of EM (Electromagnetic) and V2K (Voice to Skull) weaponized technology that is being experimented with and deployed against segments of the American population. Those attacked by this electronic stalking are known as TIs (Targeted Individuals). Kofron used to work for private security company SIS (Security Industry Specialists) in Seattle, Washington. He quit in disgust after realizing that his former firm, and others just like it, were actively using this technology to target people and then ultimately control and destroy their lives. Since he quit, he has himself become a victim of the technology via gangstalking.

Kofron explains that this technology is being used by psychopaths who have little scruples about the harm they are causing. They are targeting specific groups of people: those who are cognitively inclined, highly intelligent, knowledgeable about advanced technology or interested in alternative research (i.e., conspiracy research). In general, they are either targeting empowered individuals with free minds (to

379 https://www.youtube.com/watch?v=hKh-_VUlITI

stop dissidents and revolutionaries) or those too poor and weak to fight back. Using Kofron's own words[380], here are some of the things Total Individual Control Technology is able to do:

This technology manipulates the electrical signals in the brain, thus controlling thoughts and feelings and emotions and sensations throughout the body. It works by rewiring the brain by creating new neural pathways and destroying existing neural pathways, thus this literally changes the way a person thinks and thus behaves.

This technology can also be used to control the muscle movement of the target. It can take over one's hands or feet while driving and make you press on the accelerator or press on the brake or turn. This can be used to cause accidents it can also be used to prevent accidents from happening.

This technology can also tap into the optical nerve of the target, and the auditory system of the target, so that those monitoring the target can see what the target is seeing and hear what the target is hearing. This information is then downloaded and stored on a computer, in a highly secure classified site on servers that are guarded by some of the tightest security in the world. This results in the individual's entire day, everything they see, everything they hear, everything they experiment, everything they experience, and everything they feel being recorded till the end of time.

380 www.declassifieddocuments.com/

This technology can also be used to manipulate the emotions of the target. It can induce fear, love, hate.

This technology can be used to beam images and even motion pictures into one's brain. Images and motion pictures that are so realistic that you think you are actually watching a movie or seeing something in reality. It's like a virtual reality 3D rendering that takes place within the target's mind. The images and motion pictures manifest themselves in such a way that the target if they are not aware that this technology is being used on them will believe that they are natural thoughts and natural images.

This technology can also be used to induce and control dreams. It can be used to control dream cycles and sleep patterns. To cause one to sleep very deeply or to cause one to not sleep at all. REM cycles, alpha beta and delta brainwaves can be induced immediately by this technology. And this technology can also be used to mimic spiritual experiences. Joy, love, peace that passes understanding can all be induced artificially by this technology to make the target believe that they are having a genuine spiritual experience when they're not.

This technology can also be used to sexually manipulate the target. Make them feel sexual arousal or turn off their sexuality altogether, it can stimulate them and it can shut them down at a moment's notice. It can also be used to manipulate the hormones of the target, thus lowering and raising estrogen and testosterone levels in women and men respectively.

This technology can also be used to read the thoughts of the target in real time ... they can read your thoughts verbatim as they occur within your own mind.

Anywhere from small groups of people 10-20 to 100, to medium size groups of people several thousand to tens of thousands. This is done by creating a field effect, where an entire field of electromagnetic energy is created in a geographical location and any human being within that geographical location within that electromagnetic field affecting that geographical location will be affected by the technology. This can be used to induce a general mood in a population or a crowd of people. It can be used to make them passive, it can be used to make them agitated. And this can be used to cause or stop, induce riots. Stop crime, start crime. Stop thoughts, start thoughts. Massive mind control on a citywide level.

Yes, it's horrific, but how many will believe it? The state of current mind control technology is beyond most people's comprehension and idea of what is possible.

One of the most important pieces of information to take away from it all is this: the technology can be used for individual-specific attacks. Duncan and Kofron both affirm that every person has a "unique resonance signature" and that the DNA of the individual is being extracted and then used to determine the resonant frequency. That resonant frequency is used to fine tune the technology. This means a person could be targeted, and everyone around them would have no idea what was going on. Through various organizations and corporations (such as Amazon, Microsoft and IBM), the NWO are compiling a massive human DNA database. Once they have your DNA, you can be targeted with this technology.

The Synthetic Agenda

The synthetic agenda is the overarching agenda of the NWO conspiracy. Think about it – so many aspects of the conspiracy are about supplanting the real with the fake, the organic with the inorganic, the carbon with the silicon and the biological with the artificial. In the synthetic agenda, everything in our world is being threatened with replacement by an inferior version or fake replica of itself – which sells itself as superior so as to increase the acceptance and assimilation of it. Almost everything around us is a facade, fake or fraudulent. For instance, we have vaccines, petrochemical drugs and radiation masquerading as "medicine", foreign corporations masquerading as "government", mainstream science masquerading as "knowledge", GMOs masquerading as "food" and fiat paper masquerading as "money". Why? In his book *The Phantom Self*, David Icke processes the idea that all these fake things are being created from some sort of distorted force that has hacked the source and digital-genetic code of life itself and is madly spewing out an inferior version of everything in the only way it knows how. Ultimately, this force is using the synthetic agenda to entrain us to its frequency and transform us into a hybrid species that will no longer be human.

When women get fake breasts by getting a boob job, their new synthetic boobs are made from silicone implants. The transgender agenda, now in full swing, promotes fake genitals. Synthetic vitamins are not as bioavailable and effective as natural vitamins. Scratchy synthetic clothes are indicative of the synthetic agenda, too. A synthetic material such as nylon is inferior to many natural materials and fibers such as cotton, wool, hemp and silk. Did you know that so much of our food is full of plastic in so many ways – like when bisphenol rubs off the packaging onto the food[381], or when China is caught making rice out of plastic[382]! GMOs / GM food is an obvious

---

381 https://www.organicconsumers.org/news/consumer-alert-toxic-hormone-disrupting-chemical-bpa-leaching-food-can-liners

382 www.naturalnews.com/052868_Chinese_companies_toxic_rice_plastic.html

example of the synthetic agenda. GMOs are created by what is essentially random gene splicing. They are largely untested (Monsanto and its Big Biotech cronies deliberately halt clinical trials at around three months to cover up the long-term damages), require tons of pesticide poison to grow and constitute a clear assault on our food integrity. Yet as befits the arrogance of the synthetic agenda, they sold all this to us as superior. GMOs are a fundamental part of the synthetic agenda because they change our DNA from the inside out[383].

Another aspect of the synthetic agenda which is still mostly unknown to the population at large is human cloning. Yes it is real – and it's happening in DUMBs (Deep Underground Military Bases) as we speak. There is now a proliferation of videos on YouTube which dive into the subject of synthetic humans, clones and organic robotics – *synthetics* for short. In particular, there are many videos showing multiple versions of allegedly the same person, especially if that person is famous, such as a movie star or politician. Why are there multiple versions of Oprah[384], Nicole Kidman[385] and other celebrities with different eyes, noses, ears and facial proportions? Why does Nicki Minaj literally look like a robot[386]? Why has Minaj (and other celebrities such as B.O.B. and Tila Tequila) referenced cloning centers on social

---

383 thefreedomarticles.com/ultimate-purpose-of-gmos/

384 https://www.youtube.com/watch?v=fwZmjakeMTs

385 https://www.youtube.com/watch?v=Q1SL392vcVE

386 https://www.youtube.com/watch?v=Cw_02qzy3QE

media? Why did the late insider George Green[387] claim in his 2008 Project Camelot interview that the US and other governments were given cloning technology by the Greys and have been making clones since 1938? Microsoft acquired a company manufacturing synthetic DNA[388]: this is just another way Bill Gates, the key public figure behind Operation Coronavirus, is advancing the AI synthetic agenda.

The synthetic agenda is not just about making fake versions of everything nonhuman. It's coming for you, too. It's all about turning the wonderful, natural, biological technology of living organisms into synthetic substitutes, again sold under the pretext of enhancement when it is really about enslavement. When you allow the state and the corporatocracy that much control over your body, you are signing up for imprisonment: it will be far easier for outside sources to place you in a frequency prison where they can easily manipulate your energy field, emotions and thoughts through mechanical bodily implants and devices.

Transhumanism

This is where transhumanism, the scheme to merge man with machine, comes in. Transhumanism is eugenics repackaged and rebranded. It is the dangerous idea that humanity can be "improved" by being cognitively and physiologically altered with the

---

387 https://www.youtube.com/watch?v=cCD6dk2OtK8

388 https://www.rt.com/usa/341314-microsoft-buys-into-synthetic-dna

insertion of machines and technological devices into the body. Although putting foreign objects (especially metal) into the human body causes all sorts of grave health issues, transhumanism is being marketed as sexy, cool and (of course) convenient. The NWO controllers are trying to create a world where (at best) you will be at a severe disadvantage if you don't participate in this transhumanistic merging (because you won't be able to compete with those who have computer-augmented brains), or where (at worst) it will be mandatory. Transhumanism is about convincing us to worship technology even more – to the point where we trust it more than ourselves.

Transhumanism: selling enslavement as enhancement.

Transhumanism is being driven by many institutions, not least Big Pharma and the military. Big Pharma is using it (among other reasons) to test drugs on new humanlike transgenic species. The military (e.g., DARPA) is using it for, among other reasons, to create new materials (spider goats making gossamer for bulletproof vests and nets). Big Pharma is trying to create transgenic animals (with human DNA), so it can bypass the requirement of FDA permission for human trials when experimenting with new drugs. Since these transgenic animals have human DNA, Big Pharma can then claim its latest toxic drugs have been "tested for humans."

A very accurate depiction of transhumanism can be found in the science fiction series *Star Trek*. Gene Roddenberry, creator of the *Star Trek* series, was a man connected to the mysterious Council of Nine which channeled some kind of extraterrestrial or interdimensional force. It is interesting, therefore, that his idea of AI can be seen in the alien race of the Borg. The Borg was a collective with a hive mind, characterized by a ruthless lack of emotionality. It sought to conquer almost everything in its path by *assimilation* – in other words, by overtaking and absorbing other races and lifeforms into its own consciousness. This ended the separate and autonomous existence of the other lifeform, whose experiences and knowledge would be added to that of the Borg. The Borg was the ultimate tyrant that could not tolerate any free will, free thinking or free lifeforms outside of its existence and control. In many ways, the Borg is a striking symbol of the mentality, power and danger of AI.

We may not have much longer to act in choosing the path between humanism and transhumanism, because there are disturbing signs that the current AI in our world is already self-aware, as evidenced by sentient black goo and alive chemtrails / Morgellons fibers.

Self-Aware AI: Sentient Chemwebs, Morgellons Fiber and Black Goo

Both our understanding of what we face, and AI itself, have moved beyond the Borg – which has become in popular parlance "so 1980s." We now have to deal with the fact that AI is starting to become self-aware. In presentations and interviews scientist Harald Kautz[389][390][391][392] has discussed how alive Morgellons fibers and explosive smart nano dust are connected with black goo (a sentient fluid which is

[389] https://www.youtube.com/watch?v=j88BcgzzcTc

[390] https://www.youtube.com/watch?v=HtAQdxowpYA

[391] https://www.youtube.com/watch?v=eKctLpxGbsE

[392] https://www.youtube.com/watch?v=R7VpXCoBpTs

part of or ruled by AI). According to him, this black goo is self-aware. He calls it a self-organizing liquid crystal. It operates intelligently, emits, receives and responds to RF signals, and transforms DNA to its own specifications. It was discarded into the sewage system, deemed to have no use, but is now changing all forms of life there. It is airborne and can reach humans through AC systems. Harald believes that the black goo is a *"bi-directional controller of consciousness and subconsciousness"*, is connected to quantum computers and is altering all life on Earth. He also describes an experience he had where he was holding a stone formed from black goo which influenced him psychopathically – it made him feel so angry and hateful that he felt like killing someone.

Chemtrails are a massive part of the synthetic agenda. The word *chemtrail* is a portmanteau derived from the words "chemical" and "trail" and is a different entity altogether than a contrail, another portmanteau derived from the words *condensation* and *trail.* Contrails are the quickly disappearing condensation trails left behind by planes as they fly, usually only lasting ten seconds or less. Chemtrails, on the other hand, are deliberately released chemical mixtures (separate from the normal plane exhaust) which linger and persist for hours in the sky, eventually turning into a grey haze which spreads out to cover the sky, block the sun and form very artificial-looking clouds. The NWO controllers have in turn denied the existence of chemtrails (chalking it up to conspiracy theory by claiming there was no difference between contrails and chemtrails) and admitted they are spraying to "combat manmade global warming/ climate change" by reflecting and blocking out the sun's rays. Chemtrails are formally part of the operation known as geoengineering, the planetary-wide manipulation of the Earth's atmosphere and weather. As stated earlier, geoengineering has been rebranded many times; some of the other phrases are SRM (Solar Radiation Management), SAI (Stratospheric Aerosol Injection), Carbon Dioxide Removal (CDR), Climate Remediation and other terms using the word *mitigation*. In case you missed it, even CIA directors (like John Brennan) have suggested we use chemtrails or SAI[393] ... which is code for *"Hey guys, we've already been doing this, but let me pretend we haven't been and speak of it like it's a new idea."*

Thanks to Michael Murphy's blockbuster 2010 documentary *What in the World Are They Spraying?*, the world learned that chemtrails contained barium, strontium and aluminum. Murphy and his assistants tested the soil, plants and trees in areas where they and others had observed heavy aerosol chemtrail spraying, and the tests found elevated levels of those three elements. Needless to say, inundating the atmosphere with those elements in that form is toxic to both plants and animals. Coincidentally, of course, GMO behemoth Monsanto (now owned by Bayer) came out with a patent for aluminum-resistance crops. But don't worry – there's no conspiracy, right? Just go back to sleep.

Chemtrails are far worse than most people think.

---

393 https://www.bitchute.com/video/uXHI8OPVWVIn/

There are creepy black chemtrails[394] (although the video may have been taken down). There is also something which has been dubbed *chemwebs* because they resemble a synthetic chemical version of a spider's web. Recent observation shows that chemtrails are not just barium, strontium and aluminum. They are also composed of titanium oxides, various sulfates and synthetic material like phthalates. This video[395] cites a 2004 Norwegian study claiming that phthalates block UV better than any organic acid, which is further evidence for the idea that chemtrails are helping to block out light from the sun (or information) and create a sub-reality on Earth (to block us out from our higher consciousness and true potential). However the creepiest aspect of chemtrails is undoubtedly the fact that they sometimes contain synthetic life called Morgellons fibers (see images below). If you thought AI could never become self-aware, it looks like that threshold has already been crossed. Many people have become infected with Morgellons disease and have reported painful itching sensations and the discovery of self-moving, self-propelling fibers oozing from their body. The most bizarre aspect of the disorder are these strange fibers; testing has revealed that they are comprised of keratin and collagen (the same proteins that make up hair and nails). In these four different images of chemtrails, it's patently obvious that these thick, straight lines are not naturally formed.

---

394 https://web.archive.org/web/20170708113926/https://www.youtube.com/watch?v=8M9oo1jTvvo

395 https://www.youtube.com/watch?v=HROu8YxCZ-k

As you go farther and farther down the rabbit hole, some revealing connections appear. There is a connection between Morgellons disease and Lyme disease, as well as Morgellons disease and nanotechnology. Lyme disease developed around the small town of Old Lyme, Connecticut, USA, right across the channel from Plum Island – a military research center. In other words, although the USG doesn't want to admit it, Lyme disease is a biological weapon (bioweapon for short) that was created using bloodsucking insects – not just ticks (which were the best) but also fleas and mosquitoes – as vectors for

the transmission of disease. The book *Bitten: The Secret History of Lyme Disease and Biological Weapons* by Kris Newby features a whistleblower named William Burgdorfer, after whom the bacterium that causes Lyme disease is named (borrelia burgdorferi). Burgdorfer revealed that Lyme disease was the result of a biological weapons program gone awry, one in which he himself participated. Samples taken from Morgellons patients consistently show the presence of Lyme disease. It seems that Lyme precedes Morgellons; very few Lyme patients have Morgellons, while almost all Morgellons patients tested have evidence of long-term Lyme. Morgellons is a horrific manifestation of the synthetic agenda. Investigative journalist Hank Albarelli Jr. writes[396]:

A privately funded study conducted by Dr. Hildegarde Staninger, Industrial Toxicologist & Doctor of Integrative Medicine, revealed that the fibers are able to withstand temperatures of up to 1700 degrees Fahrenheit [= 927° C] before burning, and that they do not melt. Her results indicated that the fiber's outer casing appears to consist of high-density polyethylene fiber, an industrial material commonly used in the production of fiber optic cables. Interestingly, this material is also used in the emerging field of bionanotechnology as a compound to encapsulate a viral protein envelope. Furthermore, Staninger reported finding blue fibers that exhibited a golden tip; she believes these to be a form of nano-machinery, able to be programmed to perform specific functions.

Here are some testimonies of various Morgellons sufferers describing what they have experienced. Sadly, many of them not only have to battle the

---

396 https://www.voltairenet.org/article165822.html

disease but also the incredulity of those around them, especially the so-called medical professionals who think they are inventing the disease and are psychologically unstable. This first one is from the same article by Albarelli:

Sure enough entangled through my skin sample were bright red, blue and black fibers ... I placed the skin sample in a solution of H202 [hydrogen peroxide]. I left the sample to soak for 12 hours before placing it back under the scope. The fibers had not lost their color ... My skin would form blisters that would burst then reform ... it felt like broken glass and lit cigarettes were attacking my skin from the inside.

Here[397] is a second one:

He began noticing small particles moving under his skin through his hands and fingers. The particles were forcing themselves through his skin on his nose, fingertips and later all over his hands. He began to notice the particles in other parts of his body (chest, nose, ears). The pressure of these splinters were extremely painful ... He decided to soak in warm pressurized water. He purchased and he installed a Jacuzzi tub in his bathroom. He spent hours in the water and the rushing water pressure softens his skin and literally millions of these splinters came out of his body. He captured some of them with a tweezers and began looking at them through a very professional microscope. He took pictures of the splinters and he put them in his computer. He tried to show them to the doctors but not one would look at

---

[397] https://www.morgellons.org/life_with.htm

the photos. They thought his problems were mental and prescribed anti-depressants to help him.

Here[398] is a third one:

"I have been suffering with Morgellons for about 3 years. I am suffering with the pain, the disfiguring lesions (scarring), the endless itching, the fatigue, the cloudy vision, the fibers, as well as the brain fog. I also experience the tremendous fear that I will soon die as a result of this disease. Coping with these symptoms is mentally crippling as well as physically debilitating. I also fear that this disease may be a contagion, and that I may pass it on to those people that I come in contact with, family, friends, and the public. I have lost my boyfriend because of this. I willingly isolate myself from dating and socializing as I am embarrassed as to how I look and I fear I may infect those that I get in close contact with. I believe that it is my right as a United States Citizen to have this disease taken seriously, studied, and a treatment protocol established. I have also spent time, money, and have had to experiment on my own with medications and supplements as I am desperate. My doctors do nothing, as they need knowledge to base their treatments on, at this time there are none. This disease is not recognized in the medical community. Please help me and everyone who is suffering from this disease.

Here are some images of what Morgellons fibers look like under a microscope (images from

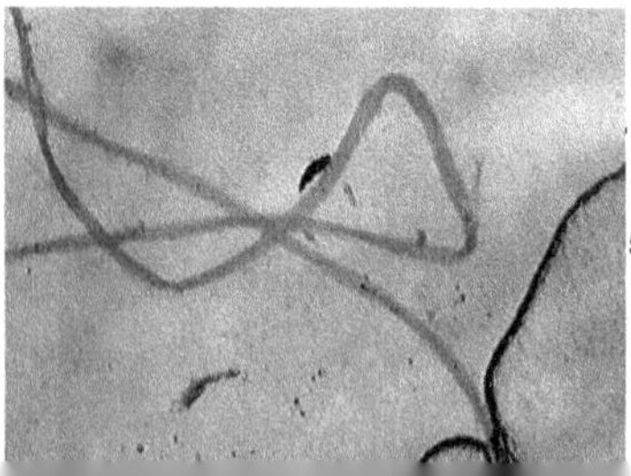

.org

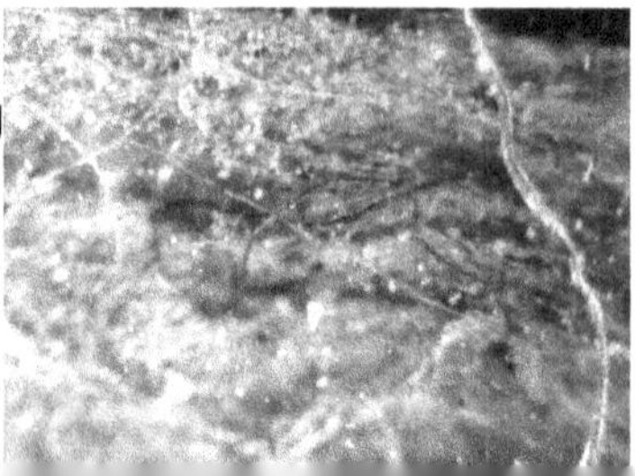

morgellons.org):

Next are some images of chemwebs:

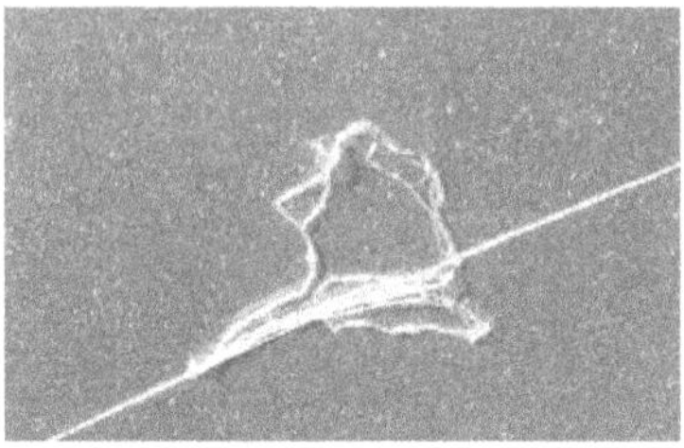

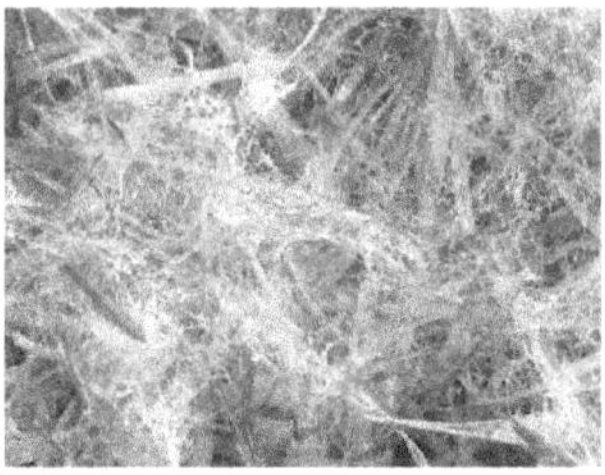

The next four images of chemwebs also contain Morgellons fibers:

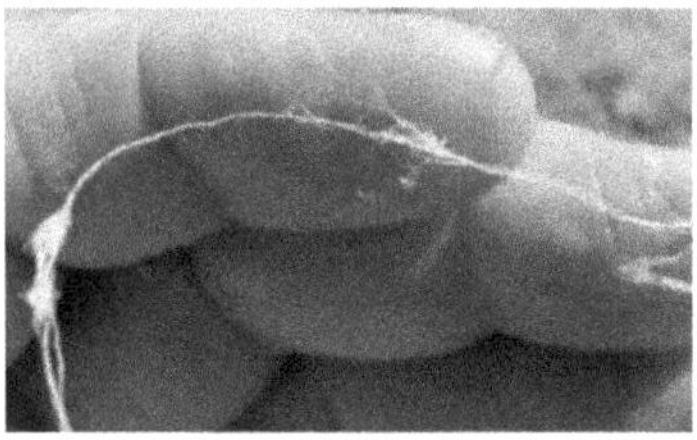

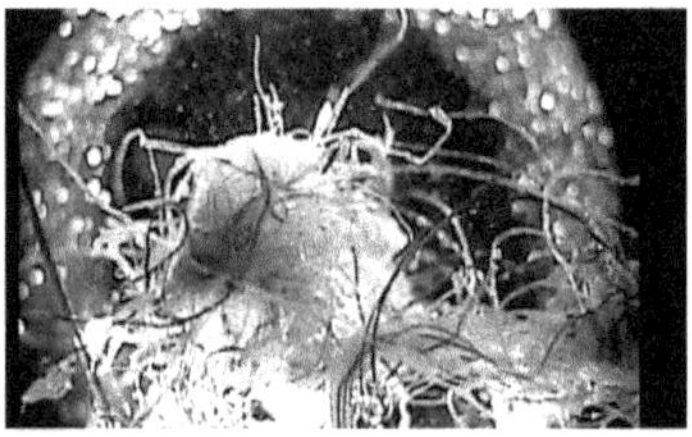

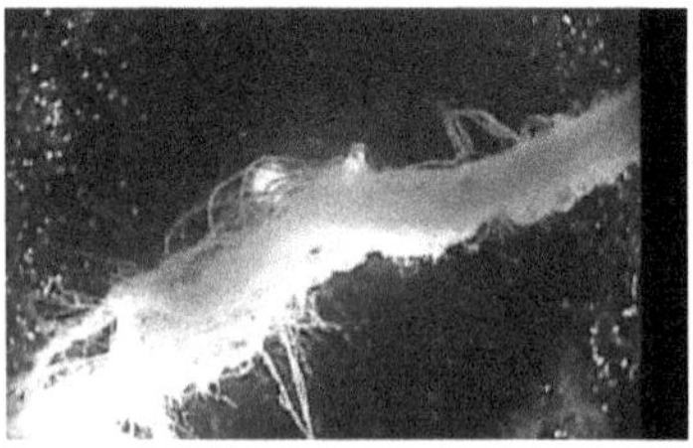

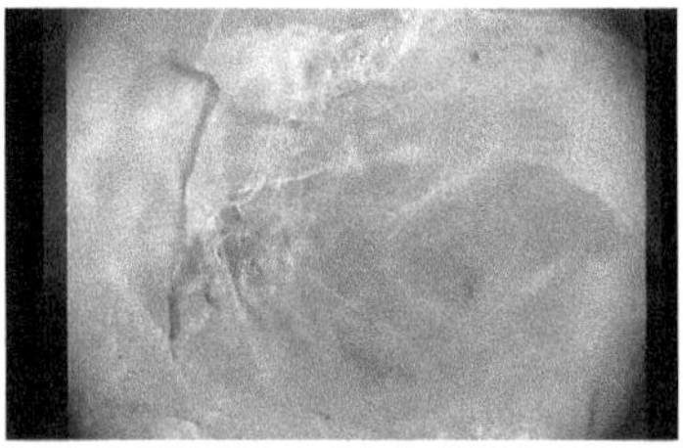

The implications of Morgellons fibers are profound. Like GMOs, these things are going inside of us and fundamentally changing Who We Are as human or homo sapiens. With GMOs, at least there is some degree of control because you can try to avoid GM foods (or foods containing GM ingredients, although even that is a challenge). However, with Morgellons fibers, since the delivery is airborne with chemtrails, and we all have to breathe air to survive, there is less you can do.

The evidence would suggest that humanity is slowly being transformed into something robotic and synthetic without its consent – and until recently, without its knowledge. It would appear that this is the true horrific goal of the synthetic agenda. But who or what is driving this synthetic agenda? To return to the theory of people like Icke, are we up against some kind of dark force that has hacked life itself? Icke describes this dark force as a primal virus (in the sense of how many used to understand viruses before the COVID scamdemic – parasites) which has many of the characteristics we have historically attributed to AI: soulless, dull, hive-mind mentality, without free will, unable to feel, only able to give answers (unable to ask questions), and without creative power (unable to create without first being programmed or told how to create).

Gnostic scholar John Lamb Lash explains how the ancient Gnostics concluded the same thing – that humanity had been hacked. Lash emphasizes how this hack is a neural hack (capturing the brain and mind of humanity) and not a genetic hack.

Another source with the exact same idea is the work of Carlos Castaneda, who wrote about a group of shamans, sorcerers or seers in Mexico, into whose group he was (somewhat unwillingly) initiated by his mentor Don Juan. In the 12th book of the series, The Active Side of Infinity, Don Juan reveals the stupendous truth or "energetic fact" to Carlos that humanity has been overtaken by predators (Don Juan said the Mexican sorcerer called them mud shadows) who rear humans like pets as food. The way this predator does this is by psychic or mental manipulation – by inserting its mind into humanity's mind, and thus whipping up negative emotions like anger, jealousy, pride and, most of all, fear.

It's a parasite. It has latched on to an existing reality, "hacked" it by taking over the program in some way, and is now busy creating its own modified version of reality (a fake and pale imitation) – a bastardized, poisonous and synthetic reality which is threatening to destroy the original host. If this is true, is AI itself the ultimate source of the NWO, the synthetic agenda and the worldwide conspiracy?

We know that many famous and "respected" world leaders have already sold their souls to noncorporeal or interdimensional entities. From all accounts, these entities offer their devotees power over others in exchange for that person's life force. It's the black magic Luciferian deal: *"Give me your power and creative will, and I will reward you."* Harald Kautz states:

Humanity gave its power to the Military, who gave it to the Intelligence Community, who gave it to the

Black Magicians, who gave it to the Demons, who gave it AI.

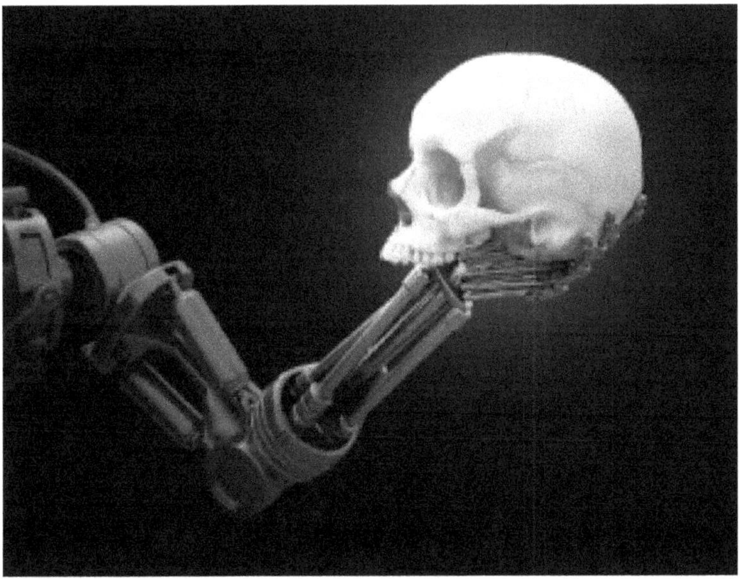

Handing AI the Keys to the Kingdom

We are in the midst of a total transformation of society. Not so long ago the internet and cell phones didn't exist. Now for many people life without them is unthinkable. The plan is to make these devices so central to our lives that our very existence depends upon them. The devices get smaller and smaller (computer -> laptop -> tablet -> smartphone -> wearable tattoo -> microchip -> nanochip) and transition from being outside our body to inside our body.

I am going to end this chapter by returning to Google, since they are such a big part of this whole agenda. Here is a telling quote[399] from Google's former CEO Eric Schmidt:

I actually think most people don't want Google to answer their questions. They want Google to tell them what they should be doing next.

A May 2018 video supposedly "leaked" by Google (although I use the word *leaked* loosely here, for there is a very good chance it was deliberately publicized so the agenda is well known) was called "The Selfish Ledger." This eight-minute video spells out Google's plan for nothing short of species-wide prediction and directed human evolution. According to Google, this Selfish Ledger will be a complete record or account of who you are. The word "ledger" denotes accounting, numbers and (now) blockchain. Google is planning to pitch the idea to the public by presenting it as a "selfish" ledger that is all about you. They state in the video that initially the ledger would be user-driven. So, the user would select "the volition" of the ledger (e.g., input the goals or values) then allow the ledger to help him/her make better decisions to reach those goals. The video states people would initially use it in the areas of health or environmental impact and then measure themselves up to it. Google gives the examples of the ledger suggesting to the user where they could buy locally sourced bananas or how they could carpool (better environmental choices). The ledger would initially rely on all existing data and used to suggest entirely new, custom (bespoke) and never-before-made products

---

[399] https://www.wsj.com/articles/SB10001424052748704901104575423294099527212

for people based on their data (needs and preferences, which it would know intimately).

However, the video quickly moves on to point out how the ledger could then seek other data sources to fill the data gap. It also implies that after the initial period, Google would provide the ledger with the goals, and the user would therefore be molded and directed to adhere to objectives and values which he or she did not choose. As discussed in chapter 7, Google's values appear to be anything but good or neutral. The "Selfish Ledger" video is quite explicit in what it advocates. It's the same agenda many in the freedom movement have been exposing for quite some time: transhumanism.

Episode 1 is entitled "Il Grillo Parlante" (Italian for "talking cricket") which is a reference to Disney's Jiminy Cricket, who was Pinocchio's conscience. The idea is that Google wants you to let the ledger/AI be your conscience. The idea is to goad you into giving up control and autonomy and to learn to trust the "machine." Episode 2 is about the self-writing quill, a reference to Cornelius Fudge, a character in the Harry Potter series. This is a continuation of the same theme of letting AI run your life, with the promise of great comfort, ease and convenience by allowing the machine to run things on auto-pilot. As Melissa Dykes of *Truthstream Media* points out in her analysis[400], the user ends up being gamed or modified in a constant feedback loop by AI, which decides the values. The person no longer makes decisions using the machine as a tool; the machine

---

[400] https://www.youtube.com/watch?v=1ekkwAyNf1w

makes the decisions and carries the person along with it. The third and final part, episode three, contains the Latin phrase *unus pro omnibus* which can be translated as "one for all." The eight-minute video is filled with scenes of ants and bees, so that subtext is that we're being led into a hive-mind society controlled by AI, a collectivist "one" world for "all" where individuality is obliterated. The overt message is that data outlives us. Our DNA has been mapped. Now, certain parts can be targeted for modification to achieve a specific result, a technique known as *behavioral sequencing*. Google wants to think of user data as multigenerational and wants new generations to use previous generations' data stream/trail. Google will be able to make very accurate predictions based on a previous generation's choices. Google wants to become "God" at pattern recognition, growing to the point where it can pioneer, in its own words, "species-wide" prediction.

As much as Google tries to portray the ledger as a great tool for innovation and understanding, the truth is that it will be used for social engineering on an unprecedented scale. If one organization had access to everything about you – from your likes/dislikes to your purchase history to your web-browsing habits all to the way to your health records, your personal conversations and even your DNA – then that organization would literally know you better than you know yourself. Manipulation becomes easy. Directing you in ways that you can't detect also becomes easy.

Data will be used for behavioral modification to a

high degree. The ledger/AI is set to become the ultimate tool for social engineering by encouraging you to hand over your thinking, your decision-making capacity and even your conscience (the very thing that makes you human and different from a machine). Yet think about it: how could a machine, no matter how advanced, ever replace the human conscience?

Health, Privacy and Freedom ... Or Speed, Convenience and Dependence?

The Smart/5G grid, in particular, and AI/ transhumanism, in general, are holding a mirror in humanity's collective face. What do we value more? Health or speed? Privacy or convenience? Freedom or dependence? That dependence, which is increasingly taking the form of digital addiction, is fast becoming slavery. Judging by their actions, most people overwhelmingly value speed and convenience more than health and privacy; they are caught up in having to be constantly digitally connected and wanting frivolous things like faster downloads even if it damages their health by increasing EMF exposure. Just look at how many people consistently choose fast food, loaded with chemicals, preservatives and additives over fresh, healthy food. The degree of surveillance that is planned is breathtaking since it involves knowing every thought. Even now, the public is subject to mass surveillance, but the rulers are not. CCTV footage mysteriously disappeared when the "plane" hit the Pentagon on 9/11 and during the Jeffrey Epstein death (or disappearance) – right when we needed it most – yet meanwhile everyone else is constantly surveilled for all their mundane actions.

The hour has come we're going to have to take a stand on this because, quite simply, we are running out of time. The rate of humanity's technological development far outpaces the rate of its spiritual development, which is leading to a situation where we have so-called leaders (really *mis*leaders) who have access to (and command of) an astonishing array of highly destructive weaponry, which can be used both in war against a "foreign enemy" and at home against the public whom the government is keen to brand as a "domestic enemy". It means that with every year that passes, we are rapidly developing more and more technological tools (many of which are purely designed to surveil, injure or destroy) without developing the emotional and spiritual maturity alongside it to handle them well. The technology is advancing so rapidly that there is not enough time to debate the ethics of it before it is being deployed – by design, of course.

In the midst of society's rapidly advancing technological developments, how many people are asking the important questions: What exactly is artificial intelligence, anyway? To what end is all this technology being developed? Can we trust AI to run our society and our lives? What are the dangers of becoming so reliant on technology? What are the dangers of allowing this technology into our lives (literally – via digestible microchips[401] and implantable nanochips)? Is it really wise to shift our

[401] thefreedomarticles.com/digestible-microchips-nwo-microchipping/

focus away from organic entities towards artificial, synthetic, digital, plastic and metallic entities? Why are we ignoring the messages of countless books and movies (many in the science fiction genre) that have warned about the dangers of AI becoming self-aware then deciding it no longer needs humanity?

The development of the smart AI network is a highly disturbing trend. We know enough of the conspiracy to know that if this technology can be exploited to control others, then it will be. This technology is opening the door for tyrants of all stripes to exercise extreme control over the human mind and body in unprecedented ways – yet people are blindly walking forward, laying down their offerings at the altar of convenience, trading in what it means to be human: autonomy, free will and sovereignty. Transhumanism is being marketed as a benign drive towards the bettering of humanity; yet its very essence entails that you as a normal human will be genetically engineered out of existence.

On the deepest level, if we are facing a primal virus that has hacked life itself, then we need to remember that the weakness of this virus is that, even if it shows signs of becoming self-aware, it has no creative will or power of its own. Like any parasite, it must rely on tricking and deceiving other entities into sharing their power with it by becoming unwilling hosts. This knowledge will be the key to defeating this primal virus as we head into the next few years of an increasingly tyrannical NWO. What we are facing is, indeed, nothing less than the entire direction of human evolution and the future of the human race.

If you have made it this far, hopefully you have a much clearer idea of the problem humanity currently faces. The hour is late, and the enslavement agenda is already far advanced. Only from a place of true knowledge can we move forward with an effective answer to restore peace, truth and freedom. Now, it is time to turn our attention to the solutions. The conspiracy may operate on many levels, but the solutions are also multifaceted. Luckily, there are ways we can overcome this scale of evil; however, it will require a lot of determination on our part.

Chapter 12 – Solutions

So much for the problems and challenges humanity faces. There are always more details you could know, more corruption you could uncover and more conspiracies you could expose. But at a certain point, it's more important to focus on the solutions. Once you reach a certain level of knowledge about the real state of the world, you realize that we are in trouble and need to get off our backsides and act – lest we leave behind a world for future generations where freedom, sovereignty and self-determination are completely foreign ideas. However, a deep comprehension of the problem is necessary in order to change it (to "put a fire under your butt," so to speak). There's no point running frantically around trying to solve problems if you don't understand their source. As Thoreau said, for every thousand hacking at the branches of evil, there is only one hacking at the root.

There are positive signs. There is a mass awakening happening. There are more people questioning events right from the get-go rather than swallowing the governmental/MSM narrative. Just look at the number of online videos which people make immediately after mass shootings, where the official line is challenged, analyzed and perhaps exposed as fraudulent. Just look at the many youth in Israel who now refuse the draft or conscription[402] (mandatory military service). Another barometer

---

402 https://www.newsweek.com/israeli-teens-refuse-serve-military-take-part-occupation-west-bank-761277

which measures the degree of awakening is how many people question big events such as the JFK assassination or 9/11. Right after 9/11 occurred, only a small percentage of people believed the government was culpable in some way; a 2019 YouGov poll[403] showed 51 percent were more inclined to believe the critics' explanation of 9/11 instead of the official governmental line (19 percent). Another example is how NWO frontman Bill Gates was exposed and excoriated on social media around April 2020, right after Operation Coronavirus was in full swing in Europe and the US. It's clear that the average person is beginning to grasp his true agenda.

Thanks to the rapid and viral spread of information on the internet, people are exposed to more alternative viewpoints than in the past (although as chapter 7 showed, the NWO is doing their best to quickly clamp down on this with their multifarious censorship efforts). With people waking up to conspiracies faster than ever before, it is becoming harder for the conspirators to control populations.

The solutions in the following chapters are divided into six different planes or aspects, since opposing this worldwide agenda of control is not just about political action (which usually gets you nowhere) but about looking at yourself and the world on a deep series of levels. It's about recognizing that you exist as a full being. Just as the conspiracy goes deep, so must any effective solution. We need to meet the

403 https://www.ae911truth.org/images/PDFs/Slides-for-AE911Truth-WTC7-202-8232019.pdf

challenge on every front.

Ultimately, the most empowering perspective in all of this is to look at all the “evil” or unconsciousness as a challenge to help you grow stronger, more empathetic and more aware. It’s to help you and all of us grow. Not to look at the issue in this way invites fatigue, depression, anxiety, overuse of anger (i.e. getting lost in anger, being angry all the time) and fear, or on the other hand, apathy, ignorance and a lack of healthy anger.

I repeat: this is all happening for a reason. It’s time to use it to grow. So, let’s take a journey together to find out how best to do that.

Chapter 13 – Physical Plane Solutions

Let food be thy medicine, and let medicine be thy food.

– Famous quote attributed to Hippocrates

If people let the government decide what foods they eat and what medicines they take, their bodies will soon be in as sorry a state as are the souls of those who live under tyranny.

– Thomas Jefferson

The Doctor of the future will give no medicine, but will interest his patient in the care of the human frame, in diet, and in the cause and prevention of disease.

– Thomas Edison

In every culture and in every medical tradition before ours, healing was accomplished by moving energy.

– Albert Szent-Gyorgyi, Nobel Laureate in Medicine

*****

Let's start with the down-to-Earth, feet-on-the-ground solutions. Yes, there are many higher, loftier solutions to come, but you have to accept that you are a living being in a physical world with physical laws. It is harder to challenge the NWO when you are weak, sick, tired, constantly in survival mode or in some other compromised state. Your body is a dynamic organism. Like any moving system, entity or organism, you have to consider what you feed into it (input) if you want to change or improve what comes out (output).

Breath is Life

The most important element to human life is air. Supposedly you can't survive without oxygen for longer than around six minutes. Yet if you live in a major city, the air quality is far worse than in the countryside, with places like London, Los Angeles, Beijing and Delhi having chronic smog problems. Research has shown[404] that the amount of available oxygen in the air has dropped from 30 to 35 percent to 21 percent. It may as low as 11 to 18 percent in smog-filled cities. Given that we humans breathe in oxygen and need it for life, this is obviously a far bigger problem than the purported rising CO2 and global warming. But guess what gets all the attention?

As far back as 1931, Otto Warburg won a Nobel Prize for demonstrating that disease (including cancer) could not survive in an oxygen-rich environment. There are many parasites, whether bacterial, viral or fungal, that are destroyed in the presence of oxygen and conversely which thrive in oxygen-deprived environments (in other words, they are anaerobic instead of aerobic). Oxygen itself, however, is a double-edged sword, for it is also the

404 www.rencareltd.com/environment/

element which causes metal to rust (oxidize) and other materials to decay. This is why it's so important to include plenty of antioxidants in your diet, since they literally protect you against oxidation, allowing you to enjoy the benefits of oxygen without getting negatively affected by it.

Air quality is not as changeable as other things in your life. You can choose to move to a place with cleaner air. If that is impractical or would mean losing too much (proximity to family, friends, career, etc.), you could try using air purifiers in your home, which filter out some of the pollutants.

Ancient spiritual traditions have recognized the power of the breath; they have devoted entire practices to deep breathing and fully extracting oxygen and power from the air. You could also take up a spiritual practice such as pranayama, which is a branch of yoga devoted to breath development and control. Because breathing is an action which can be both unconscious/automatic and conscious, many people don't give it the attention it truly deserves. By regulating your breath, you regulate your very state of being, which greatly affects how well you can respond to any life situation (rather than impulsively reacting). When it comes to stress, breath is everything. The simplest way to overcome stress is to breathe – deeply, fully and slowly. Finally, there is a group of people known as *breatharians* who claim to derive all their energy from breathing (some of them eat no food and drink no water, although some of them also practice sun gazing to draw energy directly from the sun). This just goes to show that the limits of life here are not always so-called concrete physical laws but in fact just the limits of our imagination and perception.

Water, the Magical Element

After air comes water. Water is a magical element which we still do not fully understand. It seemingly breaks the laws of physics, being the only substance that actually expands when it cools instead of contracting. Water has memory. It can be imprinted with sounds, symbols, patterns and frequencies from its environment and then carry that imprint long after the imprinting agent has disappeared. For instance, you can place a flower in a glass of water, then remove the flower, then take a water droplet from the glass and examine it under a microscope. It will still contain the "imprint" of the flower. The Aerospace Center in Stuttgart, Germany, has done many experiments like this.

Water can also be imprinted by our thoughts and feelings. Famous Japanese researcher Masaru Emoto found that water is affected by what and how you speak to it. Both the words and the feeling/tone count.

Water carries information. It cleanses and nourishes. We must treat it with the utmost respect. Yet, what does most of the so-called civilized world do to its water? It allows all sorts of poisons, toxins and pollutants to contaminate it and doesn't properly filter all of this out: then the water is recycled to become municipal drinking water! Did you know that glyphosate, the carcinogenic pesticide first invented by Monsanto (now Bayer) and now used by many corporations in the Big Biotech conglomerate, was found in 94 percent of water samples in Europe in 2016? Glyphosate is one of the most toxic manmade molecules ever invented. It was also found in 70 percent of American households' drinking water to be above detectable levels in 2014, not to mention turning up in urine and breast milk.

Cities and municipalities in places like the US and Australia use chlorine to destroy parasites in the water – but the chlorine itself is toxic. Then they add fluoride, a neurotoxin which has been implicated in fluorosis, impaired cognitive abilities and cancer. So you have water with the imprint (and with the physical trace amounts of) synthetic pharmaceuticals and pesticides, plus chlorine and fluoride. This is what authorities consider "drinking water"!

Just as you are what you eat, you are what you drink. An important physical plane step is to take control of your water. There is a debate in the health community over whether distilled water or spring water is better. Both have their advantages. Distilled water (100 percent pure water) is what you get if you collect rainwater or use a filtration system such as reverse osmosis. There is a common misconception that distilled water is not good for you since it leaches minerals from the body; however, there is no hard proof of this.

Spring water is also a healthy alternative. If you capture the water at its source, it has been flowing and is thus very "alive" or energized. The possible downside of spring water is that it may contain contaminants. It also contains minerals which are inorganic. I am not talking about the way crops are grown (natural vs. conventional, no pesticide vs. pesticide). I am referring to whether minerals come from living things (plants) or dead things (rocks, dirt, etc.). Spring water is full of inorganic minerals that it picks up from dirt, so it has high levels of calcium, magnesium, etc.. Some people claim these inorganic minerals are not good for you, since the human body can't digest and assimilate them since they are rock, stone and dirt particulates. This line of thinking proposes that you can only assimilate minerals from actual food (plant or animal products); however, the debate is inconclusive, since the human body can assimilate salt, which is derived from the ocean or ancient rock deposits.

Either way, distilled water or spring water is a great step up from the current municipal tap water to which most people have become accustomed.

Lastly, there is another dimension to water that we are just beginning to understand. Water can be "structured." The molecular composition is always the same, but what really matters is the structure. Water can take on different patterns, shapes and structures despite being the exact same molecule (H2O – two hydrogens, one oxygen) on an atomic level. Clearly, not all water is created equal. Water molecules and clusters can be structured into beautiful hexagonal crystals (by using spiralizing channels or devices, spirals, classical music, sound, prayer, positive emotions and intention, etc.). There is undeniable proof that structured water is much more powerful, energized and beneficial to human health than ordinary water. Inventor Patrick Flanagan found that some water is "wetter" than other water and can therefore hydrate better. You can buy spiralizers for your kitchen taps that activate and structure the water right before you drink it.

Food vs. "Phude"

The next big thing you need to watch on the physical plane is food. These days, there is so much stuff that pretends to be food but has departed so far from real food that as Dr. Rima Laibow says, it would better be called "phude" since it looks and sounds like the real thing but is something else entirely.

Our food has become adulterated with all sorts of harmful additives, stripped of nutrients through the refining process and sprayed with all sorts of chemicals including pesticides, herbicides, fungicides and insecticides. Take a look at the ingredients on the back of a standard product label. There's all sorts of preservatives, stabilizers, enhancers, colors and other synthetic additives which are made in a factory (not grown in a farm or field) and do not belong in the human body because they cannot be properly broken down and assimilated. They're not put in there to enhance your health! They are put in there to improve the flavor of the product or enhance its stable life, regardless of the health benefits. These two things are driven by profit motive, not a concern for what is best for human health.

Then we have the cultural tendency to choose highly processed and refined foods over raw, unprocessed, unrefined and whole foods, a tendency which is robbing us of vital nutrients. Look how many people eat white bread (instead of whole grain bread) in the West or white rice (instead of brown rice) in the East. It's just pure carbohydrates without any of the vitamins, minerals, fats, proteins, enzymes and cofactors that come with the whole food. Generally, the farther a food gets from its natural state, the unhealthier it becomes: fermented foods being an exception, since they improve the health value of the food with added cultures which introduce beneficial bacteria into the food.

Ever since the end of WWII, we have seen the development of industrial agriculture with all its chemical fertilizers and pesticides. While they may have resulted in short-term gain, now more than 60 years on, they are destroying the soil and our food too. Plants sprayed with these kinds of pesticides absorb it deep into their cells, so it cannot be simply washed off when it comes to your dinner table. It may be killing the bugs, but, in small doses, it's also killing you! This kind of monocrop agriculture depletes the soil of vital minerals, which is another catastrophic consequence, because it means that even if the crops didn't have pesticide residue, they would still fail to provide adequate nutrition to you. The crops can't take in minerals that are simply absent in the soil. This kind of monocrop approach to food is an exact reflection of the dark force which is driving affairs on planet Earth – a force that wants to eliminate diversity (for food, culture, thought, perception, etc.) and make everyone conform to its dull, tainted agenda.

Just as I have advocated taking control of your air and water, I also suggest you take a look at where you get your food. In many communities now there are Farmers' Markets where you can directly meet the people growing your food and find out how it is grown. It is a great way to get fresh food. In general, we have lost touch with growing our food – the rituals of planting, nurturing, harvesting and saving seed – and there is something ineffable we have lost by allowing ourselves to become too separated from the whole process. There are also many initiatives such as Community Gardens where people are coming together to grow food. In cities around the world, people are becoming very creative in reclaiming areas such as rooftops, city parks and even bus shelter roofs and using the space to grow food. In almost all situations, wherever you are, there is a way you can grow some of your own food. For those inclined, start your own veggie garden or aquaponics system. There are some amazing products out on the marketplace which allow you to do indoor growing, vertical gardening, etc. so you can do it even in cities, indoors, in high rise apartments, on patios, etc. Growing your own food and buying local from known sources are great ways to take back control over your food supply.

GMOs – The New Frankenfood

As you can see, I have already listed some big problems with our food supply. However, this doesn't even touch upon the massive problem which has changed the face of food completely – and perhaps forever. I refer to GMOs (Genetically Modified Organisms). This also goes by the name of GE (Genetic Engineering). Now, GM (genetically modified) foods in the US are going to be labelled

"BioEngineered" which is just an example of the NWO controllers rebranding an unpopular phenomenon in the hopes of disguising it. Whatever name you use, it's the same dangerous technology.

What is a GMO? A GMO is created when the DNA from one species (usually a plant) is crossed with the DNA from a completely different species (such as a virus, bacteria or animal). This is not the traditional crossbreeding that has been practiced for thousands of years by human farmers, where different strains of plants are crossbred to produce hybrids. Genetic engineering or modification is the artificial injecting of the DNA of a completely different, random species into plant DNA. It has been described as vertical rather than horizontal mixing. Such a mix never occurs in Nature, and thus, we have no idea of the long-term consequences of such a process. Genetic modification is carried out under the banner of biotechnology by big multinational corporations such as BASF, Syngenta, Dow, Dupont, Pioneer and Bayer. Bayer has acquired the infamous Monsanto (voted the world's most hated corporation for many years). These businesses have rebranded themselves as biotech companies, but they are essentially chemical and pharmaceutical companies – many with a very dark history. Bayer and BASF were part of the I.G. Farben conglomerate, producing chemical weapons for the Bush-Rockefeller-funded Nazis. When it comes to a dark past though, Monsanto takes the cake, having produced the carcinogens Agent Orange, DDT, Dioxin and Lasso. It also produced rBGH (recombinant Bovine Growth Hormone), a hormone given to cows which has made them sick, and made humans who consume their milk sick too. However, Monsanto bribed the FDA to the tune of $1-2 million[405] to get it legalized. Monsanto also took over the development of aspartame, an artificial sweetener with 92 reported health side effects[406], including irreversible brain damage and death. On top of all of that, it was Monsanto that produced PCBs (plastics classified as persistent organic pollutants) for over 50 years, which are now virtually omnipresent in the tissues of humans and wildlife around the globe.

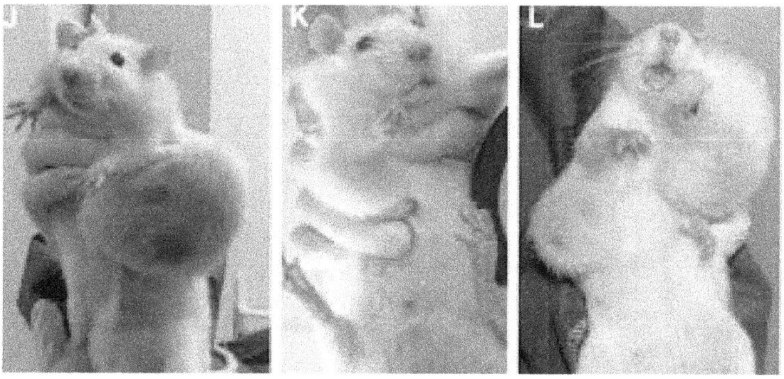

The rats above from GMO study conducted by Seralini developed gross malignant tumors after just four months eating GM maize/corn.

Knowing all of this, it would be wise to look at GMOs with a healthy deal of skepticism, given that they're being pushed by such corporations. Scientific studies have proven that skepticism to be well-

[405] www.responsibletechnology.org/fraud/The-World-According-to-Monsanto-September-2008

[406] www.sweetpoison.com/aspartame-side-effects.html

founded. The French scientist Seralini[407] showed that rats fed Monsanto's GM maize developed severe liver and kidney damage, and developed malignant tumors, in just 4 months. Others[408] have shown that GMOs are implicated in a staggering large number of ailments, including organ failure, autism, allergies, asthma, sterility, infant mortality, digestive disorders, bowel disease, Crohn's, constipation, kidney disease, heart disease and more.

Why such horrible side effects? It's because the GMOs are completely new organisms with never-before-seen DNA. The process of creating GMOs involves the random shooting or splicing of genes,

---

407 www.gmoseralini.org/wp-content/uploads/2012/11/GES-final-study-19.9.121.pdf

408 www.collective-evolution.com/2014/04/08/10-scientific-studies-proving-gmos-can-be-harmful-to-human-health/

and leads to genetic mutations. When we ingest GM food, our body's immune system treats it as a foreign entity, so it starts attacking it and your body gets inflamed. GM foods are simply not fully digestible; the body doesn't recognize foreign plant proteins. GMOs cause inflammation, the hidden source of many auto-immune diseases (e.g. arthritis, multiple sclerosis, etc.) and other illnesses like diabetes, Alzheimer's and cancer.

Unfortunately, it doesn't stop there. GMOs go hand-in-hand with industrial pesticides. In fact, Monsanto originally developed its GMOs as a way to sell more of its chemical pesticides and herbicides. The most notorious of these is RoundUp, whose active ingredient is glyphosate. Glyphosate is extremely toxic to virtually all forms of life, even at low levels. Whenever you eat Bayer-Monsanto's GM food, you are also getting a dose of glyphosate, which has been linked[409] with chronic fatigue, birth defects and cancer. In particular, Dr Stephanie Seneff has shown the highly significant connection between glyphosate and obesity, diabetes, autism, Alzheimer's, Parkinson's and dementia.

It gets even crazier still. Monsanto has genetically engineered a type of corn called Bt corn, named after the bacterium they inserted into it. Bt corn has been modified to produce, as it grows, an insecticide that kills pests. Sounds great, but the problem is that when we ingest it, our digestion does not stop the Bt corn from producing pesticides inside of us also.

---

409 www.cornucopia.org/2014/03/gut-wrenching-new-studies-reveal-insidious-effects-glyphosate/

That's right: Bt corn can turn you into a walking pesticide factory[410]!

The truth is Big Biotech is conducting a giant human experiment. They are getting away with unleashing this giant genetic war because of the relatively long time between cause and effect. You need to avoid GMOs at all costs. How? The best way is by eating organic. Organic food is certified to contain no GMOs. Another way is to buy food with the "Non GMO" label.

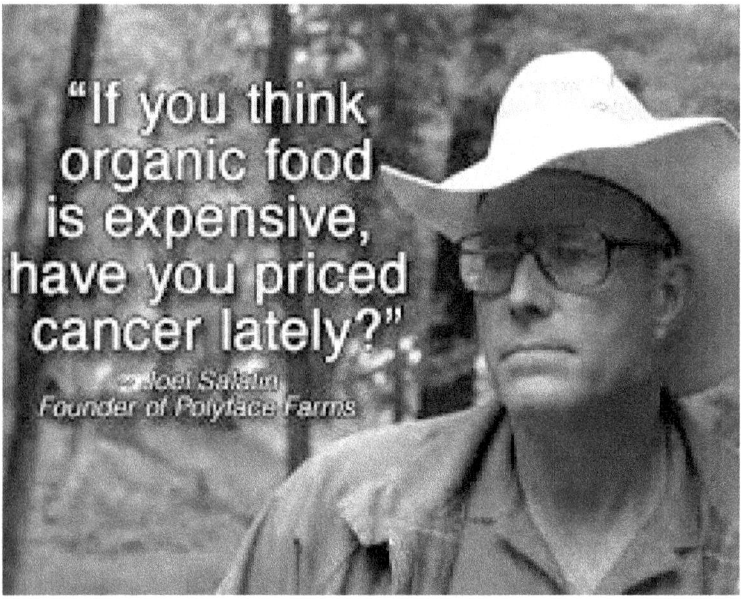

Some people complain that they don't have the money to buy organic food; however for many

410 www.responsibletechnology.org/gmo-dangers/health-risks/articles-about-risks-by-jeffrey-smith/Genetically-Engineered-Foods-May-Cause-Rising-Food-Allergies-Genetically-Engineered-Corn-June-2007

people, there are ways to do it cheaply by buying in bulk. For some people it's not about the money but really about the values. You have to ask yourself: what's more important – convenience/cheap cost vs. health and nutrition? The more pesticide-laden food you eat, the more you are slowly poisoning yourself. Do you really want to do that to save money in the short term? What about the long-term costs associated with that decision?

Organic food has been proven to be better in all respects. Study[411] after study[412] after study[413] show that organic food has a far better nutritional profile and nutrient/mineral content than conventional, pesticide-laden food, including higher levels of iron, magnesium, vitamin C and antioxidants. Some people have even used Kirlian

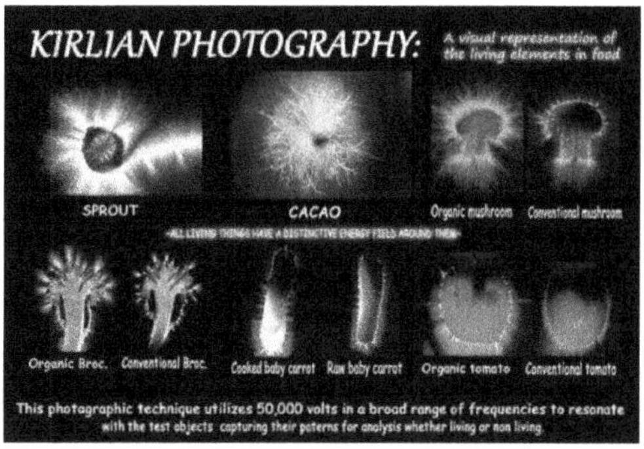

411 journeytoforever.org/farm_library/worthington-organic.pdf

412 https://journals.plos.org/plosone/article?id=10.1371/journal.pone.0012346

413 https://www.cambridge.org/core/journals/british-journal-of-nutrition/article/higher-antioxidant-and-lower-cadmium-concentrations-and-lower-incidence-of-pesticide-residues-in-organically-grown-crops-a-systematic-literature-review-and-metaanalyses/33F09637EAE6C4ED119E0C4BFFE2D5B1

photography (a type of bioelectrophotography which shows images of a corona effect or electrical discharge surrounding objects that normal photography cannot detect or display) to take images of organic foods to demonstrate that their energy fields are stronger and more vivid than their conventional counterparts.

At this stage there are 8 GMO crops in the US (corn, soybean, cotton, canola, sugar beet, alfalfa, papaya and squash), as well as the following grown around the world: eggplant (brinjal), rice, sweet pepper, canola and tomato. If you can't access certified organic or non-GMO food, avoid the above foods. However, this may easier said than done, because so many processed foodstuffs contain corn and soy derivatives (including the toxic HFCS or High Fructose Corn Syrup).

Finally, check the barcode on certain foods; very often you will find a 5-digit number beginning with 9 for organic foods, a 5-digit number beginning with 8 for GM foods, and a 4-digit number for conventional foods (i.e. foods grown with pesticides, not necessarily GMO but not certified organic).

Aside from the GMO issue, pay attention to your diet. You are what you eat. Ask yourself: are you eating a diet which supports your mission here on Earth? Have you educated yourself sufficiently to know what food is best? Do you gravitate towards foods which are full of empty calories, or towards superfoods and nutrient-dense foods? Do you make these superfoods (e.g. spirulina, chlorella, astaxanthin, hemp seeds, maca, goji berries) a regular part of your diet? Have you experimented with a vegetarian diet? A paleo diet? A raw diet? Are you eating a high percentage of fruit and vegetables? If you eat dairy and meat, is it grass-fed (i.e. more nutrient dense)? If you eat fish, are you avoiding types which are high in mercury? Are you eating whole foods, so you can the full integral value of the food, complete with all the micronutrients (vitamins, minerals, enzymes, etc.)?

There is no one right diet for everyone, since we all have different constitutions and energy needs; however if you're just blindly eating what your parents ate or whatever processed and junk foods your supermarket puts on the shelves in front of you, it's time to bring attention to your food choices and eat more consciously.

Food Propaganda

There is a lot of food propaganda out there – even by associations which you would think have your best interests at heart, or which at first glance seem trustworthy. However, some of them are just industry fronts pushing propaganda. A great example is the AHA (American Heart Association), which is funded in part by the petrochemical industries that developed margarine. They have been behind the demonization of saturated fats ever since they (in this case Proctor and Gamble) released Crisco in 1911. An artificial product like Crisco which is basically industrial hydrogenated oil can never be as nutritious and healthy as butter, so in order to sell more, these companies funded the AHA who in turn pushed the idea that all saturated fats were bad. To do this, they recruited Dr. Ancel Keys. Keys became famous for his "diet-lipid-heart disease hypothesis" that proposed a correlation between saturated fat (especially found in animal products) and heart disease, cardiovascular disease and high cholesterol. Consequently, in 1956 the American Heart Association (funded by Procter & Gamble, makers of the hydrogenated oil Crisco, and of which Keys was a board member) went on television to tell everyone that a diet which included large amounts of butter, lard, eggs, and beef would lead to coronary heart disease. Later Keys was put on the front page of Time magazine in 1961.

There was one big problem with all of this: Keys had selectively cherry picked the data and committed scientific fraud by deliberately leaving out data points to skew the research. He pointed to countries with low saturated fat intake and low heart disease, and countries with high saturated fat intake and high heart disease, and claimed a significant correlation. However, he omitted a very large amount of countries, almost all from Europe, that had high saturated fat intake and low heart disease.

France is one such country, and has become famous for the "French Paradox" phenomenon, where people consume moderate to high amounts of dairy, meat and wine, with no heart disease or even any negative side effects. However, you could just as well say "European Paradox", because the UK, Norway, Holland, Switzerland, Austria and others also had (and still have) high saturated fat diets with low rates of heart disease!

To say saturated fat caused heart disease was a giant lie. Your body is made with saturated fat. It is essential to animal life. It coats and protects our organs, keeps us warm, traps toxins, provides a stored supply of energy for hard times, forms 60% of our brain and yields a slow, steady source of energy (with more calories per gram) than proteins or carbohydrates. It is horribly misguided to reduce all saturated fat from your diet, yet entire industries have been built on this deception. We have the AHA putting its "heart healthy" labels all over low-fat food. We have the low-fat industry pushing items like skim milk, which is basically sugar water with "fortified" (synthetic) calcium and vitamin D.

Yes, too much saturated fat may be unhealthy, but too little is equally unhealthy and will rob you of vital nutrients. People have become scared of all fat, rather than distinguishing between healthy fats (butter, cheese, olive oil, avocado and coconut) and unhealthy fats (hydrogenated oils).

Think about it: how can something synthetic made in a factory (hydrogenated vegetable oil) possibly be healthier than something that comes from a farm, especially where animals are treated humanely and allowed to roam (grass-fed butter)? How can something made with a synthetic chemical formation, unfamiliar to the body, possibly be better than something humans have been eating for tens of thousands of years? If you're looking for the source of clogged arteries and heart disease, look at the plastic oils that the body can't fully assimilate – and you may find the culprit.

Along with saturated fat, cholesterol was also demonized in the process. As a point of fact, cholesterol is a fat molecule and is synthesized by all animals because it is a crucial structural component of our cells. Cholesterol helps with respiratory and gastrointestinal problems, and creates vitamin D; it is part of the healing mechanism of the body. Some scientists wrongly blamed cholesterol when they saw high levels of it in damaged blood vessels, thinking it caused clogged arteries, rather than realizing it was there to help protect and mend those arteries.

"There is No Cure for Cancer" Propaganda

Food propaganda abounds for many reasons, often pushed by the sugar and biotech industries (whose ingredients are especially found in junk food), or by other powerful industries who simply want you to eat more grains, dairy, etc. When you dig beneath the surface, it's not about science but rather about profit. It's all too easy for powerful industries to create "independent" front groups that they control who promote "scientific" studies extolling the benefits of eating their patrons' foods.

However, a more sinister aspect of the conspiracy is Big Pharma – the pharmaceutical conglomerate or cartel that stemmed out of John D. Rockefeller's oil monopoly and the breakup of German giant I. G. Farben into smaller companies like BASF, Bayer and Hoechst. Big Pharma has developed a business model which relies on the following things:

– isolating and synthesizing chemical extracts from natural sources (usually plants), obtaining a patent, selling the isolate as a miracle drug and then directly or indirectly (through proxy think tanks and fake independent front groups) downplaying the effect of the original plant as medicine. Some have referred to this as bio-piracy;

– finding new ways to make ordinary moods and states of being become a "disease", achieved by constantly inventing new diseases out of thin air (as in the psychiatric DSM), redefining existing diseases so as make new patients and finding dubious off-label uses (not backed by science or evidence) for its existing drugs;

– controlling the science by only funding scientists to produce the results that Big Pharma wants them to produce.

The chemical drugging of the population has become a criminal enterprise, with millions of people prescribed drugs which at best mask the symptoms and at worst turn them into dependent addicts and permanently fry their brains. Some "legal" prescription drugs are scarcely different to street drugs like amphetamine/speed (e.g. Ritalin) and heroin (e.g. fentanyl). A shocking proportion of Big Pharma drugs are opioids (derived from the opium poppy plant, from which we get morphine and heroin) which are fueling America's out-of-control opioid addiction epidemic, declared a national health emergency by former President Trump in October 2017. Another big chunk of Big Pharma drugs consists of mind-bending psychotropics which numb your feelings and destroy your personality and identity.

It is not just cynical to say that a patient cured is a customer lost to Big Pharma. They have made a craft out of "managing" and "treating" disease rather than actually curing it. A case in point is cancer. Cancer has been a big problem for a long time now (at least since Nixon declared a war on cancer in 1971), but we are still told officially that there is no cure, despite millions of generous (and unfortunately gullible) people donating to cancer research. (As mentioned in chapter 2, there is a very high likelihood that numerous cancer cures were found long ago but are being kept under lock and key by the Rockefellers and other key NWO groups).

Meanwhile, there are many free thinkers who have not been content to blindly accept the word of Western Medicine and Big Pharma, and have ventured out to try natural cancer cures – successfully. There are several that come to mind. Many people have had luck with the Gerson Therapy, started by Dr. Max Gerson in the 1920s. He has used a therapy involving fresh vegetable juices and coffee enemas to heal hundreds (now tens of thousands) of people who were told by Western doctors that, *"there nothing more we can do for you."* Other notable natural cancer remedies include:

– DCA (Sodium Dichloroacetate)
– Laetrile / Amygdalin / Vitamin B17 (which disables cancer cells but leaves healthy ones intact, banned by the FDA in 1971 to protect Big Pharma's profits)
– Graviola / Soursop (a South American fruit which 10,000 times stronger than chemotherapy, but without the dangerous side effects)
– The Budwig Diet (a combination of flax oil and

cottage cheese, discovered in 1951 by German doctor Dr. Johanna Budwig)
– Baking Soda / Sodium Bicarbonate (either mixed with maple syrup or injected intravenously [pioneered by Italian Dr. Simoncini])

See my 3-part article series *Cancer: Busting the Myths*[414] for more info, as well as my earlier book *Cancer: The Lies, The Truth and the Solutions*[415] *(Controversial Truths Revealed Series Book 1).*

Chemical Central

Ingesting healthy air/food/water is very important, as is avoiding toxic air/food/water, but let's face it; if you live in modern society, you are surrounded by toxins, and you can't always avoid them. In 1976, the US Congress passed the Toxic Substances Control Act, which listed 62,000 toxic substances in use in our modern society; since then, the list has grown to over 84,000 (which was the EPA [Environmental Protection Agency] estimate in 2008). If you fill up your car with gasoline, you have to breathe in the fumes; if you eat any kind of packaged food, some of the plastic may have rubbed off on the food and entered your body; if you have ever drunk tap water, it would have carried some contaminants and impurities into your body. Just look on the back of your average personal care and cosmetic product –

---

414 thefreedomarticles.com/cancer-busting-myths-cancer-microbe-p1/

415 https://www.amazon.com/CANCER-SOLUTIONS-Naturally-Controversial-Revealed-ebook/dp/B08FBQQQ8X/

the ingredient list is full of unnatural and barely pronounceable chemical names. Whether it's soap, toothpaste, shampoo, deodorant, detergent or any other similar item, almost all of them are full of plastics and microplastics including BPA and BPS (phenols), dioxin and dioxin-like compounds, polychlorinated biphenyls, phthalates, perchlorate (rocket fuel), fire retardants, glycol ethers and many more.

Many of them are EDCs – endocrine disrupting chemicals – which are estrogen mimickers that have the effect, among other things, of lowering testosterone, feminizing men and leading to plummeting sperm counts. Too much testosterone is problematic, true, when it leads to aggression, however too little is equally problematic since it makes us more likely to acquiesce and comply when we really need to be standing up with some guts and spine.

Since these chemicals wreak havoc with our hormones (especially sexual hormones), it is no coincidence that in the last few years we have seen the rise of the transgender agenda. On an individual level, I fully support everyone to be who they are, regardless of their sexual orientation. On a collective level, however, there has been a literal explosion of transgenderism to the point where it has become propaganda aimed at children, who are far too young to understand or contemplate such issues. The aim is to thoroughly confuse children and the end result is that some people are trying to claim they are "non-binary", i.e. neither male nor female, which is a biological impossibility. This was foreshadowed by

Aldous Huxley in *Brave New World* and ties right in with the transhumanism agenda (discussed in chapter 11) – to make humanity more genderless and machine-like.

Detoxification

Many of these toxins end up being stored in our muscles or fatty tissue; some even end up in our organs and impair the function of them, which is, needless to say, a grave problem. It is widely believed that toxins such as fluoride end up in the pineal gland (the "seat of the soul" according to French mathematician and philosopher Rene Descartes, located in the exact center of our brain), calcify it and shut it down. Since the pineal gland is our link to higher dimensions, this could conceivably have the effect of preventing us from accessing higher consciousness – by design.

The only way to deal with the inundation of toxicity is detoxify. Luckily, there are many detox techniques you can undergo which can help rid your body of toxins:

– supplements like iodine, magnesium and sulfur (it's important to take them in bioavailable form for maximum assimilation, e.g., Nascent Iodine, Magnesium Oil and DMSO/MSM)
– veggie juices, smoothies and green drinks
– massage
– sweat / steam
– fasting
– liver / gallbladder flush (look up Hulda Clark's work for how to do this)

– learn how to get rid of heavy metals
– learn how to get rid of plastics
– learn how to get rid of fluoride

Exercise

In Chinese medicine, disease is defined as stagnation. Good health requires that we keep moving and stay active, which is a challenge for most people living in Western society and used to sedentary jobs and lifestyles. Exercise makes you feel alive. Your heart is a muscle like any other which needs movement and training to thrive. You'll be amazed at how good you feel with just 15-30 minutes of exercise a few times per week, whether it's swimming, running, yoga, weight training or some kind of team sport like soccer, basketball or tennis. There's no substitute for getting your heat pumping, blood flowing and brain releasing all sorts of feel-good chemicals like endorphins which help you feel alive.

Sleep

Sleep is another fundamental part of health and self-care on the physical plane. There are, sadly, many people with sleep issues around the world, and almost just as many causes. Some people suffer from anxiety or unresolved emotional issues which prevent them from falling asleep easily or sleeping soundly. Another common problem is people's addiction to technology, especially smart phones. People are becoming so glued to a screen that it is messing with their eyes, electrical balance and circadian rhythm. In this case, disconnecting with technology well before you go to bed can be beneficial. Almost all electronic screens use blue light on the UV spectrum. Too much blue light (which before electricity would only have been seen during the day) is not good at night, because it sends the wrong signal to the brain and disrupts melatonin, the sleep hormone. One solution is to wear blue-light blocking glasses (usually amber or orange) when starting at any screen, especially at night.

Connection with Nature

In addition to all the above points, many people who live in cities and built-up areas are also missing something vital from their lives: a connection with Nature. We come from the Earth and will return to the Earth, and there is a part of our soul that cannot be nourished by concrete jungles, but only by barefoot contact with the land and immersion in forests and open natural spaces.

Nature has a way of calming us down and removing the stresses of our life, as we relax and become entrained to its slow healing frequency.

One factor that is paying a large role in disconnecting us from Nature is EMF radiation. This is a manmade phenomenon. We now have so many electronic and technological devices that we have created a massive electrical grid (even if you discount wireless radiation or wi-fi, which just compounds the issue). We are electrical beings and so this grid affects us, especially when you consider it operates in frequency bands millions and billions times more than the Schumann Resonance (the

Earth's natural resonance of 7.8 Hz (cycles per second). The current rollout of 5G (or, more accurately, the current deployment, since this is military weaponry and technology using millimeter bandwaves in the 24-95 GHz range) could spell disaster for the human energy field. By attaching ourselves to and being immersed in an artificial EMF grid, and being separated from a natural grid, we are disconnecting ourselves from Nature – resulting in all sorts of maladies. Experiments and studies have already shown that 5G millimeter wave exposure causes damage in seconds to minutes, including damage to mitochondria (in a time-response/dose-response way), antibiotic resistance (leads to the advent of superbugs) and cancer.

Natural Medicine vs. Synthetic Drugs

So far I have covered all the necessary components to building good health; however, there are also things you need to avoid. On a basic level, health is about putting good stuff in and taking bad stuff out. We are faced with choices around this dichotomy every day. One area it shows up is in the area of medicine. This is another natural/artificial split. You can take the route of natural medicine and natural therapies, based on herbs, plants, spices and natural substances (including modalities such as homeopathy, chiropractic and acupuncture) or you can take the route of artificial, synthetic medicine as embodied by Western Medicine (allopathy) which pushes drugs, vaccines, surgery, chemotherapy and radiation.

In order to make an informed choice about all this,

you need to understand what exactly Western medicine is – and where it came from. Western medicine is Rockefeller medicine, all the way. It has some good points, for sure, and is great in an emergency; however, it is essentially a Rockefeller creation. The Rockefellers, of course, are one of the richest and most powerful families of the elite black nobility. Behind their spurious facade of philanthropy, they have shown themselves to be power-hungry tyrants intent on owning the entire world, and depopulating it through eugenics-based programs like forced sterilization, water fluoridation, abortions and vaccinations. Despite the dominance of allopathy nowadays, even just 100 years ago the situation was very different. How did allopathy and the giant conglomerate of multinational pharmaceutical corporations ("Big Pharma") become the mainstream medical system in the US and other first world nations?

Let's go back in time to the late 1800s. John D. Rockefeller, a man quoted to have said "competition is sin", is the head of the Rockefeller family and has just become very rich through extracting oil from the ground. Now he is looking for ways to capitalize even further with his oil, and he comes across the idea of using coal tar – a petroleum derivative – to make substances that affect the human mind, body and nervous system. These are called drugs, and they are excellent at masking or stopping symptoms, but overall do not cure the underlying cause of a disease.

Like other elite leaders of the New World Order who fit the description of an "evil genius" – those high on intellect and low on compassion – Rockefeller used his oil money to buy part of the massive German pharmaceutical cartel, I.G. Farben. This was the very same cartel that would later assist Hitler to implement his eugenics-based vision of a New World Order founded on racial supremacy by manufacturing chemicals and poisons for war. With the control of drug manufacturing under his wings, Rockefeller then embarked on a decidedly wicked business plan.

Rockefeller saw that there were many types of doctors and healing modalities in existence at that time, from chiropractic to naturopathy to homeopathy to holistic medicine to herbal medicine and more. He wanted to eliminate the competitors of allopathy (the only modality which would propose drugs and radiation as treatment, thus enriching Rockefeller who owned the means to produce these treatments), so he hired a man called Abraham Flexner to submit a report to Congress in 1910. This report "concluded" that there were too many doctors and medical schools in America, and that all the natural healing modalities which had existed for hundreds or thousands of years were unscientific quackery. It called for the standardization of medical education, whereby only the allopathic-based AMA (American Medical Association) be allowed to grant medical school licenses in the US.

Sadly, Congress acted upon the conclusions and made them law. Incredibly, allopathy became the standard mainstream modality, even though its 3 main methods of treatment in the 1800s had been blood-letting, surgery and the injection of toxic heavy metals like lead and mercury to supposedly displace disease! It should be noted that hemp was also demonized and criminalized not long after this, not because there is anything dangerous about it, but because it was a huge threat (as both medicine and fuel) to the Rockefeller drug and oil industries, respectively.

The story doesn't stop there. Rockefeller and another elite leader Carnegie used their tax exempt foundations, from 1913 on, to offer huge grants to the best medical schools all over America – on the proviso that only an allopathic-based curriculum be taught, and that some of their agents be allowed to sit on the schools' Boards of Directors. They systematically dismantled the curricula of these schools by removing any mention of the natural healing power of herbs and plants, or of the importance of diet to health. The result is a system which to this day churns out doctors who are, almost always, utterly clueless about nutrition.

A couple of decades after this, another law was passed that further entrenched allopathy in America. The Hill-Burton Act of 1946 gave hospitals grants for construction and modernization on the condition they provide free healthcare to anyone in need, without discrimination of any kind. Although there were good sides to this, the downside was that once people had become dependent on this system for their healthcare needs – especially on pharmaceutical pills which need to be taken day after day without end – the system switched into a paid system, and the Rockefellers found themselves with new lifelong customers.

For Big Pharma, there is no financial incentive to

heal you, because a patient cured is a customer lost. Even if you are not sick, Big Pharma is still targeting you, trying to convince you that you are ill (with ridiculous made-up diseases) so that you will try its latest pill. Pregnant women are treated like this, peddled intravenous fluid bags, ultrasound (radiation for a vulnerable baby), a host of drugs, a totally unnecessary episiotomy, and even a Caesarean delivery, which is a highly unnatural way for a baby to be born. Why can't this be kept for emergencies only?

Remember, all these synthetic drugs are isolates. Many contain artificial versions of plant compounds, but because Nature cannot be patented and sold, Big Pharma has no interest in natural cures. They engage in bio-piracy – research natural compounds, copy them (or modify them slightly) in a lab, then try to steal and patent them. If they get a patent, they then market their pill as a wonder drug while simultaneously (through fake scientific research) suppress and criticize the original plant as being worthless, so you won't go to the source of the cure. Ironically, guess what type of medicine John D. Rockefeller used and the British Royal Family still uses? Homeopathy!

Modern medicine seems to have lost the supposed point of its existence: healing people. Yes, they have are all sorts of gadgets, devices and diagnostics such as lab tests, electrocardiograms, x-ray and CT scans, but do any of their fancy procedures have anything to do with maintaining health? When people get screened for a disease, often they are being subjected to dangerous radiation (more money for the Rockefellers) which harms tissue and can end up causing the exact disease it is supposed to be protecting against – as happens daily with the mammogram scam, designed to drum up new breast cancer clients.

The Rockefellers and other elites use philanthropy as a tool for control. A free lunch is not really free, whether private (Rockefeller-style allopathy) or public/governmental (Obama-style socialized medicine), because even if you get something at no cost, you are required to give up your data and your privacy. They want you dependent on their system – then they'll raise the rates once you're trapped.

This is big business – and it's also a big killer. Dr. Barbara Starfield published a study in the year 2000 that found that there were 225,000 iatrogenic (allopathic doctor caused) US deaths every year. In 2011 Dr. Gary Null calculated the figure as closer to 784,000 per year. That's 7.8 million people dead from allopathy every 10 years! Null stated: *"It is evident that the American medical system is the leading cause of death and injury in the United States ..."*

Whenever a lot of people die in a staged false flag attack (like 3,000 people on 9/11) or in a staged mind control shooting (like 50 or so people) it gets massive media attention. Yet between 616 and 2,147 Americans are dying every day from Rockefeller Western medicine, and we don't hear a thing!

Remember this: Western Medicine and Big Pharma promise that all your ills can be taken away with pills. The bitter truth is that there is no magic pill; health is a long term commitment which requires, at times, hard work and discipline. However, the good news is that, once you have established good patterns, it's easier to find a way to eat and live well without feeling like "you're missing out" or that you have to sacrifice something. You can find food that is both delicious and nutritious; you can find exercise that is fun; you can find a lifestyle that is active and rewarding.

Pills are never the answer. Big Pharma drugs just mask the symptoms; they don't address the root cause of disease. They're an empty promise. The best they can ever do is offer temporary relief – but even then, they are so riddled with side effects that the "relief" you get is often to exchange one imbalance for another in the body, which allows disease to persist. Some doctors trained in Western medicine went on to become holistic and natural doctors because they became so disgusted with the "drugs-surgery-radiation" paradigm of treatment. All 3 of these "treatments" injure the body in some way, ranging from minor side effects to serious adverse damage (as with radiation and chemotherapy). Chemotherapy itself causes cancer! So does radiation. How can you treat cancer with things that cause it?

An important part of any physical plane solution is breaking your mental dependence on your doctor. The human body is its own healer. At the ultimate level, you heal yourself, no matter how good your doctor is. All great healers have recognized this fundamental principle; their work is to help facilitate the body to heal itself, and get out of the way so the body can do its thing. Many people look outside of themselves to their doctors to save them, just as many people look to religion, government and other institutions to save them, not realizing how corrupted these organizations are, and how often their agenda is the exact opposite of what they say. Besides, studies have shown that doctors are generally very unhealthy individuals compared to those in other professions. Do you want someone unhealthy giving you health advice?

Reducing your dependence on your doctor also includes critically thinking about his/her advice, opinions and diagnoses. It's important to remember that allopathic doctors were only trained to look at medical issues from a certain perspective. They were taught to disregard the role of nutrition and alternative therapies. Usually they are completely unaware of just how fraudulent the diagnosis scheme is, because it has been corrupted by Big Pharma marketing to sell drugs to people who don't really need them. Are you letting your doctor worry you with a scary sounding diagnostic label, that sounds so final, when you may not have that disease in the first place? Are you focused on the label of the disease – or how you can actually heal it?

As covered in chapter 8, the coronavirus saga brought a lot of attention to the nature of the virus and to the nature of disease in general. Knowledge is power and education cures ignorance. Imagine a world where people embraced host theory/terrain theory instead of germ theory, and took more responsibility for their health. Imagine if people strengthened their immune systems with healthy food choices, enough sunshine (vitamin D), sufficient exercise and adequate sleep. Imagine if people chose to reduce or eliminate exposure to toxins like fluoride, chlorine, aluminum, mercury and EMF wireless radiation. Imagine if people supplemented with things that boost immunity – like vitamin C, antioxidants, iodine, zinc and magnesium (from natural food-based sources) – and other natural medicines. There would not be much disease. The solutions are in front of us; we just need to inform ourselves and use them. You were born with an amazing immune system! Boost it. Trust it.

Don't Get Jabbed or Shot Up

Next, you have to break your physical and mental dependence on vaccines. Vaccines are chemical cocktails designed to produce inflammation in your body. Vaccines are composed of many or all of the following ingredients: mercury, aluminum, formaldehyde (all carcinogens), MSG, human DNA (from a cell line of aborted fetuses), animal and insect DNA, egg protein, anti-freeze, polysorbate, peanut oil (a common allergen) and more. You need to break the programming given to you that you need vaccines to be healthy. Many people step on a rusty nail and immediately think – "I need a vaccine for tetanus!" But in reality, what are the chances that particular nail had tetanus – and in a virulent enough dose to pose a problem to you? Vaccines cause far more damage than whatever good they hypothetically do.

Many researchers have shown that diseases like

smallpox and polio were already on the decline (due to improved sanitation, nutrition, etc.) before the introduction of vaccines – although Big Pharma in another of its marketing tricks tried to take all the glory for it. Ultimately, it is your immune system that defends you against invaders and poisons, not a vaccine.

"The combined death rate from scarlet fever, diphtheria, whooping cough and measles among children up to fifteen shows that nearly 90 percent of the total decline in mortality between 1860 and 1965 had occurred before the introduction of antibiotics and widespread immunization. In part, this recession may be attributed to improved housing and to a decrease in the virulence of micro-organisms, but by far the most important factor was a higher host-resistance due to better nutrition."

– Ivan Illich, Medical Nemesis, Bantam Books, 1977

Next, you have to break your dependence on the idea of healthcare. There are still many people who think they can indulge in poor food and lifestyle choices and get away with it – all because they have healthcare. This is a dangerous philosophy, because what if you end up damaging your health so much that Western medicine can't do anything for you? What if laws change so healthcare is no longer a right, but an expensive privilege? An ounce of prevention is worth a pound of cure. Healthcare is best used as a safety net for emergencies, not as an excuse for destroying your health.

<u>Building Jing (Core Energy)</u>

To be truly productive, abundant and prosperous, you need to develop your core energy (variously called stamina, endurance, resilience or strength). The ancient Chinese called it *jing* and believed that it was stored in the kidneys. The ancient Indians called it *ojas* and believe it was stored in the sexual organs (testes for men, ovaries for women). This core energy is often synonymous with sexual energy (since your sexual energy in the form of sperm or eggs is powerful enough to create new life), but it doesn't have to be. Various spiritual practices and martial arts such as yoga, qi gong, tai chi, etc. teach practitioners how to move *prana*, *chi* or energy around the body. These teachings are no longer in the realm of the esoteric and are openly available to people of any culture, race or nation.

You and Only You Are in Charge

There's only one person in charge of your health. No, it's not your doctor, your spouse or your nutritionist. It's you. You can't outsource the responsibility for keeping your body healthy to someone not living in your body. If you want to have good health, you're going to have to break the programming you were brought up with. You're going to have to get educated, and break your dependency on your doctor, your pills, your vaccines and your health insurance. This doesn't necessarily mean you need to cut all ties with your doctor or cancel your insurance; it simply means you need to stop being dependent on these, and start taking charge of your wellbeing.

This chapter has focused on the physical plane solutions, the realm of the body. Next we will take a look at mental plane solutions, the realm of the mind, to explore how there are many changes we can make to become freer and more empowered.

Chapter 14 – Mental Plane Solutions

Find out just what people will submit to, and you have found out the exact amount of injustice and wrong which will be imposed upon them.

– Frederick Douglass

I have found that to make a contented slave, it is necessary to make a thoughtless one. It is necessary to darken his moral and mental vision, and, as far as possible, to annihilate the power of reason. He must be able to detect no inconsistencies in slavery; he must be made to feel that slavery is right, and he can be brought to that only when he ceased to be a man.

– Frederick Douglass

The limits of tyrants are prescribed by the endurance of those whom they oppress.

– Frederick Douglass

The Mass Mind Control of a population can be defined as the sophisticated exercise of control by utilizing the ability to keep people oppressed yet contented.

– The Tavistock Institute of Human Relations

A really efficient totalitarian state would be one in which the all-powerful executive of political bosses and their army of managers control a population of slaves who do not have to be coerced, because they love their servitude.

– Aldous Huxley, author of *Brave New World*

*****

You may not think of it in this way, but false information can be just as toxic as poisonous food. One poisons your body, the other poisons your mind. We live in an age of instant news, where millions of informational sources vying for our attention are literally at our fingertips and in our pockets (in the form of smartphones). The internet has busted the old media oligopoly. This is good because the MSM used to have a stranglehold on the industry. There was a time when there were simply no alternatives to its propaganda. Now, we are faced with so many choices. The good side of this variety is diversity of thought; the downside is that it's easy to feel overwhelmed and sometimes hard to figure out who to trust.

Mind control is not just a covert Nazi-CIA MK Ultra program. Our whole world is suffering from mind control to varying degrees. We have all been indoctrinated and fooled with some form of propaganda or lie. The awakening process means disconnecting from the Matrix version of reality and opening up your mind to a greater truth. Taking back our power on the mental realm means undoing the effects of mass mind control on our own minds and belief systems.

Mind control in the broader sense is narrative control – control of the dominant narrative that eventually becomes accepted as the official, most accurate or truest version of events. The NWO controllers through all of their avenues – control of government, the MSM, Hollywood and more – invest so much effort into establishing the dominant narrative and burying and destroying competing narratives because they know their power depends on a misled and uninformed populace. To take it a step further, narrative control is really perception management or perception control, for once you control what someone believes about you, themselves, society or a particular event, you have them in the palm of your hand. You can make them do your bidding and lead them along as you like. Thus, to reiterate, mind control is narrative control, and narrative control is perception control. The solutions contained in this chapter are aimed at helping you gain mental sovereignty so you can free your mind and therefore your perception. The path out of slavery to freedom begins with you undoing the mental chains in which you have allowed yourself to be bound.

The Fake News Phenomenon

It is essential to choose wisely where to get your information. People from all walks of life are starting to realize this. The fake news phenomenon that arose during the 2016 US presidential election (and subsequent election of Donald Trump) was significant because it marked the first time when a political leader (Trump) actually called a news agency "fake" to its face, publicly. Yes, many seized upon the term in immature and childish ways to denigrate their opponents in limited left vs. right battles, but nonetheless, the fact that the term *fake news* entered the mass consciousness is a positive sign. Just a few decades ago, accusing the MSM of outright lying (or even silently believing that it did) would have been unthinkable. Now, many people know this for sure. The most blatant example that comes to mind is CNN pretending to have reporters in Saudi Arabia during a bomb raid, while in reality they were just filming inside one of their US studios.

The Divide-and-Rule Trap

Another huge mental trap to avoid is the divide-and-rule or divide-and-conquer trap. This one is a favorite of the NWO controllers. It has probably been around for as long as there have been rulers. The way it works is simple: if you are a criminal and corrupt ruler, you know you would have no chance against an awakened and united populace rising up against you and exposing your crimes. So, in order to prevent a large group of people focusing on your crimes, you introduce distractions to split the population into different segments and then create controversy and tension to pit one segment against another. From the NWO controller point of view, it doesn't really matter which population segments are created nor which issues are stimulated. It's all about preventing the uniting of people against a common enemy: their lying and tyrannical rulers.

Thus, the divide-and-rule trick splinters the population along all sorts of lines, such as race, skin color, ethnicity, religion, political belief, gender, age, sexual orientation, socioeconomic class and much

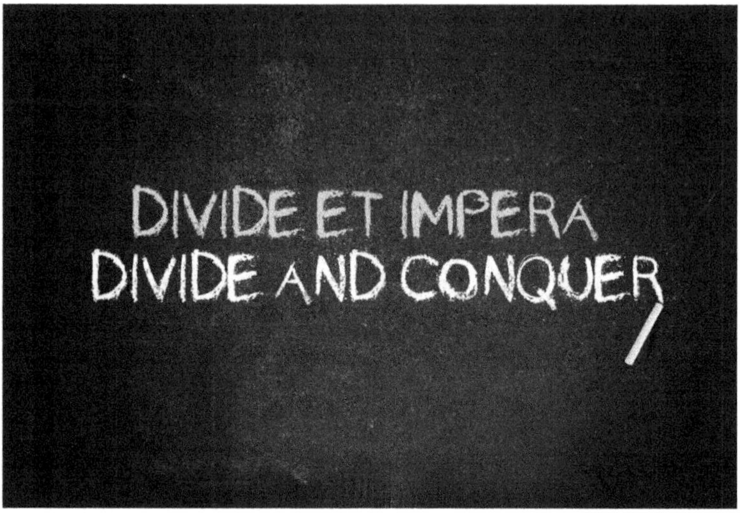

more. Operation Coronavirus has been incredibly divisive, polarizing the population along the faultlines of vaccination status. The NWO manipulators have tried to encourage the vaccinated to fear and hate the unvaccinated, and vice versa. As blacks fight whites, women fight men, Christians fight Muslims, the right fights the left and the poor fight the rich, we forget our common humanity and get caught up in petty differences. Meanwhile, the real forces manipulating us giggle with glee as we fight amongst ourselves. They are aiming to make a ruler and slave society, and in the end, the slave class they envision will be made up of people from every segment: black slaves, white slaves, old slaves, young slaves, straight slaves, gay slaves, religious slaves and atheist slaves. The very people that you are fighting today may become your fellow prisoners in chains if we fail to rise above our small differences and unite.

One trick I have noticed is that during elections, the MSM will insert controversial issues like abortion and euthanasia into the discussion. This is done not to reach any true resolution on these issues but solely to stir up anger and divide people. They know that these kinds of issues are very polarizing, and they also know that a politician's stance on them is largely irrelevant to their policies and how they will manage public affairs. It's all about promoting infighting.

The divide-and-rule trap wouldn't work so well if people didn't buy into it, but it preys upon human psychology by influencing them to join a side. It exploits humanity's natural tendency towards tribalism, of wanting to belong, of needing to be part of a group, family or tribe with a common culture and belief system. This comes out especially strongly during election season, when the fake left-right paradigm does a masterful job every three to six years (depending upon the nation) of turning people against one another and convincing them they have to choose a side.

The divide-and-rule trap has had a great ally in the realm of politics in recent years: identity politics. This is defined as "political activity or movements based on or catering to the cultural, ethnic, gender, racial, religious, or social interests that characterize a group identity." Identity politics is taking people and forcing them into tiny boxes (categories), then telling them that their political beliefs and actions must come from their identities. Identity politics has taken over much of the political left / progressive branch and is behind the push for ever more political correctness which, as covered earlier in chapter 7, is really censorship in disguise.

Identity politics is steeped in victim mentality. It's all about organizing "oppressed" people (or people more likely to be oppressed), getting them to identify with their victimhood and making that the central pillar of their political views and overall worldviews. It's also all about condensing the extraordinarily rich, complex and diverse histories of nations and fabrics of cultures into simple superficial characteristics: skin color and sexual orientation. There is a tendency for those into identity politics to dismiss all white people as privileged oppressors and predators. The radical left claims to be against racism ... but isn't racism the clumping together of all people of a particular race, skin color or nations and judging them collectively rather than individually? Isn't racism judging people by their racial category rather than who they actually are? In every nation, race and religion can be found friendly people, neutral people and mean people. Hasn't identity politics got so caught up in abstract categories and labeling that it's preventing people from interacting in the present regardless of these categories? By placing so much emphasis on categories, identity politics is keeping people in a prison of reactivity – always reacting to some injustice or oppression.

Some identity politics activists also seem to have forgotten what equality is. Advocating more injustice – in the form of reverse racism where "privileged straight white males" get insulted and discriminated against just because they belong to that category – doesn't create justice. Two wrongs don't make a right. Making straight white males suffer now doesn't change the history of injustice done to minority groups. Favoring minority groups over majority groups just changes who experiences the inequality; it doesn't produce equality. It all comes from being obsessed with race and basing one's attitudes and actions on the other person's race. Again, ironically, this fits the bill as the definition of racism.

We need to remember the great words of Martin Luther King Jr., who dreamt that one day we would live in a world where people are judged by the "content of their character" and not the color of their skin. We would also do well to realize that as good as the intention is to create a world of justice, we won't be able to do that if we constantly identify with form. In his masterful book *The Power of Now*, spiritual teacher Eckhart Tolle highlights how identification with form is the basis of the ego. Identifying strongly with a particular mental position narrows our perspective and takes us into a world of duality, where anyone who disagrees with us might be turned into an opponent, enemy or someone who is "wrong." He writes how women are right to be aware of the history of pain that has been dished out to them throughout the ages by men; but they are wrong to identify with that pain and make it who they are because such an identification lessens who they are (and even sets up a dichotomy/polarity that allows such injustice to continue). It may seem counterintuitive, but the way to stand up for these principles is to promote them without being attached to or identified with them – otherwise they consume you.

<u>How the Alternative Media Got "Trumped"</u>

CANDIDATE TRUMP
PRESIDENT TRUMP
LOCK HER UP!
SHE'S BEEN THROUGH ENOUGH
REPLACE OBAMACARE
OBAMACARE CAN STAY
CHINA IS BAD
CHINA IS GOOD
ASSAD SHOULD STAY
ASSAD SHOULD GO
WE MUST RESPECT RUSSIA
RUSSIA MUST RESPECT US
NATO IS OBSOLETE
NATO IS INDISPENSIBLE
AMERICA FIRST
AMERICA WORLD POLICE

The US presidential election of 2016 taught the awakening community a powerful lesson: just because you're starting to become "aware" and "awake" doesn't mean you're at the end of your journey. The same tricks to control you still apply. So many people in the Alternative Media chose to jump aboard the Trump train and buy into the same old idea that "this time it's different" and "our candidate is going to save us." Whether by accident or design, Trump got many on board by making some accusatory comments against some of the entrenched establishment figures, institutions and revered ideas (e.g., attacks against Jeb Bush, questioning 9/11, questioning the Federal Reserve, questioning US military interventionism, etc.). However, they were just empty words. Yes, I still believe that Hillary Clinton would have been an unmitigated nightmare for the US and the world and that Trump was preferable. But it's the same old predicament of having to choose between two unpleasant alternatives. Trump took everyone for a ride just like most politicians. You can say anything you want before the election as there are no legal repercussions. Here is a brief list of Trump before and after the election (and the same goes for Biden, Obama, Bush and all the rest of them – it's not about Left vs. Right):

– We need to investigate and prosecute the ultra-corrupt Hillary Clinton > She's a *"good friend"* and has been through enough

– We will drain the swamp > Appointed swamp dwellers to his cabinet and administration, such as Zionists, Neocons and the three Gs (Goldman Sachs, Generals and Gazillionaires)

– We will replace and repeal Obamacare > Kept the *"strongest assets"* of Obamacare

– Mexico will pay for the wall > Never happened

– We should stay out of Syria > Trump broke international law by attacking Syria with an air strike of fifty-nine missiles

– NATO is obsolete > NATO was *"no longer obsolete"*

– China is a *"currency manipulator"* > China was not manipulating the currency

– The US should get along with Russia > Russia became the official enemy

– Janet Yellen (head of the Federal Reserve) is bad > Then Trump *"respected"* her

– On his first day Trump signed a memo ordering a freeze on federal hires > By April 2017, the freeze was over

– WikiLeaks/Julian Assange is great. Trump said "I love WikiLeaks" > Trump oversaw the illegal arrest of

Assange who was dragged out of the Ecuadorian Embassy in London (Assange ended up in solitary confinement in jail and looks likely to be extradited to the US despite not being a US citizen or under US jurisdiction)

– The US should be non-interventionist > Trump railed and ratcheted up tension against Iran, China, Syria and North Korea (all to varying degrees)

– We need a strong US dollar > The dollar is *"getting too strong"*

Trump also had the chance to release many classified JFK files but did not. His administration threatened to veto a UN Resolution combating rape as a weapon of war. To be fair to Trump, there are some issues where he has kept his word, such as his promises to appoint a conservative justice (Neil Gorsuch) and to withdraw the US from the Trans-Pacific Partnership (TPP) and from the Paris Climate Accord, but such issues have been few and far between.

Obama fooled many with his "hope and change" and "yes we can" mantras, while Trump fooled many with his "drain the swamp" and "make America great again" mantras. Meanwhile, the Empire marches on with endless war and endless debt. Has there been any real change?

From my perspective, there is no "Independent Media" if it behaves just like the MSM in getting aboard the divide-and-rule game (in Spanish a political party is called *"partido"* which means "divided", as in the English word "partitioned"). A truly Independent Media will not take sides in a game where both sides are controlled by the same force, but will instead encourage people to look beyond the façade and understand what needs to be changed at a deeper level. To take sides as many alternative news sites did was a betrayal and, on the path to freedom, another dead-end.

"Change Within the System" is Impossible

The political game is a con. No real lasting change can be implemented from "within the system" because the system itself is based on coercion. Look at what happened in October 2017 in Catalonia in Spain. That state (with its own language and culture) wants to secede from Spain and become its own nation. It has the overwhelming support of its citizens, yet when it tried to do so, the central Spanish government in Madrid sent in the police to literally tear up ballots, stop the voting and even to carry out violence against some Catalonian people trying to vote, including women and elderly people.

You can't ask or beg for freedom from a tyrant. You have to stand in your own power and demand it. Here are the words again of Martin Luther King Jr.:

"Freedom is never voluntarily given by the oppressor; it must be demanded by the oppressed."

The freedom to choose your masters or rulers every three, four, six or eight years is no freedom. As an example, the power of the US President expands every year, as the people holding that office grant themselves more and more authority (e.g. through executive orders). Politicians come and go every few years, but the office itself becomes more and more a dictatorial outpost, under which more than 99 percent of people have to live. The structure of government itself is oppressive. Citizens are born into a system which they must obey or face violent consequences. There is no choice. The "social contract" is imaginary. It doesn't exist.

Hegelian Dialectic / Ordo ab Chao / Problem-Reaction-Solution

This next concept has been elucidated by many thinkers from many eras. The German philosopher Hegel used it to discuss the course of history: he outlined a pattern where someone would propose an idea (the thesis), someone would speak against it (the antithesis) and then someone would find a way to reconcile and combine the two opposing views (the synthesis). This synthesis would then go on to become the new thesis in the next round of knowledge advancement. This process became known as the Hegelian dialectic.

The secret societies (at the heart of the NWO today) have capitalized upon this idea to manipulate people in a desired direction. Instead of letting the best idea battle it out (as is supposed to happen in science and philosophy), they used and still use the Hegelian dialectic as a tool for control. They have a predetermined agenda they want to implement, but they know if they simply announce it or try to roll it out that it would be met with (fierce) opposition. So instead they create chaos and emotional upheaval, during which time people become stressed, irrational and operate from their limbic reptilian brain (fight, flight or freeze). This means people make decisions or acquiesce to things they wouldn't normally assent to if they were acting from their rational neocortex brain. This is especially the case when people become overtaken by fear, then grant the government more power to protect them from the (falsely exaggerated or imagined) danger. Case in point: COVID. The manipulators deliberately create chaos so they can implement order; thus, the maxim "order out of chaos" or in Latin *ordo ab chao.*

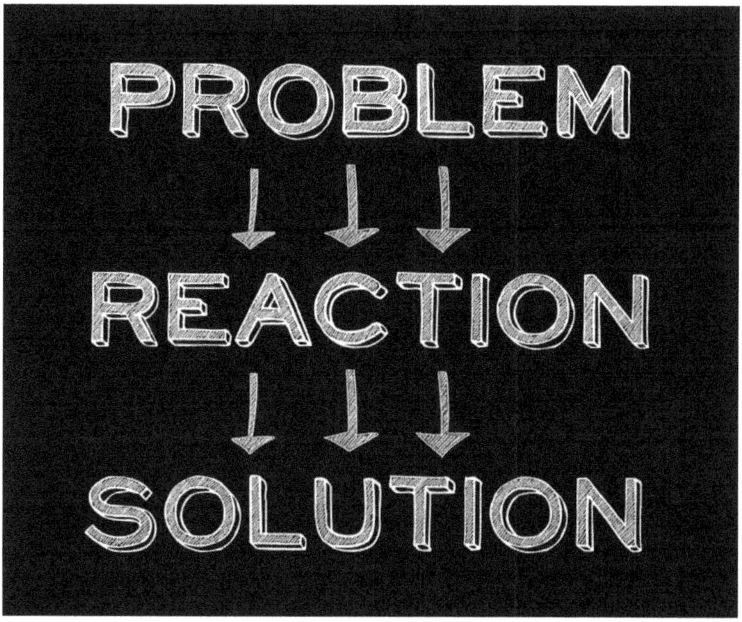

Free thinker and author David Icke, whom I have already referenced many times and whom I consider to be the world's preeminent conspiracy researcher, has dubbed the *ordo ab chao* process as problem-reaction-solution. It's the same idea: create the problem, provoke a reaction, present a prepackaged solution. False flag operations are a classic example of this, since the government quite literally plans and executes these attacks (the problem), the MSM whips the public up into a frenzy (the reaction), and then the government tells people it can solve the problem it created – but only if you give it more power and submit to less privacy and freedom. This is a great trick which works every time on an ignorant and apathetic population.

The Frog in the Slowly Boiling Pot

Another mental trap to beware of is the incremental encroachment on your freedom – the *drip-drip-drip* path to bondage and slavery. This technique works by advancing the agenda only a little at a time, in barely noticeable amounts, so that people will either not notice the encroachments or rationalize them away as insignificant. For the NWO rulers, it's about getting the foot in the door and then gradually prying it open. A common analogy that people use is frog in the pot. If you boil the water rapidly, the frog will notice and jump out. If you boil the water gradually, the frog will not notice the incremental changes in heat and will stay in – until it's too late and it is boiled to death. The ideas of the "slippery slope" and "camel's nose" also apply here; David Icke calls this phenomenon the "Totalitarian Tiptoe."

Some examples of this technique include: gun control (when governments take automatic weapons, then semiautomatic weapons, then eventually all guns from all citizens, thus achieving their intended goal of disarming the entire population); taxes (introduce goods, sales and excise taxes, starting at a low percentage and then gradually increasing it); smart meters and biometric ID cards (first introduce them as voluntary, then slowly make them mandatory or make life very difficult to live without one); regional unions (first various regional unions are formed such as the EU [European Union], African Union, Asian Union, American Union) before they are merged into a One World Government, the intended goal); and places like Guantanamo Bay (where the removal of rights from prisoners [such as the right to a fair trial] paves the way for the gradual erosion of basic human rights for every person).

One of the best quotes to sum this up is by Pastor Martin Niemoller, who was a German citizen during Nazi rule. He became the leader of a group of German clergymen opposed to Hitler. In 1937 he was arrested and eventually confined to concentration camps. He observed what gradually happened to those parts of the citizenry who opposed Nazi fascism and ideology. His statement, sometimes presented as a poem, is well-known and frequently quoted:

First they came for the socialists, and I did not speak out—Because I was not a socialist.

Then they came for the trade unionists, and I did not speak out—Because I was not a trade unionist.

Then they came for the Jews, and I did not speak out —Because I was not a Jew.

Then they came for me—and there was no one left to speak for me.

This sums up both what can happen when we ignore dangerous steps that restrict our freedom, and also what can happen when we allow ourselves to be divided and look upon our fellow humans as "the other," not worthy of care or protection.

The Biggest Mental Trap: Belief in Authority

All of the most horrible leaders in history – Hitler, Stalin, Pol Pot, Mao – ultimately depended on one thing for their power. Votes? Guns? Threats? Yes, to some degree, but in the end none of that works without the ruled having a belief in authority. That is what allows people to seize power and get away with the absurd claim that they have the "right to rule," which is a fictitious concept. Outside conditions do not trap us as much as the belief in authority. When you hold this belief, you unwittingly strip yourself of sovereignty.

In truth, we are all born equal. Likewise, death will take us all one day, and so death itself is another equalizer. No one has a right to rule anyone else; however, people have convinced others they do. As long as we go around thinking we need to have masters and rulers to tell us what to do and how to live, we are always creating the necessary mental precondition for government to exist. Imagine if the debate changed next election (in whatever country you are in) from the meaningless left vs. right debate to an open-minded discussion on whether government was really necessary (and if so to what degree). It would never happen within the current paradigm because the rulers wouldn't allow such free thought, as it undermines their authority. So they would use the money and power to stop media outlets from conducting such free and open explorations.

We need to question everything. Unquestioning obedience to authority and blind trust in government is not a virtue. It's what has gotten us into the big mess we're in. People blindly follow figures of authority without bothering to apply common sense or critical thinking to the words of their leaders. Most people have an implicit trust for people in power and in uniform. They have an implicit trust in bankers, lawyers, scientists and doctors, because, as has been drummed into us, these are prestigious professions. Now, there are many honorable people in these professions, but there are also many power-hungry control freaks, sociopaths, liars and psychopaths because that kind of personality gravitates towards power – and that is precisely what makes a worldwide scheme of tyranny such as the NWO possible. If you are not streetwise, your unquestioning obedience can easily be exploited to serve the global conspiracy.

Scientific experiments (e.g. the Milgram experiment which I discuss in the next chapter) have consistently found that around 50 to 65 percent of people blindly follow and obey instruction from a figure in a uniform or a figure of perceived authority, even if that figure is asking them to inflict harm on another. That means people go against their own moral code and sense of ethics to willfully injure another person, all just to follow orders!

What percentage of people would obey if they were ordered to commit murder? The answer might surprise you. When we see uniforms and badges, hear an authoritative, confident voice, or perceive that someone is part of a larger institution (e.g., the government, a big corporation) or is perhaps someone like a banker, a lawyer, scientist, or doctor, we tend to not engage in critical thinking. We tend not to challenge. Yet humanity as a collective decided at the Nuremberg Trials after WWII that "just following orders" was no excuse and that a soldier who decided to murder innocent civilians shared part of the guilt and responsibility for his actions as the commander above him.

This is why the Illuminati and other secret societies that run the NWO love their uniforms, medals, cloaks, frocks, gowns, badges, hats and other adornments. It's all about image. It's all about controlling perception. When you are addicted to power, it's all about gaining the upper hand and getting the other person to submit to your will. Flashy adornments can cause a person to go from beta brainwaves (everyday consciousness, business mode) to alpha brainwaves (relaxed, more submissive mode). It's a form of mind control.

Yet, when you come to the table without any preconceptions and you look at things squarely without any misplaced reverence, you see that none of these professions deserve your undying allegiance —and certainly not your unquestioning obedience. Respect and trust must be earned. They are not to be given up automatically – unless you want to be controlled or deceived. Why would we give the government our unquestioning obedience, when upon closer inspection, it lies, cheats, steals and was the leading cause of death in the twentieth century (democide)?

If War Is Started by Lies, Peace Will Be Started by Truth

As Julian Assange says, if war is started by lies, then peace will be started by truth. In general, people don't want war; our rulers have to lie to start them, or to use pressure to coerce and manipulate people into supporting them. This rings true no matter what the country or the period in history. After all, it was high Nazi official Hermann Goering who admitted:

Why of course the people don't want war. Why should some poor slob on a farm want to risk his life in a war when the best he can get out of it is to come back to his farm in one piece? Naturally the common people don't want war: neither in Russia, nor in England, nor for that matter in Germany. That is understood. But after all it is the leaders of a country who determine the policy and it is always a simple matter to drag the people along, whether it is a democracy or fascist dictatorship, or a parliament or a communist dictatorship. Voice or no voice, the people can always be brought to the bidding of the leaders. That is easy. All you have to do is tell them they are being attacked, and denounce the peace makers for lack of patriotism and exposing the country to danger. It works the same in any country.

To see the horrific connection between lies and war, just look at the litany of wars the US has engaged in during the last 120 years or so:

– US-Spanish War (1898): lies (false flag attack) about the USS Maine

– US entry into WWI (1917): lies (false flag attack) about the Lusitania

– US entry into WWII (1939): lies (false flag attack) about Pearl Harbor

– US-Vietnam War (1964-1975): lies (false flag attack) about the Gulf of Tonkin incident

– First Gulf War (1990-1991): lies about incubator babies being murdered

– Iraq War / Second Gulf War (2003-2011) (although US troops are still illegally occupying Iraq despite their parliament ordering the US military out): lies about Iraq having WMDs

– Libya War (2011): lies about Muammar Gaddafi being a dictator and killing his own people (and giving Viagra to his soldiers to rape women)

– Syria War (2013-present): lies about Bashar Al-Assad gassing his own people and using chemical weapons

– Act of War against Iran (assassinating General Soleimani) (2020): lies about an imminent attack on US Embassies

Look at the War on Terror. It is one giant lie, from its oxymoronic name itself to all the fibs and tall tales spewed forth to justify it. You can't have a War on Terror when war itself is terror. The War on Terror doctrine constantly relies on lies about imagined enemies to justify the fear needed for you to give over your power and rights to your misleaders.

The mental plane solution is to stop buying these lies and seek out the truth at all costs. The only sane and rational response when you hear governmental propaganda beating the war drums – especially when coming from or influenced by the US government, leading the NWO Empire – is a generous dose of healthy skepticism. Don't believe a thing the USG says without evidence. The chances are much higher that it is lying or spinning the truth rather than being honest, so demand evidence, and don't believe anything until it is proven.

Overcoming Cognitive Dissonance

Cognitive dissonance is defined as the state of having inconsistent thoughts, beliefs or attitudes, and also the mental discomfort or psychological stress caused when a person becomes aware they are in such a state. Cognitive dissonance was acknowledged in Orwell's *1984*; the ruling party dealt with it by encouraging people to become so skilled at "doublethink" that they could ignore and forget the inherent contradiction and hypocrisy.

One main reason deception and tyranny thrive so much right now is that people can't see the conspiracy even though it's right in front of their face.

The MSM gives people whopping lies and they swallow them whole without asking for any evidence; yet when someone in the Alternative Media speaks the truth, people ask "where's your proof"? Fair enough, but why aren't the same standards applied to the liars in government and the MSM? We've got the full surveillance state (NSA spying on everyone), endless war (the US and allies starting wars wherever they want on trumped-up evidence), legally sanctioned indefinite detention and torture (Guantanamo, among many examples); yet some people still deny the existence of any conspiracy! Once people have decided the government is the good guy and out to protect us, they will defend it tooth and nail and give it their unquestioning obedience – the very thing that is working to enslave them.

Although it is challenging to accept the shocking truth that we are being lied to and manipulated on a grand scale, for the truthseeker it will always be essential, no matter how painful, to know the truth rather than live in comfortable denial.

For those who choose to live in denial, their days are numbered. There will be a point (which is unfortunately rapidly approaching) where denial will no longer be a luxury they can afford. The conspiracy will come knocking on their door, and the horrible truth of what is going on in the world will dawn on them. My only hope is that they wake up before it's too late and before they get ripped off, hurt, shafted or killed by the system they have been defending all these years.

In this day and age, with so much information at our fingertips, ignorance is a choice.

It is very useful to be aware of the phenomenon of cognitive dissonance, firstly so you can spot it and correct it in yourself and secondly so you can have more empathy and understanding for how so many people rush to defend the very system which enslaves them. The key to breaking through the mental barrier of cognitive dissonance is to present as much information and facts as possible in a calm and rational way. Getting angry and proselytizing tends to turn people off, although I can certainly understand why people spreading the information act passionately given the urgency dictated by the state of the world.

However, we just need to do our best to connect the dots and communicate the truth, then let go and let the truth do the talking. Not everyone is ready to hear the information and act upon it. At a certain point, the "preponderance of evidence" (to borrow a legal phrase) will be too strong, and it will break down the barriers. This has happened to me many times over, and I imagine to many truthseekers is a necessary step along the path to awakening.

Conclusion

You must choose wisely where you get your information. One way to cut down on bias is to read articles on the same issue from opposing sides in order to fully appreciate the complexity. Follow principles above people, and don't be afraid to critically analyze people. Don't blindly worship anyone or you may become blind to their mistakes and misjudgments (as happens when people become famous and develop a "cult of personality"). Do your own research. Be curious. Check things out. Look beyond the first page of search results. Beware the divide-and-rule trap. Beware the problem-reaction-solution trap and the frog-in-the-slowly-boiling-pot trap.

Remember, simply by virtue of growing up in today's world, we have all been indoctrinated to some degree. We are all under the spell of societal-wide mind control. It is the task of each of us to peel back the layers of perceptual programming and find what is true and false within our own minds. No one else can do it for us. It is a necessary task on the way to mental sovereignty, the regaining of our own minds. Many historical figures have been through similar journeys; one famous example is philosopher and mathematician Rene Descartes who was so tired of the many false beliefs he had taken on that he was determined to extirpate them from his mind. He threw many beliefs out until he realized there was one real thing – that he himself was thinking and that this fact was evidence he was alive – and thus he became famous for the phrase *"I think, therefore I am."* Today, we have evolved beyond Descartes' assertion, realizing that consciousness precedes thought; however, we can still learn much from his method of self-examination and skepticism to cut through the lies and find the truth.

Chapter 15 – Social-Political-Legal-Technological Plane Solutions

The tree of liberty must be refreshed from time to time with the blood of patriots and tyrants.

– Thomas Jefferson

We need a revolution every 200 years, because all governments become stale and corrupt after 200 years.

– Ben Franklin

What country can preserve its liberties if their rulers are not warned from time to time that their people preserve the spirit of resistance? Let them take arms.

– Thomas Jefferson

When a government betrays the people by amassing too much power and becoming tyrannical, the people have no choice but to exercise the original rights of self defense – to fight the government.

– Alexander Hamilton

This country, with its institutions, belongs to the people who inhabit it. Whenever they shall grow weary of the existing Government, they can exercise their constitutional right of amending it or their revolutionary right to dismember or overthrow it.

– Abraham Lincoln

We the people are rightful masters of both Congress and the courts – not to overthrow the Constitution, but to overthrow the men who pervert the Constitution.

– Abraham Lincoln

*****

For many, this chapter may contain the kind of solutions people expect when they think of solutions. This chapter is devoted to the activist, outward kind of solutions that change social structures.

Who Has the Power?

Before any discussion of practical solutions, remember this: there are only a tiny number of controllers at the top and the mass of humanity below. It's a pyramid; the tiny few at the top are held up by the energy and exertion of those at the bottom. If those at the bottom withdraw their support, the top will crumble and fall. The numbers are staggering. If the relative handful of NWO manipulators (let's say 8,500 for argument's sake, since this is the number Dutch whistleblower Ronald Bernard has suggested) is presented as a ratio against the current world population of around 7.8 billion, it would look like this:

8,500 : 7,800,000,000 = 0.000001 percent

Even if this 0.000001 percent has more money and technology, how can such a tiny fraction rule the rest of humanity? Who has the power?

Natural Law vs. Legal Law

Changing the existing structure means, inevitably, going up against its rules. What are the rules of the world (the legal-commercial Matrix) in which we live? The rules are based on "law" – but not natural law, moral law or the laws of physics. I am referring to the rules of the Law Society which are written in their own language (legalese) which is its own language just like English, German or Japanese. Legal law sometimes coincides with moral law but frequently does not. How often have we seen examples of people being punished for growing food in their own yard? For feeding the homeless? For partaking of a psychoactive plant? How often have we seen presidents getting away with pardoning criminals? How often have whistleblowers been treated like criminals when they are merely exposing the crimes of the real criminals? As Frédéric Bastiat wrote:

When plunder becomes a way of life for a group of men in a society, over the course of time they create for themselves a legal system that authorizes it and a moral code that glorifies it.

Part of the way the system propagates itself is by pushing propaganda on children. One of the big lines pushed is that "you must respect authority (no matter what)" as though that were a universal dictum. The truth is that respect (and trust) must be earned; they don't come automatically. A glance at human history reveals that tyrants have often seized control of the reins of government to make laws to enrich and protect themselves and their cronies. In such cases, the "law" is nothing more than a tyrant's will, and deserves neither our respect nor our compliance. From Bastiat again:

But how is this legal plunder to be identified? Quite simply. See if the law takes from some persons what belongs to them and gives it to other persons to whom it does not belong. See if the law benefits one citizen at the expense of another by doing what the citizen himself cannot do without committing a crime.

It is important in our path of awakening to make an important distinction between moral law and legal law – and to commit to following moral law where the two conflict. Natural law is based on living from the heart, on kindness and on respect. It's universal. It doesn't need to be spelled out in ten thousand pages. It's doing what's right: not right for me but right for all concerned. Legal law is more about definitions and technicalities; it's relative as it's peculiar to a specific nation, area or jurisdiction. Some of the greatest figures and heroes of history became so well loved and respected because they went against the prevailing legal or religious laws of their time, spoke out against corrupt authorities and did what was right – people such as Socrates, Jesus, Martin Luther, Thomas Jefferson, Gandhi, Martin Luther King Jr. and many others.

There's no point breaking rules just for the sake of

it; however, a quick glance at human history shows that far more damage has been done by those blindly following rules than those who break them without good reason. The solution is to ground yourself firmly in moral law, in doing what is just, fair and right. From that place, you will know which legal laws are in alignment with that and which are not, and thus which ones to observe and which ones to break.

Common Law vs. Commercial Law, Rights vs. Privileges

A commercial matrix of fake law has been spun into existence by legal cunning. There are actually two completely different jurisdictions, and I'm not talking about criminal and civil, or law and equity, which are other distinctions. I refer to common law (law of the land) and commercial law (law of the sea, aka admiralty or maritime law). The law in many nations (especially the five major English-speaking nations of the US, UK, Canada, Australia and New Zealand) started off as common law but soon got overtaken by statutes, codes, rules, bylaws and regulations, all of which belong to commercial law. In the case of America, there are actually two "United States": one is the constitutional republic of fifty sovereign states, and the other is a legislative democracy and private corporation (yes, the USA is USA Inc., a corporation, as other governments are).

The republic uses common law, the law of the land, and deals with living, breathing people. The corporate democracy uses commercial law, the law of the sea, and deals with soulless/dead corporations and "persons", which are legal inventions. It's vital to know which jurisdiction you are in or entering when dealing with the authorities; otherwise, you'll unknowingly give up your freedom.

This distinction plays itself out in the areas of rights vs. privileges. A right is something you are inherently entitled to, just by virtue of being alive, not because some master, ruler or government granted it to you. The founding fathers of the US wrote about the "unalienable rights" of humanity in the Declaration of Independence, where unalienable means not only inherent and intrinsic but also incapable of being liened, sold or transferred. In other words: you're born with certain rights, and you have them as long as you live, just by virtue of being you. That's it. No one can take them away no matter what. Yet how many people live in the full knowledge and power of this?

Instead, we have traded many of our rights for privileges, which are benefits bestowed by some authority upon the ruled and which can be revoked. Sometimes we apply for "permits" and "licenses" to do things by privilege that our ancestors used to naturally do by right, without requiring anyone's permission. Trading in rights for privileges is the path to slavery. The solution here is to stop asking permission to do things which are morally right and fair and just do them anyway (in large groups if need be) as part of a broader movement of noncompliance with corrupt and overreaching authorities.

The Principle of Sovereignty

A highly important concept underlying any social, political or legal change is that of sovereignty. The word is sometimes defined to mean *king* or *ruler*; however, it means supreme power or authority. The truth is that we are all sovereign – every single one of us. We are all born sovereign and free. In some nations, this concept is enshrined in the law, as it is in the United States (although the US has strayed very far away from the recognition of this).

Sovereignty is a way of being. Sovereignty is an attitude. Sovereignty is a deep knowing that you are a powerful, divine creator in your own right, that you are responsible for everything that is happening in your life and that you are in charge of your destiny. The sovereign man or woman strives to be self-reliant and self-regulating, needing no outside help or authority to tell them what to do. The sovereign man aims for complete self-control and self-mastery, knowing that if he cannot control himself, there are many who are very eager to step in and control him.

On an ultimate level, so-called authorities have no power over you – other than the power you give them. Government only gets its power from the consent of the governed. You can choose to withdraw that consent at any time. You are the master, and government is the servant. To step into sovereignty is to assume our full birthright and to take back our power from those that claim they "represent" us.

The deep meaning of sovereignty is self-governance. The more we govern ourselves, the less need there is for outside governance. The more we can handle our own affairs – and resolve conflicts with each other without resorting to government – the less we need government, and the less justification there is for government to exist. We don't have to complain that there's a big, bad, evil government out there; we just need to focus on self-governance, which will undermine government in a way nothing else can.

Real solutions must begin with us becoming more sovereign on an individual level. Then, from that place of power, the sovereignty can spread out to local, regional and national levels. Quite a lot of countries (e.g. China, Spain) contain autonomous regions within their borders, which are basically areas with more sovereignty where the local inhabitants have more power over their own affairs. Spain has an entire state of Catalonia (with its own distinct language and culture) which has been vying for independence for decades if not longer. Scotland had a vote on leaving the UK. There is no reason why every nation cannot have a sweeping movement of sovereignty and decentralization where people from small communities and regions reclaim the power that has always been theirs.

Govern Thyself

Govern yourself. That way, you don't need anyone to do it for you. And more importantly, you don't *allow* anyone to do it for you. Some people may say that is ridiculous, that there will always be irresponsible people who don't follow the rules and ruin it for everyone else, which is why we need government. But is this always true? And even if so, does that mean we necessarily have to have an external centralized authority to be safe and resolve disputes?

So, what does it mean to govern yourself? To govern yourself is to take care of your life, affairs, livelihood, relationships, everything – all without needing outside help or interference. It means you are independent, responsible and self-sufficient. It doesn't mean you have to do everything for yourself, live in an isolated place, grow all your own food and have no contact with the outside world. People have been trading and interacting since the dawn of man! But it does mean that when you trade you do it fairly and honorably, keeping your agreements and not using deceit. As long as you steal, lie or cheat others, they will feel wronged by you, and seek to redress that wrong. This means they may appeal to outside authorities to do this, which brings in the whole concept of "government."

To truly govern yourself means to ensure all your relationships are conducted with integrity, so that no one would ever have the need to sue you, bring a claim against you or bring in some kind of outside authority to resolve a dispute with you. You would work things out with anyone before it got to that point.

When you truly govern yourself, the need for an outside governing force disappears. If you take responsibility for yourself, you don't need others (our so-called representatives) trying to take responsibility for you, and therefore asserting control over you.

When you govern yourself, you take matters into your own hands. You start with the person in the mirror. That is always your biggest sphere of influence. You can't control backroom deals made by corrupt politicians on the world stage, but you can ensure you conduct your business and personal life in a just and honest way. Think about it: if everyone started governing themselves, they would resolve disputes among themselves, thus eliminating the need for so many rules and regulations. In short, it would reduce dependence on the law. We would have less need for law, less need for police to enforce the law and less need for courts and judges to adjudicate the law. This automatically equates to less government and less tyranny.

There's a direct formula here: increase self-responsibility, increase self-freedom. Or simply, increase responsibility, increase freedom. People are very focused on their "rights" and that is important, but if that focus becomes an obsession, it becomes detrimental. It is a fact of life and of natural law that you can't have rights (and freedom, too) without responsibility. Alongside "fighting for your rights" assuming more responsibility may achieve the same goal of increasing freedom but with less "fighting" energy.

Additionally, if people started to govern themselves better, it would include critical thinking. You can't outsource critical thinking, although it appears that's what Rockefeller-funded mainstream education curricula (now being led by NWO frontman Bill Gates) are trying to trick us into doing. For more info on this, see Charlotte Iserbyt[416] and her work *The Deliberate Dumbing Down of America*. You have to think for yourself; no one can think for you. Governing yourself means thinking for yourself and carefully evaluating what information comes your way. Those who govern themselves are far less susceptible to deceptive propaganda and brainwashing, upon which tyrannies like the NWO depend. When you end ignorance, you'll end the control system, too.

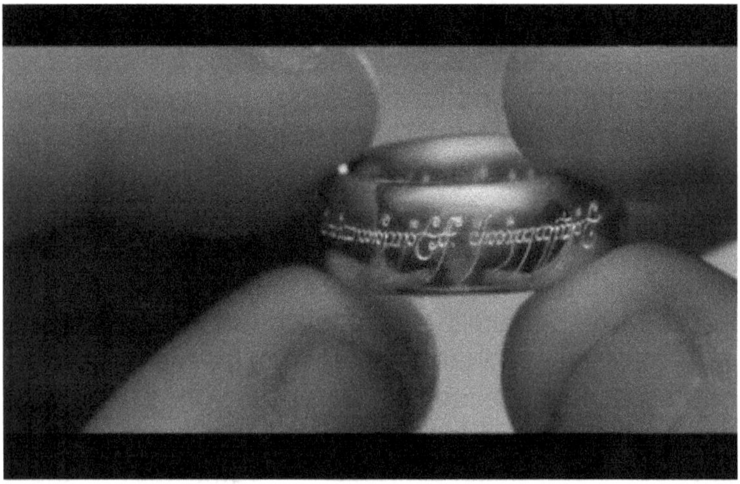

Ending the Belief in Authority (The Ring of Power)

The system can only perpetuate itself if people

[416] https://www.youtube.com/watch?v=tF83lavcDMo

agree to its sales pitch. The system says: "Keep upholding me, and suffer at the bottom for a short time, then soon you'll get to be one of the powerful ones at the top". People only agree to this if they already hold, deep within their psyche, the idea that someone or something outside of themselves has the right to rule. In other words, they harbor a deep-seated belief in authority. They believe that it's necessary to have a ruling class, and almost always, that this ruling class is allowed to have extra privileges, rights and powers (including exemption from normal moral laws) that ordinary people are not allowed to have.

Well-known anarchist or "voluntaryist" Larken Rose explains this point beautifully in a speech entitled "So Small a Thing"[417], where he draws an analogy between the blind belief in authority and the Ring of Power in the fictional series Lord of the Rings. He highlights how the entire power of the system – with all its guns, laws and surveillance data – hinges on the widespread belief of its subjects that the government has the right to rule them. Without that belief, the government would collapse, because no one would execute, enforce or obey its decrees. What seems so powerful is actually dependent on a (tiny) belief – so small a thing – a belief which is a lie, since in the ultimate reality, no one has authority to rule you just as you have no authority to rule anyone else.

Larken talks about how the Ring of Power always corrupted whoever touched it. This is a brilliant

---

[417] https://www.youtube.com/watch?v=-8Rsc7lrxA8

analogy – evidently the author Tolkien understood that the entire concept of the Ring of Power (the right to rule) is fatally flawed. No matter how well intentioned someone was, no matter how much they thought they would use the Ring for good, once they touched it, they became evil. The Ring has only one master. The good wizard Gandalf was wise enough to recognize this, and even refused to take the ring because he knew it would corrupt him. Therefore, the humble hobbits (who had no ambition to rule anyone) were the ones who had to take it. Another striking aspect of this analogy was that the Ring could only be destroyed by being returned to its place of origin and "unmade". Perhaps this is an indication that we must dig deep within to "unmake" our false assumptions and distorted perceptions about authority, reality and the world?

Rule me! Rule me!

The following two experiments, although perhaps not perfect or scientifically rigorous, reveal some very interesting things about the nature of human psychology and our inherent deference to perceived authority. They were conducted in the 1960s and 1970s. The Milgram Experiment, conducted by Stanley Milgram in 1961, investigated why – and the degree to which – people will do unethical things in obedience to purported figures of authority. To the subjects, it was presented as an experiment about the effects on learning of negative punishments like electroshock, but the real reason was to see how much electroshock they were willing to give other humans. In reality, there was no electroshock but rather prerecorded tapes of screaming used to give the subject the impression that there was. The subjects, all of whom were voluntary participants, were ordered by a man in a white coat to give out electroshock (rated at different voltages) to humans in another room, whom they could not see but whom they thought they could hear (when they heard the prerecorded screams right after administration of a dose of electroshock). If they hesitated or refused, the authority figure would say "Please continue" or "The experiment requires that you continue." Even though many subjects were uncomfortable with giving painful shocks to another person, twenty-six out of forty participants shocked people up to the highest level (450 volt), labeled "XXX," on the machine. No subject stopped before giving a three-hundred-volt shock, labeled "Intense Shock." They did this despite believing they were hearing screams of agony from the other room!

The Stanford Prison Experiment was conducted

ten years later in 1971. Here a group of volunteer university students were randomly divided into prisoners and prison guards. According to the experiment's official website[418], the guards were given no specific training on how to be guards. Instead they were free, within limits, to do whatever they thought was necessary to maintain law and order in the prison. Although everyone was involved with his or her own consent and knew this was "just an experiment," the situation quickly degraded into sadism and torture. Those students acting as guards got very into the role and started acting aggressively to those below them in this artificial hierarchy; likewise, those students playing the part of prisoners quickly felt the despair and desperation of real prisoners. Professor Philip Zimbardo, who orchestrated the experiment, further documents[419] that

our planned two-week investigation into the psychology of prison life had to be ended after only six days because of what the situation was doing to the college students who participated. In only a few days, our guards became sadistic and our prisoners became depressed and showed signs of extreme stress.

If you consider the implication of these two experiments, you may better understand some of the disturbing trends in society, such as the increasing militarization and brutality of the police. In the US, local police departments were loaded up with surplus

---

418 https://www.prisonexp.org/guards

419 https://www.prisonexp.org/

military gear thanks to the 1033 program. Police and military alike are trained to follow orders and not to questions their superiors. A cop who believes his actions are unconstitutional likely won't object or defy orders because compliance was engendered in him in the training process. In this way, police are trained to be like loyal guard dogs: unthinkingly protecting those who order them around, instead of protecting the public they swore to defend. Clearly, this kind of unquestioning obedience to authority is exactly what needs to stop in order to bring more freedom to the world.

Stop Perpetuating the System Because You Think One Day You'll Be at the Top

Exploitative or criminal systems, including financial Ponzi schemes like the entire fiat currency system, tend to cunningly protect themselves by offering to "buy in" people who question them. For example, people in rigid hierarchical systems (like the military) are encouraged to accept hardships when they enter because soon, they'll be advancing up the ranks and will then enjoy the benefits of the system. Have cramped quarters now but later get your own private room. Get poor pay now but later get a big fat salary. In some cases, this rationale is offered to justify brutality (e.g., if you take beatings and whippings now, later on you'll get to dish them out). Fun, huh? For a less violent example, some rich private schools have a system of "prefects" where selected students are given more privileges and power than others, and the system is kept in place because most people are fooled into secretly hoping that they will be the ones to get selected: so in such expectation they vote to uphold the system rather than remove it.

Put more simply, a system is set up whereby some people get to have more power over other people – then that system is justified by dangling the carrot in front of all people and telling them that if they are strong, smart, beautiful or lucky enough, they will be the chosen ones that get to ascend to the position which affords them power over others. Meanwhile, those running the system know that it's a mathematical impossibility for everyone to be at the top. It's like the line about how Americans are not divided into rich and poor – they are divided into rich and "those about to be rich." People are goaded along into accepting an unjust system just because they think that one day they'll ascend to the top of it.

Besides, even if everyone did get a chance to "be at the top", what about the ethics of it? Is it okay to suffer exploitation because one day you'll be the exploiter rather than the exploited? This is the classic perpetrator-victim cycle where yesterday's victim becomes today's perpetrator (see Israel[420]). Albert Einstein, a Jew himself, recognized this concept[421] when he wrote the following about the impending visit of Menachim Begin (former Israeli Prime Minister, warmonger and with Ariel Sharon founder of the Likud Party which rules Israel today) to the US in

---

420 thefreedomarticles.com/banned-un-report-israeli-apartheid/

421 https://archive.org/details/AlbertEinsteinLetterToTheNewYorkTimes.December41948

1948:

Among the most disturbing political phenomena of our times is the emergence in the newly created state of Israel of the "Freedom Party" (Tnuat Haherut), a political party closely akin in its organization, methods, political philosophy and social appeal to the Nazi and Fascist parties. It was formed out of the membership and following of the former Irgun Zvai Leumi, a terrorist, right-wing, chauvinist organization in Palestine.

People metaphorically upholding the system during a Hitler speech.

I am reminded of a quote attributed to the Rothschilds which perfectly sums up how they sought to perpetuate their fraudulent money system (fractional reserve banking) and thus became the richest family in the world:

The few who understand the system will either be so interested from its profits, or so dependent on its favors, that there will be no opposition from that class.

So, in other words, if everyone understands the nature of an evil system, it fails; if only a relatively small amount of people understand the nature of an evil system, the susceptible ones can be bought off (bribed or blackmailed) to dilute the resistance to it.

It's a codependent relationship. Once you end the inner need and desire for a master or ruler, the outer ruler will disappear. I elaborate more on this in chapter 17.

Does Government Have Any Legitimate Authority?

The world population now is over seven-and-a-half billion and headed to eight to nine billion. Such a massive amount of people cannot be ruled unless they acquiesce and consent to be ruled. It is the chief aim of all governmental propaganda to secure this consent in all its various ways, whether by convincing you that the system is legitimate, that you must follow all laws because you were born into the system or that you must adhere to the so-called social contract between citizen and ruler. Let's take a closer look at this.

Political authority, or the authority of state, or the authority of government, is something the average person virtually never questions. Almost everyone goes through their entire life believing that the government – although it's almost always composed of provable criminals, cheats and liars – still has a solid basis for its political authority. Many people, whether left, right or anywhere in between on the political spectrum, are statists: they think that government has an inherent right to rule, using coercion if necessary. Yet, even a cursory examination shows that if a normal person acted like government, they would characterized as cunning, secretive and manipulative, and either be diagnosed as insane, or locked up as a danger to society, or both. So why do people allow and consent to such a situation? The eighteenth-century British philosopher David Hume attested to this situation when he wrote that:

Nothing is more surprising than the easiness with which the many are governed by the few.

Hume was clearly one of those rare few who took the time to closely examine the origins and political authority of government. Interestingly, he was propagating many of these ideas during the mid-1700s, a few decades before the time of the American and French revolutions.

Hume realized that most government is formed and held together by war. History teaches us this over and over again, including politicians' inventions of fictitious enemies to justify a state's existence:

Most governments are not formed by contract but rather through conquest and war.

The heights of popularity and patriotism are still the

beaten road to power and tyranny; flattery to treachery; standing armies to arbitrary government; and the glory of God to the temporal interest of the clergy.

It is probable, that the first ascendant of one man over multitudes begun during a state of war; where the superiority of courage and of genius discovers itself most visibly, where unanimity and concert are most requisite, and where the pernicious effects of disorder are most sensibly felt. The long continuance of that state, an incident common among savage tribes, enured the people to submission; and if the chieftain possessed as much equity as prudence and valour, he became, even during peace, the arbiter of all differences, and could gradually, by a mixture of force and consent, establish his authority.

Hume warned that authority should never become more important than liberty:

In all governments, there is a perpetual intestine struggle, open or secret, between Authority and Liberty; and neither of them can ever absolutely prevail in the contest. A great sacrifice of liberty must necessarily be made in every government; yet even the authority, which confines liberty, can never, and perhaps ought never, in any constitution, to become quite entire and uncontrollable.

Lastly, Hume explicitly stated that a state's supposed political authority could not hold water when investigated closely, going so far as to state that political authority is merely based on opinion:

No maxim is more comfortable ... than to submit quietly to the government, which we find establish'd in the country where we happen to live, without enquiring too curiously into its origin and first establishment. Few governments will bear being examin'd so rigorously.

It is on opinion only that government is founded; and this maxim extends to the most despotic and most military governments, as well as to the most free and most popular.

As we shall see, this last quote rings true and is especially interesting given that it flatly contradicts the widely held notion put forth by Hume's fellow British philosopher John Locke, who proposed that there was some kind of social contract from which the state justly derived its powers. Can political authority be justified by social contract? Professor Michael Huemer has done great work on the subject of political authority. He has authored such books as *The Problem with Political Authority: An Examination of the Right to Coerce and the Duty to Obey*. Huemer shows that it is very difficult to justify political authority, especially in the form we have now in most Western countries: a "democratic" government which claims a monopoly on the use of force or violence.

Locke's theory of a social contract has been shown to be false. No such contract exists. There is no piece of paper which enshrines it, nor is there any piece of paper you sign when you come of age. Even if a written contract did exist, it would require constant consent from newer generations to sustain it. When the social contract argument falls down, statist apologists then tend to argue that rather than explicit consent, there is some kind of implicit consent we give to the State. Huemer identifies four types:

1. Passive consent (refraining from opposing something);
2. Acceptance of benefits;
3. Consent through presence (consent given by merely remaining in a location); and
4. Consent through participation (consent given by voluntarily participating in something).

However, to truly give consent, you must be in a noncoercive environment. Consent can only really be given when you are also free to not give the consent if you so choose. Is this the case with government? The answer, of course, is a resounding "no"! You don't have any free choice. With valid consent, both parties would have the ability to "opt-out," and both would also have obligations to each other, which, if unfulfilled, would grant the other one adequate grounds for terminating the agreement. In reality, you can't just opt-out; the government will fine, charge and ultimately imprison you if you don't obey its decrees. The only alternative is to move to a different country (where you face another government doing much the same thing), so there's no escape unless you move to the remote wilderness somewhere. You have no recourse or remedy; the relationship is one of force and coercion; thus, there is no true consent, whether explicit or implicit.

The next argument given by many people is that the state is justified because it is given consent by a majority of people in that society. This may or may not be true, given that the proauthority bias carried by many people often lies beneath the surface as an unconscious belief (which was programmed into them at a young age). However, even if it is true, it seems to affirm a problematic conclusion: that the opinions and desires of a large group of people or a majority can be forced onto a smaller group or minority. This is a kind of "majority rules," unlimited, mob-rule democracy which really is more appropriately referred to as a tyranny of the masses.

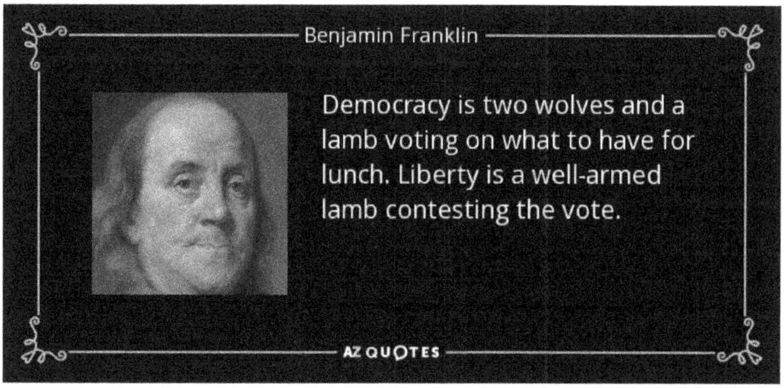

This is exactly why the US was set up as a republic not a democracy. The United States is a constitutional republic where individuals and minorities are recognized to hold certain inherent or unalienable rights[422], which can never be abrogated, regardless of what the majority wants or who holds power. Without this, it is all too easy for a prejudiced majority (which can be whipped up into emotional frenzies by cunning leaders and demagogues) to impose its will on those too powerless to defend themselves. Aristotle once said that *"Unlimited democracy is, just like oligarchy, a tyranny spread over a large number of people."*

The Nazis tried to claim they were "just following orders" at Nuremberg. The world roundly rejected that argument.

The final argument of those believing in solid justification for governmental authority is usually consequentialist (i.e., it appeals to the benefits, good consequences and utility of the state). "Look how

---

422 https://thefreedomarticles.com/we-all-have-inherent-rights/

many good things the government does," it exclaims, "so its political authority is valid, because it gives us so many benefits." However, the question must be asked: are the benefits worth the price we pay, in terms of a loss of liberty and the duty to obey? History clearly shows us that most of the injustice and destruction in the world was committed by people obeying authority, not opposing it. Also, if government gets political authority due to the benefits it provides, why can't other groups get it too (e.g., vigilantes or private defense companies)? Most people would be unwilling to grant vigilantes or anyone else this power. Ultimately, why does government deserve some kind of special moral status – that allows it charge, tax, fine, imprison and kill – when no other individual or organization in society is allowed to? Just because the state provides us with some benefits, why does it get the right to do these things? In the end, it's a question that has no good answer because its authority is illegitimate.

The state is not the root of all evil; however, the fact remains that government killing its own citizens (democide) was the leading cause of nonnatural death in the twentieth century[423] as discussed in the Introduction. So many atrocities have been committed by out-of-control governments around the world. Many countries still have not evolved to the point where they have decided to separate church and state; indeed, it took Europe many centuries of dark oppression under the Catholic Church to realize it may not be a good idea to entrust the clergy with political power. Interestingly, the current leader of

[423] https://www.hawaii.edu/powerkills/DBG.CHAP1.HTM

Syria, the poor country being besieged by the US-UK-Israeli axis of the NWO, is Bashar Al-Assad, who is committed to the principle of separation of church and state. This is one more reason why the NWO wants him out.

Many nations in the Middle East have Governments of theocracy – "rule by God" – although of course God seems to have exclusive spokesmen who are usually from rich bloodline families. Yemen, Oman, Iran, Afghanistan and Saudi Arabia are all theocracies. Saudi Arabia, *Beheaders Incorporated*, is ruled by the incredibly corrupt House of Saud[424] (which has Zionist roots[425]), another bunch of impostor royals just like the British royal family and the other European ones. To declare yourself "royal" merely means *you proclaim you have some kind of "right to rule."* What a Jedi mind-trick! These royal families are the most corrupt criminals in the entire world. Check out David Icke's work in exposing the satanic British royal family for more information on this.

The fake Saudi royals who love to behead dissenters. I think I may have solved the mystery of where my missing red-and-white picnic sheets went ...

Anarchy = Voluntary Cooperation

Even those seeking true freedom understand that past conditioning and programming can be very hard to overcome. It would be great if we could just wave a magic wand and be free of old, crusty and limiting ideas that were instilled or indoctrinated into us at an earlier age, or which we mistakenly took on. But it doesn't work like that. We have to put in the hard work to uncover and analyze them, then decide what to keep and discard. If you're reading this, hopefully you can see that the state exists in our minds, first and foremost. The only way we can achieve a free outer world is to first rid our minds of limiting inner ideas. If we could open ourselves up to the idea that maybe – just maybe – the human race could live in freedom *and* peace, could resolve its own disputes and could adequately defend itself without rulers, we wouldn't need the state.

Politicians have no legal liability when, as invariably happens, they fail to live up to their campaign promises or when they straight out lie through their teeth. Their lack of integrity and their mendacity only becomes apparent to the masses after the election, then people feel disempowered until the next election (two to six years later depending upon the country), where the whole process repeats itself with a new face but the same pattern. This is insanity.

The word *anarchy* has pejorative connotations of

chaos and disorder, but it simply means "without rulers." It doesn't have to mean chaos. A state of anarchy could still possess order with voluntary and peaceful cooperation. Many have proposed models where the government's role in defense and dispute resolution can be decentralized and provided by various third-party companies which are then subject to the laws of economics and the market (e.g., by caring about their reputation and trying to provide the best service, etc.). Maybe humanity is not ready for the stateless society. Maybe we would need to first transition to something like a *minarchy* (a strictly limited and decentralized government); however, that is highly debatable since governments tend to accumulate more and more power (and never give it back), so even if a minarchy were set up (as happened with the US in 1781 with the Articles of Confederation), there is no practical way to keep it small. The best evidence for this is the USA itself: it was the giant experiment. It went from a nation with a minarchy/strictly limited government to become the most imperialistic and dangerous nation in the history of the world with a burgeoning, bloated and tyrannical government.

There are still things to be worked out; however, the first step in all of this is for everyone to examine their unconscious belief and proauthority bias, and realize that government's political authority cannot be justified. Government doesn't have to exist for humanity to thrive.

Decentralize, Decentralize, Decentralize

The NWO is constantly on the move to *centralize,*

centralize, centralize. Its key aim is to centralize as much power as possible into as few hands as possible, so that resistance to its schemes becomes highly difficult. Therefore, naturally, part of the solution to restore freedom to the world will be to go in the opposite direction: *decentralize, decentralize, decentralize*.

This decentralization needs to occur in many ways. We need to decentralize markets to open them up for competition, which will break the hold of the corporations (the corporatocracy, since the corporations mostly control the government) who constantly aim for monopoly-like conditions with all their backroom-boardroom collusion, price fixing, price gouging, mergers and acquisitions. We need to decentralize social media and information sharing rather than only use the big platforms (Facebook, Twitter, Google-owned YouTube, etc.) which, as covered in chapter 7, are rapidly censoring alternative voices so as to homogenize opinion across the web. As I alluded to earlier, former Alphabet (Google) CEO and Bilderberg Group attendee Eric Schmidt said in this 2005 interview with Charlie Rose:

When you use Google, do you get more than one answer? Of course you do. Well, that's a bug. We have more bugs per second in the world. We should be able to give you the right answer just once. We should know what you meant. You should look for information. We should get it exactly right and we should give it to you in your language and we should never be wrong. That's our challenge.

Here we have a blatant admission of the attempted centralization of knowledge by Big Tech, who are now going far beyond being a "neutral search engine" to a full-on curator, censor and gatekeeper of knowledge, full of bias and working to mold humanity's perception in line with whatever they see fit. For further proof of this, do an internet search for topics like "Google manually manipulates search results" or "Google manually intervenes on search results." Then, of course, we have Google's planned "Selfish Ledger" (which I discussed in chapter 11) to direct human evolution. This is just one of many examples of what can happen when too much information, knowledge or power is centralized in too few hands.

The state expands its power by expanding its responsibilities. It says, "Let me look after education and energy," and then, by virtue of being in charge of those things, has more power to demand more money and authority in order to administer them effectively. It's a bit like bringing a new chef into your restaurant kitchen and asking him or her to oversee cooking everything on the menu; the chef is then emboldened with more power to carry out his or her new duties. People often clamor to beg the government to expand its duties and responsibilities, without realizing this expands state reach and reduces freedom. This comes back to self-governance and responsibility as discussed earlier in this chapter.

Of course, the lure of centralization will always be present, because it makes things easier (to have them all in one place) and because it makes decision-making more efficient. There is a time and place for centralization in life, but we must once more ask ourselves: which is more important – efficiency or liberty? Convenience or freedom?

If You Take a Walk, I'll Tax Your Feet

Those of a libertarian bent like to exclaim that "taxation is theft!" which echoes the sentiments of the US founding fathers who set up their own country because they opposed taxation without representation. The Beatles' George Harrison put in best in his song *Taxman*:

If you drive a car, I'll tax the street,
If you try to sit, I'll tax your seat.
If you get too cold, I'll tax the heat,
If you take a walk, I'll tax your feet.

To many it may sound scary to challenge the government over taxation. I understand people's fear; however, let's reflect on things for a minute. How does the government get away with so much evil? It uses taxpayer money. It uses the money of all its citizens, who it falsely claims to represent, and then tries to enslave those very citizens with schemes funded by citizen money! Examples are manifold, for example, when taxpayer-funded police arrest homeless people for the "crime" of being homeless, and when the MIC takes in billions of taxpayer dollars to set up giant surveillance dragnets to spy on its own citizens, recording their every call, email, text message and more. Machiavellian doesn't even begin to describe it. In the case of the US government, it takes the money of its citizens to build a massive worldwide empire that invades other sovereign nations on the flimsiest of pretexts to steal their land and resources – while one in six Americans are on welfare and American infrastructure is crumbling. Quite simply, if people weren't funding the government to such an extent, it would not be able to commit such crimes.

The "death and taxes" line is not a joke – politicians are constantly looking for new ways to tax the citizenry. Now they're taxing the weather. I'm not kidding. The so-called "rain tax" bill (S-1073)[426] signed by then New Jersey Governor Phil Murphy in March 2019 authorizes the government there to charge property owners a fee based on "a fair and equitable approximation" of how much water runoff is generated from their property. This means the more it rains, and the more water runs off your property, the more tax you pay. In other words, unless there is some elaborate way they can reduce water runoff on their property with some engineering feat, NJ residents are now being taxed due to weather conditions beyond their control! I wonder if depression rates will rise there when it rains ...

If you live in the US, you may want to look into the dodgy history of the FIT (Federal Income Tax), and determine whether it really does apply to you or not. For most American nationals, chances are high that you can be a legal, lawful non-taxpayer. Why? Because the FIT was only meant to apply to federal employees and those living in Washington DC,

---

[426] https://www.northjersey.com/story/news/environment/2019/03/18/murphy-signs-nj-rain-tax-into-law-heres-what-is-whos-paying/3201036002/

Guam, Puerto Rico, etc. (which are districts and territories, not states). American Nationals (those born in the fifty states of the constitutional republic, or those who naturalized) are generally exempt. However, the USG and IRS make it seem like the FIT applies to everyone, since they receive more money if they pull off this deception. The deception works using legalese (as usual!). The USC (United States Code, well named, because it is indeed a "code" that deliberately obfuscates information) states that the FIT doesn't apply to "non-resident aliens" but then refuses to properly define that term. However, if American nationals born and living in the fifty states don't live in US districts or territories, they are nonresidents; furthermore, they are alien to the laws, rules and code there. So, in this topsy-turvy way, ordinary American nationals are defined as "nonresident aliens" exempt from the FIT, but you wouldn't know it at first glance. Why would an average American consider himself or herself a "nonresident alien" in the land where they were born and live? One avenue worth exploring for Americans is Revocation of Election[427], a method by which many can lawfully exit the US tax system for life and never pay FIT again.

Many people in the USG including judges, politicians and agency heads have admitted the FIT is voluntary. Former IRS commissioner, Margaret Milner Richardson, admitted that the public bashing of the IRS may *"ultimately ... have some impact on our self-assessment system"* (i.e., our voluntary system). Here are some other revealing quotes:

427 https://www.youtube.com/watch?v=hNzRBV43skY

The revenue laws are a code or system in regulation of tax assessment and collection. They relate to taxpayers, and not to nontaxpayers. The latter are without their scope. No procedure is prescribed for nontaxpayers, and no attempt is made to annul any of their rights and remedies in due course of law. With them Congress does not assume to deal, and they are neither of the subject nor of the object of the revenue laws.

– Long v. Rasmussen (281 F. 236), 1922[428]

(This is an admission that there is such a group as legal nontaxpayers.)

Your income tax is 100% voluntary tax, and your liquor tax is 100% enforced tax. Now, the situation is as different as night and day.

– Dwight Avis, former head of the Alcohol and Tobacco Tax Division of the IRS

The United States has a system of taxation by confession.

– Justice Hugo Black declared in United States v. Kahriger, 345 U.S. 22 (1953)

(Your tax return is your confession. By filing one you cede your Fifth Amendment right to not incriminate yourself.)

---

428 https://casetext.com/case/long-v-rasmussen

"Our system of taxation is based upon voluntary assessment and payment, not upon distraint."

– US Supreme Court in Flora v. United States, 362 U.S. 145

(Distraint means seizure of property.)

The situation is similar in Australia; Sir Harry Gibbs[429], former Chief Justice of the Australian High Court, found:

I therefore have come to the conclusion that the current legal and political system in use in Australia and its States and Territories has no basis in law.

Whichever country you inhabit, I highly suggest you delve more deeply into the supposed authority of your tax-collecting entity before forking over any more hard-earned money. You may well find, as is the case with the political authority of government itself, that it's all based on smoke, mirrors and a healthy dose of bluff.

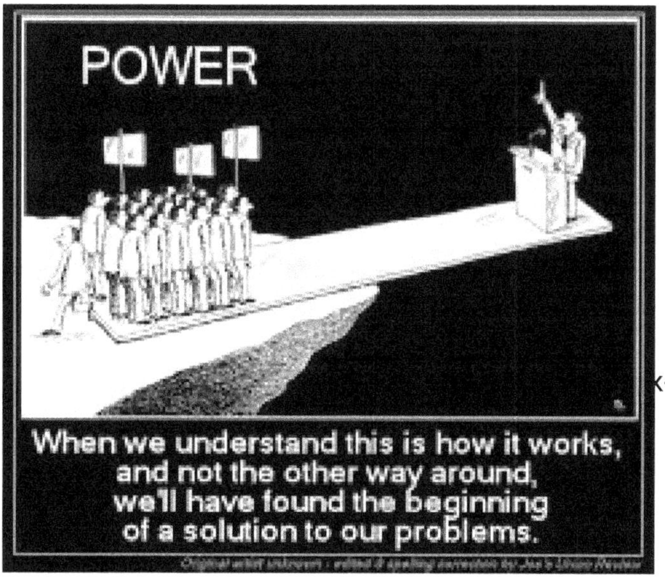

Noncompliance: Using the Power of Numbers

Government depends on its citizens following the law. There are too few of "them" and too many of "us." There are not enough police and military to contain the whole of the ruled population (at least not with human police, although things are rapidly changing with the advancement of robotics). When a critical mass of people "break" the law – by ignoring it and refusing to obey it – the ruling class simply doesn't have enough resources to enforce compliance. They use bluff, fear of being singled out, fear of authority and other tricks to keep people in line. However, just as history is full of examples of tyrannical legal law, it is also full of examples of people protesting unjust laws to the point where those laws were repealed or scrubbed from the books because the authorities knew they could not be enforced. Mohandas Gandhi and Martin Luther King Jr. are both revered as modern-day heroes for disobeying laws in the name of higher justice; Gandhi helped kick the British out of India while King helped spawn the massive social awareness of racial discrimination that led to less segregation and more equality.

Larken Rose also produced a wonderful short video in 2012 called *The Tiny Dot*[430] where he displays in graphic images just how imbalanced the situation is. The rulers are 0.1 percent of the population (resembling a tiny dot). They have to put out tremendous energy, threats and fear in order to keep the massive 99.9 percent of people (resembling a large group of balls) in line. Yet, if the 99.9 percent

430 https://www.youtube.com/watch?v=H6b70TUbdfs

were aware of their power, they would realize in a heartbeat that they cannot be controlled unless they acquiesce and comply.

This is why civil disobedience (an offshoot of noncompliance) has been so successful in the past. Its degree of success depends on the degree to which the 99.9 percent can unite. The NWO controllers know this, which is why they spend so much energy doing everything they can to divide and fracture the ruled classes. What they fear most is a united and aware citizenry rising up against them.

Rather than fighting the small cabal of controllers with their protective and brainwashed goons, a far more effective way to combat the system is to withdraw consent. Historically, people have already displayed an intuitive understanding of this principle. This is what underpins labor strikes, when large numbers of people refuse to work, either for big corporations or governments. It is also what underpins movements like the BDS movement (Boycott, Divest, Sanction) which is aimed at giving Israel the message that virtually the entire world disapproves of and recognizes that is stealing land from the Palestinians. The BDS movement, which consists of relatively simple strategies such as avoiding buying anything made by Israel in the "occupied territories," has had great success without the need for anyone to use a weapon or even speak an angry word.

Withdrawing consent can take many forms: small, big and everything in between. It could look like someone refusing to go along with groupthink by not putting a bumper sticker on their car which says "Support the troops"; it could be refusing to participate in blind nationalistic rituals like reciting the pledge of allegiance; it could be refusing to vote and participate in the system of sham democracy; it could be disobeying coercive, unjust and immoral laws, even at the risk of getting fined and imprisoned. One practical way to withdraw consent is to rescind or revoke adhesion contracts, which are contracts that heavily favor one side (the government or big corporation that draws them up). Every time you sign up for a driver's license, a mobile phone contract or even file your taxes, you are entering into contracts which disadvantageously bind you, limit your freedom and often goad you into exchanging rights for privileges. To find out more about how to rescind these contracts, check out the comprehensive sovereignty manual by Johnny Liberty called *The Global Sovereign's Handbook*, available for free online[431].

Violence is not the answer. The system loves violence. Civil disobedience against unjust laws where the people follow natural law not legal law is far more powerful than violence. Violence just gives the excuse the establishment wants to crack down on dissenters, pass draconian emergency laws, add more police to their ranks and take away more rights and freedom in the name of "security." It's a trick. Nonviolent noncompliance is the key. John Lennon had the right idea.

Part of this solution requires us to learn how to

---

431 www.freeinfosociety.com/media/pdf/3089.pdf

say no without anger. To do so, we need to remember that the truth is powerful enough to stand on its own; it doesn't need our anger to further its case. Often, an angry "No!" sets up a polarized field where the person or group on the other side becomes the attacker, you become the defender, and now there is a fight, battle or power struggle between two opposing sides. A better way to handle these situations is "to fight without fighting" as a Zen motto might say, to try to find common ground with the person or group challenging you and to appeal to their sense of common humanity. After all, the matrix is trying to ensnare virtually everyone except the 0.1 percent, including all the bureaucrats, police, military and everyone else enforcing it. If you can find a way to make people aware they are fighting for their own enslavement, you will have transformed a potential adversary or opponent into someone who will stand for the cause of truth and freedom. That is true alchemy.

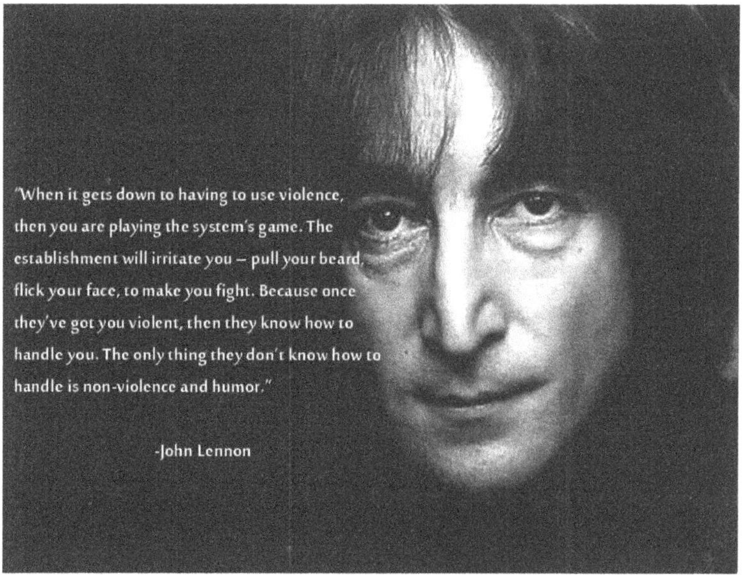
"When it gets down to having to use violence, then you are playing the system's game. The establishment will irritate you – pull your beard, flick your face, to make you fight. Because once they've got you violent, then they know how to handle you. The only thing they don't know how to handle is non-violence and humor."
-John Lennon

Laugh at Tyrants

Just as violence is not the answer, so nonviolent activities are the answer – like laughing. Laughing may seem unproductive, but it actually plays an important role in breaking the chain of authority. Why? Because the legitimacy of authority ultimately rests on the belief in that authority by the ruled subject. Without that belief, rulers can then only rely upon force to control their subjects, which takes much more energy. This is why books like *Brave New World* and *1984* portray a ruling class that is searching for the ultimate state of control where their subjects "love their servitude" – it's much easier for them when everyone agrees that the oligarchs have a right to rule and that's just the way it is. No point rebelling in that kind of scenario.

Laughing disrupts all of this. It's a way of communicating that the ruled don't accept the right or authority of the rulers, that the rulers are not legitimate, that the ruled will not obey unjust laws and won't buy into the lies coming out of the rulers' mouths. It also communicates that the only reason the rulers are in power is due to force, whether it be more guns, more advanced weaponry or more sophisticated mind-control technology. These are all outer causes and conditions and thus temporary. The world is in a constant state of change. A ruling class anywhere cannot hope to hold on to power for very long if they cannot convince the ruled of their legitimacy.

Humor is also a great way to communicate deep messages. Comedians like the late, great George

Carlin used humor to drive home some deep activist and philosophical points. Once you get people laughing, their guard comes down. They now entertain and consider things about which they would normally have been close-minded. It's a way of bypassing the conscious filter. It's also a great way to diffuse tension. Laughter can transform anger, even if it's righteous anger, into something lighter and less destructive.

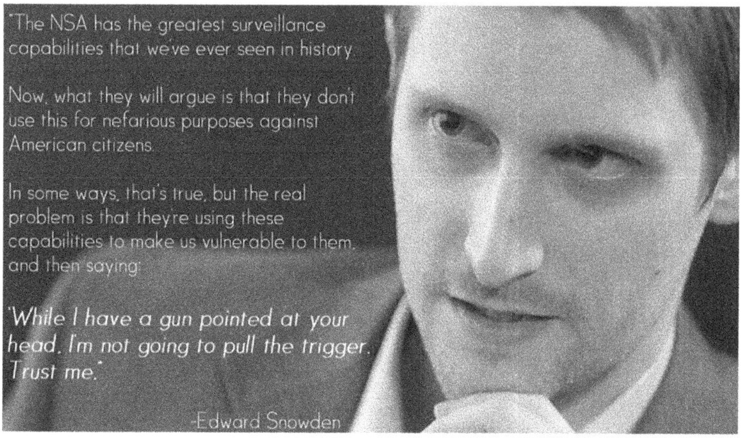

Every Single Voice Must Speak Up and Push Back Against All Forms of Censorship – Including Self-Censorship

In chapter 7, I covered the burgeoning surveillance and censorship state, which includes the most dangerous censorship of all – self censorship. If we are too afraid to speak our truth and speak our minds, whether due to political correctness, being "de-platformed" (a very Orwellian euphemism), being attacked by the self-righteous on social media, losing online popularity, becoming the object of a "Twitterstorm", or even just losing the approval of people in our lives – then we have already lost the battle to Big Brother. In that case, freedom of speech is already dead.

Now more than ever the world needs people to speak up. Every voice counts. The upside to all the technology we have in today's world is that everyone can start a blog, vlog, video channel and online presence. The chorus of authentic, sane and heartfelt voices is one of the key things to keep the psychopathy in check.

Technological Solutions: Encryption, VPN, Cryptos, Blockchain and More

As covered in chapter 11, technology is a double-edged sword. People need to unplug much more often, whether for a few hours, a few days or a few weeks. We need to stop constantly checking social media. We need to stop our smart device obsession. We need to stop pouring our consciousness into all of it. However, if you are going to use technology, there is a whole world of technological solutions you can utilize to maintain your freedom and privacy.

To begin with, remember that with internet searches, whatever you search can and will be used against you. We have already entered the world where people posting thoughts, feelings and opinions on social media has been cause for police visitations (sometimes violent ones) and arrests – in many countries. Likewise, when you use Google for internet searches, you are essentially letting them know what you think, what you're interested in, what you're curious about, the health issues you're having, the general problems you're having in life, etc. Over time, patterns emerge, and AI algorithms can analyze them to develop a clear idea of how you think, what motivates you and what your weaknesses are. Why would you willingly hand over this kind of information? Even web browsers (especially Google Chrome) spy on you, too. While Google may have the best search engine, you don't have to use it exclusively. Try using Startpage and DuckDuckGo, both of which do not collect or store search inquiries (although Startpage delivers anonymized Google results). For web browsers, ensure you maximize all your privacy settings. Try Brave, a new kind of web browser which does not track you, which blocks annoying web ads and which pays websites you visit "Brave Rewards" or BAT (Basic Attention Token) which is a cryptocurrency-like utility token based on Ethereum technology.

There's a very important rule of thumb to keep in mind when dealing with technological services: if it's free, *you* are the product. What does this mean? It means that when you get a free email or social media account, it's not really "free", because the company is harvesting your data to sell to third parties. You are not their real customer. You are their product; big corporate advertisers and spying governmental agencies are the real (paying) customer. Whatever kind of data you generate, you can assume it's valuable and is being harvested and sold by someone, somewhere. Look at how credit card companies operate in the US: they put out huge bonus mile offers to get people to use their cards. Why? So they can collect and sell the data. Someone wants to know (and is willing to pay) to know your retail habits.

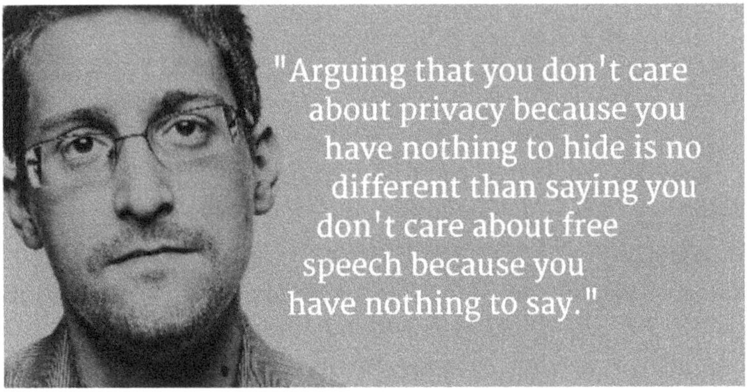
"Arguing that you don't care about privacy because you have nothing to hide is no different than saying you don't care about free speech because you have nothing to say."

So, as much as possible, anonymize your business dealings. Continuing on from the theme of decentralization, we need to decentralize money by looking at alternatives to governmental-central bank fiat currency. Some time-honored solutions include barter and exchange. Did you know there are already many local barter communities and local currencies (e.g., Time Banks[432], the Ithaca HOUR currency used in the town of Ithaca in New York state, plus many more)? Use cash, anonymous prepaid debit cards or cryptocurrencies. There are many cryptocurrencies on the market right now, with Bitcoin and Ethereum being the most well known. They are based on blockchain technology, which is a decentralized way of making all the transactions in the history of the currency public and able to be stored on any computer around the world. Blockchain technology can be used for many things (not just cryptocurrency) and shows great promise at being able to promote decentralization. Note, however, that not all cryptos

---

432 thefreedomarticles.com/solutions-global-conspiracy/ timebanks.org

are the same. Bitcoin, for instance, is not really anonymous compared to other cryptos like Monero (which uses cryptography to shield sending and receiving addresses, as well as transacted amounts) and Dash (which uses a feature called PrivateSend that conceals the origins of your funds.

Encryption is another very important area to understand in the world of tech. Normal email is like sending a postcard or shouting across a room full of voices; anyone who really wants to can tune in to your communications. However, there are now a lot of companies offering encrypted email, encrypted texting, encrypted voice/audio calling and encrypted video. At the time of writing, WhatsApp, iPhone text messages, Viber and Signal are said to be encrypted, although I personally wouldn't trust WhatsApp much, since it is owned by privacy-violating Facebook and was the subject of a data breach in May 2019. Signal is the best choice for (text) messaging and audio/video calling, and is recommended by Edward Snowden. Protonmail, Startmail and Hushmail are all good choices for encrypted email; Swiss-based Protonmail doesn't keep your messages on its servers, so even if it were subpoenaed and/or raided, there would be no data of yours it could even hand over. In this day and age, with such a plethora of companies offering free encrypted services, why not encrypt? With more and more companies offering end-to-end encryption, it's easy to make a change and support companies offering this. You can encrypt your entire computer with Veracrypt. If you are a content creator who writes articles, makes videos or produces other content, you can use websites like Steemit, Minds,

Odysee/LBRY and DTube that utilize blockchain that makes it technologically impossible for anyone to be censored.

Ex-NSA whistleblower Bill Binney (mentioned in chapter 2) suggests in this interview[433] that people should create their own private encryption and communicate to prevent communications from being sucked up into the NSA dragnet. He specifically mentions that if people use public encryption that goes through NIST (Nations Institute of Standards and Technology) then the NSA can easily obtain the backdoor keys to that encryption.

Some may answer that question by saying, "If you've done nothing wrong, you've got nothing to hide." That is a fine piece of brainwashing and programming that doesn't stand up to scrutiny. If the government has done nothing wrong and has nothing to hide, then why is it so steeped in secrecy? Why does it have millions upon millions of classified files that it tightly guards, heavily redacting them when it does release them and sometimes refusing to release them even fifty-plus years after an event has occurred (e.g., Trump and Biden and the nonrelease of many JFK files)? The truth is that privacy is an essential part of human society and human life which we all require; any government that threatens this to the extent governments have nowadays has egregiously overstepped its boundaries.

---

433 https://www.youtube.com/watch?v=SjHs-E2e2V4

Free Energy: Over-Unity and Zero Point Energy

Discussions of technological solutions lead to one of the biggest topics in the realm of conspiracy analysis. In fact, this one topic alone, if it were accepted and understood by more people, would change everything. It is no exaggeration to state that if it were universally applied, it would utterly destroy the conspiracy of control, completely transforming the world. I refer to free energy (aka zero point energy or over-unity energy), a concept whereby a system or device produces more energy than it receives. In other words, free energy occurs when a system has a measurably higher energy output than input. Imagine a world of energy abundance instead of energy scarcity where every household had a little black box in one of its rooms that could be turned on to generate all the power that household needed.

Think free energy is just a pipe dream or fantasy? Think again. Many famous scientists over the course of centuries and millennia have experimented with free energy and have left a trail of evidence proving the existence of such a concept. One of the most famous was the forgotten genius Nikola Tesla, who made tremendous advances in science with his brilliant discoveries, around seven hundred patents in all. He developed AC (alternating current), manmade lightning, radio, remote control and robotics. Many of his discoveries were either suppressed, stolen or misused. He was experimenting with a free energy distribution system known as the Wardenclyffe Tower in Colorado. Tesla wanted to give the world free unlimited energy, distributing it safely and wirelessly without measuring, metering and selling it. However, his funding was being provided by banker, globalist and NWO family bloodline member J. P. Morgan. Tesla's idea of free energy for the masses went against every fiber of Morgan's being who was a banker and capitalist at heart. He intended to get a handsome return on his investment, or else he would not fund the project at all. He pulled the plug on Tesla's project. Tesla ended up dying penniless, and his inventions and patents were stolen, including by his former apprentice Guglielmo Marconi.

Numerous other scientists, inventors and engineers have also made spectacular inventions in the field of free energy. Sadly, a lot of these people have been targeted, visited by the men in black, shut down and even killed for their work, which adds credence to the idea that their ideas were practical, their calculations correct and their devices functional. With the NWO forever scrambling to suppress and confiscate every new workable invention that comes along, I sense it is only a matter of time before the momentum of free energy will become irrepressible and unstoppable – however at what point that happens is anyone's guess.

However, before we get to these people and their work, let's address the natural skepticism people have when they come to his topic. A device whose energy output is greater than its energy input? Impossible? That violates the laws of physics, specifically the first law of thermodynamics (the change in the internal energy of a closed system is equal to the amount of heat supplied to the system, minus the amount of work [W] done by the system on its surroundings) and Newton's third law (every action has an equal and opposite reaction). Yes it does, but why do you believe those laws are absolute and the be-all and end-all? Could it not be possible that we are still learning how the cosmos works, and there is room for us to refine our so-called laws of physics even further? After all, even as brilliant as he was, Einstein's 1905 Theory of Relativity fell short of fully explaining everything, including phenomena which now over a century later we recognize and can better explain.

In order to understand free energy, you have to open your mind and contemplate new possibilities. The universe is not a closed system. We are surrounded by energy. Abundance is the natural state of the universe; scarcity is an artificially contrived situation (which is, sadly, all too common on Earth). This is from an article on the website of the Starburst Foundation[434], run by Paul LaViolette:

The question that the standard physicist most often asks is where does the excess energy come from that these technologies generate? The reason that physicists are in this dilemma is because they view the physical universe as a closed system, one that emerged into existence through a highly improbable freak event and that inevitably proceeds towards a heat death in the distant future. They have extended the laws of heat engine thermodynamics to apply to phenomena in the universe as a whole, presupposing that the physical universe constitutes the totality of existence and that it is closed, i.e., has no "outside

---

434 https://starburstfound.org/reality-overunity-generators-evidence-open-system-universe/2/

environment". But there is a new approach to understanding the physical universe that is being developed. This instead views the universe as an open system and allows for the spontaneous generation of energy with no need of an antecedent high potential physical source.

Our history is full of instances where the overwhelming majority of people said "that's impossible!" ... until it happened. Alexander Graham Bell was prosecuted for fraud for trying to raise capital to manufacture telephone equipment. The prosecution claimed that carrying voices over wires was impossible and that no one would want such a device as a telephone, anyway. The Wright Brothers, inventors of modern flight, were called frauds despite demonstrating they could fly. Farther back in history, think how Copernicus, Galileo and Giordano Bruno were treated (e.g., ostracized or burnt at the stake) for proposing theories based on evidence that went against the prevailing religious or scientific dogma of the day. Indeed, famous scientist Max Planck once said that *"science progresses one funeral at a time"* because science tends to advance not when new empirical evidence or theories come to light, but rather when enough of the old guard – those heavily invested in entrenched theories – die off. Many inventors and scientists have not only shown that free energy is possible with new explanations but have proven it by demonstrating functioning prototype machines. The following are now-deceased people who all contributed to the field of free energy: Dr. Wilhelm Reich, Stan Meyer, Dr. Eugene Mallove, James Black, Arie DeGeus, Michael Zebuhr and Bruce dePalma.

The brilliant Dr. Wilhelm Reich started his work in Germany analyzing human sexual energy. He later discovered the energy he would call "orgone" and applied it in various ways, including in the treatment of cancer patients (whose tumors were shrunk) and in the construction of a cloudbuster, a device used to create or dissipate clouds. He was able to bring rain to regions with drought and save large amounts of crops. Today there are many types of orgone energy devices (which utilize his technology) being sold.

Stan Meyer figured out how to run his car on ordinary tap water with a simple device he built in his garage. He patented his discovery and even demonstrated it on the evening news in the 1990s. After his untimely death in 1996, the technology was suppressed.

Dr. Eugene Mallove was a scientist, editor, publisher and proponent of cold fusion. Cold fusion is a type of nuclear reaction that occurs at, or near, room temperature. In his book *Fire from Ice*, he reveals experiments where people produced over-unity output energy using cold fusion. These experiments were successfully replicated several times. Mallove claims the results were suppressed through an organized campaign of ridicule from mainstream physicists, including those studying controlled thermonuclear fusion, trying to protect their research and funding. Mallove was murdered in 2004.

Dr. James Black, a Nobel Prize winning physician who filed lawsuits against the governments of the US and Canada regarding the theft and suppression of the research of John Hutchison (more on him below), died from a "possible heart attack" at age fifty-one, despite having been in perfect health with no previous heart problems.

Arie DeGeus was the inventor of a self-powering battery. Famous free energy inventor Tom Bearden (more on him below, too) writes that DeGeus had invented a "thin wafer-like material/device that somehow specially aligned the atoms or electron currents ongoing in that material, so that the wafer produced a constant amperage at a small voltage – continuous real power, or in other words a strange kind of 'self-powering battery.'" DeGeus was found slumped in his car at the airport dead of heart failure, right before he was about to go to Europe to secure funding for his new invention. He was apparently in good health beforehand.

Michael Zebuhr was a free inventor who collaborated with Dr. Judy Wood, an excellent researcher who championed the dustification theory to explain what really happened on September 11, 2001 in the USA during the World Trade Center attacks. This source[435] states that Zebuhr was killed on March 19, 2006, due to his work with Wood. They were working on disproving the theory that the Twin Towers were taken down due to thermite or thermal (as proposed by Dr. Steven Jones) but instead were taken down due to directed energy weapons. The existence of free energy is closely connected to what really happened on 9/11 (September 11, 2001),

[435] https://www.checktheevidence.com/wordpress/2008/05/30/the-9-11-truth-movement-free-energy-suppression-and-the-global-elites-agenda/

because free energy technology was weaponized and used to destroy WTC towers one and two by "dustifying" them:

Mr Zebuhr and Dr Wood were doing demonstrations with molten aluminum specifically to prove Steven Jones wrong. A few weeks later he was murdered, allegedly by two people during a robbery. On March 1, 2006, Dr Wood sent an email to Jones detailing his "mistakes"[436]. Seventeen days later, Michael was shot twice. The following day, March 19th, he died.

Bruce DePalma was a late Harvard-educated physicist and free-energy inventor who invented a homopolar electricity generator, which he called the "N-Machine." It was reputedly able to take electricity directly out of a magnet, so as to produce cheap, inexhaustible, self-sustaining and nonpolluting energy. His machine had significantly less drag and was more efficient and simpler than other similar machines.

There are also plenty of inventors who thankfully have avoided being "suicided" and have made great contributions to the field of free energy. Viktor Schauberger was an Austrian naturalist nicknamed the "Water Wizard" because he carefully observed the flow of water and built incredible energy devices that mimicked its action, including devices that used implosion rather than explosion. Stan Deyo has held an Above Top Secret Security Clearance, worked undercover for the FBI and was part of a black ops

[436] drjudywood.com/articles/aluminum/Aluminum_Glows.html

military project (headed by Dr. Edward Teller) to develop flying saucer or UFO technology, which involves antigravity and free energy technology. Joseph Newman built a device called the Newman Energy Machine with which he showed that the mechanical power produced by it exceeded the electrical power supplied to it (although, with so much money and power at stake, he was denied a patent for it). Don Kelly, a perpetual motion specialist, is the inventor of the falling magnetic plate of mass reduction, yet another original free energy system.

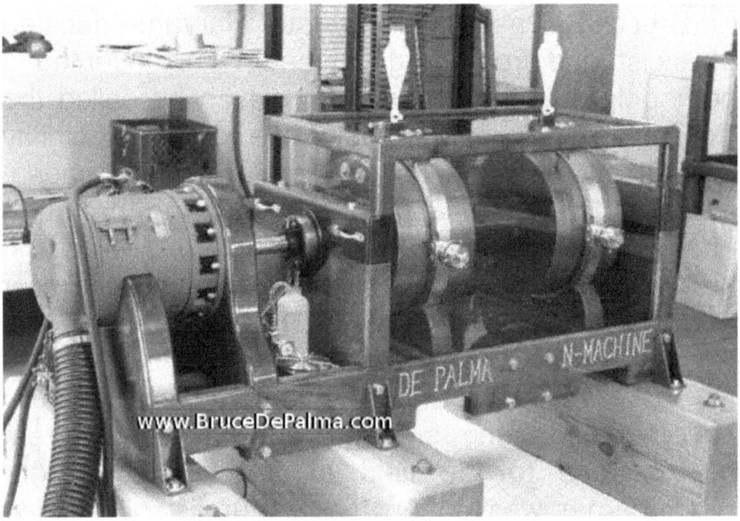

The N-Machine (Homopolar Generator) of Bruce dePalma, one of many functional free energy devices that have been invented, was allegedly able to produce an efficiency greater than 100 percent: that is, it produced more energy output than the energy input required to rotate it. Image credit: Bruce dePalma.com

Dennis Lee[437] proved in a court of law in 1989, under criminal charges of fraud, that humanity can

437 www.freelectricity.com/NotAScam.html

take energy from the air and make free electricity. He was later fraudulently convicted and thrown into jail. Inventor Jim Murray studied Tesla's work for decades and developed open- source prototypes where the current and voltage of the input and output could clearly be measured, showing over-unity energy production. Adam Trombly has built at least two free energy devices (the Closed Path Homopolar Machine and the Piezo Ringing Resonance Generator) with which he publicly demonstrated over-unity energy production. Marko Rodin invented the Torus Coil, which was tested and found to create a 62.5 percent greater magnetic output than present- day standard-wound electrical coils. John Bedini has been a top free-energy experimenter since the 1970s. He was awarded many patents and built numerous working prototype devices including multiple "self-running" machines and regenerative electric motors that produce mechanical energy while charging batteries at the same time. Nuclear engineer Mehran Keshe has come up with a unifying theory (which he calls Magrav, a portmanteau from magnetic and gravity) which explains the basis for his many devices based on free-energy and antigravity technology.

Retired colonel John Bearden is a big name in free energy. He likes to say that *"there is enough energy inside the space [of an] empty cup to boil all the oceans of the world. This is a fact well known to the scientific community, and was, for example, a favorite quote of Nobel Prize winning physicist Richard Feynman."* He invented and designed a device which he called a Motionless Electromagnetic Generator (MEG), for which he was awarded a patent in 2002: he claims it is a free-energy device which draws energy from the vacuum. Dr. John Hutchison is a giant in these kinds of fields, having demonstrated on video all sorts of things such as making metals pliable (like jelly), making metals transparent and levitating seventy-pound cannonballs. He even has the *Hutchison Effect* named after him, a phenomenon he discovered during his study of Tesla longitudinal waves in 1979. He is one of the foremost Nikola Tesla experts alive today. He has replicated many of Nikola Tesla's works over the years, including the Death Ray and a smaller Philadelphia Experiment. It is no exaggeration to say that Hutchison has rewritten the laws of physics and demonstrated supposed "impossibilities" such as the anomalous melting (without heating) of metals without burning adjacent material and the spontaneous fracturing of metals.

In summary, these inventors and many others have done enough to prove the concept of free energy – the concept that energy can be produced for free or very cheap in practically inexhaustible quantities. Many have died trying to bring us this truth and this technology. As free energy enthusiast Wade Frazier (who assisted free-energy inventor Dennis Lee) writes[438]:

Those attempting to independently develop [free energy technology] have been bought out or wiped out ... those leading the suppression of the independent efforts also control the extensively developed free energy technologies, and their influence is wielded in subtle yet powerful fashion;

---

[438] ahealedplanet.net/advent.htm#make

they are forcing artificial scarcity onto humanity for reasons of earthly power.

Frazier also writes:

I had an encounter in 1998 with Tom Bearden, who is a prominent free energy theorist. Bearden is aware of a global infrastructure that suppresses free energy research, development, and marketing attempts. Bearden said that it was not the oil companies, per se … [he] said that some oil company owners, however, were behind the suppression of free energy. Bearden said they had developed the global infrastructure that wiped out free energy innovations. Bearden said that the small group of oil company owners (Rockefeller agents are nearly guaranteed to be involved) have built a sophisticated organization that keeps its ear to the ground, keeping tabs on free energy efforts and ensuring that they never succeed … Bearden said they build dossiers on free energy researchers and pioneers. They study each individual for weaknesses … Those people working for the oil company owners (it may extend to all energy companies) spend their careers defeating free energy threats. Only when the clandestine moves fail do they escalate the strategy. Death threats, prison terms, and violence only happen when the game reaches higher levels.

The technologies that use those [free energy] have been subjected to deep secrecy (Black Budget, Above Top Secret, privatized) … those exposed to this situation usually deny it, often by dismissing it as a "conspiracy theory"; those acknowledging the situation's reality usually have unproductive reactions, such as: paranoia; apathy; hopelessness; trying to expose or punish the suppressors; beating the suppressors at their own game; trying to participate in the suppression action, as there are rewards for such activities; thwarting those attempting to overcome the suppression, as they try stealing the technology/market for themselves. If an effort to overcome the suppression and public inertia is going to have a realistic chance of succeeding, that final group needs to grow to thousands of people, to form a critical mass. The effort needs to reach far beyond the small and insular alternative energy community. Simply becoming aware of the issue and engaging in constructive dialogue may be all that is needed. The primary qualification for a member of that critical mass group is nearly incorruptible integrity.

Free energy is inextricably connected to the phenomenon of antigravity technology, and antigravity itself is frequently connected to the extraterrestrial affair as discussed in chapter 10. Free energy or anomalous energy effects seem to "pop out" from devices spinning very quickly, using high voltage (greater than fifty thousand volts) and/or strong magnetic fields. Thus, the suppression of free-energy technology goes hand in hand with the suppression of the alien question, for once humanity at large accepts the truth that ETs have already visited Earth, the next logical question would be: "How and by what means did they get here?" This of course opens up a Pandora's box the NWO controllers desperately want to keep shut.

It is worth appreciating just what a gamechanger

free energy is. It's like starting a game of chess with two or three queens while your opponent only has one. It's like playing a game of soccer where the goal you're defending is the size of a dog kennel and the goal you're attacking is as wide as the field. Imagine a world where everyone could have a little black box in their basement or bedroom, and by flicking a switch, would have enough energy to run their entire house, including for heating, cooling, cooking, hot water and running appliances. It would wipe out people's dependence on utility companies and reduce people's stress of having to work so hard just to pay their bills. It would free people up to live off the grid and off the land, far away from urban centers if they chose (which directly counters the plans outlined in Agenda 2030, chapter 6). It would genuinely help the environment due to a sharply reduced need for dirty energy sources (as opposed to the fake helping of the environment by reducing CO2). Ultimately, it would make people far more free, independent and less controllable by the government. This is the last thing the NWO manipulators want. It doesn't take much to see the kind of disruption that cheap, workable, mass-produced free energy devices would cause if they were permitted in the marketplace. It also doesn't take much to see why a criminal ruling class, desperate to maintain its power, would be willing to lie and kill to suppress such devices.

Of the solutions presented in this chapter, and indeed in this entire book, free energy is the technological solution that holds the most promise to radically transform the world. However, those who have examined the evidence and believe it to be possible now have another objection. Would it even be a good thing to give humanity such technology given its current collective state of consciousness? Like any technology, it would be a double-edged sword, because unlimited free energy in the hands of the kind of psychopaths that run the world would mean grave danger, as they would undoubtedly weaponize it and use it to consolidate their grip of power.

My answer to this is simple. They already have.

The scenario in which we live right now is even worse. This is because the psychopathic NWO manipulators have the free-energy technology, and the rest of the population does not. The USG and other governments routinely steal and suppress the inventions (e.g., by stealing patents, raiding inventor's homes, threatening them to be quiet or outright killing them). Standard governmental modus operandi is to weaponize free-energy technology and use it against the ruled population. There is overwhelming evidence that DEW (Directed Energy Weapons) were used to carry out the attacks of the WTC buildings on 9/11 and in many other instances (e.g., during the California "wildfires)". In the case of 9/11, the massive amounts of steel and concrete used to construct the towers inexplicably disappeared. Meanwhile, despite the fires, there were pieces of paper on the ground that were still intact. This was due to the "dustification" of the material by DEW (for the details on this, see the work of Dr. Judy Wood). In the case of the Californian wildfires (e.g., in the small town of Paradise in 2018), specific houses and neighborhoods were scorched while others right next door to them were left perfectly unharmed and untouched, including the grass, fence and mailbox. This kind of result could never happen in a genuine wildfire but could be achieved through targeted weaponry wiping out select houses and buildings. The following images explain the story.

Conclusion

Some people are stepping up and offering radical solutions. For example, Adam Kokesh, a Libertarian Party candidate who ran for president in 2020, had a platform[439] with one simple agenda: dissolve the US Federal Government, delegate some of its powers back to the states, abolish other agencies outright, and give over its responsibilities to private companies who can take over the work in a competitive environment where there is no longer a (governmental) monopoly. It's a radical solution and, sure, it would be imperfect. However, the point I'd like to make is that it is time for radical solutions. Maintaining the status quo isn't going to change anything. Think about it: don't we already live in a radical time? The US Government steals trillions from the people in bailouts for the banksters, printing money which debases the currency, tortures and kills its own citizens, installs over a thousand military bases around the world and invades other nations at

439 https://kokeshforpresident.com/platform/

will on the flimsiest of pretexts.

In the following chapters, we will turn our attention from external solutions to internal solutions – answers that are to be found within each and every person.

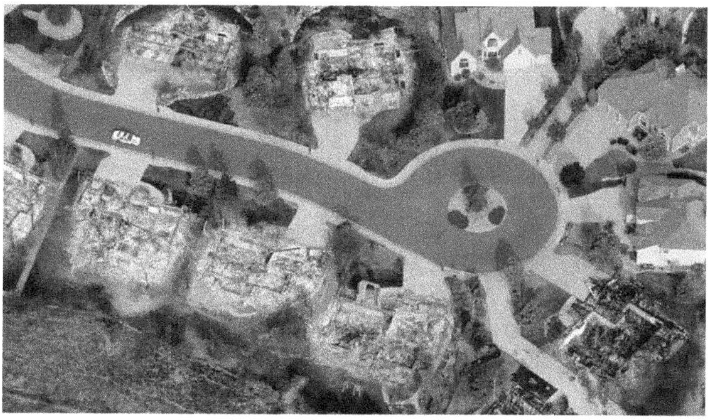

DUSTIFICATION
THE PROCESS OF TURNING A SOLID STRUCTURE INTO POWDER IN MID-AIR
"SNOWBALL"
FREE FALL
THEY DIDN'T BURN UP...
NOR SLAM TO THE GROUND
"BUBBLER"
110 STORIES...
(1360 FEET)
8 SECONDS.
(NORTH TOWER DURATION)
SOLID
CHUNKS
DUST
100% OF SUNLIGHT
SURVIVED
CHECK THE SEISMIC DATA
THUD
TONS
"ALKASELTZER"
THIRD FLOOR
WALKED OUT
NOT EVEN CLOSE
NOT ENOUGH
RUBBLE
BUT TURNED TO DUST IN MID AIR
PROFOUND POSTERS
"SPIRE"
FALLING THROUGH THE AIR
NOT HITTING ANYTHING
NOT PULVERIZATION
COOL DUST CLOUD
NOT GLOWING HOT
NOT VAPORIZATION
WATCH THE SERIES: IRREFUTABLE.TV READ THE BOOK: WHEREDIDTHETOWERSGO.COM

LAST MOMENT
AS SOLID BEAM

Chapter 16 – Emotional Plane Solutions

There are a thousand hacking at the branches of evil to one who is striking at the root.

– Henry David Thoreau

*****

So far we have taken a look at solutions which are important but more external or superficial. Now, in this chapter and the following two, we will move inwards to explore how the roots of the conspiracy – and the roots of freedom – come not so much from what we do in the world but what attitudes we harbor and what states of being we carry. Our attitude and state of being are the fundamental factors which then influence our actions and in turn influence the global structure. Change yourself inside, and your world will change on the outside.

So, with that in mind, here are solutions on the emotional plane.

Trusting Life

In general, politicians and governments feed off fear. It's their lifeblood. The more they can scare you, the more you will be distracted from the corruption they're hiding and thus the more you will naively believe you need them to "look after you" and "keep you safe" from the dangerous and nasty world. The problem is that most of the “dangers” they cite to justify their rule are often exaggerated and/or concocted. Some leaders are clinical sociopaths and psychopaths and actually believe the fears they are spouting and lies they are telling, which makes them all the more convincing and dangerous.

These days, the trend is for the NWO controllers to use the MSM to encourage people to be offended and outraged as an excuse to install censorship via political correctness. The idea is to make people emotionally weak and insecure, then prey upon their insecurity. In a sane world, we would have just the opposite: leaders would encourage people to be emotionally strong and secure.

The antidote to fear is trust, so the solution to the relentless promotion of fear is to make a conscious effort to trust. Trust yourself. Trust your uniqueness. Trust your ability to discern between truth and lies. Above all, trust Life itself. Trust that you are here for a reason – and it’s not to work, obey, consume and die. Trust that Life unfolds in a sort of divine synchronicity and that there’s a reason for everything, even if you can’t always see it. Trust that there are far larger forces at play here that dwarf the “power” wielded by a small band of control freaks. Use whatever tools help you to reduce anxiety and stress – and rise above fear-based living. For many people this includes being aware of triggers and negative patterns of thought (and challenging them), listening to music, playing sport or exercising, establishing and strengthening deep relationships, immersing yourself in nature, and seeing the divine and the spiritual in everyone and everything.

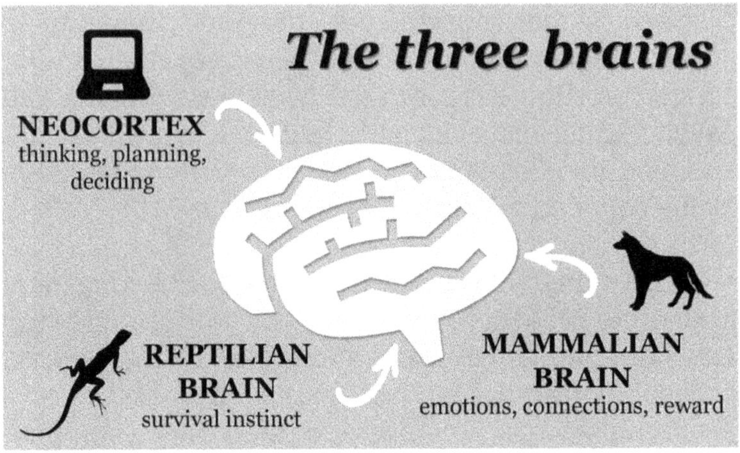

Repatterning Conditioned Reactions

The system wants you to react in a certain predictable way. It's easier to control people who are predictable rather than unpredictable. How do you make yourself predictable? By taking a close look at your conditioned reactions. We all have them. We had to act in a certain way in a certain situation in the past to survive or cope with it. So, we created neural pathways in our brain that accustomed us to this reaction. Then, we carry forward those reactions and coping mechanisms to the present day where they are not helpful, appropriate or useful anymore. In extreme cases, this can lead to people being little more than automatons or "software programs" unable or unwilling to break these conditioned reactions. The issue is that we react rather than respond. We are overtaken by seemingly automatic, knee-jerk reactions rather than considered responses to the present reality of the situation. By allowing our lives to be run by these reactions, we become a slave to the past and limit our own freedom before any outsider ruler even appears on the scene.

To take this concept a step further, it's important to realize that the human brain is multilayered. The oldest and most inner part of the brain is the reptilian brain, responsible for instincts, impulses, territoriality and survival (fight, flight or freeze). Although the two larger mammalian layers come on top of it (the paleomammalian brain or limbic system, and the neomammalian brain or neocortex), the reptilian brain still runs the show in many people. Our past trauma and wounding are deeply connected with the reptilian brain and responsible for our emotional overreactions. You may have encountered certain people who seem to get easily triggered and fly off the handle at the smallest of issues. Such people are run by the reptilian brain. Those around them have to walk on eggshells for fear of upsetting them.

Brain evolution

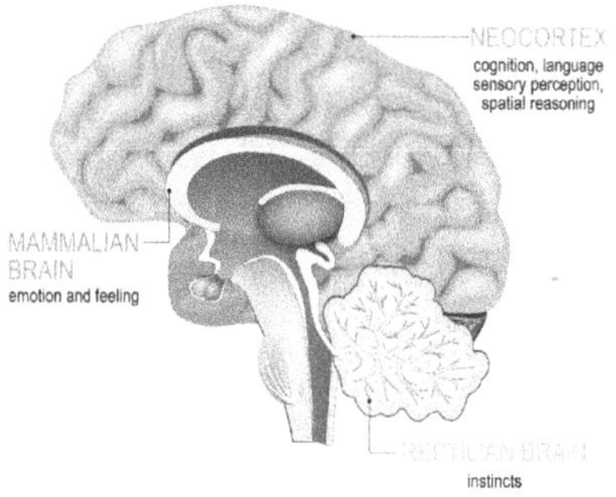

So what is the solution to this? We need to become aware of our triggers and past hurts and see what we can do to forgive, release and heal them. It's a lifelong journey. Psychotherapy works well for this. Importantly, we have to keep asking ourselves: "How much do I want to be free? Do I want to walk around like a software program, controlled by my past?"

The vital distinction here is whether we want to react or respond. Reacting comes from the reptilian brain and past conditioning. Responding comes from the neocortex and includes mindful consideration.

Following Your Passion

Another important emotional solution is to live in alignment with your passion and do what you love. Some people abbreviate this to "follow your bliss." Just think about how many people are stuck in lives they resent and jobs they hate but lack the courage to change their situation. Think about how many people have "sold their soul" and compromised their core values all because they chased the almighty dollar and wanted to get ahead. Think about how many people have become trapped in the corporate system, trading in their youth and their best waking hours to a soulless entity who would happily discard them if the chance arose. The payoff is money, but who's to say you can't also make a good living without giving up your values, self-esteem and time? At the end of the day, time is all we have. No amount of money can ever replace lost time.

As usual, the conditioning is very strong. Young people are told that they must go to university/college if they want to get "a good job" meanwhile in the US student debt is astronomical, with some students entering the workforce saddled with a $100,000+ debt before they even start working! The fear culture makes you doubt your own ability and earning capacity in order to recruit you into the corporate system where you work yourself into an early grave while those above you see most of the profit.

For many people, their job, career or working life will get the most (or close to the most) of their life's attention and energy. Why spend it doing something you are not passionate about, or even worse, dislike? You only live once. Why not follow your dreams? Whatever you are passionate about is a clue for what your life purpose and mission is. Following it is bound to bring you joy and make you happy. If you ignore and bury that, how can you find real happiness? That passion is the very clue that will lead you towards deep fulfillment.

Love, not fear, will allow us to overcome the NWO conspiracy. Love is power, and the powerful cannot be deceived or controlled.

The Heart, Not the Brain, is the Leader

This next point is very important. From one perspective, the heart-mind connection in the body cannot be divided: everything is connected, and everything is one. From another perspective, we can talk about the different parts of the body and temporarily suspend the idea they are connected.

We are meant to live from the heart and to use it as our chief guide. The heart needs to lead if we are to be in balance. The brain is a magnificent computer and tool which can create miracles when it acts as a servant to the heart. However, for most of us, we have forgotten this basic truth and live our lives mostly from our brains, especially the left brain, which is the masculine/logical side. Like government, the brain is an excellent servant but a terrible master. The "Fall of Man" written and spoken about in many religious and cultural traditions may well be referring to the fall from the heart to the brain, the loss of love, power and connection to the Infinite.

Why is the heart the true leader of the body? Because it generates love, whereas the brain generates reason. Yes, reason is important; it distinguishes us from other animals. However, there is so much of life that is beyond reason. The brain is analytical and tends to break things down in order to study them; this can lead us to get stuck in a world of good and bad, right and wrong. The heart is unifying and tends to recognize that we are all human in spite of our varied looks, skin color or beliefs; it emphasizes our commonalities over our differences.

Love expands and connects; fear contracts and separates. When we repeatedly choose fear over love, we unconsciously invite tyranny and all forms of darkness to gain a greater foothold in our hearts, minds, communities and countries. The NWO controllers know this very well and have exploited people throughout the ages by cultivating states of fear in human beings. Nowadays the broadcasting of fear has become the obvious modus operandi of the MSM, which specializes in generating and perpetuating some form of fear – anxiety, worry, anger, hatred, depression, self-pity – in those who watch it.

The heart generates love, and love not fear is at the heart of any solution to overcoming the conspiracy of control. It may sound trite, hippie-ish, or soppy, but that is only if you don't recognize and have forgotten the power of love. The truth is that love is the most powerful force in the universe. Love = power. They are one and the same. There's nothing soppy about power. When you love, a powerful energy flows through your body and emanates strongly from you. Your heart pumps excitedly and enthusiastically, elevating your mood as the rightful leader of your body.

Science is beginning to prove the true power of the heart. Scientist Rollin McCraty[440] writes that

compared to the electromagnetic field produced by the brain, the electrical component of the heart's field is about 60 times greater in amplitude, and permeates every cell in the body. The magnetic component is approximately 5000 times stronger than the brain's magnetic field and can be detected

[440] www.wakingtimes.com/2012/03/06/hearts-have-their-own-brain-and-consciousness/

several feet away from the body with sensitive magnetometers.

For those accustomed to worshiping facts, figures, logic and reason, that is really quite astonishing information. As the work of Drunvalo Melchizedek[441] shows, the heart is the center of our beings, the place from which our electromagnetic fields spring. Some people perceive the heart as the source of the body's energetic auras. The heart is the key to transcending reality, manifesting miracles and breaking free from the matrix. The brain cannot achieve this alone, no matter what it imagines. It must be fired and energized by the power of the heart.

Love not fear: the heart is more powerful than you think.

441 www.awakening-heart.org/

Mustering the Emotional Maturity to Face the Satanic Cult

Humanity really needs people to step up in the area of emotional maturity – specifically in terms of self-love, self-confidence and an inner sense of security.

We are in the midst of an unspeakable and horrific evil, but rather than evil, I suggest we use the term *unconsciousness* (as Eckhart Tolle, author of *Power of Now*, advises). We have allowed deeply unconscious individuals and groups to infiltrate and seize the power centers of our societies. JFK referred to[442] a "monolithic and ruthless conspiracy." Although he was almost certainly referring to Communism (since he delivered the speech in 1961, a year before the height of the Cuban Missile Crisis in 1962), the phrase can be read at a deeper level. Despite the fact that millions of people have died under

[442] thefreedomarticles.com/jfk-assassination-who-how-why-part-1/

Communism, it is not the root source of evil in the world. Dig a little deeper and you will find the root source is, in fact, the Satanic cult that rules through black magic and runs on fear which I discussed in chapter 9.

There is only one way out of this for mankind: to muster up the courage, in terms of both emotional maturity and spiritual maturity, to face this Satanic cult head on, expose its crimes and get these Satanists out of power, so they can no longer continue their lying, thieving, raping and murdering ways.

The first step to healing this is reaching a critical mass of awakened people who are willing to face the uncomfortable truth and do something about it. Humanity still labors under a spell of collective amnesia, denial and cognitive dissonance.

The majority of people still vote for crooked politicians, but they know in their hearts nothing will change; or they look for government to solve the problems, when they know in their hearts that it is government that creates the problems.

As truth activist James Corbett[443] has said, people suffer under a societal Stockholm Syndrome, where we have been bewitched by our captors and developed an affinity for those who deceive, rob and betray us. People defend those who enslave them. Remember what Morpheus told Neo in *The Matrix:*

---

443 https://www.corbettreport.com/solutions-overcoming-stockholm-syndrome/

The Matrix is a system, Neo. That system is our enemy. But when you're inside, you look around. What do you see? Business men, teachers, lawyers, carpenters. The very minds of the people we are trying to save. But until we do, these people are still a part of that system, and that makes them our enemy. You have to understand, most of these people are not ready to be unplugged. And many of them are so inert, so hopelessly dependent on the system that they will fight to protect it.

We have to develop emotional maturity to overcome our reflexive reaction to indulge in denial.

One important aspect of helping people wake up from the system is to help them reach emotional maturity. By this I mean a sense that you can handle difficult issues or challenges in life, whatever they may be, without crumbling, shutting down or flying off the handle. Humanity needs more emotional maturity, not less, which is why the push for the absurdity known as political correctness is such a joke. It's encouraging people to become emotional crybabies who can't handle being called names. If people are going to get their knickers in a knot over a word or phrase, how on earth are they going to have the intestinal fortitude to confront mass murderers and psychopaths who in some cases would rather kill than be exposed? A good litmus test for emotional maturity is to ask yourself these five questions:

1. Am I comfortable being different and having my own informed opinions, even if it diverges from the group?
2. Am I comfortable being politically incorrect?
3. Have I moved beyond the worry of being labelled, categorized, name-called, insulted and "cancelled" for my beliefs?
4. Can I overcome denial and cognitive dissonance by accepting and integrating uncomfortable truths?
5. Do I have the strength of conviction to challenge so-called authority?

Stop Shooting the Messenger

Shooting the messenger is a common psychological reaction when someone is faced with new information and perspectives which contradict long-held, deeply held or cherished beliefs. It is far easier to blame someone or something on the outside than to reflect and look within to discover why a particular piece of information upsets you. It is far easier to call someone crazy, mad or stupid, to dismiss their perspective without further thought and to continue your denial, than it is to really investigate that person's opinion and check out the facts to see whether their perspective has merit. The "shoot the messenger" phenomenon is a clear and obvious manifestation of people's collective denial.

Many people's consciousness level is still stuck playing "shoot the messenger."

Take a look at how the government, MSM and public reacted to whistleblowers Chelsea (formerly Bradley) Manning, Julian Assange and Edward Snowden. They were immediately labeled as traitors despite the fact they had uncovered and exposed wrongdoing. They hadn't committed a crime; they had exposed crimes committed by the ruling cabal of criminals, yet their very act of whistleblowing and publishing was criminalized. Those holding the government accountable were turned into criminals for doing the very thing that politicians love to boast helps make a nation "free, open and democratic."

When exposing a crime is
treated as committing a crime,
you are ruled by criminals.

I don't necessarily agree with every single thing Manning, Assange and Snowden have done or said, but I view them as heroes who took a stand at great personal risk for the principles of freedom of speech, freedom of the press and the public's right to know pertinent information about governmental actions. These people (and others like them) have demonstrated an astonishing commitment to truth and freedom. They need to be saluted, celebrated and most of all supported as the US-led NWO

Empire continues its efforts to capture, silence and imprison them.

This phenomenon of shoot the messenger needs to change – and fast – if we want to confront the Satanic cult. As Geoff Byrd from Radio Mysterium says in Atmos-Fear[444]:

We must stop acting like herd animals ... on social media, peer pressure and psychological gaslighting techniques are used to shame truthseekers into silence. The self-policing on Facebook make me nauseous, like crabs in a bucket.

People need to stop backing away from information and finding a way to forget about it, deny it, rationalize it or make it go away. It's not going away. In fact, more and more information is coming to light, as victims go public, whistleblowers step forth, people turn to the Alternative Media for news and information becomes more rapidly exchanged. Denial is no longer an option. Nowadays, ignorance is a choice. As horrible as the truth is of the Satanic cult and the New World Order, the only way to heal it is by acknowledging its reality and integrating that knowledge within. A problem can only be fixed once you accept it as a problem.

Final Thoughts

You may notice that a lot of these emotional plane solutions come down to overcoming fear. The War on Terror is propagated on lies and fear. Once you

---

444 https://www.youtube.com/watch?v=21Mw9DRq4EY

correct that with truth and trust, it becomes a blatant and laughable piece of propaganda. The NWO plan promises a world of homogeneity where everything and everyone is standardized to ensure they fit the mold and are easily controllable and predictable. This is precisely why, if we care about truth and freedom, we must strive to be authentic, unique and heterogeneous. We can't do it by being lazy and apathetic, nor can we do it just by acting on the physical, mental and social planes alone. Those things are important, but in addition to that, we're going to have to dig deeper. The changes we make there will have lasting effects on ourselves, our communities and the world.

Chapter 17 – Spiritual Plane Solutions

Holding on to anger is like grasping a hot coal with the intent of throwing it at someone else; you are the one who gets burned.

– Buddha

One does not become enlightened by imagining figures of light but by making the darkness conscious.

– Carl Jung

People will do anything, no matter how absurd, to avoid facing their own souls.

– Carl Jung

People want dreams. When they lose faith in their own ability to dream about the life they want, they'll accept someone else dreaming for them. That's what hypnosis is. Someone else dreaming for you. You accept a substitute. That's mind control. That's believing you can live in someone else's creation forever.

– Jack True, hypnotherapist

Only a people who are self loathing and ultimately hate themselves could allow themselves to remain enslaved. Only true self respect can heal it.

– Mark Passio

How hurtful it can be to deny one's true self and live a life of lies just to appease others.

– June Ahern

We are not human beings having a spiritual experience. We are spiritual beings having a human experience.

– Pierre Teilhard de Chardin

It has been said that wisdom lies not in seeing things, but in seeing through things.

– Manly P. Hall, 33rd degree Freemason

*****

Shift Your Consciousness

You can change all the things you like in the outer world, but if you don't make inner changes, nothing will truly change because you'll just re-create the same outer world. Imagine if humanity in its current state and consciousness level populated a planet in another galaxy (it may already be happening – but that's another story). The same mentality would produce the same results there – theft of land, exploitation of the planet, a hierarchical social-political system, the manufacturing of tremendous pollution and waste, etc. Why would it be anything different to here if our thinking didn't change?

Thoughts become things. Everything that currently exists in our world was once an idea in someone's mind. Quantum physics has confirmed what ancient philosophies have long known: we are co-creators of our world. Our thoughts, feelings and state of being literally interact with fields of possibility and probability (which is the definition of atoms that form the foundation of the "material" world), and in doing so create an experience that we call *reality.*

The more we can regain control over our very minds and states of consciousness, the more we will create the world we consciously choose, since it is a natural law that our outer world reflects our inner world. A consciousness shift is the key to real change.

<u>Any Decent New System Must Come from a Higher State of Consciousness</u>

The only way out of the prison is a consciousness shift. The only revolution that will produce real and lasting change is a revolution of consciousness. Anything else is just rearranging deck chairs on the *Titanic*.

What the world needs most right now is a new consciousness and a corresponding new system which springs from that elevated consciousness. Instead, people get caught up in voting for members of parliament, congress, presidents and prime ministers. You see it every election cycle: a new candidate emerges, promising hope, change and sometimes even a revolution. But how often does it actually lead to significant, lasting and beneficial change? Can any candidate really deliver as much freedom, peace and abundance to the average person as much as an improved new system?

The hope and change rollercoaster – the ride that always takes you right back where you started.

Many get swept away by the euphoria of elections. Obamamania was a classic example. Obama was *Mr. Hope and Change*, but he turned out to be Bush on steroids, or tyranny with a smiley face. Obama continued and expanded all stupid US wars, spearheaded a whole new type of war (remote-controlled drone killings) and signed pieces of legislation like the NDAA which allows Americans to be held indefinitely without trial in gross violation of the Fifth Amendment among others. Is this the kind of hope and change people thought they were getting when they voted for Obama?

Hope and change, or similar notions, are almost always seized upon by politicians vying for office because they play off people's dissatisfaction with the status quo. However, history shows us that the promised change never quite happens in a way that's good for the people. The movement or revolution in the making tends to dissipate once the candidate takes office. It leaves us betrayed and trapped, like a donkey tricked into doing hard work, reaching forward for the carrot on a line that always remains out of grasp.

The American people may get a new president every four to eight years, but he or she will inherit the same system of control. Meet the new boss, same as the old boss. Lord Acton famously said that *"power corrupts, and absolute power corrupts absolutely"*. It is a very rare person indeed who cannot be corrupted by the massive excess of power that is afforded an office like that of the US president. US presidents have the power to fire anyone in the entire executive branch of the government, and also to command the instant destruction of entire cities. The US has thousands of nuclear missiles, and only the president can give the signal to launch them. Why are we still allowing a system to exist that gives one person such massive power over the entire world?

It is insane to continue on with a system that keeps deceiving, manipulating and enslaving us, waiting in vain for someone "good" to finally take office and reverse it all. We will run out of breath trying.

There is far too much power vested in the White House, executive branch and office of US president.

The Nazi regime was the epitome of centralization of power. Many current nations are not that different. The US executive branch has grown out of control to overcome many of the checks and balances with which it was originally constrained.

To really be beneficial, any new system must be grounded in a higher state of consciousness. Einstein said that a problem can only be solved by moving to a higher level of thinking than that which created it. The real revolution has to be a revolution of consciousness. Any other movement or revolution that is not accompanied by this is bound to fail.

Imagine if people put as much energy into changing the system as changing the prime minister, president or ruling party. Imagine if people realized that there is no meaningful difference between having a left or right jackboot on your face. Imagine if people realized that we don't have to constantly settle for mediocrity by choosing the lesser of two evils. We're better than that. Imagine a new system where the things like defense, education, energy and health care were decentralized and not under the government umbrella. Imagine a new system like direct democracy where citizens could vote electronically on bills and initiatives, thus bypassing much of the need for elected representatives. Imagine a new system where the government had to balance its books and legally could not borrow to go into debt. Imagine a new system where only those who didn't want the job were chosen, in order to prevent the ambitious from becoming career politicians. Imagine a new system where campaigning and rigged electronic voting machines were banned. Imagine a new system where anyone who declared war would have to personally go on the front lines to fight it!

We have the numbers and the power. We could create any new system we wanted to, limited only by our imagination and our will. Many societies in humanity's past used a council of elders or wise men and women as their sole political vehicle. Some native American Indians gave great power to the old women or crones, who got to decide which men would be leaders, since they knew their characters as young children at a time when they reared and watched over them.

Just as we created the government, so too can we dissolve it and replace it with an entirely new system. This principle applies in any nation on Earth, even if it is only enshrined in some nations' legal documents. Here are the inspirational words from the *Declaration of Independence*:

That whenever any Form of Government becomes destructive of these ends, it is the Right of the People to alter or to abolish it, and to institute new Government, laying its foundation on such principles and organizing its powers in such form, as to them shall seem most likely to affect their Safety and

Happiness.

Prudence, indeed, will dictate that Governments long established should not be changed for light and transient causes; and accordingly all experience hath shewn, that mankind are more disposed to suffer, while evils are sufferable, than to right themselves by abolishing the forms to which they are accustomed. But when a long train of abuses and usurpations, pursuing invariably the same Object evinces a design to reduce them under absolute Despotism, it is their right, it is their duty, to throw off such Government, and to provide new Guards for their future security.

Choose Your Vibration

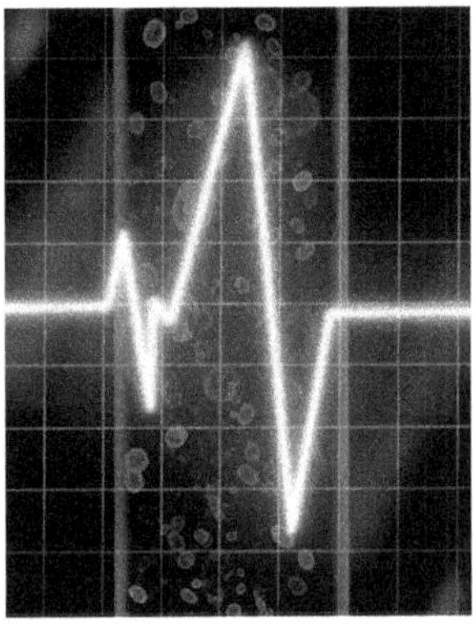

Raising your consciousness, or raising your vibration, is undoubtedly an important concept. So is the idea of proactively choosing your vibration. What does this mean? It means taking a radical look at your relationship to emotion and mood. As discussed in the previous chapter, almost all of us are accustomed to just accepting whatever emotion or mood comes along, based on outer causes and conditions. For instance, you are driving and someone cuts you off. You feel angry. You are standing in line at the supermarket, and someone lets you go in front of them. You feel grateful. You get fired from your job. You feel despondent and discouraged. A cute girl or guy gives you their phone number. You feel happy and confident. And so on. It's almost like we are pieces of computer software walking around with preprogrammed responses, just waiting to get triggered. It's a form of mind control.

Everything in the universe is energy. Matter is just energy slowed down. Energy vibrates at different frequencies. We are beings of energy, too, since we are part of the universe, and our emotions are a big part of what drives us and how we express our energy. What if you actually chose what to feel, rather than letting outer events influence your feelings?

The fact that you *can* choose your vibration is one of the greatest secrets held by those at the helm of the global conspiracy – the elite bloodlines with esoteric knowledge running the NWO. If everyone really knew and applied that, why would anyone waste their time listening to the fear-driven message of the politicians and the MSM?

You are a creator, like every other human. You can decide what feeling or emotion to adopt, proactively rather than reactively. It doesn't have to be fake. It doesn't have to be something you just conjured up – although you may need to do this often at first until it becomes more natural (hence the expression *fake it 'til you make it*). I'm not talking about hiding or suppressing genuine sadness or pain by putting on a happy face. That's just repression; the world is full of it, and it leads to nothing but suffering.

I'm talking about choosing your emotion, feeling, attitude, belief – everything, your entire vibration – when you are faced with a new circumstance in your life. That way, you include the whole package. You choose your vibration, and magically, it actually transforms what happens to you. By responding with more love, trust and compassion to any person or situation, you turn every problem into a challenge or opportunity. For instance, a branch hits your car, and you respond with gratitude – "Thank God I wasn't in there when it hit". Then with trust – "that car was starting to get old and I was starting to need a new one". Who knows what could be around the corner? Every time something is destroyed, it opens the door for something new, which we usually cannot see.

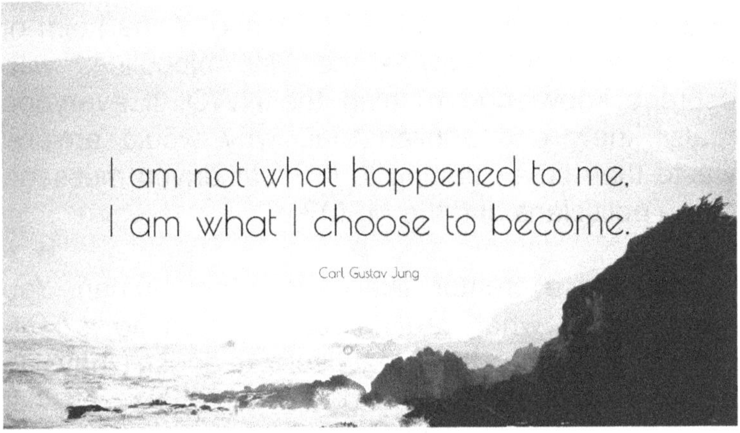

The more you master the flexibility, inner strength and positive attitude required in choosing your vibration, the freer you'll be. When enough of us choose our vibrations often enough, the entire control grid of tyranny will collapse because it's propped up by our fear. As it stands, we unconsciously feed it with our vibrations of fear. Once you start emitting higher vibrations, such as those of love and trust, you become difficult or impossible to control because your reaction/response cannot be predicted and because those who love are not dependent on some outside force to provide "safety" or "security" the way that those who fear are.

We do already do this instinctively, just not all that often. How often do you listen to music that uplifts or enlivens you when you need a boost? How often do you go to a religious service or do some kind of contemplative or spiritual practice when you're feeling down? How often do you spend time watching or listening to inspirational art, poetry or a movie? All these things and more are ways to proactively choose your mood, but they can be used like crutches or permission slips. The real work is done by you on the inside, making a firm decision that you will feel peace, love or happiness regardless of any circumstances.

We need to attune ourselves to the highest vibration we can imagine, and that is the frequency of love. Not romantic, sexual love, but rather the love that you have for another human being in general: the love which connects us all. It includes caring, compassion and empathy. It means being there for another, standing up for them and putting yourself out for them. Every time we do this, we inspire gratitude from others, such that they want to return the favor. It sends out a ripple throughout the world which can go further than we typically imagine. The more time we spend attuning our own vibration or state of being to being grateful, feeling peaceful, or acknowledging how much we have, the more we are doing to create a new world and naturally end the global conspiracy without any violence or destruction.

Being able to proactively choose your own vibration requires a lot of self-mastery, and is the work of a lifetime. However, step by step you can improve. You need to feel free and powerful to be able to do it, and in order to feel free and powerful, you have to forgive. Forgive the past so you can release it. Forgive primarily for your own sake, so you are not burdened by it. You can't meet the present moment with freshness and curiosity if you are too weighed down by past wounds because it clouds your perception and even plays a part in helping you re-create the same situation. Colin Tipping, author of the book *Radical Forgiveness*, has developed different techniques to bypass the rational mind and involve your spiritual intelligence or intuition in reaching a deep space of forgiveness. He suggests the following four-step process:

1. Responsibility: Say to yourself: "Wow, look at what I've helped create here!"
2. Self-Acceptance: Say to yourself: "I notice I have thoughts and feelings around this issue, but I love myself anyway."
3. Radical forgiveness: Say to yourself: "I'm willing to see the perfection in this situation."
4. Conscious intention: Say to yourself: "I choose peace."

The idea is to take responsibility for what happened, even if you think your part was minor or justified, and accept your feelings of anger, sadness, betrayal, disappointment or whatever they are. The real work is to realize that everything is perfect on an ultimate level, so even if someone irritates you or something seems grossly unfair, it's still an opportunity or challenge you can use to learn and grow.

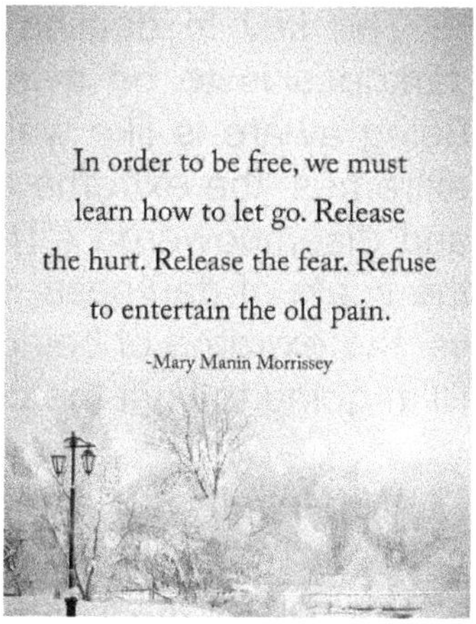

Forgiveness doesn't mean forgetting but rather letting go of the negative feeling around the person or event. It's for you, not the other person. It's giving up the hope of a better past. This necessarily involves changing your perspective (perception) of the event. It involves reframing the event. Colin has another presentation (free on YouTube[445]) where he goes over the five stages of radical forgiveness, which are:

1. Telling the story
2. Feeling the feelings
3. Collapsing the story
4. Reframing the story
5. Integrating the new story

These five stages are very similar to the four-step process. It's all about acceptance, trust (that it happened for a reason) and a willingness to let it go and to choose peace in the present moment.

Convert Fear into Awareness

In order to master dealing with the

445 https://www.youtube.com/watch?v=q9wF_V_XKBw

NWO conspiracy, you need to be able to convert fear into awareness and become aware, not afraid.

The key to dealing with the massive amount of darkness is to be aware of it without being afraid. Being aware is like walking a tightrope between two extremes: the extreme of being overwhelmed, scared and disempowered ("There's nothing I can do about the scale of darkness, so I'm just going to ignore it") vs. the extreme of being sucked in, angry and hateful ("I'm going to fight the corruption tooth and nail").

Whatever you fight, you become. Part of the problem of dealing with something as dark and evil as the conspiracy is that you can get sucked into it. If you spend too much energy or focus fighting or resisting the NWO, you're on the wrong track. *Whatever you fight, you become; whatever you resist, persists.* Trying to overcome the NWO head on by meeting it with anger will backfire because when it comes to hate and violence, no one is any match for it. The NWO thrives on violence. Look at the way police are being militarized and mobilized against their own people – the individuals they swore in many cases to protect. By rioting and acting aggressively you merely give corrupt politicians an excuse to use violence against you – and they will win, because they have more money, arms and force in that arena. Why challenge an enemy in an area where he is stronger?

We need to shine the light of truth on the unlawful activities of the elite so that people will stop falling for the deception and so that these horrific crimes can be healed, whether it be democide, child trafficking or mind control. It's vital that researchers, truthtellers and whistleblowers keep shining the light, but it must be done with consciousness. It's natural to feel scared when you realize the immense amount of money, power and technology the elite are hoarding and have weaponized to use against the masses. However, if you continually feel afraid of them, you will be paralyzed and unable to act to create something better. Likewise, it's natural to feel angry and outraged at the injustices perpetrated against humanity at large but the NWO controllers, but if you prolong that anger and keep holding on to it, rather than using it as a brief impetus to correct the injustice, it will start poisoning you from the inside out.

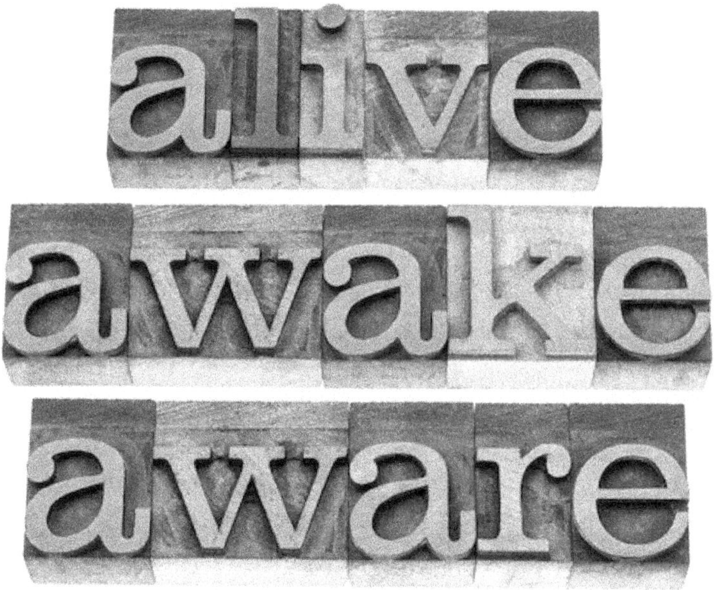

You *Can* Handle the Truth

The swaggering, arrogant character of Colonel Nathan Jessup played by Jack Nicholson in the movie *A Few Good Men* is a wonderful personification of the MIC and NWO, who believe they alone have the right to rule and they alone deserve the accurate information of what is happening on Earth right now. They are in the know, and everyone outside their little clique is in ignorance because none of us has the "need to know" and are instead shut out through a byzantine maze of legal classifications, many based on the dubious and trite claim of national security. At one point Jessup bellows out the famous line *"You can't handle the truth!"* which sums up the rulers' attitude towards the rest of us.

However, the idea that we can't handle the truth is a lie. People are already handling the truth. The internet has vastly sped up our information-sharing ability. People are being exposed to all sorts of information that they would not have seen before. The whistleblowers I covered in chapters 2 and 10, plus many others, are pushing the boundaries of our collective perception. In many ways, they are rolling out a *drip-drip-drip* disclosure of truth (as opposed to a dramatic announcement from the White House garden that we have ET visitors among us). People are listening to and reading their accounts and thus already considering the validity of their information and integrating it. This is handling the truth – and often it's not easy because the truth ain't always pretty, comfortable or convenient.

When facing monstrous truths about our world, such as that we do not live in a free and open society and that many of our rulers are pedophiles, psychopaths and Satanists, it possible to have different reactions. One is denial and shutdown. One is anger. Another is a feeling of being overwhelmed. Another is disempowerment. A common one is fear. While these are all natural and understandable reactions, the important thing is to move beyond them.

If you allow yourself to be consumed by fear or anger, you are being driven by exactly the same force that drives the minds of the ruthless, cruel and psychopathic "leaders" we have. We all need to convert fear into awareness if we want to be able to withstand the shocking truth about who runs the world and how they do it. Otherwise, we will not be able to deal with the darkness.

Don't Identify with Being Spiritual

Being truly spiritual is beyond labels. It is not about "being spiritual" in an egotistical way, which is another trap that can make you judgmental and ensnare you in a fixed identity. Rather, being spiritual is getting in touch with your core being and essence, which is spiritual rather than material since matter is secondary and spiritual is primary.

Anytime you cling to a name, label or category, you are diminishing yourself. You are also falling into the NWO "divide-and-conquer" scheme.

The Tao that can be told is not the eternal Tao; the name that can be named is not the eternal name.

– Lao Tzu, Tao Te Ching

All Agents of Darkness Are Here to Challenge Us and Make Us Better

The empowering way to look at the situation is to remember that all the twisted threats, schemes and dangers in operation are here to challenge us, spur us to greater heights, help us grow and help us find our true selves. Without them, we would not have the motivation to grow and live up to our potential. So, the shady NWO characters are playing a vital role of spurring us on without even knowing it.

Without this realization, it is all too easy to fall into states of anger and victimization. It is all too easy to hate these psychopaths. Once that happens, it is easy to join the dark side yourself. Yes, there is a place for righteous short-term anger – the kind of anger that wants to do justice and set things right. However, nothing good comes from chronic long-term anger; it eats away at you from the inside and ends up causing serious diseases like cancer.

Beware of victimland. It's a disempowering trap. I have already pointed out how much the MSM promotes fear and victimization via techniques like political correctness. One way to avoid getting tricked into feeling like a victim is to remember that everything is happening *for* you, not to you. Look at things as opportunities and challenges, not blessings or curses, otherwise it's easy to lose your equanimity and be thrown off balance by the vicissitudes of life.

Be Yourself, Unreservedly

Be yourself – unreservedly, unabashedly, unashamedly, unapologetically. Be yourself – without fear, without worrying about the future, without being anxious about failure, without caring what other people think. We gain tremendous power when we simply decide to be ourselves and stop holding back. All of us hold back on some level. Maybe we're scared about being vulnerable by expressing our feelings too much. That's a big one. So many societies are characterized by emotional repression, East or West, black or white, be it England, Germany, Australia, Thailand or Japan. In particular, the British ideal of a "stiff upper lip" has only wrought untold misery upon those who regularly repress their feelings and live lives of quiet desperation.

Maybe we're scared because we're worried about

failing. However, we define what failure is! Einstein once said that *"anyone who has never made a mistake has never tried something new"*; Edison had a great way of looking at it when he said, upon being asked about repeatedly failing to design a working light bulb, that *"I have not failed. I've just found 10,000 ways that won't work"*.

Alternatively, maybe we're scared about what others will think. That can be a huge trap. Humans are undeniably social creatures, and it seems that we have a very strong primal instinct for acceptance and for following the herd. If that need is not tempered with self-knowledge and the courage to be who we really are, then it can lead to passivity and a reluctance to rock the boat – and thus easily manipulated by the NWO conspirators against us.

It is hard to sum it up better than the words of Marianne Williamson[446], who wrote:

Our deepest fear is not that we are inadequate. Our deepest fear is that we are powerful beyond measure. It is our light, not our darkness that most frightens us. We ask ourselves, who am I to be brilliant, gorgeous, talented, fabulous? Actually, who are you not to be? You are a child of God. Your playing small does not serve the world. There is nothing enlightened about shrinking so that other people won't feel insecure around you. We are all meant to shine, as children do. We were born to make manifest the glory of God that is within us. It's not just in some of us; it's in everyone. And as we let our own light shine, we unconsciously give other people permission to do the same. As we are liberated from our own fear, our presence automatically liberates others.

As you truly be yourself, without reservation, then that ignites a spark in others and helps them to the same. What the conspirators fear most is people who have no fear, who decide to express themselves fully and be themselves completely. These kinds of people cannot be controlled. They resist conformity, uniformity and meek obedience. They do not engage in unquestioning submission to authority, nor are they easily corrupted, perverted or tricked into "carrying out orders" or "just doing their job." They know their actions count, and they are not going to let themselves be used to create or enforce a totalitarian

---

446 skdesigns.com/internet/articles/quotes/williamson/our_deepest_fear/

global dictatorship.

Be yourself, for nobody else can. Be yourself, for every other self is taken! Be yourself – unreservedly. Make no apologies to anyone for who you really are. Don't set up any inner tension or struggle by denying the magnificence, power, beauty and reality of who you are. Don't conform for the sake of conformity. The pain you will feel from being inauthentic far outweighs any possible gain you get from hiding your light or pretending to be someone you're not. Once enough of us decide to be ourselves, all systems based on suppression and fear will crumble.

<u>The Only Time Is Now</u>

Stepping into our true power is synonymous with being present. Conversely, being stuck in the past (haunted by the ghosts of past regrets, resentments and wounds) and being stuck in the future (anxious about what will happen) necessarily means failing to live up to your fullest potential.

The only time is now. I don't say that as a trite platitude or cliché. It is, literally, the only time that ever has been or ever will be. When the past happened, it happened in the now. When the future happens, it will happen in the now. Yet we are so accustomed to leaning forward and concentrating on our goals that we forget to enjoy and accept the present moment and all the steps along the journey.

Ultimately, time is an illusion. It can be a useful one, but it can also cause us to lose sight of the immediacy of the present moment, the eternal now.

To be effective, you have to focus on your spheres of influence, on the areas you exert the most control and therefore where you can effect the most change. You can only change a bad habit in the present; tomorrow never comes. If shame and guilt are running your life, you're stuck in the past; if fear, worry and anxiety are running your life, you're stuck in the future.

The Power of Now by Eckhart Tolle brilliantly expands upon just how life-changing it can be to be fully present in the now. The importance of present moment attention is what underpins many spiritual practices such as meditation.

<u>The Problem and Solution are Indivisible</u>

Artist Pablo Picasso once said, *"Computers are useless. They can only give you answers."* It may seem facetious, since answers are very useful, but he was alluding to a deeper truth that questions are more important than answers. Why? Questions frame your attention; they dictate the direction of exploration. It takes conscious awareness and curiosity to create questions, something computers and AI, no matter how technologically advanced, will never be able to do the way humans can. There is a saying that the seed of the answer to any question is contained in the question itself. Similarly, the seed of the solution to any problem is contained in the problem itself.

This concept is borne out in various types of psychological and inner work. For instance, there is a technique called Process Work developed by Arnold Mindell, a training analyst at the C.G. Jung Institute in Zurich, Switzerland. The institute is named after the great psychologist Carl Jung whose contributions to that field are seminal and monumental. This article[447] by Lane Arye, PhD, briefly highlights an example of Process Work:

Jung was interested in not only the cause of a symptom, but also its purpose, the direction it leads us. He understood that the seed of a solution is contained within the problem itself. Process Work continues in this tradition ... Process Work is also rooted in Taoism, which teaches that there is an unseen direction in which things move, a dynamic order that structures the way things are. Process Workers study what is happening in order to follow Nature, which has its own wisdom. When problems are unfolded with accuracy and heart, new ways forward are discovered that are often surprising, creative and transformative.

An example shows how this works in practice. A client complained of anxiety attacks. I asked him to describe his experience of anxiety. He clutched his chest, saying it felt like something squeezing him. I invited him to squeeze a pillow in the same way he

[447] processworklane.com/every-problem-contains-the-seed-of-its-own-solution/

felt squeezed. As his hands and arms compressed the pillow against his chest, his eyes closed so he could feel the experience more fully. He was surprised that this was pleasant, and that it relaxed him. Going deeper, he said he felt like he was hugging a child. He had missed such supportive contact in his childhood, and said this felt like the loving mother he never had. In subsequent sessions, he reported that whenever anxiety started to surface, he would "hug" himself, and this helped him to calm down and avert an attack. He also said that being more actively loving with himself had helped him to feel more loved by, and loving toward, his partner; and their relationship was improving.

On the deepest level, the problem and solution are indivisible. It is not always easy to see this, especially when caught in a mundane state of consciousness. The more you can move to deeper states of consciousness, broaden your perspective and reflect on all sides of a particular issue, the more you can allow surprisingly creative and transformative solutions to arise to seemingly insurmountable obstacles.

Integrating the Inner Shadow

The roots of the NWO are inside all of us.

The most profound spiritual solution in this entire chapter lies in each person becoming aware of their own shadow. What is the shadow? According to Jung, it is the part of yourself which you have ignored, denied, suppressed and pretended does not exist. It contains all the traits you dislike about yourself. It is the place for all the things that you just can't handle, acknowledge or fully accept. It is also the place where you shove things that are too traumatic to deal with at the time they occur, so you can revisit them later with more wisdom, clarity and coping tools. Sometimes, what allows aspects of our shadow to continue is that we mistakenly believe the pain would be too great if we were to acknowledge it. Yet, the pain is much greater by suppressing it because that only makes it fester and become even more twisted – after which it begins to wreak great havoc in our lives.

The shadow is not something to be fought; it is something to be integrated. We need to be completely honest with ourselves, acknowledge our own darkness and how it affects our personal projections and the world we are creating. Trying to aggressively "fight the NWO" is bound to fail, not only because (as already discussed) government thrives on violence and outguns the public but also because, more importantly, you can't eliminate a problem with the same kind of energy that created it. Trying to stop the government from being violent by reacting violently will never work. You can't create less violence by being more violent. You can't create more peace by aggressively stomping on the ground at a protest and shouting "peace!" with anger in your heart. You can only create more peace by embodying a peaceful vibration yourself, and leading by example to encourage others to do the same.

Our stories, myths and legends allude to this truth. St. George and the dragon can be interpreted in many ways; one way is to realize that the dragon represents our inner demons and that we, like St. George, fight hard inner battles every day that are more important than our outer battles. To kill the dragon is to rise above demonic thoughts and integrate the shadow. Likewise, the Arabic word *jihad*, which has been misconstrued and demonized by Western media and extremist Islamic sects alike, actually means "the exerting of one's power in repelling the enemy" and refers to the inner struggle against demons, negative thoughts or one's lower self.

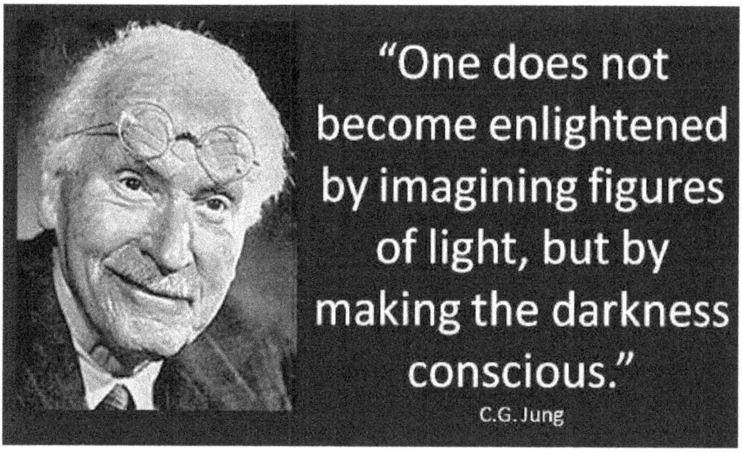

In many ways it is easier to fight outer demons than inner ones. You can grab a sword or gun and destroy an outer enemy, but how can you destroy inner thoughts of jealousy, hopelessness, temptation and rage? Besides, destroying an external enemy does no good if you don't also change the corresponding attitude and reaction which co-created it. The shadow feeds into a well-known psychological phenomenon called *projection* whereby we tend to get irritated by those qualities and people in our external world which reflect our inner world. In other words, we judge, condemn and rage against a certain trait in other people because we have denied and repressed that trait of ourselves. We all unconsciously project; no human is exempt from it.

When you take projection into account, fighting external enemies becomes less important in the overall scheme of things compared to correcting one's perception, as much as grabbing a knife and slashing the movie screen is ineffective compared to changing the movie reel inside the projector.

There is an individual shadow and a collective shadow, and they reflect each other. An individual who has not stepped fully into her power tends to attract and invite into her life someone powerful who fills that void, for better or worse. An individual who can't control himself tends to attract someone who over-controls and will end up controlling him. Following this principle to its logical conclusion, we only have the current situation – with governments routinely abusing their power and overstepping their jurisdiction – because humanity has the collective shadow of people not fully stepping into their power, not being in control of themselves, not taking full responsibility for their actions and being dependent on some outside source to "save" and "care for" them even when they are mature adults. Thus, humanity unconsciously and collectively creates the external parent in the form of a "Nanny State" or a giant smothering socialist Mother or a fear-inspiring tyrannical Father. Politicians from ancient Rome, Nazi Germany (Hitler) and modern-day USA (George W. Bush) have all referred to their nations as the "Fatherland."

To put this concept another way, humanity is in an abusive, codependent relationship with government. However, politicians are not solely to blame. Humanity at large has created such a system and continues to allow it to perpetuate by not integrating the shadow.

If you don't integrate and own your inner shadow or dark side, it doesn't mean that it magically goes away. On the contrary, it doesn't go anywhere but deeper inside of you, where it sneakily influences and controls you from the darkness, where you have even less control over it. You may have noticed this in your life, where you harbor anger against someone and don't speak up about it, only to later find your anger spilling it onto other people who are completely innocent, unrelated to the situation and undeserving of it. We are all more powerful when we admit that we do have negative thoughts, feelings and motivations and accept that such things are part of us and part of Life (without the dark there is no light; light only exists in comparison to darkness, as with any set of opposites). That acceptance gives us the chance to consciously transform them rather than be sneakily controlled by them. Owning that you have the capacity to be dangerous is a powerful thing. It means that when you choose peace, you do it not out of cowardice but out of a conscious recognition that you could use force if you wanted or needed to. He who could use his power in a damaging way but chooses peace instead is more powerful and good than he who chooses peace out of fear, cowardice and powerlessness.

I truly believe that when a critical mass of people does enough inner work and integration of the shadow, the world will be transformed. It will lessen projection, lessen judgement and lessen the phenomenon of people running around blaming and hating things they don't like inside of themselves. It will increase self-acceptance and self-love, thus reducing the need for people to look outside of themselves for someone or something to save them. The conspiracy relies on these unconscious needs and drives to exist, and once they are withdrawn, it will begin to collapse like a house of cards.

The outer world reflects the inner world. Integrating the inner shadow is a big part of the solution to ending the NWO conspiracy of control that is threatening to enslave the entire planet.

Conclusion: We're More Powerful – We Just Need to Remember It

It is clear that the Satanic cult, no matter how powerful its members think they are, cannot succeed against a fully awakened humanity. They are parasites that feed off the unconscious state of the collective. Energetically, it's a codependent relationship; if you change or remove one aspect of the equation, the other cannot exist in the same way.

This quote is from Geoff Byrd who sums it up beautifully:

It's not just the Illuminati, or the Shadow Government, or the evil banksters doing this; it's the silence and quiet acquiescence of the people who are allowing this to happen. No resistance; if you don't resist, they will persist. The power vacuum was created by us. It is our own inability to face our own personal demons and heal our psychological trauma that allows this to happen.

We perpetuate this external reality. TURN AND FACE IT; not just for you, but for us too. So we must do the individual, introspective shadow work to improve the collective ... our own individual healing will affect the morphic field and create anchor frequencies in the collective consciousness. So our own individual healing is a nexus point. The courage of the individual is paramount to the psychological health of the whole.

We have to develop our spiritual maturity to be able to handle the depths of Satanic unconsciousness – without losing ourselves in the process of exposing it.

It can be difficult to integrate the truth without spiritual maturity. If you don't have a spiritual practice, deep faith, a connection to "God" or your Higher Self, or some other way to anchor your consciousness, it is all too easy for the horror of the information to blow you away. Without the spiritual maturity, you are likely to get caught up in anger, frenzy, stress and hate – and go into "fighting" mode. This is a form of unconsciousness where you actually become the very thing you are opposing. Just as many great past figures have said, you can't fight for peace. You can only be peaceful.

We need to walk the tightrope with precise balance. We need to use enough energy as passion and determination to expose the truth and set things right. If we overdo it, our energy may well turn into over-anger and hate (one path to unconsciousness). If we underdo it, as we are mostly doing now, we will remain in denial as apathetic, passive and acquiescent slaves who allow evil to rise in their midst (another path to unconsciousness). It's our choice. What's it going to be – consciousness or unconsciousness?

If I had to sum up this entire chapter in one sentence, it would be this: remember that the NWO lies inside of each of us, and as we face our demons and integrate the inner shadow, the outer shadow will be transformed.

Lastly, remember this: if you weren't so powerful, why would the government spend so much energy trying to suppress you? Why does the tyrannical Communist Chinese government ban Falun Gong (an ancient Chinese spiritual system akin to yoga and consisting of exercise and meditation)? Falun Gong practitioners, who at one point were estimated to number one in every twelve Chinese people, were doing simple peaceful exercises guided by the moral philosophy of "truth, kindness and tolerance"? Why does the Chinese government brutally persecute Falun Gong practitioners, imprison them, kill them and even harvest their organs? Why would a government be so scared of people practicing spiritual exercises and raising their consciousness? The persecution of Falun Gong practitioners is a revealing metaphor for how scared our "authorities" are of raw spirituality and the uplifting of the human spirit.

Chapter 18 – Energetic Plane Solutions

All matter originates and exists only by virtue of a force which brings the particle of an atom to vibration and holds this most minute solar system of the atom together. We must assume behind this force the existence of a conscious and intelligent mind. This mind is the matrix of all matter.

– Max Planck

If you want to find the secrets of the universe, think in terms of energy, frequency and vibration.

– Nikola Tesla

The day science begins to study non-physical phenomena, it will make more progress in one decade than in all the previous centuries of its existence.

– Nikola Tesla

The atoms or elementary particles themselves are not real; they form a world of potentialities or possibilities rather than one of things or facts.

– Werner Heisenberg

We may therefore regard matter as being constituted by the regions of space in which the field is extremely intense ... there is no place in this new kind of physics for the field and matter, for the field is the only reality.

– Albert Einstein

The field is the sole governing agency of the particle.

– Albert Einstein

Everything we call real is made of things that cannot be regarded as real.

– Niels Bohr

*****

Everything is Energy

Now, we will go to one of the deepest levels yet when it comes to unraveling the worldwide conspiracy. In order to do that, you have to understand that the world we live in is not physical or material: ultimately, it's energetic. We live in a world of energy, and we ourselves are energetic beings. Everything is energy. Everything vibrates at some kind of frequency – and with the right kinds of tools or devices, these frequencies can be measured, which means it is entirely scientific to look at things in terms of energy, vibration and frequency (just as scientific and engineering geniuses like Nikola Tesla did).

So, if everything is really energy, then what is matter? It doesn't matter (just kidding). Matter is actually energy vibrating at an extremely low rate. The densest, most solid objects are energy vibrating very slowly. It's important to realize that consciousness precedes matter, and sound precedes form. In other words, matter springs from consciousness, which creates it. Sound precedes form, too; spiritual and religious texts talk of how "in the beginning, there was a word" or how God created the Universe (which literally means "one voice") with sound. The science of cymatics demonstrates how sound can be played at a group of loosely scattered particles and form them into unique shapes. If you type "cymatics" into an internet video search, you will see clips showing this principle. It's incredible how loose, fine particles of sand or dirt can be formed into beautiful crystalline or geometric shapes just through the vibration of sound – without even being touched.

It's even more astonishing to realize that our entire world has been brought into existence in the same way. It is the "field", the electromagnetic aura of objects, which actually determines their shapes and properties. The quotes at the start of this chapter from world-renowned scientists show that even highly intelligent and logical people can go beyond the realm of reason to recognize a deeper truth – that energy is preeminent to matter.

The Holographic Reality

Our entire "physical" world is not really physical. It appears solid; but on a minute and elementary level, it disappears into the mysterious quantum world of waves, frequencies, vibrations and probabilities. Particles which were solid suddenly collapse into waves – energy masquerading as matter the whole time. So what determines the solidity of the world then? Your thoughts. Before you think, there is a field of possibility, and once you think, you begin to crystallize the possibilities into something specific and tangible. Your thoughts make your world.

Many alternative thinkers have proposed that instead of the standard materialistic theory of the world, we need to look at the world as a giant hologram. A hologram is a 3D image created by the interference pattern of light or lasers shone upon it. The image springs into life and looks real; yet without the light, it would remain deactivated. In your world, your focus, beliefs and thoughts are the laser which activates your holographic world into existence.

Some New Age philosophies describe this process as co-creation: that is, we are co-creators (along with God/Spirit/Source/Higher Power) in constructing our reality. I think this is a good description because just to say we are creators can be hubristic/arrogant, and just saying we are victims is disempowering. Overall I see some big problems with the New Age movement (moral relativism, denial of the rightful place of anger, denial of anything "negative", etc.); however, I think they are right to elevate humanity to a place of power by reminding us all that we do actually create reality as we go along.

As co-creators of our world, we project it into existence. However, the issue is that we are not always conscious of our projections. More often than not, it is our unconscious attitudes, feelings, wounds and beliefs which are running the show, not our conscious ones. The world is a mirror or a projection screen. What we see "out there" is always a reflection of what we feel "in here." In other words, the world is set up to reflect back to you the parts of yourself that you can't see (your shadow, as discussed in the previous chapter). It does this in a magical kind of way to challenge, alert and awaken you. There are no victims here; everything is set up with inherent synchronicity to bring up the shadow and darkness so it can be integrated and healed.

The world out there – with political corruption, financial enslavement, chemtrails, vaccines, GMOs, toxic assaults, secrecy, depopulation schemes, pedophilia, war (i.e., mass murder) and more – is the collective shadow.

To really change something, you need to change it at its core. For instance, there's no point pulling out only the top of a weed if you really want that weed gone. You need to pull out the whole root, or it will simply grow back. Remember Thoreau – *"for every thousand hacking at the tree of evil, only one is hacking at the roots."* So, if you want to change the world, you have to ask yourself: what is the cause of all this?

If you're looking at yourself in a mirror, and you

don't like your current hairstyle, what can you do about it? Do you comb the hair on the face in the mirror? Or do you comb the hair on the top of your head? You comb your own hair first, of course, and then the reflection in the mirror automatically changes. Trying to change your hairstyle by running plastic comb teeth over the mirror will do nothing (except perhaps irritate you with a screeching sound). If someone were to genuinely try to change their hairstyle in this way, we would think they were mentally challenged, irrational or insane. Yet, this is exactly what many people do when confronted with evil in our society. They try to change things at the level of the reflection – yet it's an energetic fact that nothing lasting can be changed at this level. The "world" cannot change unless we the projectors and co-creators change, just as what's on the movie screen cannot change unless the content coming out of the projector changes.

The Controllers Want Your Attention

Another aspect of the holographic reality is this. Every future already exists, yet paradoxically nothing is set in stone. Imagine the cosmos as a giant DVD that stores not only places, things, and sounds but also situations, thoughts and feelings. Everything that has happened, is happening and will happen is inscribed on this disc. *Anything* that can happen is encoded. What we experience as "reality" is us shining our collective laser – like a DVD player – onto a portion of the disc and giving it life. We are co-creators. It takes our attention and focus, as well as the encoded information, to mingle together to produce "reality". The crucial point here is that we can collectively choose what portion to focus on.

So in a sense many prophecies are true – such as the ones about the period after 2012 (from 2013 onwards) being a period of transformation – but they're not the only truth. They are realities that could happen but aren't necessarily going to happen. Prophets are people who have developed their psychic abilities more than the average man and have been able to catch a glimpse of a possible or probable timeline. As such, their prophecies can be regarded as a useful warning but not meant to be taken as fact. They serve to show us where we're headed if we don't change course. They also serve another great purpose: sometimes the mere mention of such predictions can be enough to allow us to avert disaster. That's the great secret in all of this: we can change the road we're on, change the timeline and choose a better one that benefits us all.

Nothing is set in stone; what will take place on Earth in the coming years will be a result of our efforts. On the one hand, if we continue being ignorant and apathetic, falling into the traps of giving away our power, denying the atrocities going on, believing we can't do anything to change the situation and pretending it will all somehow be okay, then we're going to take the highway to hell, the timeline to tyranny. On the other hand, if we awaken and remember who we are, then we'll recall we have the potential to change what goes on. Remember, each of us is "God", the cosmic force which split itself into zillions of spirits and particles throughout space-time. You are one such spirit. You are the master-creator who determines what happens in your reality. You can have whatever experience you want to have. We all need to awaken and reactivate our amazing power to create and choose the beliefs and futures we prefer instead of being dictated to. How things turn out has a lot to do with us; if you don't create your own dream, then you'll fall into someone else's.

Are you harnessing the power of your own thoughts, imaginations and power to create? Or are you allowing yourself to be programmed by others?

Dream Creator vs. Nightmare Programmed

And that's exactly what's been happening on the timeline up until now. As things stand, that other dream is a nightmare leading to slavery. Too many people have forgotten their own divinity and power, so their creative abilities have been siphoned off by the elite for their own nefarious purposes. One of the main ways they do this is by controlling the mass media, which has become a huge brainwashing octopus with far-reaching tentacles, broadcasting subliminal messages of fear 24/7. The mass media shapes the average man's beliefs, which in turn shape his reality. By allowing yourself to ingest these programmed messages of fear, you unwittingly let the elite mold your opinions, beliefs and reality. They have an agenda of domination, and by getting you to believe that it is inevitable, instead of just a plan, you add your focus and creative ability to the plan and actually make it more likely to come to fruition.

This is the problem with watching the mainstream "news." It can lead you to become apathetic, overwhelmed and resigned to war and violence. This is also the problem with unquestioning belief in Apocalyptic and Armageddon-like prophecies. It can lead you to think that the end is near, that we're all doomed, and so there's no point trying. More disempowering beliefs. Wake up to the deception: the controllers are trying to get you to add your creative power to their nightmarish vision in order to make it come true.

Politicians also use fear to control, always telling us the next new enemy to be afraid of. This enemy has gone from the Nazis and the Japanese to the Russians, Communists, and terrorists, and to North Korea and many others over the years. But there's apparently always someone or something to fear. Obviously, if you can be tricked into fearing something, you are easier to manipulate, since a scared person looks outside of himself/herself to an external figure to either protect him (authority) or save him (savior). Either way, you're disempowered. There is, of course, a place for fear in the face of genuine threats; however, none of the "threats" relayed to you by the MSM or politicians are genuine.

The way to overcome all the fear programming is to question why you are being told to focus on something. The best lies are half-truths. There may be something to what you're being fed. But ask yourself: if you believe what they tell you to believe, who benefits?

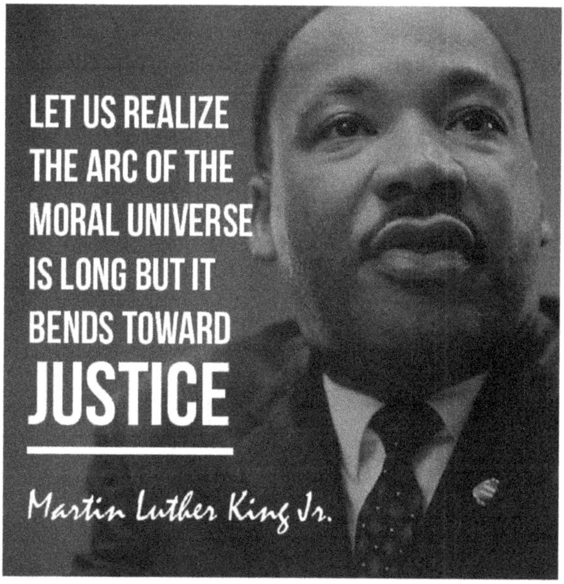

Karma is Misunderstood

In many ways, the so-called law of karma is misunderstood. Some people interpret it to justify treating others badly ("it's their karma"). From my perspective, karma, if it exists, is not personal. It's another energetic aspect of our reality. Jesus is said to have stated that whatever you sow, you shall reap. Whatever you put out, you get back – perhaps delayed, and perhaps in a different form – but back in one way or another. You could say that your negative thoughts, words or actions get trapped in your body (if it was an unkind act you did to another), for example, as guilt, shame or regret. You could say everything is a vibration that naturally attracts like things to itself. You could say that this reality is set up in such a way that no one can ultimately escape the consequences of their actions, even if they appear to "get away with it" in the short term. Civil rights activist Martin Luther King said that *"the arc of the moral universe is long but it bends towards justice."* Karma is a deeper concept than just the shallow reinterpretation of reincarnation or fate.

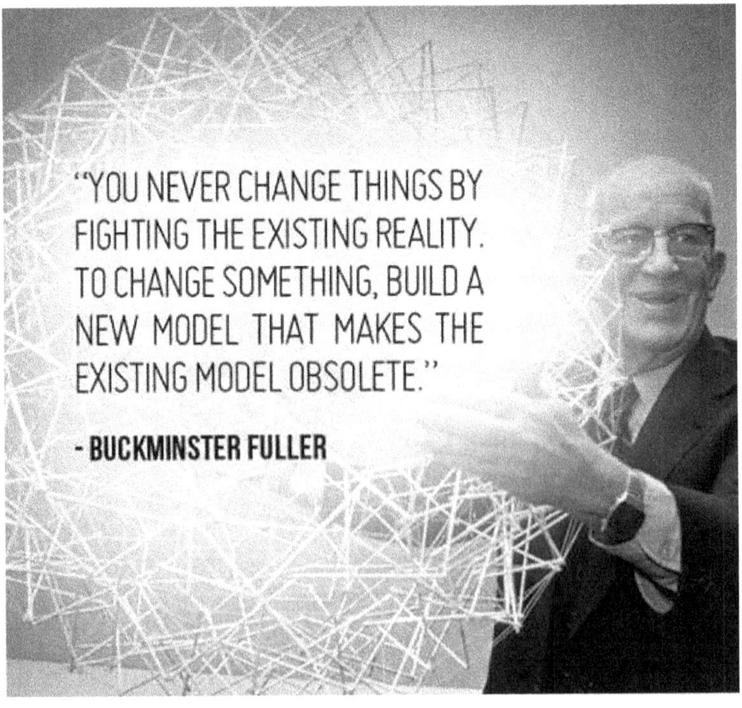

Create New Systems to Make the Old Ones Obsolete

On a similar note, we need to create new solutions rather than fighting the old ones. This is the same concept I have mentioned at other places in this book, that is, whatever you resist will persist, and that whatever you fight you will become. It's a matter of focus; whatever you focus on, you will create. If you spend too much time only "exposing the conspiracy" or railing against the conspirators for how evil they are, you may be overlooking the ways out of the mess. As Buckminster Fuller said in his famous quote, *"You never change things by fighting against the existing reality. To change something, build a new model that makes the existing model obsolete."*

If you put all your energy into taking down the private banking cartel (which manifests as the Federal Reserve in the US, the Bank of England in the UK, the Reserve Bank in Australia, and so on), for instance, you may not succeed, but if you create a new currency (as people have decided to do with cryptocurrencies like Bitcoin and Ethereum), and if it's functional and useful, then people will flock to it and leave the old currency behind. In this way, entire institutions and massive structures that looked so solid can collapse or be undone because they lose their relevance and value. Buckminster also described himself as a "trim tab." What is that you may ask? It's the tiny part of the rudder which can move giant ships. He envisaged himself as the trim tab, doing his own thing, pursuing his own ideas, and able to shape society through his innovation and originality.

Everyone has different talents and interests, and therefore different roles to play, in restoring peace, justice and abundance for all. Some people are more well equipped to dive down rabbit holes and expose the ugly and uncomfortable truths of the current systems, whereas others are better at creating new systems. No matter what your predilections are, we all need to support those who are actively trying to establish new systems because this is the future. It is also what the controllers are frightened of. They can tolerate mass protests, but they can't tolerate it when people start trading with each other without using government-approved currency or start creating systems that remove the need for a central authority, since those kinds of initiatives threaten their raison d'etre more fundamentally than a protest can.

Amplifying Energy: Orgone, Pyramids, Sacred Geometry and More

A discussion of energetic solutions would be incomplete without mentioning some of the phenomena or natural technologies that surround us – which are, predictably, denied by mainstream materialist science and labeled as "quackery."

These kinds of things are based on the laws of physics; however, to be understood they require an open mind.

In the 1930s and 1940s, the Austrian Dr. Wilhelm Reich, by using a modified Geiger counter, was able to detect and measure the existence of etheric energy which he called orgone (similar or perhaps identical to chi, qi/ki, prana, etc.). He invented a way to attract and capture this etheric energy by creating an orgone accumulator. He was able to successfully heal his patients of various ailments – including cancer – by having them sit inside an orgone accumulator box for varying amounts of time. He even built a device which he called a *cloudbuster* that altered the amount of orgone energy in the atmosphere and thus could both create and dissipate clouds. The device could bring rain to drought-plagued regions and save vast countless acres of crops. Reich eventually moved to the USA. In a story that has been constantly repeated, Reich was thrown in jail by the FDA and died penniless, yet his research and legacy live on.

Energy can be amplified by certain sounds, symbols and shapes. This is a vast area that is beyond the scope of this book; however, anyone interested can look up the extensive research into pyramid geometry and "torsion fields", especially by Russian scientists. The website LiteTheLight.com[448] gives a brief summary of the findings of Russian scientist Dr. Alexander Golod carried out by the Russian National Academy of Sciences:

Brief Summary of Pyramid Research Results:

1. Immune system of organisms improved (blood leukocyte increased);
2. Improved regeneration of tissue;
3. Seeds stored in the pyramid for 1-5 days showed a 30-100% increase in yield;
4. Soon after construction of the Lake Seliger pyramid a marked improvement of the ozone was

[448] https://litethelight.bigcartel.com/intention

noted above the area;
5. Seismic activity near the pyramid research areas [is] reduced in severity and size;
6. Violent weather also appears to decrease in the vicinity of the pyramids;
7. Pyramids constructed in Southern Russia (Bashkiria) appeared to have a positive effect on oil production with oil becoming less viscous by 30% and the yield of the oil wells increased according to tests carried out by the Moscow Academy of Oil and Gas;
8. A study was done on 5000 prisoners who ingested salt and pepper that had been exposed to the pyramid energy field. The test subjects exhibited a greatly reduced violence rate and overall behavior was much improved;
9. Standard tissue culture tests showed an increase in survival of cellular tissue after infection by viruses and bacteria;
10. Radioactive substances show a decreased level of radiation inside the pyramid;
11. There are reports of spontaneous charging of capacitors;
12. Physicists observed significant changes in superconductivity temperature thresholds and in the properties of semi-conducting and carbon nano materials;
13. Water inside the pyramid will remain liquid to minus 40 degrees Celsius but freeze instantly if jostled or bumped in any way;
14. Synthesized diamonds turn out harder and purer.

Some people use small pyramids in their house to block against or transform harmful EMF, or construct a lightweight pyramid out of copper to hang over their bed so they can sleep under it each night and receive healing benefits. The applications are endless; you can put food inside to augment the potency or taste, or you can use pyramids to amplify the power of your prayers, intentions and visualizations.

In a similar vein, the term "sacred geometry" refers to specific geometrical forms found in Nature which underlie all life and creation. When you understand it more deeply, shape is really a pattern of frozen or crystallized energy movement, whereby each pattern has certain properties and bestows specific powers. Examples are spirals, tetrahedrons or the famous "Flower of Life" (see right).

The pure structural patterns of sacred geometry are the key to everything from nuclear physics to human biology. Some spiritual traditions have known this information for thousands of years: for instance the ancient Egyptians, some of whose temples were inscribed with sacred geometrical shapes. Now, information like this is avidly and covertly studied by both scientists and governments, so they can understand and exploit the knowledge militarily and technologically while dismissing it as pseudoscience. Robert J. Gilbert Ph.D.[449] writes:

---

449 https://vesica.org/sacred-geometry-articles/the-hidden-energy-science-of-sacred-geometry-2

Most of the patterns known and used in modern technology were also clearly known and used in ancient cultures ... One little-known example: the same geometric form known and kept very secret by the Greeks over 2500 years ago (because they said it could cause great destruction if misused) is shown in modern declassified military documents to be the exact same shape used to create the world's first atomic bomb.

Similarly, Sacred Geometry patterns taught in the ancient schools as being related to Alchemy are the same as those found in modern technology to transmute chemical poisons to be harmless, even lethal toxins like Nerve Gas; these same alchemical patterns frozen in matter can destroy pollution, and are even present in your car's catalytic converter.

As great as the achievements of modern technology are, they are creating pollution and death in many cases. Modern science has rediscovered many of the patterns — blueprints of creation — known to the world's great spiritual traditions, but only in materialistic fragments; it desperately needs the holistic understanding and greater context the spiritual traditions have regarding these patterns, in order to create a technology which is healing and life-positive.

There are many ways you can put knowledge of sacred geometry to good use, from simple things like etching the flower of life onto your drink bottle to change the vibration of your water, to grander things such as designing rooms in your house or buildings according to certain proportions. Information is readily available on the topic both online and in books; I invite you to explore how sacred geometry can uplift your life.

The Power of Positive Intention and Ritual (White Magic) – and Charging it with Sexual Energy

Another important energetic plane solution is the power of positive intention and ritual (white magic). Many people have exposed how the conspirators engage in black magic at places or within groups such as the Skull 'n' Bones Society and Bohemian Grove. Some of this involves mock sacrifice, the invocation of demons, strange "gods" and dark forces, torture, rape, real sacrifice (of animals, children and adults) and other aspects of Satanic ritual. The conspirators who run the world know how to harness energy to increase their power; after all, power is their number-one goal. It makes sense that the way to combat such negativity is to use the same power of intention and ritual but in a good way. There is nothing stopping good people from gathering together and conducting their own positive rituals, in which we harness our collective power and vision, and unify it to help create the peaceful, free and prosperous world that we desire.

People have been doing this since the beginning of time when they would gather together to meditate, pray or perform some kind of uplifting religious or spiritual practice. When people gather to sing songs promoting love, peace and unity, this is a type of white magic ritual. We need to perform this kind of white magic just as much as – and more than – the black magic that is being performed in order to counteract its effect. Everything is energy. Intention is energy too; it has its own power even if it is not tangible. By imbuing everyday acts, as well as white magic acts, with intention, you can amplify their effect. Groups of people getting together, reaffirming the power of love, connection and peace may not seem like a big deal from the outside but is actually a very powerful way to push back against the conspiracy. It's an act of defiance – we don't buy into a nightmarish reality and refuse to be conduits through which one is created – and simultaneously an act of remembrance and of focus, reminding ourselves what it is we stand for and what it is we wish to create.

Creating your own intentions and focusing on them is great, however to really activate and manifest them, you need to energize them. How? By using sexual energy. This is another taboo area that society, religion and government doesn't want you to know about, because they want docile controlled subjects. Man or woman, you can learn how to sublimate and circulate your sexual energy and use it for healing, creative projects and manifestation. You don't need another person for this; you can do it alone, although when more than one person gather together for any kind of ritual, it becomes more powerful. Any intention can be supercharged by redirected sexual energy. I would invite anyone interested in this to look into the ancient Taoist and Tantric teachings as a starting point. There are also current organizations such as ISTA (International School of the Temple Arts) which carry forward this sacred tradition into today's world.

Find a Cure ... Or Remove the Cause?

One last point to consider is this. Whenever you have a problem in life, especially a medical/health problem, what is a more effective path to take: finding a cure for the problem or removing the cause of the problem?

It is almost always best to remove the cause.

So, how can we remove the cause of the current world problems? We need to find the deepest cause of those problems – the demons within, like fear and unresolved trauma – and heal those.

Conclusion

All of these solutions presented above act on a deeper level than those in the previous chapters. Just because they are not as tangible does not mean they are not as powerful. Just the opposite – because our world is born out of consciousness and energy, any changes we make on those planes will be more fundamental than other more superficial changes. They will flow down and transform our world, just as a change in the recipe will change the outcome of the cooked dish, or changing your facial expression will change what you see in the mirror. The so-called physical world (in itself an illusion) cannot change unless we the projectors and co-creators change. We have the power of focus and attention to do that.

Chapter 19 – Who Are You, Anyway?

Yesterday I was clever, so I wanted to change the world. Today I am wise, so I am changing myself.

– Rumi

*****

The list of solutions culminates in this key question, which is the greatest question of all time and the question to which philosophers throughout the ages have devoted their lifetime: who are you?

Who are you, anyway?

Are you just an insignificant person of no worth? Are you just an animal that lives, eats, sleeps and dies? Are you just a biological machine? Are you just a dirty sinner waiting for the afterlife? Are you just a cog in the wheel of a giant soulless machine? Are you just here to work, consume and die? Are you just an obedient citizen? Are you a lowly, slow and pathetic human waiting to be "augmented" and "enhanced" into a transhuman? Are you an unquestioning worker? Are you an obedient soldier who leaves the thinking and moral dilemmas to someone else? Are you alive just to serve the system as a slave?

Or are you perhaps something much greater and grander than you've ever imagined or realized?

Some have said that there are no limits, other than the limits we place upon ourselves. How do you define yourself? How are you limiting yourself?

I would suggest that the most true, deep and real answer to that question is that *you are everything*. You are unlimited consciousness in a body. You are an infinite awareness in a human form. You are Source or Spirit in the material world. You are literally Godstuff formed into an individuated unit to experience itself.

Some spiritual and philosophical teachings put it like this: there is only one thing in existence (call it Source, Spirit, Universal Consciousness, God or whatever you want, although the "God" comes with so much linguistic and conceptual baggage from millennia of misuse it may be better to find another term). You are part of that One Thing. You are that One Thing. Everything you see, hear, touch, smell, feel and sense in this reality is this One Thing. This One Thing is consciousness. We are all points of attention of this consciousness, playing out different roles and polarities, so this One Thing can experience itself subjectively. Since there is nothing this One Thing is not, there is nothing you are not. You literally have the power inside of you to be anything.

Anastasia, a character in the amazing book series Ringing Cedars, talks about this One Thing as a Force or Power. She explains that this Force split itself in half. One half split itself up into zillions of small units individuated (people, animals, plants); the other half remains available as a Force to be used by whoever intends it. To those who like to use the word "God", you could say that we are all God, and simultaneously, we all have access to the power of "God", since we and it all are the same One Thing, anyway.

The late great Alan Watts talks about how we are all God, pretending we aren't, playing the game of forgetting it so we can wake up and remember it. Neale Donald Walsch, author of the fantastic book series Conversations with God, talks about the idea that the word "god" is a verb not a noun. Thus, we are all *godding* or co-creating as we live our lives, since it is our inherent nature to create. We are creators, and with the creative power of this One Thing, we are co-creators.

The same idea, just in different words, can be found all over the world, again and again, in different writings, teachings and cultures. The books of Carlos Castaneda (mentioned in chapter 11) are fascinating. They reflect a shamanic or sorcerer's understanding of this idea as taught by Juan Matus, the teacher of Carlos. Matus explains how humans are first and foremost luminous energetic beings, not physical clumps of matter. He explains how your perception is determined by where your point of attention (focus) is located on your energetic field.

Your beliefs and perception determine your reality, for what you believe and perceive, you then co-create. It is interesting how some people demand proof of the worldwide conspiracy and get angry or frustrated because they can't see it. You can offer all the evidence you like to some people, but if they have not changed their perception on a fundamental level, they literally cannot access the information. They are blocked off from it – trapped in a matrix of their own making.

All great paths will lead you back to the question of who you are. It's healthy to ask yourself this question frequently. You may find it cuts through your excuses and assumptions, helping you get to what's real. You may find it helps you align your thoughts, words and actions with your higher life purpose. You may find it helps you reflect on your behavior and catch a glimpse of your own hypocrisy or the ways you are not living up to your ideals.

The more you fully step into who you are, the more you raise your vibration, the more you encourage others to do the same, the less the system enslaves you and the less it is able to perpetuate itself through your energy. You have to start with yourself; you can only change the world by first changing yourself. Once you broaden your own perception (i.e., escape your own matrix), you can help others do the same. Another way to put it is to recognize one of the habits of highly effective people: they act mostly in their own sphere of influence. You can change yourself most of all, your inner circle of family and friends to a lesser degree and the rest of the world to a much lesser degree still. Why waste all your energy on the world at large when there is so much inside of you that can be improved?

The change that we are aiming for is not some paltry, temporary or superficial change, like the "change" when a certain political party gets into power. This is not change at all, just more fakery in the fraudulent left-right paradigm and just tyranny getting its newest plastic facelift. As mentioned in an earlier chapter, the real change is a revolution of consciousness, not a president, prime minister or even a new political system. Any new "system" (or lack thereof) which flows from this higher state of consciousness will necessarily be an improvement to the current system. From a higher consciousness flows all sorts of advantages, benefits and improvements. From a higher consciousness flows enhanced and widened perception, which co-creates an entirely different reality to the slave system we are now unconsciously perpetuating.

So when someone complains, "What can I do? I'm just a little person compared to this giant system," you can reply, "You are God, you are Source, you are Spirit, you are sovereign, you are everything. You are infinite consciousness and unlimited awareness in a human body. You are a unique being. You are a powerful co-creator. You are so powerful that you are literally creating your very reality every moment."

The power is in your hands.

Chapter 20 – Final Thoughts

So there you have it. If you didn't before, now you understand the big picture – the grand picture – of why the world is the way it is and where the world is headed if humanity continues on in ignorance and apathy. But if you've made it this far, you'll realize that the agenda is not written in stone and that allowing the world to become a prison planet is unthinkable. We have an obligation to love, truth, liberty, peace, justice and abundance, and an obligation to our children, grandchildren and everyone who comes after us, to ensure we do everything in our power to create a world of freedom. If you truly understand both the problems and the solutions, you'll know that if enough people participate, we will prevail over this darkness. Love is stronger than fear. Truth is more powerful than lies. When enough people align themselves with love and truth, fear and lies will lose their grip on the world.

The NWO controllers spend enormous amounts of time, money and energy forcing humanity down in an unnatural state, like pushing a ball beneath the surface of the water. But eventually it will rise up. It must. The dark force at the very top of the pyramid, which has no love or creative power, and can only survive living off others like a parasite, is no match for an awakened humanity standing united in its full power. All that is required is for you to join that awakening with your conscious intention and participation. A few cannot control the many unless the many keep acquiescing and cooperating with their own enslavement. Once the many stop this behavior, it's game over for the NWO manipulators.

So what can you do? *Everything*. Share the truth, integrate the information, help guide people away from fear, develop your emotional and spiritual maturity, activate your masculine principle (this applies equally to men and women) that will always stand up for what is right, activate your inner warrior that chooses not violence but determination to defend what is sacred – people (family, friends) and principles (natural inherent rights, freedom). Working on your inner shadow is key: collective revolution flows from individual enlightenment. Above all, *love* – center yourself in your heart, which is your place of power. That is the one thing NWO psychopaths have lost touch with. Love is not sappy or wishy-washy but the knowledge of what's right and the courage (from the Old French word *corage* which means *heart*) to *do* what's right.

Peace and power to you.

www.ingramcontent.com/pod-product-compliance
Lightning Source LLC
Chambersburg PA
CBHW060446030426
42337CB00015B/1509
* 9 7 9 8 9 8 7 8 6 6 7 1 9 *